Beyond Tordesillas

New Approaches to Comparative Luso-Hispanic Studies

EDITED BY
Robert Patrick Newcomb

AND
Richard A. Gordon

THE OHIO STATE UNIVERSITY PRESS • COLUMBUS

Copyright © 2017 by The Ohio State University.
All rights reserved.

Library of Congress Cataloging-in-Publication Data
Names: Newcomb, Robert Patrick, editor. | Gordon, Richard A. (Richard Allen), 1969– editor.
Title: Beyond Tordesillas : new approaches to comparative Luso-Hispanic studies / edited by Robert Patrick Newcomb and Richard A. Gordon.
Other titles: Transoceanic studies.
Description: Columbus : The Ohio State University Press, [2017] | Series: Transoceanic studies | Includes bibliographical references and index.
Identifiers: LCCN 2017024726 | ISBN 9780814213476 (cloth ; alk. paper) | ISBN 0814213472 (cloth ; alk. paper)
Subjects: LCSH: Comparative literature—Portuguese and Spanish. | Comparative literature—Spanish and Portuguese. | Spain—Relations—Portugal. | Portugal—Relations—Spain. | Brazil—Relations—Latin America. | Latin America—Relations—Brazil. | United States—Relations—Latin America. | Latin America—Relations—United States. | Transnationalism—Social aspects. | Culture in motion pictures. | Popular music—Social aspects—Brazil.
Classification: LCC PQ9019 .B49 2017 | DDC 460—dc23
LC record available at https://lccn.loc.gov/2017024726

Cover design by Lisa Force
Text design by Juliet Williams
Type set in Adobe Minion Pro

∞ The paper used in this publication meets the minimum requirements of the American National Standard for Information Sciences—Permanence of Paper for Printed Library Materials. ANSI Z39.48-1992.

9 8 7 6 5 4 3 2 1

CONTENTS

Acknowledgments											vii

INTRODUCTION		Bridging Tordesillas								1

PART I			LUSO-HISPANIC STUDIES AND RELATED LINES OF
			INQUIRY: A SERIES OF PROPOSALS

CHAPTER 1		Portuguese and the Emergence of Iberian Studies
			PEDRO SCHACHT PEREIRA								21

CHAPTER 2		The Case for Ad Hoc Transnationalism
			HÉCTOR HOYOS									37

CHAPTER 3		Queer Spanish, Queer Portuguese: A Series of
			Research Proposals
			DAVID WILLIAM FOSTER								54

CHAPTER 4		Before Tordesilhas, and Beyond: The Politics of Native
			Agency across the Americas
			TRACY DEVINE GUZMÁN								64

CHAPTER 5		"Blister you all": Sérgio Buarque de Holanda and the
			Calibanic Genealogy
			PEDRO MEIRA MONTEIRO
			TRANSLATED BY JAMES IRBY							82

PART II WRITTEN FICTIONAL NARRATIVE: BRAZIL AND SPANISH-SPEAKING LATIN AMERICA

CHAPTER 6 The Literary Revenant in a Latin American Comparative Context
ROBERT MOSER — 95

CHAPTER 7 Borges, Clarice, and the Development of Latin America's "New Narrative"
EARL E. FITZ — 108

CHAPTER 8 Mapping Citizenship in Luiz Ruffato's *Inferno provisório* and Guillermo Saccomanno's *El pibe*
LEILA LEHNEN — 119

PART III LUSO-HISPANIC POETRY, MUSIC, AND EXPRESSIVE CULTURE

CHAPTER 9 The *Parábola* of the Latin American Avant-Gardes
ALFREDO BOSI
TRANSLATED BY ROBERT PATRICK NEWCOMB — 137

CHAPTER 10 Brazilian Symbolism and Hispanic American *Modernismo*: Resonance across the Luso-Hispanic Divide
SARAH MOODY — 149

CHAPTER 11 Shared Passages: Spanish American–Brazilian Links in Contemporary Poetry
CHARLES A. PERRONE — 162

CHAPTER 12 *Cantigas de amigo*: Galicia and Brazil in the Lusophone Musical Space
FREDERICK MOEHN — 173

PART IV LUSO-HISPANIC CINEMA, PERFORMANCE, AND VISUAL CULTURE

CHAPTER 13 Cartography of Dissidence: In/visibility and Urban Display in Luso-Hispanic Street Projects
TINA ESCAJA — 191

CHAPTER 14 Memory, Youth, and Regimes of Violence in Recent Hispanic and Lusophone Cinemas
LESLIE L. MARSH — 204

CHAPTER 15 Cinema in Totalitarian Iberia: Propaganda and Persuasion
            under Salazar and Franco
            PATRÍCIA VIEIRA   220

CHAPTER 16 Globalization and Documentary Film: Luso-Hispanic
            Reflections
            MICHAEL J. LAZZARA   234

List of Contributors   249

Index   252

ACKNOWLEDGMENTS

THE EDITORS would like to recognize: first and foremost, our contributors, who have made this volume what it is; Iliana Rodríguez, editor of the Transoceanic Series, for her support of this project; Lindsay Martin and The Ohio State University Press, for guidance and patience; our anonymous external reviewers, who provided crucial feedback.

Robert Patrick Newcomb would like to thank his colleagues at the University of California, Davis, and Kelley Weiss, for her love and support.

Richard A. Gordon would like to thank his colleagues at The Ohio State University and the University of Georgia.

INTRODUCTION

Bridging Tordesillas

ROBERT PATRICK NEWCOMB
RICHARD A. GORDON

PERHAPS NO two literary and cultural traditions share such a natural affinity through both language and history, and yet so consistently resist comparative study, as do those of the former Spanish and Portuguese colonial empires. Of the major Romance languages, Spanish and Portuguese are the most closely related, having only diverged from one another in the Middle Ages. Today, Spanish and Portuguese are to a significant degree mutually intelligible, and in certain border regions the two languages bleed into each other, as occurs on portions of the Brazilian-Uruguayan frontier. Similarly, the histories of the Portuguese and Spanish states, and of Brazil and the Spanish-speaking republics of Latin America, have been closely intertwined. Portugal and Spain are the modern products of a centuries-long process of often-linked political evolution on the Iberian Peninsula, a landmass set apart from the rest of the European continent by the Pyrenees, and which the Portuguese novelist José Saramago imagined as a cultural—and literal—island in his speculative novel *A Jangada de Pedra* (The Stone Raft, 1985). Having been bonded in protean form during the Roman, Visigothic, and Muslim periods of rule in Iberia, much of what would become Portugal and Spain embarked during the Middle Ages on parallel processes of peninsular *reconquista*. In the late fifteenth and sixteenth centuries the two kingdoms undertook Europe's first modern overseas colonization projects, expanding into the Americas, Africa, and Asia and becoming imperial rivals. Between 1580 and 1640, Spain and Portugal were united under the Spanish Habsburgs, and while they have remained politically independent of one another ever since, they have experienced a succession of analogous historical developments. Over the past century, these connections have included a common experience of totalitarian dictatorship, under Francisco Franco and Antônio de Oliveira Salazar, followed by African decolonization and transition to democracy during the late 1960s, 1970s, and 1980s and, most recently, a not untroubled process of European integration.

In the New World, the Spanish-speaking republics and Brazil—themselves products of Iberian colonization—cut an enormous, contiguous swath across two continents, ranging with little interruption "del Bravo a Magallanes" [from the Rio Bravo to the Strait of Magellan], as the Cuban poet José Martí put it in his essay "Nuestra América" ("Our America," 1891). And like Spain and Portugal, the Spanish- and Portuguese-speaking countries so often termed "Latin America" have been subject to a number of common historical processes, including post-independence civil tensions and underdevelopment, periods of populist and dictatorial rule, complex relations with the United States, and finally, participation in the modern, globalized political and economic order.[1]

The significant linguistic, geographic, and historical similarities that exist between the regions of the world where Spanish and Portuguese are spoken underlie the comparative approaches we advocate in this volume. Yet for all of this proximity, the academic fields of Hispanic and Luso-Brazilian studies—which, we should note, were constituted in the late nineteenth century, long after the apogee of Luso-Hispanic intercommunication—developed independently and generally remain isolated from one another, even in close institutional quarters. In Iberia and Latin America, the cultural products of transnational or translinguistic traditions tend to be marginalized, leaving little room to appreciate the rich Luso-Hispanic interconnectedness that has characterized literary and cultural expression on the Iberian Peninsula and in Latin America. The persistent disciplinary separation and consequent missed comparative opportunity between the Hispanic and Luso-Brazilian traditions are perhaps more surprising in the United States, where in most research universities the two fields exist in awkward association within nominally bilingual university departments of "Spanish and Portuguese."

Beyond Tordesillas: New Approaches to Comparative Luso-Hispanic Studies seeks to confront the seemingly paradoxical relationship, the interplay of proximity and distance, between these fields and their objects of study. This introduction will offer diagnoses for the lack of solid comparative work on Hispanic and Luso-Brazilian literary and cultural materials, and the volume as a whole will showcase recent efforts to bridge this gap through the vital

---

1. See Newcomb on the ambivalent relationship of Brazil to the idea of Latin America.

contributions of scholars on both sides of the Atlantic who are exploring underexamined connections between the literary and cultural traditions of the Spanish- and Portuguese-speaking worlds. In so doing, *Beyond Tordesillas* underscores the potential of what we might term Comparative Luso-Hispanic Studies. Broadly, we understand this as an academic approach that calls for sustained, side-by-side analysis of writers and artists, cultural texts (e.g., novels, films), and intellectual paradigms originating in the Portuguese- and Spanish-speaking worlds. Further, it stands as an alternative—and sometimes a corrective—to the national philological model traditionally favored in Iberia and Latin America, and to the somewhat inorganic division of the fields of Portuguese and Spanish that occurs in the U.S. academy.

David William Foster, a contributor to *Beyond Tordesillas* and a pioneering proponent of Luso-Hispanic comparativism in the U.S., remarked in a 1992 essay on the pervasive "disconsonance" to be observed between the fields of Brazilian and Spanish American literature. The long history of Luso-Hispanic disconsonance cited by Foster would tend to puzzle colleagues who work outside of Hispanic and Luso-Brazilian studies: surely, they might ask, the linguistic closeness of Portuguese and Spanish, along with centuries of interconnected history dating back to the Romans, would lead to a greater degree of dialogue and mutual influence between the two fields? Indeed, medieval and early modern Iberia *did* play host to a vibrant linguistic, cultural, and intellectual dialogue in which Iberian men of letters circulated between regional centers including Santiago de Compostela, Lisbon, Madrid, and Barcelona. Reflecting the legacy of medieval poetic culture, in which composition in multiple Iberian languages was de rigueur, some of the outstanding Iberian writers from the period, particularly those born in Portugal, composed in both Portuguese *and* Castilian. Here we may cite the examples of Alfonso X, who wrote prose in Castilian and poetry in Galaico-Portuguese, and bilingual writers such as the playwright Gil Vicente, the poet Luís de Camões, and the writer and soldier Francisco Manuel de Melo.[2] Scholars of medieval and sixteenth- and seventeenth-century Iberia have long understood the value of the multilingualism and comparative perspectives we advocate in this volume,

---

2. Alfonso X (1221–84; r. 1252–84) was King of Castile and Leon, nicknamed "the wise" or "the learned." Gil Vicente (1465–1536/37) wrote plays in both Portuguese and Castilian. His farce the *Auto da Índia* (1509?) was written in Portuguese, but features a Castilian character (named simply "the Castilian"), who delivers his lines in that language. Camões (1524/25–1580) wrote the Portuguese national epic, *Os Lusíadas* (1572), as well as a good deal of lyric poetry. He wrote the vast majority of his work in Portuguese, but penned a small number of Castilian sonnets. Melo (1608–66) is best known for his *Historia de la guerra de Cataluña* (1645). He also wrote poetry in both Spanish and Portuguese.

and in this respect have been more forward-thinking than those of us who work on more recent periods, which are the focus of this volume.

As noted above, cross-border and multilingual dialogue continued to a certain degree, though these became substantially less common, as Portugal and Spain developed as distinct national polities with competing imperial agendas from the sixteenth century on. In part, we attribute the resistance to comparison of the two linguistic and cultural traditions to the parallel steps Portugal and Spain took toward national distinction during this period. The tendency toward intellectual and cultural disengagement became especially pronounced following the sixty years of Iberian dynastic union (1580–1640), which Portuguese nationalists retroactively cast as a period of foreign occupation and "Spanish captivity." The conjuring of disjunction continued as the two peninsular kingdoms moved away from the center of European imperial power during the seventeenth and eighteenth centuries and slid toward what many both inside and outside Iberia saw as political, scientific, economic, and cultural marginality. By this point the vibrant Luso-Hispanic dialogue of the centuries preceding roughly the eighteenth century had given way to a shared gaze toward the new centers of global influence—that portion of western and central Europe *além Pirenéus* (beyond the Pyrenees), and the Anglo-American world. When the political and cultural gazes of Spain and Portugal shifted during this time of perceived European marginality, they generally turned to territories beyond the peninsula rather than to lands across the Spanish-Portuguese border. Iberian mutual ignorance became so pronounced by the turn of the twentieth century that the writer and philosopher Miguel de Unamuno—himself a tireless advocate for Portuguese literature in his native Spain—would bemoan the tragicomic phenomenon of Spanish- and Portuguese-speaking men of letters learning of each other's work only after reading it in French translation (4: 527).

Beginning in the late nineteenth century, Portugal and Spain undertook neocolonial projects that further consolidated Iberian disjunction. Portugal's and Spain's attempts to exert control over their present and former American, African, and Asian colonies marched in lockstep with the advancement of notions of *hispanidad* and *lusofonia*, which affirmed imperial and neo-imperial linguistic and cultural unity. It was in this context that Hispanic and Luso-Brazilian letters as academic fields encompassing literary production in Spanish and Portuguese, respectively, developed. Insistence that a cultural cohesion maintained through the linguistic legacy of colonialism should be the overarching principle of literary analysis left little room for work across Luso-Hispanic frontiers.[3]

This disciplinary history is reflected in the scholarly records of Hispanic and Luso-Brazilian studies as they have come down to us today. Historically speaking, when scholars have undertaken comparative approaches within these disciplines, they have tended to establish points of contact with a Eurocentric field of "world literature," or to operate within the confines of either the Portuguese or the Spanish linguistic spheres. For example, Lusophone scholars have routinely compared the great nineteenth-century Portuguese novelist Eça de Queirós to the French realists (Balzac, Flaubert, Zola) who served as his literary models, while others have studied him alongside his Brazilian contemporary and critic, the novelist Machado de Assis. Comparisons between Queirós and his Spanish contemporaries, such as Leopoldo Alas (Clarín), Emilia Pardo Bazán, and Benito Pérez Galdós, have been less frequent. This is despite the fact that these Iberian writers used the realist-naturalist novel to engage with similar, and particularly *peninsular,* social problems, including the decline of the Portuguese and Spanish colonial empires and the tension between the Catholic intellectual tradition and European notions of modernity.[4]

To be sure, we do not question the value of comparative approaches to Hispanic and Luso-Brazilian studies that are structured as dialogues between the Spanish- or Portuguese-speaking world and the European and North American centers of geopolitical power and cultural influence, or that are situated within the individual spheres of Hispanophone and Lusophone letters. This said, as scholars specifically interested in Luso-Hispanic dialogue, we contend that serious engagement with Luso-Hispanic studies as a form of comparative literary and cultural analysis is long overdue. The Transoceanic Series, in which this volume is published, provides a privileged space for us to make this argument.

Beyond Tordesillas builds from an understanding that the former Spanish and Portuguese colonial empires are transoceanic spaces, multicontinental entities tied together not only by relationships of political and economic power, but also by waves of immigration—both voluntary and, through the

---

3. See Loureiro and Hamilton for critical assessments of *hispanidad* and *lusofonia,* respectively.

4. See, for example, Silviano Santiago's "Eça, autor de *Madame Bovary*" (1978) and João Camilo dos Santos's "Eça de Queirós, Critic of Machado de Assis—A Symptomatic Understanding" (2005). For a recent example of Luso-Hispanic scholarship on Queirós, see Estela Vieira's *Interiors and Narrative: The Spatial Poetics of Machado de Assis, Eça de Queirós, and Leopoldo Alas* (2014).

transatlantic slave trade, forced—as well as affective ties maintained within dispersed families, social networks, and on the broader terrain of national, literary, and cultural identity. As such, the Hispanic and Lusophone worlds represent an appropriate context for transoceanic analysis, which emphasizes comparison, relational knowledge, and change over time, rather than the study of self-enclosed, fixed national canons. As Joel Pace has noted, "Transnational and transatlantic studies are part of an ongoing transcendence (moving beyond) of the literary canon(s) [. . .] Transnational studies is international and interdisciplinary and complements rather than invalidates single-nation studies" (233).[5]

As mentioned previously, Portugal and Spain engaged in parallel journeys of maritime exploration and overseas colonization that occasionally overlapped, in the context of either collaboration or competition. Iberian mariners routinely served on ships commissioned by the other peninsular kingdom. Fernão de Magalhães (Ferdinand Magellan), the Portuguese-born mariner who sailed for Spain, and whose crew made the first successful voyage of global circumnavigation, is the most famous example. In a 1931 tribute to the Brazilian modernist poet Ronald de Carvalho, the Mexican humanist Alfonso Reyes seized on the image of parallel journeys of exploration in reflecting melancholically that the Spanish and Portuguese had not recognized their degree of interconnection: "Siguiendo rutas paralelas, nunca se encontraban nuestros barcos. No sabíamos que éramos unos, y los pueblos americanos vivíamos tan alejados unos de otros como tal vez de nosotros mismos—porque la ignorancia de lo semejante supone siempre, en mucho, el desconocimiento de lo propio" [Though we followed parallel routes, our ships never sighted one another. We did not know that we were one, and we, the American peoples, lived as alienated from each other as we did from ourselves—for ignorance of he who is like you presupposes, to a great degree, ignorance of oneself] (8: 158–59).

The Treaty of Tordesillas—an agreement brokered by the pope in 1494, and which tried and failed to impose a cartographic order on the fluid process of Iberian overseas colonization—divided the known world into Spanish and Portuguese spheres of influence and stands as a symbolic manifestation of the enforced mutual ignorance and animosity that Reyes bemoans.[6] In a path-breaking critical call-to-arms, "Abaixo Tordesilhas!" (Down With

---

5. The editors wish to thank Cecilia Enjuto Rangel, Sebastiaan Faber, and Pedro García-Caro for alerting them to this source.

6. In Brazil, the Portuguese failed to respect the boundary imposed by the treaty, with waves of Luso-Brazilian adventurers, the *bandeirantes*, ranging through territory to the west of the dividing line, and bringing it under Portuguese control. These territories remain part of Brazil today.

Tordesillas, 1993), Jorge Schwartz seizes on the treaty and the imaginary line created by Tordesillas to propose a "critical reflection that is capable, when considering Latin America, of duly including Brazil." Schwartz, an Argentine-born scholar who has made his career teaching at the University of São Paulo, exhorts his readers to join the "new generation" of critics, "dedicated [. . .] to the elimination of the line of Tordesillas" (195). Seizing on Schwartz's metaphorical appropriation of the line of Tordesillas as a manifestation of Luso-Hispanic self-segregation and noncommunication, *Beyond Tordesillas* seeks to give voice to the growing ranks of Luso-Hispanic comparativist scholars that Schwartz convokes. The volume features key contributions from senior scholars who, like Schwartz, pioneered this approach, including Earl Fitz, David William Foster, and Charles Perrone.[7] Further, it showcases a rising generation of Luso-Hispanic comparative scholars based in U.S. universities, whose numbers and academic production have grown significantly in the past decade.[8]

Today, the institutional possibilities for promoting comparative approaches to Luso-Hispanic literary and cultural analysis vary significantly. Whereas the distinction between "national" and "foreign" literatures tends to separate Luso-Brazilian and Hispanic studies in Latin America and the Iberian Peninsula, the prevailing "Spanish and Portuguese" departmental model in U.S. research universities would seem to offer the promise of real dialogue by placing specialists in both disciplines under a common roof. In practice, however, this model has proved less amenable to comparativism than might be expected. As Luso-Brazilianist colleagues who teach in these departments often relate, factors such as unequal institutional attention to dominant Spanish and invariably subordinate Portuguese sections, which manifests itself in battles over funding (especially acute at resource-stressed public universities), tend to foreclose real dialogue. Other institutional configurations like departments of Romance Studies or Romance Languages, which group Spanish and

---

7. See: Earl E. Fitz, *Rediscovering the New World: Inter-American Literature in a Comparative Context* (1991); *Brazilian Narrative Traditions in a Comparative Context* (2005); Charles A. Perrone, *Brazil, Lyric, and the Americas* (2010); Jorge Schwartz, *Vanguardas Latino-americanas* (1995); *Borges no Brasil* (2001); *Fervor das Vanguardas. Arte e Literatura na América Latina* (2013). See also: Raúl Antelo, *Na Ilha de Marapatá: Mário de Andrade Lê os Hispano-americanos* (1986); Leopoldo Bernucci, *Historia de un malentendido: un estudio transtextual de* La guerra del fin del mundo *de Mario Vargas Llosa* (1989); Silviano Santiago, *As Raízes e o Labirinto da América Latina* (2006).

8. See: Richard A. Gordon, *Cannibalizing the Colony: Cinematic Adaptations of Colonial Literature in Mexico and Brazil* (2009); Paulo Moreira, *Modernismo Localista das Américas* (2012); Robert Patrick Newcomb, *Nossa and* Nuestra América*: Inter-American Dialogues* (2011); Ori Preuss, *Bridging the Island: Brazilians' Views of Spanish America and Themselves, 1875–1912* (2011), Patrícia Vieira, *Seeing Politics Otherwise: Vision in Latin American and Iberian Fiction* (2011).

Portuguese together with French, Italian, and sometimes Catalan, as well as separate departments of Hispanic Studies and Portuguese and Brazilian Studies (as is the unique case of Brown University), present their own barriers to Luso-Hispanic exchange.[9]

In the best of cases, the "Spanish and Portuguese" model allows departments that are truly committed to Luso-Hispanic dialogue to facilitate fluid transitions between the two languages and traditions at the levels of research collaborations, as well as course and program design. Indeed, in recent years universities such as Vanderbilt and Ohio State have introduced PhD programs or tracks that require true linguistic and literary-cultural competency in Spanish *and* Portuguese, and that specifically encourage the comparative study of writers, texts, and cultural paradigms across the Luso-Hispanic divide.[10] Many Spanish PhD programs require graduates to study Portuguese language or support dissertation projects that are inclusive of Luso-Brazilian literary and cultural materials. Some departments incentivize undergraduates who major in Spanish to double major or minor in Portuguese, while others have incorporated courses in Spanish or Iberian multilingualism and regional identities into their curricula.[11] We strongly support all of these efforts on intellectual as well as pragmatic grounds. Further, growing interest in emerging fields such as Iberian, Inter-American, Transatlantic, and now Transoceanic studies has significant implications for Luso-Hispanic comparativism, given that all of these approaches provide opportunities for scholars to compare Luso-Brazilian and Hispanic materials, writers and cultural actors, and cases, albeit within distinct but not uncomplementary analytical frameworks.

Old habits may die hard, though the continued growth of comparative Luso-Hispanic scholarship, academic programs, and course offerings serves as evidence that the long pattern of Luso-Hispanic disengagement noted by Unamuno, Reyes, and more recently, Foster and Schwartz, may be changing, both in academia and "on the ground." Recent decades have seen a growing number of commentators in Latin America and Iberia—and an especially large number of U.S.-based scholars—call for a corrective to the "dissonance" that has traditionally impeded dialogue between Portuguese- and

---

9. In the interest of full disclosure, we both completed our PhD at Brown, in the departments of Portuguese and Brazilian Studies (Newcomb) and Hispanic Studies (Gordon).

10. Vanderbilt's Department of Spanish and Portuguese offers PhD programs in Spanish, Spanish and Portuguese, and Spanish and Portuguese with a specialization in Comparative Literature. Ohio State offers MA and PhD specializations in Iberian Studies and Latin American studies.

11. Examples include the courses "Spanish Mosaic: Catalonia, Basque Country, Galicia and Andalucia," developed by Eugenia Romero at The Ohio State University, and "Typology of Languages Spoken in the Iberian Peninsula," taught at the University of California, Santa Barbara.

Spanish-speaking writers and intellectuals. Concurrently, institutional and economic integration (MERCOSUR in South America and EU membership for Portugal and Spain), along with advances in communications technology and the much-invoked force of globalization, have facilitated Luso-Hispanic dialogue. Indeed, in 2005 the Brazilian government adopted a law (Lei 11.161) that requires all public middle schools to offer Spanish classes—a move that reflects increasing awareness of the economic importance of Spanish for Brazilian citizens. And as Pedro Schacht Pereira remarks in this volume's first contribution, the crises in Iberia and in U.S. public research universities that followed the 2008 global economic downturn have provided scholars with a particularly opportune occasion to question received ideas concerning the relationship between Luso-Brazilian and Hispanic literatures and cultures, and to challenge the assumption that these represent separate and self-contained intellectual projects.

The present moment, which holds the promise of increasing approximation between the Portuguese- and Spanish-speaking worlds, affords scholars a unique opportunity—indeed, compels us—to look back on the mutable, often fraught history of Luso-Hispanic literary and cultural relations. We firmly believe that the contributions included in *Beyond Tordesillas* demonstrate that there is much to be learned from comparative Luso-Hispanic studies, both in terms of the history of its literary and cultural expressions, and as an academic approach capable of accounting for the increasing cross-fertilization, and in some circumstances integration, of the Hispanic and Luso-Brazilian fields.

That said, the academic project presented in this volume merits explicit justification. Why a collection of essays on Luso-Hispanic studies and, by extension, why comparative Luso-Hispanic studies, as opposed or in addition to other academic projects, such as Iberian studies, Inter-American studies, and Transoceanic or Transatlantic studies? After all, don't these emerging fields address at least some of the same topics and questions? The following paragraphs present a few arguments specifically in favor of comparative Luso-Hispanic studies.

AGAINST LUSO-HISPANIC DISJUNCTION: CORRECTING THE SCHOLARLY RECORD

Comparative Luso-Hispanic analyses contribute to rehabilitating a scholarly record that has been conditioned, for reasons listed above, toward Luso-Hispanic disjunction. It is worth mentioning that the historical, ideological, and disciplinary factors that have led to Luso-Hispanic "disconsonance" have very real impacts in the present, for researchers as well as for students: in Spain, the "average" student of Spanish literature and culture, for instance, will almost certainly be less familiar with Portuguese writers than he or she will be with Catalan-language writers, or at least Catalan, Valencian, and Balearic authors who write in Castilian. This is because politically, Catalonia, Valencia, and the Balearic Islands have long been part of the Spanish nation-state (though not always willingly), whereas Portugal has not, with the exception of the 1580–1640 period. In short, writers like Juan Boscán, Eugenio d'Ors, and Jacinto Verdaguer (Joan Boscà, Eugeni d'Ors, and Jacint Verdaguer, in Catalan), along with self-identified Basque and Galician authors, can be incorporated into the Spanish national "canon" in ways that even Hispanophile Portuguese writers like Miguel Torga and José Saramago cannot, simply because the borders of the Spanish state have been viewed as synonymous with the disciplinary limits of Spanish or "peninsular" literature.[12] Similarly, successive generations of Brazilian critics—including Sérgio Buarque de Holanda and, much more recently, Jorge Schwartz—have lamented the fact that Brazilian readers typically know more about European and U.S. literature than they do about writing produced in neighboring Latin American countries, despite some prominent cases of interpersonal and thematic dialogue between Brazilian and Spanish-speaking Latin American authors. As Pereira observes, much work remains undone in elucidating these relationships. Yet he notes optimistically: "One of the upsides of the historical lack of communication between Hispanic and Luso-Brazilian Studies is the amount of work left to be done in areas that are central to both canons."

The interconnected historical, linguistic, and cultural contexts of the Spanish- and Portuguese-speaking worlds invite a variety of comparative approaches, many of which are represented in *Beyond Tordesillas*. These include the following.

Cases of literary and artistic influence, dialogue, and adaptation. As in Pedro Meira Monteiro's chapter on the "cannibalistic genealogy" that connects Uruguayan writer-critic José Enrique Rodó, Brazilian essayist and historian Sérgio Buarque de Holanda, and U.S. Latin Americanist scholar Richard Morse, and Frederick Moehn's essay on dialogues between contemporary Galician and Brazilian musicians. Monteiro's proposal to bring together Rodó,

---

12. Historically, the term "Spain" (*España, Espanha,* etc.), as the linguistic descendent of the Latin *Hispania,* referred to the whole of the Iberian Peninsula, irrespective of political boundaries. For instance, the Portuguese Renaissance poet Luís de Camões referred to the Portuguese as being from Spain in his Portuguese national epic, *Os Lusíadas* (1572). It is also curious—and frustrating, for scholars of Portuguese literature—that in the U.S. academy, peninsular literature refers exclusively to literature produced within the Spanish nation-state.

Buarque, and Morse so as to "trace [...] the curve of that Latin Americanist line of thought that envisions *another* kind of America, the other side to the mirror of America" is representative of a tendency in comparative Luso-Hispanic scholarship toward the demarcation of alternate Latin American and Iberian intellectual and artistic genealogies. Indeed, Moehn engages in such demarcations, and his contribution reminds us that alternate geographic poles, such as Galicia, or for that matter the *gaúcho* frontier between the Brazilian state of Rio Grande do Sul and Uruguay, the Amazonian headwaters, or U.S. cities with significant Spanish- *and* Portuguese-speaking populations, such as Boston and Miami, "can serve to draw our attention away from Lisbon and Madrid, and trace alternative relationships between Iberia and the Americas."

Broad literary, artistic, and cultural parallels, as well as intertwined cultural phenomena and cases of asynchrony. As in Leila Lehnen's essay on contemporary Latin American urban narrative, Sarah Moody's contribution on turn-of-the-century Latin American poetry, Robert Moser's discussion of the figure of the literary revenant, Patrícia Vieira's analysis of cinematic production under the Portuguese and Spanish dictatorships, and Alfredo Bosi's chapter on the Latin American avant-gardes, which proposes that "the avant-garde be a bridge with traffic running in two directions."

Theoretical and interdisciplinary approximations to Luso-Hispanic studies. As Héctor Hoyos, who makes the case in his chapter for "ad hoc transnationalism," reminds us, "geography is no substitute for theory." Several contributions to *Beyond Tordesillas* take Hoyos at his word, and apply a broad range of theoretical and interdisciplinary approaches to the study of Luso-Hispanic source materials. These include Pereira's essay on Iberian studies in relation to Luso-Brazilian studies; Tracy Devine Guzmán's comparative analysis of a Brazilian, Spanish American, and U.S. novel, which she analyzes under the broader rubric of hemispheric Native American studies; David William Foster's proposals for the study of "queer" Portuguese and Spanish; Earl Fitz's and Charles Perrone's comments on the role of Luso-Hispanic content in inter-American literature and trans-American lyricism, respectively; and Leslie L. Marsh's and Michael J. Lazzara's analyses of Luso-Hispanic narrative and documentary film in the context of post-dictatorial memory and globalization studies. As Lazzara observes, "studying globalization serves as an invitation to comparative scholarship," in this case Luso-Hispanic comparativism, "mainly because the critiques of globalization that appear in different kinds of cultural production seem to transcend national and even regional boundaries."

MUDDYING THE WATERS: THE REFLEXIVE CHARACTER OF LUSO-HISPANIC COMPARATIVISM

While Luso-Hispanic comparativism doubtless helps us to reform the scholarly record, we do not see this as its only function. Indeed, we believe that Luso-Hispanic comparativism can play a *productively disruptive* role with regard to geohistorical categories and disciplinary boundaries. As Robert Patrick Newcomb argues in his book Nossa and Nuestra América: *Inter-American Dialogues* (2011), comparative Luso-Hispanic studies should be understood as a necessarily reflexive project. In other words, by contesting the disciplinary separation between Luso-Brazilian and Hispanic studies, Luso-Hispanic comparativism challenges the claims of these canons, traditions, and fields to specificity and "purity," by illustrating the extent to which they are "contaminated" by one another. In this way, Luso-Hispanic studies can complement similarly reflexive initiatives such as Iberian studies and Inter-American studies.[13] Further, by "muddying the waters" of the Hispanic and Luso-Brazilian literary and cultural traditions, Luso-Hispanic studies provides us with a platform to interrogate and historicize apparently stable—though in actuality contingent and relational—categories like "Latin America" and "Iberia," and to pose potentially disruptive questions such as the following: Can Brazil be both *marginal* and *central* to Latin America, a part of the world frequently imagined as monolithically Spanish-speaking? Can Portuguese national identity be simultaneously constructed in opposition to Spain *and also* embrace its Iberian dimension, as writers like Torga and Saramago have suggested? We might ask the same question of Brazilian national identity with regard to Brazil's Spanish-speaking neighbors. And finally, is the idea of "Spain" contiguous with the Spanish nation-state? Or, as the Portuguese writer Almeida Garrett suggested at late as 1825,[14] does Spanish identity transcend Spain's borders so as to be accessible to the Portuguese as well—even as political and cultural actors in Catalonia, Galicia, and the Basque Country have challenged the notion of a cohesive Spanish identity from within the state's borders? All of these fraught, but also exciting and vital questions, can be posed by bringing Luso-Brazilian and Hispanic literary and cultural materials into dialogue.

---

13. See among other titles: Jeffrey Belnap and Raúl Fernández, eds., *José Martí's "Our America": From National to Hemispheric Cultural Studies* (1998); Joan Ramon Resina, ed., *Iberian Modalities: A Relational Approach to the Study of Culture in the Iberian Peninsula* (2013).

14. In a note to the first edition of his biographical poem *Camões* (1825), Garrett declared of his fellow Portuguese: "Espanhóis somos, e Espanhóis nos devemos prezar todos os que habitam esta península" [We are Spaniards, and all of us who live in this Peninsula should take pride in being Spaniards] (432).

BRAZIL'S EMERGENCE, THE EU CRISIS, AND OTHER CHANGES

Recent changes in the Luso-Hispanic sphere have the potential to significantly shift the ground from under the feet of Portuguese- and Spanish-speaking cultural actors. Taken together, these changes make the case for comparative Luso-Hispanic studies more urgent and compelling. Brazil's ascent to the status of Latin America's unchallenged economic leader, and its more recent emergence as an important political force in attempting to reconcile Latin America's left- and right-leaning blocs, have dramatically raised the country's international profile, even as its ongoing political drama and the challenges associated with preparing for the 2014 World Cup and 2016 Olympics have demonstrated that Brazil's rise has not been untroubled. These changes make the perennially thorny question of Brazil's relationship to "Latin America," which successive generations of Spanish American writers and intellectuals (Simón Bolívar, José Enrique Rodó, José Martí, Alfonso Reyes, Roberto Fernández Retamar, etc.) have understood as a Spanish-speaking *madre patria* or *nuestra América*, all the more pressing.

Similarly, Portugal's and Spain's roles in the European Union, in the years following the 2008 global financial crash and ensuing sovereign debt crisis, have been called into question. We may ask: If economic downturn, budgetary imbalances between northern and southern European member states, government austerity on the Iberian Peninsula, and the 2016 "Brexit" vote cause integration to stall or even reverse, will this lead to decreased Spanish-Portuguese flows? Or will Spain and Portugal's shared membership in a group of "southern" European pariah states (the unfortunately named PIIGS) bring them closer together at the expense of Europe, as prophesied by Saramago in *The Stone Raft*? In any case, the ongoing European crisis and austerity in Spain and Portugal have resurrected very old questions concerning Iberian particularity and the peninsula's troubled historical relationship with Europe *além Pirenéus*.

ORGANIZATION OF THE VOLUME

The essays of *Beyond Tordesillas* respond to each of these arguments in favor of comparative Luso-Hispanic studies. In addition to providing a rich resource for future comparative work—the contributors and others currently engaged in comparative Luso-Hispanic studies have only scratched the surface of this approach—we hope that this volume will act as a catalyst for the reconsideration of hybrid categories, institutional configurations, and the relationships between the countries of the Spanish- and Portuguese-speaking worlds. *Beyond Tordesillas* focuses chronologically on the twentieth century and beyond. In order to emphasize the geographic sweep and transoceanic interconnections essential to this emerging field, we have organized the volume according to object of study. The chapters are divided into four subsections that underscore the breadth of the volume with regard to genre, region, and topic, as well as theoretical and methodological approaches.

Theoretical and Disciplinary Proposals

Beyond Tordesillas places its first chapters in direct dialogue with the overall scope and aims of the project. This section of theoretical and disciplinary proposals begins with Pedro Schacht Pereira's essay, "Portuguese and the Emergence of Iberian Studies," which assesses how the ongoing globalization of academia and the disciplinary reassessment of "Hispanism" have created the potential for greater dialogue between Hispanist and Luso-Brazilianist scholars. The second contribution, "The Case for Ad Hoc Transnationalism," is written by Héctor Hoyos. Through a wide-ranging historical and institutional analysis, Hoyos argues "for a certain suppleness of mind when approaching Latin American literature in a transnational context." Further, he warns "against the shortcomings of the overinstitutionalization of certain transnational models." Notably, Hoyos includes among these models the "bipolar understanding of Latin American literature as the sum of Brazilian and Spanish American literatures." The next chapter is by David William Foster, who in "Queer Spanish, Queer Portuguese: A Series of Research Proposals" proposes a deconstructive "queering" of Luso-Hispanic studies as a means to investigate how linguistic normalization has contributed to sedimenting Hispanic and Luso-Brazilian studies as separate disciplines. For her part, Tracy Devine Guzmán, in "Before Tordesilhas, and Beyond: The Politics of Native Agency across the Americas," analyzes three novels—one Brazilian, one Spanish American, and one North American—that examine how Native and non-Native actors have interacted to engage and represent the experiences of indigenous peoples inside and beyond national borders. She contends that as members of groups that trace their collective ties *across* and *before* Tordesillas, indigenous intellectuals, activists, and artists offer a crucial and understudied perspective on how and why to rethink the Americas, beyond categories such as "Brazil" and "Latin America." While Devine Guzmán offers a close reading of three texts, the manner in which she brings Native American studies to bear on Luso-Hispanic comparativism merits her chapter's inclusion in this first section. In "'Blister You all': Sérgio Buarque de Holanda and the Calibanic Genealogy," Pedro Meira Monteiro draws on the work of Brazilian historian and critic Buarque and U.S. Latin Americanist scholar Richard Morse. Monteiro argues that the most effective way to "jump" Tordesillas is to look at how Brazilian and Spanish American writers have imagined a North American "Other" as an enemy to be fought against, or as a power to be emulated.

Written Fictional Narrative

Robert Moser provides the opening essay of the volume's second section, which focuses on literary prose. His chapter, "The Literary Revenant in a Latin American Context," looks to the figure of the revenant, or literary ghost, in exploring how Brazilian and Spanish American prose writers have grappled with, expressed, or negated forms of ambiguity, whether ontological, aesthetic, or gender-related. Earl Fitz's "Borges, Clarice, and the Development of Latin America's 'New Narrative'" compares the work of Jorge Luis Borges and Clarice Lispector as cultivators of Latin American "new narratives," and argues that while Borges's innovative short stories are largely sui generis, Lispector's novel *Perto do Coração Selvagem* (Near to the Wild Heart, 1943) is the logical product of a coherent, cohesive tradition of experimental fiction in Brazil that remits to Machado de Assis's highly original work at the turn of the twentieth century. Leila Lehnen's essay, "Mapping Citizenship in Luiz Ruffato's *Inferno provisório* and Guillermo Saccomanno's *El pibe*," concludes this section. Her contribution examines the conjunction between urban space and the constitution and erosion of citizenship in selected stories from Brazilian writer Ruffato's *Inferno provisório* (Temporary Hell, 2005–11) and Argentinian Saccomanno's *El pibe* (The Kid, 2006). She argues that the texts reveal the dynamic processes of citizenship, along with its unequal implementation, and how material and imaginary cartography reflects and reinforces these disjunctures and transformations.

Poetry, Music, Expressive Culture

Alfredo Bosi, one of Brazil's preeminent literary scholars, opens the third section. His essay, "The *Parábola* of the Latin American Avant-Gardes," argues that apparent differences between Latin America's many avant-garde literary movements (including Brazilian *modernismo* and Spanish American *vanguardismos*) must be examined in light of the "colonial condition" under which Latin America has historically been subsumed. In this way Bosi ties his comparative study of the Latin American avant-gardes to the provocative analysis he undertook in his now classic study of Brazilian literature, *Dialética da Colonização* (Brazil and the Dialectic of Colonization, 1992). Sarah Moody's chapter, "Brazilian Symbolism and Hispanic American *Modernismo*: Resonance across the Luso-Hispanic Divide," revisits the same Latin American poetic context as Bosi, and argues that despite limited contact between Brazilian Symbolists and Spanish American *modernistas*, they are linked through a shared reading of the French Symbolists. There existed, she argues, "a field of shared innovation across national and linguistic divides in Latin America," such that "the Brazilian Symbolists and Hispanic American modernists bear more similarities than have previously been noted." In "Shared Passages: Spanish American–Brazilian Links in Contemporary Poetry," Charles Perrone analyzes a wide range of recent lyric poetry and events organized by artists and academics from the Americas, all of which reveal the flourishing of a transnational poetics, not only across but also beyond Latin America's Luso-Hispanic divide. The closing essay of the section, "*Cantigas de amigo*: Galicia and Brazil in the Lusophone Musical Space," by Frederick Moehn, explores from an ethnographic perspective a music festival in the Galician city of Pontevedra, in Spain. He argues that this artistic, and at the same time political, event treats Galicia as a Luso-Hispanic bridge by capitalizing on Galicia's close historical and linguistic ties to the Portuguese-speaking world. These also allow Galicia to assert its autonomy within Spain.

Cinema

The first essay of the final section of *Beyond Tordesillas*, "Cartography of Dissidence: In/visibility and Urban Display in Luso-Hispanic Street Projects," is by Tina Escaja. By investigating two examples of performance that are related to gender violence, one from Brazil and the other from Spain, Escaja highlights correlations between the two in terms of parallel contexts of protest and resistance through art and collective interaction. In "Memory, Youth and Regimes of Violence in Recent Hispanic and Lusophone Cinemas," Leslie Marsh explores intersecting cinematic representations of dictatorship from across Latin American countries. She asserts that her case studies from Brazil and Spanish America, despite their differences, illustrate that "memory in cinema remains an ongoing, ever-changing process." Further, she contends that the particular films she analyzes look to a traumatic past in order to envision a better future. Patrícia Vieira explores an earlier era and, in a sense, the other side of the political-artistic coin, in "Cinema in Totalitarian Iberia: Propaganda and Persuasion under Salazar and Franco." Her essay traces the roughly parallel and occasionally intersecting histories of films produced in dictatorial-era Portugal and Spain, and focuses on films that received direct and intentional, or indirect and/or coerced, support from these regimes. The volume closes with "Globalization and Documentary Film: Luso-Hispanic Reflections," in which Michael J. Lazzara studies the trend in both Latin America and Iberia toward a "personal" documentary style. This trend tends to problematize the reliability of cinematic truth construction. Lazzara examines how films from Brazil, Mexico, and Spain use the juxtaposition of "microhistories" and "macrohistories" to evaluate "the homogenizing impetus of globalization" and to challenge its effects.

The essays in this volume represent only a small fraction of the work to be done in the area of comparative Luso-Hispanic studies. We hope the chapters that follow will act as a catalyst for more and more scholars and students to access a rich array of literary and cultural comparisons between the Hispanic and Luso-Brazilian traditions by looking beyond Tordesillas.

WORKS CITED

Foster, David William. "Spanish American and Brazilian Literature: A History of Disconsonance." *Hispania* 75.4 (1992): 966–78.

Garrett, Almeida. *Obras*. Vol. 1. Porto: Lello & Irmão, 1966.

Hamilton, Russell G. "Lusofonia, Africa, and Matters of Languages and Letters." *Hispania* 74.3 (1991): 610–17.

Loureiro, Ángel. "Spanish Nationalism and the Ghost of Empire." *Journal of Spanish Cultural Studies* 4.1 (2003): 65–76.

Newcomb, Robert Patrick. Nossa *and* Nuestra América: *Inter-American Dialogues*. West Lafayette: Purdue UP, 2012.

Pace, Joel. "Towards a Taxonomy of Transatlantic Romanticism(s)." *Literature Compass* 5.2 (2008): 228–91.

Schwartz, Jorge. "Abaixo Tordesilhas!" *Estudos Avançados* 7.17 (1993): 185–200.

Unamuno, Miguel de. "Español-Portugués" [1914]. *Obras completas*. 9 vols. Ed. Manuel García Blanco. Madrid: Escelicer, 1966–71.

PART I

LUSO-HISPANIC STUDIES AND RELATED LINES OF INQUIRY

A SERIES OF PROPOSALS

CHAPTER 1

Portuguese and the Emergence of Iberian Studies

PEDRO SCHACHT PEREIRA

FOR SOME TIME now the academic fields known as Luso-Brazilian studies and Hispanic studies have been undergoing significant reconfigurations, prompted in no small measure by the receding of the Humanities—and Literature in particular—from the curricula and the budgets of a research university constricted by the market-oriented demands of neoliberal globalization. Much has been said about the lack of appeal that, in a time characterized by extremely competitive access to diminishing financial resources, traditionally configured Hispanic studies has had for students who increasingly see a college education as an opportunity to learn a trade;[1] in the case of Luso-Brazilian studies, the slow but steady nationwide growth of enrollments in Portuguese language classes risks being mistaken for a genuine interest in the literatures and cultures of the Portuguese-speaking world.[2] It might still be premature to ask how effective these reconfigurations will be in staving off a crisis that to a

---

All translations mine unless otherwise noted.

1. For challenges to Hispanic studies—with particular emphasis on the Peninsular side of the equation—see Faber.

2. The Modern Language Association's report "Enrollments in Languages Other Than English in United States Institutions of Higher Education" (Fall 2009) lists a growth from 8,385 to 11,371 in enrollments in Portuguese between 2002 and 2009. Between 2002 and 2006 the percentage change was 22.4, and between 2006 and 2009 it was 10.8. The report also shows a significant discrepancy between enrollments in introductory and advanced classes, suggesting that indeed the association between studying the language and studying the cultures and literatures of the Portuguese-speaking world is not necessarily an immediate one in the minds

large degree transcends the realms of each of the two disciplines; but I would like to contend here that the crisis has at least created the opportunity for scholars in these disciplines to reassess their institutional configuration in the U.S. academy, which I would characterize as a situation of false proximity.[3] My contribution for this volume is envisioned as a preliminary attempt, through the discussion of two texts that have eloquently brought this issue to light, to create the conditions for an exercise of the disciplines that makes such proximity more productive and desirable.

The evidence for this false proximity can be found by anyone who peruses the documents issued annually by the Modern Language Association on the occasion of its annual convention: in programs and forms, so-called Luso-Brazilian studies is configured as merely an atemporal subsection of Hispanic studies, with the same weight as, say, "Golden Age Spanish Literature," or "Nineteenth-Century Latin-American Literature." Yet, as everyone who works in any of those fields knows well, such representation does not correspond to the reality experienced daily by scholars and teachers of Spanish and Portuguese. And it never has. For better or for worse, the study of the literatures and cultures of Spanish and Portuguese expression have always constituted separate fields in their own right, with the occasional meeting points being explored by medievalist and Golden Age scholars, periods in which Portuguese literature is often considered—falsely—as a development peripheral to Hispanism. The discussion as to why this has never been the case might not yet be settled, but few would contest that the possibility of Portuguese inhabiting the periphery of Hispanism evaporated after 1640, when the acclamation of João IV as king of Portugal put an end to sixty years of a dual Hapsburg monarchy. In this sense, 1640 is arguably a more ominous date than 1494 and Tordesillas. While the former constitutes one of the principal markers in a long-lasting history of mutual estrangement and imperial competition between the two Iberian monarchies, the latter happens at a time when, for the most part, both countries shared a common worldview, and Portuguese colonial ventures in Africa and the Americas—especially slave traders—greatly benefited from and participated in Spain's empire.

The history of the peculiar relationship that emerged out of the institutional configuration of Spanish and Portuguese studies in the United States is

---

of students: a good number of students who take introductory classes do not go on to pursue a minor or major.

3. By "crisis" I refer to a plurality of symptoms discernable in today's U.S. academy: the crisis of the Hispanic Studies paradigm, the crisis in Humanities-based education, and the global financial crisis, whose effects have been felt on so many college campuses across the country.

too complex to address within the limits of this essay, but what is at stake is the opportunity that current academic trends present to these disciplines for an increased mutual awareness and productive conversation.[4] My presumption, in accordance with Héctor Hoyos's contribution to this volume, is that institutional reconfigurations constitute valuable opportunities for pursuing new ways of thinking. I believe there are signs that a rapprochement between the two disciplines is possible and is already happening in certain corners of the system.

Among the recent developments in U.S. academia that I see as having a potentially positive and lasting impact on the relationship between Hispanic and Luso-Brazilian studies is the advent of what has come to be called Iberian studies. Issuing from a debate internal to Peninsular Hispanic studies, centered on the epistemological, political, and historical foreclosure of the ideology that has traditionally informed so-called Peninsular or Peninsular Spanish studies (i.e., Hispanism), the idea of Iberian studies has been debated in colloquia, conference panels, and a slowly growing number of publications, which have attracted the attention of university administrations.[5] In 2011 alone, two Iberian studies working groups bringing together scholars in Spanish and Portuguese—as well as scholars whose work focuses on the cultures of Spain's other languages, such as Catalan, Euskera, and Galician—were formed, one in California and another in the Midwest, and important curricular and institutional reconfigurations have taken place at some institutions. At The Ohio State University the section of the Department of Spanish and Portuguese previously called "Peninsular" has reinvented itself as a unit devoted to Iberian studies, and perhaps most notably at Stanford University, Joan Ramon Resina directs a new program in Iberian studies under the aegis of the Europe Center, defined as "an interdisciplinary initiative to promote relational knowledge of the various cultures of the Iberian Peninsula" (http://europe.stanford.edu/research/iberianstudies/).

Resina has also for a while offered what is arguably the most articulate but also controversial validation of the aforementioned paradigm shift in essays such as "Hispanism and Its Discontents" (1996), the introduction to the essay compilation *Del hispanismo a los estudios ibéricos: una propuesta federativa para el ámbito cultural* (2009), and the more recent *Iberian Modalities: A Relational Approach to the Study of Culture in the Iberian Peninsula* (2012),

---

4. For a brief overview of this history, see Jackson.
5. Among such publications I will mention Faber's "Economies of Prestige," and the volume that Mabel Moraña edited for Vanderbilt, *Ideologies of Hispanism*, which was followed by an issue of the *Hispanic Journal* with the same title, and co-edited by Moraña and Reyes Coll-Tellechea.

a volume he edited for Liverpool University Press.[6] The first essay is a good example of the epistemological cul-de-sac that Resina effectively attributes to Hispanism: on one hand the essay makes no secret of the fact that it still situates itself within the confines of the discipline it proposes to reshape; on the other hand, and in so small measure because of such discursive positioning, the essay unsuccessfully flirts with the idea of including Portuguese literature and culture within the purview of a renovated Hispanism—a gesture which merely reenacts the Hispanist tendency to confine such literature and culture at best to the periphery of Hispanism. Conversely, the second essay—published a good thirteen years after the *Siglo XX/20th Century* essay—conspicuously speaks from a different location, one that the essay charts for itself in the process of being written, and in which Portuguese literature and culture are not so much predicated upon but are rather, as we will see, already an inalienable part of its core. That is, in the volume in which Resina revisits the issue of the foreclosure of Hispanism from a Catalan perspective, the paradigm shift he began advocating at least thirteen years earlier is brought forth, and Iberian studies is born.

The underlying premise in "Hispanism and Its Discontents" is that the cultural system of the Iberian Peninsula has historically been distorted by the hypertrophic manifestation of one of its components:

> The cultural system of the Iberian peninsula, hitherto conceived as a relatively unproblematic continuum of the "Spanish" tradition, can be studied to advantage as a process of differentiation of cultures which constitute the system's internal environment. From the point of view of this model, it is obvious that the system cannot be grasped through one of its components only, and that it is distorted if this one component becomes the guiding viewpoint for the entire systemic environment. (89)

Attempting to provide an explanation for why "Hispanism has long been a poor relative of the other branches of literary studies," and more recently why its modern so-called Peninsular wing has been "steadily losing ground in American universities" (86), Resina proposes an assessment of the historical and institutional trajectory of the discipline through its three core areas of development: the German, Anglo-American, and Spanish university systems. This exercise, inspired in part by Niklas Luhmann's theory of social systems,

---

6. The controversy has emerged mostly within Hispanic Peninsular Studies, where Resina's Catalan-centered approach has been met with skepticism. But on the side of Latin American Studies questions have also been raised. For an example of a discussion of Resina's work from the point of view of Latin American Studies, see Trigo.

is carried out with the awareness that these specific historical contexts imply a "functional variability" (88) of Hispanism as an institutionalized discourse, and that such variability opens up the possibility of conceiving new, and potentially disruptive inflections. One can easily surmise that the embryo of what would become Iberian studies finds its germinating space in this opening. I will not reprise here Resina's discussion of the historical development of the three core areas of Hispanism. For the sake of expediency, let me just note that in my view the most significant trait of his argument is the provocative thesis that it was the "modernization and rapid development of a national consciousness in Catalonia" (107), coinciding with the Spanish-American War of 1898—and not the war and consequent loss of the colonies itself—which prompted "the construction of a core Peninsular identity to dam the political erosion on Iberian soil" (107). The concern with the idea of regenerationism displayed by the writers of the famous *Generación del 98* would have consisted of "a compensation for the ascent of the periphery" and contributed to "the reactive nationalism that dominates Spanish politics in the twentieth century" (107). While this thesis surely caused a stir among certain hispanists, it also shows the core location of the Catalan question in Resina's early articulation of the project of Iberian studies.

If, according to Resina, the discipline of Hispanism is still coming to terms with the "cultural reality unveiled by the political reforms of the Spanish state for more than a quarter of a century" (163), the disciplines associated with the idea of Luso-Brazilian studies have already undergone two processes of reconfiguration whose temporalities can of course be traced back to the social, political, and cultural transformations that in varying degrees and modes have shaken the entire Portuguese-speaking world, first with Portugal's loss of Brazil in 1822 and the ensuing colonial expansion in Africa at the end of the nineteenth century, and then the anticolonial struggle that challenged Portuguese colonial rule in Africa from the 1960s to 1974. The first set of events explains why the designation "Luso-Brazilian" remains problematic to this day: as is well known, Luso-Brazilian commonality of ideas and purposes, as well as the self-perception of Brazilian and Portuguese elites, effectively ceased to exist by the second decade of the twentieth century. It could be argued that the ideology of Luso-Brazilianism symbolically met its demise with the death of Brazilian intellectual and diplomat Manuel de Oliveira Lima (1867–1928).[7] The second set of events unleashed a process of reevaluation of

---

7. On the role of Oliveira Lima as mediator and precursor of the ideology that would come to be named—by none other than his former student Gilberto Freyre—Lusotropicalism, readers can consult my "Fermento da República, bolor do Império: Civilização Ibérica, excepcionalismo e o legado luso-brasileiro do lusotropicalismo." The death of this Portuguese-

Portuguese national identity that reached peak moments in 1986, with Portugal's entry into the European Union, and in 1998, when the last World Expo of the twentieth century took place in Lisbon. Ana Paula Ferreira aptly explains what a new discipline of "Luso-Afro-Brazilian Studies," as an alternative to the Luso-Brazilian studies paradigm, should look like at the beginning of the new century:

> Rather than a purely descriptive, trans-historical space or category of analysis, Luso-Afro-Brazilian Studies (or whatever other designation they may be given) illustrate the anti-disciplinary, anti-nationalist, anti-colonialist structure of thought that, in many ways, prepared and accompanied the wave of political, social, economic and cultural changes occurring since at least the last quarter of the 20th century in most parts of the world where Portuguese is spoken. ("Integrating" 76)

The uncertainty about which designation to give to this new discipline denotes the change in process in what has been inadequately called Luso-Brazilian studies, and is also an indication of the kind of epistemological challenges being faced by the field, some of which were mentioned by name in Ana Paula Ferreira's essay.[8] The challenges and the change occur in response to an empirical reality that Ferreira perceptively describes:

> From the moment that the political, economic and cultural privilege of the nation-state begins to falter; from the moment that the imaginary unity of the national community is contradicted by the presence of peoples, systems of thought, symbolic expressions and material practices that are temporally and spatially disparate, disciplinary and national definitions become unfixed, opened to re-articulations outside strict definitional boundaries. (76)

As these quotes suggest, the epistemological challenges facing both Hispanism and Luso-Brazilian studies today are strikingly parallel, even if the historical

---

educated Brazilian diplomat and intellectual coincided with the rise of Brazilian *Modernismo* and the drive for Brazil's definite cultural emancipation from its former colonial power. In the last years of his life Oliveira Lima grew estranged from Brazil's Republican establishment, dying in Washington, DC, in 1928.

8. The main challenge is to foster an interdisciplinarity that transcends the space-time of the Portuguese language, since the sites of encounter and conflict that gave shape to the cultures that share that language were never monolingual nor monocultural. In a more recent essay, "Specificity Without Exceptionalism: Towards a Critical Lusophone Postcoloniality," Ferreira addresses other, more long-term specters that have haunted and continue to haunt the discourses of Luso-Brazilian studies, such as Lusotropicalism. Such specters are not entirely different, in their silencing effects, from those haunting Hispanism.

conditions that have unraveled the cultural systems studied by those disciplines were not and are not synchronous. As some recent curricular reforms in Portugal attest, the historic transformations that have swept across the Portuguese-speaking world since the 1960s have made it harder for a Luso-centric worldview to prevail at the academic level (if not in the sociopolitical sphere, where it definitely still holds considerable ground), in Portugal and more so in Brazil.[9] It is unlikely that such a Luso-centric view would hold sway in existing and new programs in universities in the Portuguese-speaking African countries.

Almost seventy years ago the Portuguese Hispanophile Fidelino de Figueiredo (1889–1967) elevated to law what he called the "paralelidade e assincronia" [parallelism and a-synchronicity] that characterized the history *and* the cultures of the two Iberian states, which for him explained the repeated failure of the various attempts made by politicians and intellectuals alike to approximate them. While I am not sure that Figueiredo's language can withstand the test of time unscathed, given the reified understanding of the terms it promotes, I must confess affinity for the idea of a-synchronicity, not as the manifestation of a rigid law but rather as a sort of music of chance, a ground from where Iberian studies might chart its not always stable course.[10] In this particular case, it may provide the chance for a nuanced comparative study of the difficulties as well as the opportunities made possible by the demise of the cultural systems that for too long have legitimated an unproductive institutional relationship.

Granted, Resina's Iberianism, which is markedly different from nineteenth-century forms of *Iberismo*, deliberately transcends the scope of the relationship between Spain and its westerly neighbor, and, fundamentally, that of the

---

9. In most programs of Portuguese studies, recent reforms have emphasized the role of both Brazilian and African studies in the curriculum. In Brazil, for several years the Program in Comparative Studies of the Literatures of the Portuguese-Speaking World at the University of São Paulo has led the way.

10. Fidelino de Figueiredo's formulation runs as follows: "And the law, which I would propose as the regulating formula for that insistence on an approximation to Spain and its constant failure, would be that of parallelism and a-synchronicity" (82) [E a lei, que eu proporia como fórmula reguladora dessa insistência da aproximação espanhola e do seu constante fracasso, seria a da paralelidade e assincronia das histórias das duas nações peninsulares]. One telling historical example of this law for Figueiredo was the fact that "in 1930 the physiognomy of Luso-Brazilian relations does not facilitate Portuguese collaboration in Ibero-American politics, to which Spain devotes itself enthusiastically" (91) ["em 1930 a fisionomia das relações luso-brasileiras não facilita a colaboração portuguesa na política ibero-americana, a que a Espanha se aplica com entusiasmo"].

relationship between culture and the state.[11] After all, one of the premises of his thinking—ascertained more forcefully in the later essay—consists of establishing as an "epistemological advantage" the idea of "going beyond the State as hallmark of the legitimate knowledge of cultures whose geographical and historical relations precede and will outlive the present political configuration" (163).[12] But it is perhaps prudent to ask whether the wholesale omission of the issue of the state along with that of Portugal's language having its main center of gravity—and also one of the main cores of development of Luso-Brazilian studies—outside Portugal, does not run the risk of taking the balkanized reality of Luso-Brazilian studies in North American universities a bit too much for granted, as if this state of affairs in North American academia mirrored any sort of empirical reality.

To be fair, nowhere in "Hispanism and Its Discontents" does Resina establish as even a remote objective the issue of defining Portugal's role in the new discipline of Iberian studies. One cannot fault the text for failing to fulfill a promise that it does not make. But in a text invested in persuading readers that Hispanism "amputated ample segments of the Peninsula's cultural image," and that it "does not stand the exhaustive scrutiny of the sum of documented culture, nor of the Peninsula's social reality" (29); in a text, furthermore, devoted to the ideal of making viable a "supranational discipline in which the various cultures of the Iberian Peninsula (*including the Portuguese*) could be studied in a non-hierarchical relation to each other" (114; my emphasis), it is noteworthy that its author would include the Portuguese, but in what is in fact just a parenthetical remark. Doesn't the question of how to include in the discussion the entity potentially unsettle the logic of "non-hierarchical relation" and of a "supranational" dimension *within* Hispanism? Doesn't an inclusion on such grounds suggest one of those "few symbolic overtures tolerated at the margins of the discipline" ("Hispanism" 162),[13] denounced by Resina in his later writings?

My suspicion that this is the case is warranted not so much by the parenthetical confinement of the invitation, but mostly by the implicit conflation

---

11. Debates about *Iberismo* took many different forms, particularly after the publication of *La Iberia* by Catalan author D. Sinibaldo de Mas in Lisbon in 1851. *Iberismo* imagined scenarios for the union and/or federation of Iberia's many different nations, and not just its two recognized states, Portugal and Spain.

12. "ventaja epistemológica" "sobrepasar al Estado como marco del conocimiento legítimo de unas culturas cuyas relaciones geográficas e históricas preceden y sobrevivirán a la actual configuración política."

13. "pocas muestras simbólicas toleradas en los márgenes de la disciplina."

of the peripheral situation of Spain's autonomous regions and that of Portugal (and, by extension, the cultures of the Portuguese-speaking world at large):

> The most superficial analysis of the policies of cultural sponsorship by the organisms of the [Spanish] state [...] shows the extent to which the state recognizes one of the historical cultures as its one and only. The implications for Hispanism are also clear. The non-Castilian literary cultures of the Peninsula find their place as national philologies in their respective geographic-historical areas, while having virtually no presence beyond their circumscription. ("Hispanism" 114)

However urgent and welcome the question of the relation between Hispanism and its peripheries *within Spain* might be for Resina, it remains fundamentally peripheral to Portugal, an Iberian culture that does not maintain (or no longer maintains) its identity in agonistic terms with Spain. The inclusion of Portuguese in an Iberian studies conceived as a response to Spain's turbulent postimperial cultural nationalism will simply not fly. If anything, the history of the failure of late nineteenth-century Iberianist efforts serves as a cautionary tale in this regard.[14] At most, what would be accomplished would be the reenactment of Fidelino de Figueiredo's law, within a discipline where the competition for scarce resources would constitute a source of enduring bad conscience and resentment. One of Resina's crowning formulations at the end of his article is particularly telling of the insufficiency of the theoretical underpinnings of the project of Iberian studies as conceived in the mid-1990s:

> What I am proposing is patently a political program, or rather an epistemological bid that makes no pretense of political detachment. But however politicized, this bid takes its relation to the disciplinary object seriously, i.e., believes that *there is* an object. By advocating not less Hispanism but more Hispanisms, I do not suggest that the knowledge-content dissolves itself in a net of interests and self-serving tactics. (121; author's emphasis)

Without further inquiry into the adequacy of the pluralized designation of "Hispanisms," Portuguese or so-called Luso-Brazilian studies—only implicitly included—becomes the elephant in the room. And just as well, so long as the

---

14. For an overview of the history of nineteenth-century Iberianism, see Resina's insightful reading in the introduction to *Del hispanismo a los estudios ibéricos*. See also Sérgio Campos Matos's "Conceitos de Iberismo em Portugal" and "Iberismo e identidade nacional (1851–1910)," and also Fernando Catroga's "Nacionalismo e ecumenismo. A questão ibérica na segunda metade do século XIX."

goal of Iberian studies remains the reconfiguration of Hispanism, and thus to a considerable extent the reproduction at a different level of the same hierarchical logic of center and peripheries. If, however, this new field is to live up to its transformational promise, then wider epistemological (and, I dare say, political) shifts are to be sought that will open up possibilities for asking questions from the vantage point of different historical experiences and outcomes. Reluctant or absent-minded Luso-Brazilianists might just decide that this is also their debate to be had, at a time when the exclusively literary and cultural orientation of the discipline of Luso-Brazilian studies is also in question. When the nation seems to no longer be the paradigm orienting scholarship and academic debates, an Iberian studies capable of reckoning with the Luso-Hispanic borders will certainly not be the last word in the ever-evolving process of field reconfiguration. But it might help arguing more persuasively for a more transnational, decentered, and global approach to humanistic study than what the two heretofore separate, considerably different, and estranged fields have been capable of fostering. Whether the two fields will continue to evolve separately or not is something that perhaps should remain in question. But Iberian studies deserves to be embraced if, among other accomplishments, it will signal the end of the estrangement of the two fields, as well as the widening of their scope.

The cultivation of a nonhierarchical relation between the various cultures of the Iberian Peninsula is indeed possible, so long as we remain vigilant to the resilient philological prejudices that Iberian studies is intent on overcoming. More than possible, this shift toward nonhierarchical disciplinary organization is necessary, because the parenthetical entity so ambivalently invited to the conversation (i.e., the Portuguese-speaking world) happens to also be rife with philological constraints of its own, even if they run a-synchronically with those of Hispanism.[15] This a-synchronicity could well constitute the opening needed for ensuring a transformational comparatism in an uncertain academic future. Despite its shortcomings, I am convinced that Joan Ramon Resina's intervention opens up an opportunity worth exploring.

Thirteen years after the publication of "Hispanism and Its Discontents," Resina compiled in a volume several of the articles and conferences he had published on the issue of Hispanism in English-language journals between

---

15. One example of this a-synchronicity is the fact that so-called Luso-Brazilian Studies is unencumbered by the longstanding philological tradition that Joan Ramon Resina needs to reckon with from within Hispanism. In Portugal alone, the controversies around the recent project of the publication of the classics of the national literature, sponsored by the state organism *Direção Geral do Livro e das Bibliotecas* under the designation "Obras Clássicas da Literatura Portuguesa," should merit study as an anecdotal symptom of the irrelevance, in contemporary Portugal, of philology as a broker of state ideology and national identity.

1996 and 2005. The volume, titled *Del hispanismo a los estudios ibéricos: una propuesta federativa para el ámbito cultural,* includes a new introduction, which in my opinion exponentially advances the cause of Iberian studies as a nonhierarchical discipline devoted to transformational comparatism. This is accomplished in part through the rewriting of the key passage from "Hispanism and Its Discontents" analyzed above, and especially through a practice of writing that effectively brings to fruition the epistemological leap sketched out during the preceding decade. Resina himself best summarizes this type of writing in the last two pages of the introduction:

> It's neither a matter, in Iberian studies, of finding these cultures' common denominator in order to subsume them under a sterile cultural unity, nor of segregating them in airtight compartments as in a catalogue of disparate products assembled according to administrative or market whims. [. . .] *The broadening of focus that takes place with the institution of this (epistemological) demarcation uncovers interrelations that normally would be missed by the hispanist's gaze,* because they do not factor in his system of relevancies nor are they therefore given a place in the discipline's meta-narrative. (47; my emphasis)[16]

Let me note that the last sentence in the quote is doubly meta-narrative, as it signals Resina's overcoming of a significant epistemological obstacle, which weighed not only on the practice of the discipline, but also on obstacles that attended his previous writings, in which he begins to take issue with that practice: that of the exclusion (or insufficient inclusion) of the interrelations that inform the history of the cultures of the Peninsula from the discipline's meta-narrative or heuristic discussions. On the other hand, it is important to keep in mind that these remarks, and particularly the one I highlighted, do not solely constitute a declaration of principles or a strategy to be adopted in a hypothetical future; rather, they summarize and explain what has already taken place in the preceding pages of the introduction.

With the intention of providing the historical "objective correlative" of the current predicaments facing so-called Peninsular studies, while acknowledging that the "Post-imperial cultural nationalism" that marks Hispanism,

---

16. "No se trata, en los estudios ibéricos, de buscar el denominador común a estas culturas para subsumirlas bajo un unitarismo cultural estéril, ni tampoco de segregarlas en compartimientos estancos como en un muestrario de productos reunidos al azar de unos determinantes mercantiles o administrativos. [. . .] *La apertura de foco que tiene lugar con la instauración del marco pone al descubierto interrelaciones que de ordinario escapan a la mirada del hispanista,* por no entrar en su sistema de relevancias y no ocupar, por tanto, lugar en el metarrelato disciplinar."

and that fails to correspond to the social reality or the cultural record of the entirety of the Peninsula, Resina briefly revisits the history of nineteenth-century Iberianism, as an example of a crucial debate that has for the most part been passed over by the gaze of the hispanist. This leads him to discuss the role played in that debate by a figure that is key to understanding the history of inter-Iberian relations as well as the history of Portuguese literature and historiography: the Portuguese historian and thinker Joaquim Pedro de Oliveira Martins (1845–94). Through a discussion of one of Martins's canonical works, *História da Civilização Ibérica* (1879), Resina reconstitutes a debate that at several moments assumed truly inter- and transnational dimensions, with its crucial focus not on the two Iberian states but rather on Portugal and Catalonia. Oliveira Martins's work had a profound and lasting impact on at least two generations of Spanish intellectuals, and its second edition was dedicated to Juan Valera.[17] This impact in fact precedes the publication of *História da Civilização Ibérica* and dates from 1870 to 1874, when Martins worked in Spain as the manager of a mine near Córdoba, and also from his 1875 article titled "Os Povos Peninsulares e a Civilização Moderna" (Peninsular Peoples and Modern Civilization), which was published in the *Revista Occidental*, a magazine that often encouraged and sought collaboration from Spanish intellectuals.[18]

To be sure, it is not because he addresses a Portuguese source in his discussion of an issue that has important repercussions for Hispanism that Joan Ramon Resina becomes Iberian studies' first honorary citizen. Rather, it is because the Portuguese source addressed is an indispensable piece in the history of nineteenth-century Iberianism that it warrants Resina's broader gesture, which inaugurates Iberian studies. Other themes and historical periods could, and should, fall under the purview of Iberian studies: before the ominous date of 1640 almost everything written in any of the Peninsula's various regions was relevant to at least one other Peninsular culture, and it is telling that in the poem that was to become the national epic of Portugal, Camões

---

17. Unamuno mentions Martins in several of his letters and chronicles, and in one of them goes as far as to say that "this man is one of my weaknesses" [este hombre es una de mis debilidades] (*Epistolário Ibérico* 32–33). Along with the poet and philosopher Antero de Quental, Martins is one of the Portuguese writers that according to Unamuno contributed to something of a late nineteenth-century Golden Age for Portugal, a phenomenon that he desired for Spain. These writers unfortunately remain unacknowledged by most hispanist scholars who have devoted themselves to the study of the life and work of the Salamanca professor.

18. Conceived of as a pan-Iberian publication, the *Revista Ocidental* was the project of Portuguese intellectuals Jaime Batalha Reis (1847–1934) and Antero de Quental (1842–91), and it published articles by such Spanish intellectuals as Pi y Margall (1824–1901), Fernandez de los Rios (1821–80), Rafael de Labra (1840–1918), and Cánovas del Castillo (1828–97).

celebrates *as Espanhas* (the Spains).[19] The seventeenth century is arguably one of the most promising periods for comparative study, especially because scholars on the Portuguese side of the border have historically shunned it. If the bells are tolling for Hispanism, it is high time they toll for the anti-Spanish bias still hampering some Portuguese historiography of this period. The publication of a supplement to a recent issue of the Portuguese literary journal *Colóquio-Letras* (2011), dedicated to seventeenth-century Hispano-Portuguese relations is, however meager, an encouraging sign.[20] Even more heartening is the appearance, in the spring of 2011, of the annual magazine *Suroeste*, following a major exhibit of the same name that took place in Badajoz's Museo Extremeño e Iberoamericano de Arte Contemporáneo in 2010, and which garnered the collaboration of many well-known intellectuals from Portugal and Spain's various autonomous regions, including Extremadura. If *Suroeste* survives the austerity that currently ravages the Peninsula, this Spanish magazine has enormous potential, and scholars in Hispanic and Luso-Brazilian studies alike should embrace it. Two other examples I would like to mention here are Pedro Cardim's *Portugal unido y separado. Felipe II, la unión de territorios y el debate sobre la condición política del Reino de Portugal,* which signals the emerging willingness in Portuguese historiography to consider the period of the Iberian union, and *Theorising the Iberian Atlantic,* a collective volume that brings together scholars of the Portuguese and the Spanish empires (and which includes a contribution by Joan Ramon Resina), and proposes an oceanic and transhemispheric reflection on the Iberian worlds from the early modern to the contemporary period. These are just a few examples of opportunities that present themselves to scholars and disciplines wanting to broaden their gaze into at least the near vicinity.

It is this broadening of the gaze that informs the rewriting of a particularly problematic passage in Resina's essay from 1996, which we addressed above. In the epilogue to the third chapter of *Del hispanismo a los estudios ibéricos,* we encounter an almost word-for-word reproduction of his earlier declaration of intent for the new discipline of Iberian studies:

---

19. 1640 is the year in which an armed insurrection in Portugal brought an end to sixty years of an Iberian Union under Hapsburg control. The union was the result of the annexation of the kingdom of Portugal by Felipe II in 1580, in the wake of the *Cortes de Tomar,* which were convened to determine the succession of heirless King Sebastião to the Portuguese throne.

20. See *Siglo de Oro. Relações hispano-portuguesas no século XVII.* This is a supplement to issue 178 of *Colóquio-Letras,* perhaps not coincidentally dedicated in its entirety to the Portuguese poet Ruy Belo (1933–78), who lived in Spain for a period of time and famously coined the disheartened, if ironic sentence: "Madrid, uma das cidades do mundo mais distantes de Lisboa" [Madrid, one of the cities in the world the farthest from Lisbon].

> Hispanic Studies should deal with the question I formulated years back about the possibility of a new discipline which incorporates the various cultures of the Iberian Peninsula in a nonhierarchical fashion, according to thematic nuclei and without concealing the exclusion with a few symbolic overtures tolerated in the margins of the discipline. (162)[21]

The subtle difference here is that the parenthetical inclusion of Portuguese that characterized the earlier formulation disappeared, not in order to seal a de facto exclusion but rather to avoid epistemological hastiness. In order for this to happen, it was necessary that both the subject and the object of knowledge had undergone transformation, in the very act of writing. Resina himself defines knowledge as this transformation: "Such understanding changes both the subject and the object and it is this transformation that we call knowledge" (162).[22] It is still premature to ask whether this practice of writing will signal the end of Hispanism. Let's instead acknowledge that, in itself, it is not a particularly productive question. In my view it is more prudent and fruitful to ask whether Resina's model of Iberian studies will at least inaugurate a different paradigm in the cultural relations between Spain and Portugal, one that is different from Unamuno's ambivalence between condescension and true fascination.[23] I believe Resina's lesson is promising, because he consistently shows us that the choice between our love for a discipline and our commitment to the pursuit of transformational knowledge is a false one.

By making "Luso-Brazilian studies" a peripheral endeavor federated in the newly minted Iberian studies, Resina would not find many willful interlocutors in the Portuguese-speaking world, at least among those who devote their careers to the study of the cultural record (and of its constant unruliness) produced in Portuguese. But by paying dutiful attention to the relevant Portuguese materials when addressing the question of the (in)solvency of Hispanism, something that in itself remains peripherally interesting to Luso-Brazilian studies—and which is different from being forced to inhabit the periphery of Hispanism, or of any of its new iterations—Resina opens up new terrain, which this essay celebrates. He demonstrates that he already is writing in the mode he describes, already inhabiting the space he felicitously designates as

---

21. "Los estudios hispánicos deberán abordar la pregunta que formulé hace años sobre la posibilidad de una nueva disciplina que incorpore las diversas culturas de la Península Ibérica de un modo no jerárquico, en función de núcleos temáticos y no ya disimulando la exclusión con unas pocas muestras simbólicas toleradas en los márgenes de la disciplina."

22. "Tal entendimiento cambia tanto al sujeto como al objeto y esta transformación es a lo que llamamos conocimiento."

23. For an evaluation of Unamuno's paradigm, see Ángel Marcos de Dios' "Unamuno, Paradigma de las Relaciones de España para con Portugal."

Iberian studies. And this is exactly what I meant when I implied, at the beginning of this essay, that the rapprochement between what for a while longer will be called Hispanic studies and Luso-Brazilian studies is already happening. However different the (geopolitical and academic) stakes, the scope, and the degree of accomplishment, this essay arrives at the celebration of a certain inevitability of the conversation: as Joan Ramon Resina turns to Oliveira Martins in his heuristic reclaiming of the history of Iberianism, I necessarily had to turn to Resina in my determined welcoming of Iberian studies. I can attest that the only borders I had to cross in this process were those of attention, effort, and acquired competence.

WORKS CITED

Bento, José. *Epistolário Ibérico. Cartas de Pascoaes e Unamuno.* Lisboa: Assírio & Alvim, 1986.

Braun, Harald, and Lisa Vollendorf. *Theorising the Ibero-American Atlantic.* Leiden and Boston: Brill, 2013.

Cardim, Pedro. *Portugal unido y separado. Felipe II, la unión de territórios y el debate sobre la condición política del Reino de Portugal.* Valladolid: Ediciones Universidad de Valladolid, 2014.

Catroga, Fernando. "Nacionalismo e ecumenismo. A questão ibérica na segunda metade do século XIX." *Cultura, História e Filosofia* 4 (1985): 419–63.

Delgado, Antonio Sáez. *Suroeste: Revista de Literaturas Ibéricas* 1 (2011).

Delgado, Antonio Sáez, and Luis Manuel Gaspar, eds. *Suroeste: Relaciones literárias y artísticas entre Portugal y España (1890–1936).* Badajoz and Lisbon: Museo Extremeño de Arte Contemporáneo; Assírio & Alvim, 2010.

Dios, Ángel Marcos de. *Epistolario português de Unamuno.* Paris: Fundação Calouste Gulbenkian, 1979.

———. "Unamuno, Paradigma de las Relaciones de España para con Portugal." *Aula Ibérica.* Salamanca: Ediciones Universidad de Salamanca, 2007. 19–31.

Faber, Sebastiaan. "Economies of Prestige: The Place of Iberian Studies in the American University." *Hispanic Research Journal* 9.1 (2008): 7–32.

Ferreira, Ana Paula. "Integrating Portuguese Studies in Interdisciplinary Programs: A Challenge for the New Millennium." *Luso-Brazilian Review* 40.2 (2004): 73–81.

———. "Specificity Without Exceptionalism: Towards a Critical Lusophone Postcoloniality." *Lusophones Literatures and Postcolonialism.* Ed. Paulo de Medeiros. Utrecht: University of Utrecht, Portuguese Studies Center, 2007. 21–40.

Figueiredo, Fidelino. "Paralelidade e Assincronia." *Motivos De Novo Estilo.* Coimbra: Nobel, 1944. 81–91.

———. "Um Século de Relações Luso-Brasileiras (1825–1925)." Separata da *Revista de História* 14 (1925): 1–28.

Furman, Nelia, David Goldberg, and Natalia Lusin. "Enrollments in Languages Other Than English in United States Institutions of Higher Education." MLA Web Publication, 2010. 11 Sept. 2014. <http://www.mla.org/2009_enrollmentsurvey>.

Jackson, Kenneth David. "History of the Future: Luso-Brazilian Studies in the New Millennium." *Luso-Brazilian Review* 40.2 (2003): 13–30.

Martins, Joaquim Pedro de Oliveira. "Os Povos Peninsulares e a Civilização Moderna." *Revista Occidental* 1 (1875): 5–24.

———. *História da Civilização Ibérica*. Lisboa: Guimarães Editora, 1994.

Matos, Sérgio Campos. "Conceitos de Iberismo em Portugal." *Revista de História das Ideias* 28 (2007): 169–93.

———. "Iberismo e identidade nacional (1851–1910)." *Clio*, Nova Série, 14/15 (2006): 349–400.

———. "Was Iberism a Nationalism? Conceptions of Iberism in Portugal in the Nineteenth and Twentieth Centuries." *Portuguese Studies* 25.2 (2009): 215–29.

Miller, J. Hillis. *Speech Acts in Literature*. Stanford: Stanford UP, 2002.

Moraña, Mabel. *Ideologies of Hispanism*. Nashville: Vanderbilt UP, 2005.

Moraña, Mabel, and Reyes Coll-Tellechea. "Ideologies of Hispanism: Hispanic Issues." *Hispanic Journal* 28.2 (2007). 154–56.

Pereira, Pedro Schacht. "Fermento da República, bolor do Império: Civilização Ibérica, excepcionalismo e o legado luso-brasileiro do lusotropicalismo." *Estudios Portugueses* 9 (2009): 151–70.

Resina, Joan Ramon. *Del hispanismo a los estudios ibéricos. Una propuesta federativa para el ámbito cultural*. Madrid: Editorial Biblioteca Nueva, 2009.

———. "Hispanism and Its Discontents." *Siglo XX 20th Century* 14.1–2 (1996): 85–135.

———. *Iberian Modalities: A Relational Approach to the Study of Culture in the Iberian Peninsula*. Liverpool: Liverpool UP, 2012.

———. "Iberian Studies Program." <http://europe.stanford.edu/research/iberianstudies>.

Saramago, José. *A Jangada de Pedra*. Lisboa: Editorial Caminho, 1986.

Trigo, Abril. "Los estudios transatlánticos y la geopolítica del neo-hispanismo." *Cuadernos de Literatura* 31 (Jan.–June 2012): 16–45.

Various authors. *Siglo de Oro. Relações hispano-portuguesas no século XVII*. Supplement to *Colóquio-Letras* 178 (2011).

CHAPTER 2

The Case for Ad Hoc Transnationalism

HÉCTOR HOYOS

THERE ARE two components to this essay, one institutional and one intellectual. Institutions shape the way we think, while thought gives purpose to institutions. I approach this somewhat of a chicken-and-egg question with caution, emphasizing the "intellectual" element, loosely considered. I am fully aware that institutions, cultural and otherwise, have something of a transcendental effect, in that they inform our perception of what exists. However, institutional critique *is possible*. If works of art can change the ways in which museums operate, or works of fiction in which literature circulates, one can only hope that scholarly contributions, though institutionally determined, may have an effect on broader institutional configurations. Given the vastness of the topic, what follows constitutes a forcibly reductive, yet hopefully compelling, defense of what I call "ad hoc transnationalism." I argue for a certain suppleness of mind when approaching Latin American literature in a transnational context, and warn against the shortcomings of the overinstitutionalization of certain transnational models over others. The bipolar understanding of Latin American literature as the sum of Brazilian and Spanish American literatures is one among several such models.[1]

---

1. For a state-of-the-art history of the Luso-Hispanic axis, see Newcomb.

ASYMMETRICAL TRANSACTIONS

We should begin by noting that the object "Latin America" is always already transnational. As Walter Mignolo has reminded us, the term "Latin America" is equivocal. Latin, really? The term signifies by opposition to "Anglo America," whereas, in Spanish and Portuguese, "the Americas" are one geographic realm known simply as *América*. "Latin" would signal the coming of Romance languages (Spanish, Portuguese, and French) to the New World; Latin Americans would be the Romance-language-speaking peoples on this side of the Atlantic. As this coinage excludes indigenous peoples and the descendants of African slaves, one could adopt the more precise, if awkwardly lengthy coinage "Indo-Afro-Latin America." But then this term does not work evenly, as the Caribbean is relatively more Afro, the sites of pre-Columbian empires more Indo, and pockets like Argentina or Costa Rica more White—not to mention several other ethnicities that do not respond to this matrix at all.[2] The ethnocultural complexity of Latin America invites the denaturalization of the names we use to try and capture it in our discourse, academic or otherwise. At the very least, one should take "Latin America" with a grain of salt, and use the term with appropriate caution.

Now, although "Latin America" is inherently transnational, its accompanying practices in literary criticism need not be. We should account for this asymmetry. One can practice Latin Americanism locally and still speak to what is essentially a continental phenomenon. For present purposes, I understand "Latin Americanism" simply as the production of knowledge about the region. At some point, disconnects may arise between the scholarship and its object.[3] I believe this sort of disconnect was more likely before the relative massification of air travel and electronic communication, as well as the consolidation of transnational literary institutions, and at a different level, the literary blogosphere. The effects of globalization on both Latin America and Latin Americanism are profound. The scholarship and its object are becoming symmetrical, as a result of two complementary processes: first, Northern

---

2. See Ribeiro for a discussion of the different ethnic compositions of Latin American peoples. Important antecedents to both Mignolo and Ribeiro can be found in Ardao and O'Gorman.

3. Nelly Richard explores this problematic, albeit with excessive pessimism about the potential of academic discourse: "Latin American otherness constitutes itself as the opposite of the concept and of the reason fetishized by academic knowledge: a natural opposite that compensates for the abstract and reifying coldness of the theory of the Center (which is imprisoned within the walls of the university), and causes, at the level of imagination, a free flow of its own energy to course over it" (349). For an informative account of different strands of Latin Americanism, see Jenckes.

academic settings multiply their real-time connections with Latin America; second, Latin American universities gain prominence, consolidate doctoral programs, and produce more knowledge, hopefully meaningful and socially embedded. What Neil Larsen observed in the mid-1990s still applies: the South produces the raw materials of academic work—novels, survey studies, undergraduates—while the North produces theory, comparison, and PhDs.[4] But the trend is toward rebalancing this division of labor.

The underlying structural principles of the new forms of interconnection are rhizomatic and not radical. To echo Deleuze and Guattari's famous distinction: "any point of a rhizome can be connected to anything other, and must be," while the root "plots a point, fixes an order" (7). Studies on this topic are the province of sociologies of literature, except that their findings amount to something of a self-fulfilling prophecy, for they reify such structures. For some, "world literature" and its accompanying institutions carry the promise of a more inclusive, intellectually rich study of literature; for others, the opposite is true: world literature is exclusion by other means, the watering down of entire subdisciplines. The underlying questions are: what constitutes a field, and what can we do with it? The ensemble changes when some nodes have more prominence than others.

The utopia of world literature is an unhierarchical rhizome, while its reality is that, in the name of that ideal, new nodes emerge and old nodes are consolidated by different means. This is an extreme example of something that also takes place under the umbrella of various Latin Americanisms, which may downplay vast subregions, for instance Central America. Even among integrative transnationalisms that operate along a common axis, it matters under whose terms integration takes place, and with what exclusions, oppositions, and privileges. The same is true for different transnational models and their implementation.

INSTITUTIONAL CONFIGURATIONS

The nodes or points for the articulation of transnationalisms can be of different kinds. University departments and other structures with specific transnational orientations play their part. So do state-run and private cultural institutions, foreign services, publishers, and media conglomerates. Before I

---

4. For Larsen, there are several unintended consequences of "North by South" readership. A prominent one is a bad-consciousness-infused form of academic legitimacy. He calls it "self-authorization": "the emergent northern reader of Latin American texts seeks the authority for reading in a universal principle of *canonical decolonization*" (7).

devote the larger part of this essay to an exploration of different models, allow me to offer an example of two centers of gravity: the Instituto Cervantes and the Instituto Camões. They are both transnational in scope, and their transnationalism is tightly bound to the agendas of the Spanish and Portuguese states, respectively. It is in their best interest to separate Spanish from Portuguese, to distinguish these sibling languages from each other. This is the opposite of what happens in many university departments in the United States, where for historical, strategic, or casuistic reasons the two Romance languages constitute a unit, sometimes along with other related languages.

Because the common denominator for Instituto Cervantes-style transnationalism is Castilian, the languages and cultures of other regions of Spain, such as Catalonia, Galicia, and the Basque Country, will always remain second-class citizens. The Instituto Cervantes, in a nutshell, strives for a "Spain and the Rest" model. Although it would be unrealistic, given the current economic situation of Spain, to see in these diplomatic efforts a backdoor resurgence of imperialism, the project truly is one of re-Hispanicization. This new breed of enlightened pan-Hispanism posits itself as a fraternity or sorority of nations—though one in which one sibling is strongest. Similarly, the Instituto Camões gives Portugal the centrality that comes with its role as a broker between Brazil (affluent, populated, and vast) and Lusophone Africa.

Meanwhile, U.S. universities, which produce a significant portion of Latin Americanism and Hispanism, enshrine an "English and the Rest" model. The production of knowledge in American academia is so robust, relatively speaking, that a second-tier interest in Spanish can still compete with the output of any other locale. Restrictive transnational orientations within Spanish departments add to this broader, structural limitation. Anecdotal evidence abounds: curriculum committees may reject a course title such as "The Nineteenth-Century Novel," deeming it unspecific when referring to a nonmetropolitan canon, preferring "The *Latin American* 19th Century Novel." However, these committees may be perfectly fine with *implying* that it is the English or the French tradition to which one refers in proposing a course with the title of "The Nineteenth-Century Novel." "English" disappears when there is nothing other to see but English—in this case, the word does not distinguish one thing from another. This sits well with the world-literature-in-translation model, where "world" serves as a marker of assimilatory, partial inclusiveness.[5] Yet "Spanish" or "Portuguese" may disappear out of neglect, however well-intentioned such a model may be.

---

5. See the discussion of this position in Saussy (11).

The articulation of transnationalism occurs at multiple levels: locally, regionally, and globally. Latin American literature, again in terms of Deleuze and Guattari, is an *assemblage*. The Market, as Manuel De Landa has proposed, is an assemblage, too (17). It grows from the kernel of local markets and supermarkets, into regional distribution chains, until it becomes a complex multiplicity. Surely this construction describes some aspects of the "market" for Latin American literature, including phenomena of different scales and levels, from bookshops to conferences and beyond. Literary multiplicity occurs within a complex system that entails value judgments, as well as transactions of cultural prestige and modest wealth. But if one were to try and change the ensemble from a single node, no matter how influential, it would be like trying to alter the weather, another complex system. "Contemporary Latin American literature" is about focusing, retaining elements within the ensemble. And there is a contemporary *way* of studying Latin American literature that also constructs a current multiplicity. Cycles are what make the market and the weather consistent and more or less predictable, as in the ebb and flow of studies on Julio Cortázar or José María Arguedas. At the time of writing, Miguel Ángel Asturias lacks currency, Isaacs lacks scope.

CORPUS AS ERSATZ METHOD

In light of these critical developments, there is a sense of urgency in defining transnational units of analysis. As pertains to Latin American literature, the tendency seems to be to determine this unit first, by fiat, and to worry about its distinctive methodology later. Micro-comparativism by design welcomes arbitrariness—consider, for instance, the absurdity of assimilating nineteenth-century Brazil, monarchical for the most part, into the broader collection of the young Spanish American republics of the time. While it is easy to appreciate this as a casualty of a reified Luso-Spanish American model, other geography-based configurations may lead to similar findings. They produce blind spots *because* of their geographical biases, which also amounts to a lack of methodological consistency. Here transnationalism is not the result of a particular way of reading, but an a priori normative practice.

I turn now to a brief evaluation of the most important models, with the following caveats: they are sometimes overlapping; they may generate discourse, meaning, and institutional coherence, but not necessarily all at the same time or in every context; it is not clear which serves its object better than others, and yet they compete for currency and intellectual potency.

Cumulative. This model understands Latin American literature as the sum of its parts, in terms of nation-states. Here "Latin America" emerges from the sum of Argentina, Chile, Uruguay, and so forth. It may include Brazil or not. If it does, because it is the element least likely to assimilate, Brazil occupies a place of exception. A similar thing occurs with U.S. Latino culture. Exceptionalism is both prospective and retrospective: it projects the 1494 Treaty of Tordesillas into the future, as if the elusive meridian carved an actual dividing line into the continent; it assumes that the 1848 Treaty of Guadalupe Hidalgo was always in force. Not surprisingly, this is a model that has a particularly difficult time recognizing hybridity in the form of Spanglish, the language of Guillermo Gómez-Peña, or Portuñol, that of Néstor Perlongher. As in the work of a different Néstor, García Canclini, the cumulative model of Latin American literature grants sanctioned forms of hybridity adequate attention, particularly along the high–popular culture axis. This is less the case of hybrid identities and cultural manifestations that call into question the nation-state as the autonomous, integral building block of the model.

Institutional configurations of this approach include Latin American Latin Americanism, as practiced in the academic milieus of Bogotá, Lima, and Santiago. In this model, transnationalism is an effect of limited resources. The guiding principle of this university-based literary-critical practice seems to be *multum in parvo* (much in little), which is joined to an optimistic faith in representation. The hope is that representatives of all areas of knowledge, collectively, will map the broad terrain of the knowable. However, as Jorge Luis Borges's famous short story "On Exactitude in Science" reminds us, the perfect map is none other than the territory itself. Because the perfect university would be the universe itself, institutions of higher learning will always be imperfect. One can imagine a program in Latin American literature populated by at least one *mexicanista,* one *conosurista,* and so forth. In this model, the whole would be the sum of its parts. Latin American literature, as a transnational entity, would be the bringing together of discrete national spaces. If we do not achieve or even pursue this, it is often for lack of funding. At what I hesitate to call a "practical" level, this is why some job searches these days advertise positions for *andinistas,* a category that, at best, focuses on the literatures of the Tawantinsuyu, and at worst, seeks to lump together everything that happens between the two literary giants of Mexico and Argentina.

I am not suggesting that the model of Latin America as a sum of nations is incorrect, or that striving for this sort of coverage is entirely unviable or uneconomical. This cumulative approach remains a valid intellectual option, but only, I think, if it acknowledges its biases and shortcomings, and, more importantly, if it establishes a conversation with other transnational models, without assuming that it occupies some kind of default position, to the exclusion of transnational phenomena like ethnicity, gender, and class.

Supplemental. The difference between this and the previous model is that here Latin American literature is not the sum of its parts, but a supplement. Counterintuitively, not all of the works of the various Latin American national literatures "count" as Latin American. Here Latin Americanness is something that national authors aspire to. Transnationalism is not about limited resources but about limited attention. This hypercanon is the pool from which the more expansive, and yet more critically selective project of world literature takes its objects.[6] Hypercanonicity is grounded in value judgment ("the best of the best") or in representativeness ("the most of the most"). *One Hundred Years of Solitude* sits at the crossroads of representativeness and quality, for it is quintessentially "Latin American" and well crafted by conventional standards.

For one, the Cuban Casa de las Américas advocates an openly political model of hypercanonicity ("La Casa"). Its areas of focus in Latino and precolonial literatures, although examples of Latin American Latin Americanism, are more so of *Nuestroamericanismo,* the us-versus-them dichotomy established by José Martí. They are institutional vectors for expanding *nosotros* (we) over time and space, beyond the limits of the Castilian language, and for valorizing heritage over linguistic proficiency. Not all heritage is included, of course: the more politically conservative Cuban-American writers are not invited to the table. Supplemental Latin Americanism is also practiced, in a different way, by the Brazilian academy, particularly with regard to Spanish America: only the "best" or "most representative" writers and texts merit Portuguese translation and academic recognition. The supplemental model recognizes the complex dimension of regional exchange. It negotiates unity and difference, a particularly valuable feature when canonical texts speak to contemporary realities. Possible shortcomings are biases toward Argentina, Mexico, and Cuba, whose undoubtedly strong influence can become preeminent, and the reduction of regional movements, such as the *novela indigenista,* to disembodied, autonomous aesthetic phenomena, rather than socially and historically determined practices.

Comparative. More than a model, this rubric signals a question: why is Latin Americanism *not* recognized as comparativism? As scholars who deal with several Latin American national literatures at a time can attest, it takes

---

6. David Damrosch elucidates the concept of hypercanonicity with a mordant comparison: "In world literature, as in some literary Miss Universe competition, an entire nation may be represented by a single author: Indonesia, the world's fifth-largest country and home of ancient and ongoing cultural traditions, is usually seen, if at all, in the person of Pramoedya Ananta Toer. Jorge Luis Borges and Julio Cortázar divide the honors for Mr. Argentina" (48).

serious study to be able to contrast even kindred transnational phenomena, such as the cultures of post-dictatorship in Chile, Argentina, and Brazil—a task undertaken exemplarily by Idelber Avelar.[7] Disciplinary history explains part of the disconnect between comparativism and the study of the region: comparativism has its roots in German-French dialogues, ours in Spanish philology. But why has comparativism not come closer to Latin Americanism, as indeed it has to other disciplines? There are advantages and disadvantages to this separation: Latin Americanism gains autonomy, but loses interlocutors. The real drawback comes when cultural forms demand a strong comparative approach that no one seems to validate: consider the case of reading (and teaching!) Rubén Darío, and *modernismo* as a whole, vis-à-vis French Parnassianism. I believe that imagining institutional configurations that would facilitate lively, symmetrical exchange between comparativists and Latin Americanists is a worthy task.

Hemispheric. Having anticipated some of the traits of this approach, I turn to its institutional configurations and intellectual potential. Regarding the former, a notable initiative is LASER, the Latino and Latin American Space for Enrichment and Research at The Ohio State University (*LASER*). This program stands out for its institutional coherence and inclusiveness, and particularly for its ability to scale up and down from guest lectures to undergraduate working groups. The fact that it exists alongside a thirty-plus-faculty-strong Spanish and Portuguese Department suggests effective collaboration without the limitations of a zero-sum-game mentality. LASER does not take away resources from "mainstay" Latin Americanism on campus; rather, it projects its findings to a broader community.[8]

The intellectual potency of a functional, non-eclipsing hemispheric model becomes evident in a work by David Kelman, *Counterfeit Politics: Secret Plots and Conspiracy Narratives in the Americas* (2012). Kelman establishes meaningful connections between Thomas Pynchon and Ricardo Piglia that a different transnational approach would hardly allow. Under the aegis of deconstruction, Kelman proposes that conspiracy narratives model politics as a whole. More relevant for the present argument, he espouses a hemispheric archive as the site for carrying out such a study. In his later scholarship, Efraín Kristal documents tropes of Western expansionism shared by the Americas as a whole, including that of the Indian raid or *malón*. He also traces a literary

---

7. Other than the toll of dictatorship itself, Avelar builds his unit of analysis on the "'winds of democracy' and market euphoria [sweeping] over the Spanish and Portuguese-speaking Southern Cone" (22).

8. Full disclosure: the present chapter results from an invitation to give a talk through LASER.

interest in captivity and incest that suggests deeper anxieties of transculturation and conquest. It is plain to see how these approaches may broaden our understanding of Latin American culture past and present.

Subalternist. Subalternism proposes both a method and an object for transnationalism. The method, to borrow words that Gayatri Spivak used in response to a question I had the occasion to ask her, is "to focus on the differential"—by which I took her to mean that, instead of thinking of power and affluence in absolute terms (rich vs. poor, powerful vs. powerless), one should consider the distance between them. This relational approach does not reify or fetishize its object: to focus on the differential is to make way for future equality without turning a blind eye to present inequality. Paradox and perplexity are frequent travel companions of this method, because one is attempting to say the unsayable, to the extent that language, too, is embedded in power structures. Similarly, the mindful practitioner of this form of critique should also beware of the subalternizing gaze. The condition of subalternity is not written in stone, nor should it be the bedrock of an epistemological apparatus; rather, *overcoming* subalternity is the central motive for the production of knowledge. This purposefully self-cancelling method has negativity at heart: when the subaltern has spoken, the critic falls silent.

Latin American subalternism is from the get-go a chapter of a broader, complex South-South phenomenon. There is no shortage of accounts and article compilations on this topic. I will highlight that subalternism is always already a transnationalism, because (a) subalterns themselves are not constrained by national boundaries—indeed, migration is often subalternizing—and (b) in its initial institutional configuration at Duke in the 1990s, subalternism brought the South Asian intellectuals Spivak, Ranajit Guha, and Dipesh Chakrabarty into dialogue with the Latin Americanists Alberto Moreiras, Ileana Rodríguez, and Walter Mignolo, among others. In the succinct formulations Rodríguez has used in a similar context, one intent of subalternism is "to see how subalterns live, enjoy life, and organize despite all of the efforts to negate their being" (29); another, "to challenge culture to think of itself from the point of view of its own negations" (9). These continue to be valuable tasks, within the framework of the nation-state or, more often, beyond it.

Hispanist. In a 2005 essay, Román de la Campa confidently asserted that "the era in which Hispanism stood as an organic principle governing the study of Spanish and Spanish American letters seems like a dim and distant memory" (300). Clearly, this is hyperbole. One could argue that traditional Hispanism is less influential than it once was, but one could equally argue that the profession has broadened *without* compromising its long-standing Hispanist core. No longer hegemonic, but not reduced either, Hispanism is here to stay. Critical paradigms have a long life, given institutional inertia and the fact that scholars often receive their training in their twenties and then teach for four or more decades. In that essay, De la Campa provocatively compares new theoretical strands with software that we constantly update. But the comparison is of limited value: "users" are not locked out of new technologies, and can stick to their "old" software just fine. To a nonnegligible extent, the notion that "new is better" is in the eye of the beholder. Spanish-Latin bilingual medievalists, for instance, are unable to participate in a rich multilingual scholarship on the Iberian Peninsula that includes, as is historically accurate, Arabic, Hebrew, and several Romance languages. And yet they can still research and teach in those languages alone.

There are also the re-Hispanicizing forces of cultural diplomacy, mentioned above. In recent years, the Real Academia Española—as the name indicates, an institution loyal to the King of Spain—has launched commercially successful, commemorative, "critical" editions of Spanish-language classics *Don Quijote de la Mancha,* launched in 2004 for the book's four-hundredth anniversary; *Cien años de soledad,* in 2007, in time for the author's eightieth birthday and the book's fortieth anniversary; *La región más transparente,* fifty years after Carlos Fuentes, then eighty years old, first published it; and anthologies by Neruda and Mistral in 2010. (Others have followed.) Here the Academy erects monuments, living and dead, and masterfully bridges the gap between highbrow, middlebrow, and mass publishing. The often pompous, hagiographic essays included in the volumes do not reflect the state of the discipline for the study of these authors, at least not by the standards of North American academia. Nor do they acknowledge that many Latin Americanists have moved away from author and genre studies into cultural studies and other fields. Still, the cachet of this collection is hard to deny—which suggests that Hispanism is a house with many windows. Hispanism is also the most common model for secondary education wherever Spanish is taught.

Trans-Atlantic. Its most prominent proponent, Julio Ortega, from the Department of Hispanic Studies at Brown, emphasizes the long-standing connections between Spain and its former colonies, including the American Southwest. He defines his approach as a defense of particularity in a time of globality: "we believe that the global is not just the hegemonic, but the interplay among regions, the production of the particular" (my translation). Heterogeneous and inclusive, this model provides a common ground for scholars of different orientations and interests. Given the vastness of its object of study and the multiple methodologies it engages, this is something of a meta-transnational model. It combines cohesiveness and multiplicity to an extent that other approaches cannot. For self-absorbed Peninsularists and shortsighted Latin Americanists, it serves as a reminder that these traditions do not exist in a vacuum, and indeed often feed off of each other.

By the same token, its lack of specificity invites criticism: its detractors consider it Hispanism with new clothes. At times, job searches invoke the moniker "Trans-Atlantic" as a code name for "generalist." And then there is also the terminological confusion with "Transatlantic studies," a form of area studies focused on exchanges between the United States, the United Kingdom, and Western Europe. The Brown project began in 1996, exerting a considerable gravitational pull. But in 2002, the Transatlantic Studies Association held an influential conference that led to an eponymous journal, now published by Routledge. If one conducts a database search using the name, in the hopes of finding articles that coalesce around a certain orientation, odds are that the two very dissimilar projects get tangled up. One is predominantly humanist and the other veers toward political science, which makes the homonymy all the more unfortunate.

Ibero-American. Arguably the most influential critical movement in recent times, it has led to the re-founding of former Spanish and Portuguese Departments, such as the Department of Latin American and Iberian Cultures at Columbia University and the Department of Iberian and Latin American Cultures at Stanford University. The Iberian model, as a standalone approximation to the Peninsula, is a powerful instrument against Castilian-centrism. When the unit of analysis is not the nation-state, the cultures of present-day autonomous regions gain prominence and distinctness. The study of Portugal, a rarity in American academia, receives a boost. The slow historical processes that led to the current sociopolitical organization of the Peninsula come to light. Powerful and long-overdue revisions of medieval and early modern literary history gain traction, and the national complexities of the Spanish Civil War overcome partisan reductionism. Prominent proponents include Joan Ramon Resina, Sebastiaan Faber, Catherine Davis, and Mario Santana.

Where does Latin America stand in this configuration? One of the draws of the model is its capacity to stimulate innovative subfields that bridge the divide between Latin Americanism and Peninsularism. Cuba was part of the Spanish Empire until 1898, and many "Spanish" residents on the island were in fact from Catalonia. An Ibero-American lens makes visible this interesting population, which left architectural traces in Havana and other cities, and shaped early twentieth-century visions of the Caribbean in cosmopolitan Barcelona. Similarly, the study of the Republican exiles in Mexico gains awareness of linguistic difference and diasporic cultural production; the presence of Basque settlers in numerous locales in the Americas becomes an organic object of study. Potentially, new studies about contemporary Latin American immigration to Spain could emerge. The Spanish Empire fancied its international relations as a single bilateral exchange between the metropolis and each of the designated capitals. And yet not all roads led to Madrid, nor does this model explain the multilateral, bottom-up exchanges between Peninsulars and Latin Americans.

An important caveat is that Ibero-Americanism generates false symmetries. Short of an "Iberia and the Rest" effect, there is a tendency to assimilate the relationship between Portugal and the Peninsula to that of Brazil and Spanish America. There is something appealing to this commensurability. Surely, we need to think of these geographic and cultural realms together, and appreciate their family resemblances. But going too far down this path can obscure the obvious: close to 600 million people live in Latin America, roughly ten times the population of the Peninsula; Mexico alone has almost four times the area of Spain, and Brazil over five times that of Portugal; Catalan has a few more million speakers than Quechua, but it is a powerful language of commerce and high culture; the situations of Aymara, Náhuatl, and Guaraní do not easily compare to that of Basque, Galician, or Occitan; the crown of Castile exerted its colonial rule on both sides of the Atlantic, but did so unevenly.

Orientalist and others. Ignacio López-Calvo has sought to rehabilitate this term, despite its negative connotations, for the systematic study of the relations between Latin America, Asia, and the Middle East, as well as "Oriental" subcultures within Latin America. Many Cuban-Chinese fought for independence from Spain, while some remained loyal to the King. Populations of Asian descent are a significant part of Brazilian and Peruvian cultures, while third-generation Lebanese and Palestinians occupy positions of influence in Argentina. The poetry of a José Watanabe, a Japanese-Peruvian, can only be fully appreciated within this framework. Orientalist, trans-Pacific, or diasporic transnationalisms make visible phenomena that other models tend to ignore. Given the very real possibility that increasing commerce with Asia and the Middle East might lead to intensified cultural exchange, there is bound to be growth in these areas—and Northern metropolises may or may not be part of the conversation. Beyond discrete initiatives like the Centro Cultural Peruano Japonés in Lima, founded in 1967, institutional configurations of this model remain very much works in progress ("Centro Cultural").

TOWARD ACTOR-PARTICIPANT TRANSNATIONALISM

Is meta-transnationalism viable? That would seem to be the position adopted in this essay. And yet there is a de facto transnationalism in the background:

I am a Colombian, who teaches at a research university in the United States, who is also actively involved with several Latin American nations, including Brazil. Perhaps as a result, there is always a chance that the mapping proposed here is approximate and idiosyncratic. Recursiveness is an unavoidable aspect of institutional critique. Still, my site of enunciation, limited as any, allows for an informed representation of several models. The fact that this inventory is possible already suggests its conclusion: that transnationalism should proceed with caution, case by case, in recognition of its plurality and numerous possible institutional configurations. In my final remarks, I turn now to outlining three criteria that, in my opinion, may inform the cognitive and institutional flexibility that this multiplicity calls for.

Geography is no substitute for theory. I find it symptomatic that the rise of Latin American transnationalisms happens during the so-called post-theory moment. Provided that we are indeed in a post-Theory-with-a-capital-"T" moment, and provided that there ever was such a moment in Latin Americanism, revisions of the transnational field could be seen as attempts to fill this void. I find this both plausible and unfortunate. Transnationalisms alone are no substitute for methodological paradigm shifts like, for instance, the above-mentioned evolutionary and sociological turns. They may complement or even challenge them, but they do not suspend the major theoretical questions that underpin the whole enterprise of literary criticism, such as, echoing the title of Harold Bloom's not particularly theoretical book: what to read and why? The fact that certain works of art appear to function particularly well within a certain framework should be the beginning of theoretical inquiry, not its end. Yet it is tempting to reduce the act of reading to having a corpus ratify a model and then having the model validate the corpus. The cycle may accrue cultural capital in the short term, but it ultimately impoverishes the discipline.

One can reasonably suspect that the proliferation of transnationalisms is a reaction to globalization. It is less clear whether individual models offer particular insights into this phenomenon.[9] Are they attempts to grasp new forms of totality and interconnection? Transnationalisms sometimes coincide: one may visualize them as multiple layers of networks that share some or several nodes. Perhaps—for one can say this only tentatively—this multiple modality of transnationalism anticipates the emergence of a global culture, where exchanges are not unidirectional, bipolar, or easily predictable. The scenario of a multipolar, nonscripted commerce of ideas calls for a thorough revision of the method and object of Latin Americanism. Conversely, Latin American literature, with its always-already transnationalism, multipolarity, unevenness, and constant

---

9. For a Latin Americanist exploration of the problem of globalization and literature, see Franco.

negotiation, may turn out to be a model for the study of world literature. No other continental construct displays the same degree of coherence: not "European" literature, or "African," or "Asian." Cognitive and institutional flexibility may facilitate the realization of the theoretical potential of Latin American literature, along with a host of multiple transnationalisms, past and present.

Although geography is not a suitable replacement for theory, it can be a good starting point: Latin Americanism comes into its own by embracing territory and cultural specificity.

Proceed from the bottom up. Out of necessity, I have invoked some texts as examples and counterexamples for different models. The opposite, I think, holds more promise: models should emerge from texts themselves. To impose the strictures of a fixed transnational model on a cultural product may produce nonsense. A case in point is *Budapeste* (2003), the novel by Chico Buarque, adapted to film by Walter Carvalho (2009). A reified Luso-Spanish American model would call for us study them alongside other Latin American works that invoke distant locales, such as two notable films from 2002: the Argentine Marcelo Piñeyro's *Kamchatka,* or the Mexican Carlos Reygadas's *Japón.* One could indeed argue that, like in those movies, in Buarque's novel the distant locale is a metaphor for the human condition or political exile. Except Buarque's novel *takes place in* Budapest, and the dialogues in Carvalho's movie are predominantly in the Magyar language, with Portuguese subtitles. So much for suggestive symmetry.

Cultural products like *Budapeste* and its film adaptation call for multiple, overlapping transnationalisms. The affinity with Spanish American works is a viable route to explore, but not the only one. The same goes for staying within the Brazilian realm, as Rita Olivieri-Godet has done in her comparison of Buarque's novel with Bernardo Carvalho's *Mongólia* (2002) and Alberto Mussa's *O enigma de Qaf* (2004). The movie, complete with a long sequence of a dismantled, enormous statue of Stalin floating down the Danube on a cargo ship, calls for something else entirely: it should be viewed alongside other foreign representations of Budapest. Alternatively, it could also be seen as part of a modest, but not insignificant exchange between Brazil and Central Europe, which includes Sandra Kogut's documentary *Um passaporte húngaro,* the Brazilian director's attempt to reconnect with her Magyar ancestry.

Always transhistoricize. We should demand that institutions accommodate our ways of thinking about literature—not the other way around. This is a challenge for administrators and for scholars in general, for the crux of the matter is to imagine collaborative, modular, and viable transnational institutional configurations. I suggest we revisit Fredric Jameson's principle of "always historicize" to account for multiple possible histories. A combination of thinking in terms of the other, relativizing, and self-scrutinizing is needed now more than ever. In his assessment of the "lines of flight" of Hispanism, De la Campa suggested that we come to terms with how our own subjectivity is rehearsed in the process. This is true for transnationalisms at large. To historicize transnationalisms entails becoming aware of how the process of cultural globalization unfolds at the level of subjects, regions, and cultural institutions.

In a world where data and capital become indiscernible, literature resists. Reading is about much more than knowing what happens in a book, or when, or to whom. The sum of all the facts about a work of literature do not bring it back to life, any more than an anatomical study of a nightingale tells us anything about its beauty—or about the social function of a certain poem Keats dedicated to that bird. It is a false dichotomy to read for beauty or for social content, for critical elucidation or creative appropriation. Whatever our methodological and political orientation, it matters that we feed the source from where we draw our energy. In this case, we should note that the impulse toward transnationalism does not chiefly come from university departments or cultural centers. It is a reality of the world in which we live, and it feeds the imagination of the works we study.

Further research on the place of Latin America within transnationalism should engage its opposite: the transnationalism already at work within that open-ended domain we call "Latin America." This should be the occasion for more, not less, cultural specificity and relevance. The three criteria outlined above may combine in unexpected ways, such as proposing Latin Americanism as a model for World Literature, and not the other way around; enriching the close-reading of texts with the competing insights of different transnational frameworks; or building on the tension between institutional and intellectual conditions. To my mind, the most decisive step is integrating into one's critical practice a renewed awareness of our shifting sites of enunciation. Actors and participants in the new realities of globalized literature, we cannot aspire to objectivity, but to critical self-consciousness and readerly intervention.

WORKS CITED

Ardao, Arturo. *Génesis de la idea y el nombre de América Latina*. Caracas, Venezuela: Centro de Estudios Latinoamericanos Rómulo Gallegos, 1980.

Avelar, Idelber. *The Untimely Present: Postdictatorial Latin American Fiction and the Task of Mourning*. Durham: Duke UP, 1999.

Buarque, Chico. *Budapeste*. São Paulo: Companhia das Letras, 2003.

Budapeste. Dir. Walter Carvalho. Imagem Filmes, 2009.

"La Casa." *Casa de las Américas*. Casa de las Américas, n.d. 28 Nov. 2012. <http://www.casadelasamericas.org/casa.php>.

"Centro Cultural Peruano Japonés: 40 años." *Asociación Peruano Japonesa*, 5 Oct. 2007. 28 Nov. 2012. <http://www.apj.org.pe/temasemanal/10-05-07>.

Damrosch, David. "World Literature in a Postcanonical, Hypercanonical Age." Saussy 43–52.

De la Campa, Román. *Latin Americanism*. Minneapolis: U of Minnesota P, 1999.

———. "Hispanism and Its Lines of Flight." *Ideologies of Hispanism*. Ed. Mabel Moraña. Nashville: Vanderbilt UP, 2005: 300–309.

De Landa, Manuel. *A New Philosophy of Society: Assemblage Theory and Social Complexity*. London: Continuum, 2006.

Deleuze, Gilles, and Félix Guattari. *A Thousand Plateaus: Capitalism and Schizophrenia*. London: Athlone, 1988.

Franco, Jean. "Globalisation and Literary History." *Bulletin of Latin American Research* 25.4 (2006): 441–52.

Japón. Dir. Carlos Reygadas. Tartan Video, 2002. DVD.

Jenckes, Kate. "The 'New Latin Americanism,' or the End of Regionalist Thinking?" *CR: The New Centennial Review* 4.3 (2004): 247–70. Project MUSE. Web. 17 Apr. 2013.

Kamchatka. Dir. Marcelo Piñeyro. AVH, 2003. DVD.

Kelman, David. *Counterfeit Politics: Secret Plots and Conspiracy Narratives in the Americas*. Lewisburg: Bucknell UP, 2012.

Kristal, Efraín. "Interamerican Intersections: Captivity, Incest, and Historical Re-creation in the Literature of the Americas." Computers and Writing Conference Presentation. Stanford University. Pigott Hall, Stanford, CA. 26 Feb. 2009. Lecture.

Larsen, Neil. *Reading North by South: On Latin American Literature, Culture, and Politics*. Minneapolis: U of Minnesota P, 1995.

LASER: Latino and Latin American Space for Enrichment and Research. The Ohio State University, 2013. 1 Apr. 2013. <http://laser.osu.edu/>.

López-Calvo, Ignacio, ed. *One World Periphery Reads the Other: Knowing the "Oriental" in the Americas and the Iberian Peninsula*. Newcastle upon Tyne, UK: Cambridge Scholars, 2010.

Mignolo, Walter. *The Idea of Latin America*. Malden, MA: Blackwell, 2005.

Newcomb, Robert Patrick. *Nossa and Nuestra América: Inter-American Dialogues*. West Lafayette: Purdue UP, 2012.

O'Gorman, Edmundo. *La invención de América: el universalismo de la cultura de Occidente*. México: Fondo de Cultura Económica, 1958.

Olivieri-Godet, Rita. "Estranhos estrangeiros: poética da alteridade na narrativa contemporânea brasileira." *Estudos de Literatura Brasileira Contemporânea* 29 (2007): 233–52.

Ortega, Julio. "Presentación." Transatlantic Studies Project, Brown Department of Hispanic Studies, 2000. Feb. 2013.

Um passaporte húngaro. Dir. Sandra Kogut. VideoFilmes, 2001. DVD.

Resina, Joan Ramon. *Del hispanismo a los estudios ibéricos: una propuesta federativa para el ámbito cultural*. Madrid: Biblioteca Nueva, 2009.

Ribeiro, Darcy. *A América Latina existe?* Brasília: Editora UnB., 2010.

Richard, Nelly. "Intersectando Latinoamérica con el latinoamericanismo: discurso académico y crítica cultural." *Revista iberoamericana* 63.180 (1997): 345–61.

Rodríguez, Ileana. *The Latin American Subaltern Studies Reader*. Durham: Duke UP, 2001.

Saussy, Haun, ed. *Comparative Literature in an Age of Globalization*. Baltimore: Johns Hopkins UP, 2006.

———. "Exquisite Cadavers Stitched from Fresh Nightmares: Of Memes, Hives, and Selfish Genes." Saussy 3–42.

Spivak, Gayatri Chakravorty. "Aesthetic Education in the Age of Globalization." Panel discussion. Stanford University, 25 Feb. 2010. <https://fsi.stanford.edu/events/aesthetic_education_in_the_age_of_globalization>.

CHAPTER 3

Queer Spanish, Queer Portuguese
A Series of Research Proposals

DAVID WILLIAM FOSTER

IT IS no accident that the definitive effort to create standard, imperial sociolects[1] for Spanish and Portuguese coincides with the Counter-Reformation and the organization of, among other social standards, a heterosexist society that would exercise centralized administrative control over all aspects of individual life for the greater glory of the Crown and its hegemonic projects. The variability of medieval forms of the languages—and, indeed, the relative differences between Spanish and Portuguese (and Catalan, for that matter)—were to be resolved in terms of fixed linguistic identities and the regularization of the languages, which also meant the suppression of Catalan or any other neo-Latin varieties that might vie for hegemony (such as any one of the other dialects considered variants of Spanish, along with Catalan, Galician, and Portuguese). Such regularization involved even the most minute details of linguistic variation, and the creation of royal academies (the Real Academia Española in 1713, the Academia de Ciências de Lisboa in 1779), with their dic-

---

1. By imperial sociolect I refer to the emergence and development of a dominant variety of the language, often a privileged regional dialect, that serves the purposes of nation formation, state power, and, where present, imperial expansion. In the case of Spanish, this role fell to *castellano,* as opposed to other reginal dialects (e.g., *aragonés, austuriano, leonés*). *Castellano,* which becomes, then, synonymous with *español* (i.e., the hegemonic dialect of the Iberian Romance languages collectively called Spanish), is codified by Antonio de Nebrija (sometimes Lebrija) in his *Gramática de la lengua castellana,* published, by stunning coincidence, in 1492, the inaugural year of Spanish imperial conquest.

tionaries, grammars, orthographies, and general function of official imprimatur over language questions, imposing norms of behavior as strictly enforced as those pertaining to other social realms. One could debate whether such norms are any more heterosexist than pre-prescriptive variations,[2] but the principle of explicit linguistic norms that cannot without impunity be transgressed is unquestionably part of a social consciousness driven by the need to normalize social subjects and their conduct.

A research agenda under the rubric of queer Spanish and queer Portuguese would have as its goal an inquiry into the question of normalization and transgression in linguistic matters; the way in which language serves to regulate heteronormativity; those aspects of language in which heteronormativity is, nevertheless, elusive; and the practices by which the transgression of heteronormativity is sought and achieved (Queer English is already an established research agenda; see Spurlin). Such an agenda would inquire into the nature of the resistance to heteronormativity through language and what fissures exist in the Portuguese and Spanish languages in making such resistance possible and effective. It is an agenda that would be both descriptive, inventorying the record of such resistance, and philosophical, to the extent that it would foresee ways in which a nonheteronormative consciousness—a queer consciousness—would exercise an impact on the structures of the language. Finally, it would be an agenda that provides the conceptual framework for a literary criticism and a cultural critique that take into account the queer materiality of language at the levels of style, discourse, and interpretation.[3]

---

2. By "pre-prescriptive" I mean the varieties of language not yet subjected to the prescriptive force of the emergence of a hegemonic, official language (that is, the dialect made an official language by bureaucratic imposition), one reinforced with an official grammar and serving the needs of, in the case of Spain and Portugal, the imperial state. The history of the Iberian Peninsula, as elsewhere in post-Roman Europe, witnesses the gradual replacement of Latin as the official language of secular bureaucracy in favor of the neo-Latin vernacular (i.e., what come to be called the Romance languages), which ultimately achieves hegemony through bureaucratic imposition and academic codification through grammars and dictionaries.

3. It should be clear that I am not referring to a so-called queering of the curriculum, which has occurred in leading Luso-Hispanic programs through the United States, if not always yet in the Peninsula and Latin America. The examination of queer issues *in* texts of cultural production is different from, although not unrelated to, the examination of linguistic ideology from a queer perspective. Indeed, what I am promoting here is moving beyond the analysis of the queer content of—the queer reading of—cultural texts, to the analysis of the materiality of the Spanish and Portuguese language used to give linguistic form to those texts. It should also be clear that I am not directly interested in the so-called *jerga* of gays and lesbians/homosexuals/queers. However they are identified by themselves and/or by others, as important as a project of such (principally) lexical registration may be for a language as a whole or specific regional instances of it (e.g., the vocabulary of gay Puerto Ricans in New York, an MA thesis I once directed).

Of necessary initial interest for a project of queer linguistic inquiry would be the use of language by those social subjects who identify or who choose (?) to identify through language as queer. Even as basic a linguistic enunciation, heard in the case of Argentina in the period of redemocratization after 1983, and as a form of resistance to the officially sanctioned homophobia imposed by the military regime in Argentina between 1976 and 1983, the declaration "soy puto y me quiero" (I'm a faggot and I love myself [anyway]) subverts linguistic categories. This is so since it, first, involves the conjunction of two propositions that, through the internalization of homophobia pursued as an integral component of heteronormativity, are normalized as restrictively nonoccurring: a proposition of self-worth (*me quiero*) cannot co-occur with a proposition internalized as self-loathing (*soy puto*). And, second, the enunciation requires the resemaniticization of *puto*, which may mean both "male homosexual" and "male prostitute," such that the link between putative homosexuality and male prostitution is severed: *putos* are no longer necessarily homosexuals because they are male prostitutes, and male prostitutes are no longer necessarily homosexuals; indeed, *puto* as a synonym for homosexual is called into question, and there is the implicit requirement to recast the sememes of the word to begin with.

What has come to be identified as *gayspeak*[4] (where the word "gay" may refer to either supposed biological sex) is an initial manifestation of queer language that is particularly blatant, to the extent that it questions the gender binary and the stability of gender identification. It especially questions the dominant imperative that allusion to sexual desire can only be a part of linguistic enunciation if a function of overt semantic categories and never an undercurrent of other linguistic features, never something that arises surreptitiously through grammatical marking. Gayspeak, to be sure, is driven in large measure by explicit transgressive semantics, but much of its play also depends on surreptitious grammatical marking that may not be immediately evident or understandable. After all, because the lyrics are so "automatically" recalled, how likely is it for one to ponder the homoerotic implications of something so innocent as one Argentine variant of the children's song "Arroz con leche"? "Arroz con leche / me quiero casar, con una señorita de San Nicolás, / que sepa coser, que sepa bordar, / que sepa abrir la puerta para ir a jugar. / Yo soy la viudita, del barrio del frente / me quiero casar y no sé con quién. / Con esa sí, con esa no, con esa señorita me caso yo." [*Arroz con leche* / I want to marry / a

---

4. The online Urban Dictionary defines "gayspeak" as "communication between homosexual males (usually in private) who speak in a familiar manner that comes across, initially, as polite discourse but it is usually loaded with rancor and/or sarcasm" (<http://www.urbandictionary.com/define.php?term=gayspeak>; accessed 27 Feb. 2013).

lady from San Nicolás, / who knows how to sew, who knows how to embroider, / who knows how to open the door to go out to play. / I'm the old widow, from the neighborhood here in front. / I want to marry I don't know who. / With her yes, with her no, with that lady I'll get married.][5]

One does not need to trace the origins of "Arroz con leche" back to some ancestral form of gayspeak to understand that there is something surprisingly wrong with the discourse distribution of gender markers here. Such a disruption can lead to an entire range of considerations regarding the identities—or, at least, the possible erotic desires of subjects strategically deploying such identities—of those taking turns in the practice of linguistic exchange. Research on coded speech, on speech common or limited to special realms like bars and clubs, and on occasions that might permit for the broaching of nonconventional (e.g., non-heteronormative) identities, is essentially sensitive to transgressions of linguistic categories, whether on the level of morphosyntax or semantics, or on the level of discreet linguistic units or stylistic vectors. With the dramatic increase in what are rather synecdochally/metonymically called gay rights in Brazil and certain other Latin American nations, and with the geometric increase of equivalently marked publishing and cultural activity, the linguistic analysis of still encoded, but no longer veiled, queer expression becomes almost an interpretive imperative. Somewhere along the spectrum running from resistance to homophobia to outright self-declarations of non-heteronormativity, there is now much production to be analyzed.

Retrospectively, one rereads Borges, with his (queer) deconstructions of epistemology and metaphysics;[6] the unwilling lesbian and children's writer María Elena Walsh; the cultural anthropologist Mário de Andrade, whose nonhero Macunaíma may be the first modern Brazilian queer social subject; and the novelist João Guimarães Rosa, whose ambivalent Diadorim from *Grande Sertão: Veredas* (1956), a cross-dressing female *jagunço* whose biological sex is only revealed to the protagonist Riobaldo at the conclusion of the novel, and who masks more than a case of mistaken gender identity. Retrospective readings are highly problematic, as they imply the untroubled validity of attributions that only seem clear from a contemporary perspective. Yet they are valid to the extent that they open a cultural tradition up to a scrutiny that is not circumscribed by the norms of an interpretive tradition that is oriented less toward imposition than it is toward revision,[7] particularly when

---

5. I am grateful to the Argentine writer Ana María Shua for providing me with this example.

6. See Altamiranda on the queer dimensions of Borges's writing.

7. By revisionism I understand a process that proposes, in a categorical fashion, a new interpretation of the material in question. I am referring here to the validity of speculative

the latter is handled with intellectual rigor, subtlety, and due sensitivity to the dominant (but yet not exclusive) semiotic practices of the time in which a text was created.

In the deconstructive process of queer analysis, it is important to acknowledge the contribution of feminism to the forging of a consciousness of how linguistic structures are hardly natural and somehow beyond the bounds of social construction. That is, if feminism does not categorically refute the concept of language structure as essentially arbitrary, it at least calls it into question in ways that allow for languages—conceived as something other than mere lists of words—to be remodeled so as to adjust to changing perceptions of the social world. Queer theory has asserted that our society is obsessed with sexuality and especially with policing the explicit and implicit sexuality of others (so much of Michel Foucault's work is grounded in this perception). Thus, it is not surprising to find that real-world languages—as opposed to artificial or predicate-logic languages—embed questions of sexuality and gender in ways that cut across the broad spectrum of all of the subsystems of morphology and syntax. This fact may make it difficult to envision a reformation of language structure that would be radical enough to take into account the multiple forms of sexism that feminist scholarship may identify with language. In the process, we must also call attention to the vast internal contradictions of linguistic structures, their slippages and their aporias. These internal constructions allow for a queer manipulation of language that provides for far-ranging poetic and affective performances that are the quintessence of language queered in a resistance to and transgression of heteronormativity.[8]

The extent to which heteronormativity is understood as a vast ideological hegemony brings with it a queering of equally extensive proportions: Cherríe Moraga's "Queer Aztlán" necessarily segues from those elements within Chicano culture that are queer, such as her lesbian resistance to masculinist supremacy, to Aztlán as a queer sociohistoric enterprise resistant to Anglo-Protestant pretensions of *gabacho* superiority to *la raza*. One might well investigate the same point with regard to Afro-Caribbean (*santería*) and Afro-Brazilian (*macumba, candomblé*) religious practices, with their dimensions of transgendered spirituality as resistance and transgression of bourgeois Euro-

---

considerations, of the "what if" variety, that stop short of substituting received knowledge with an alternative one.

8. I would begin an inventory here with the sonnets of Luis de Góngora, especially poems such as "Mientras por competir con tu cabello," which, contrary to the inherent structures of the Spanish language, accomplishes fourteen lines of erotic encomium without identifying the gender of the addressee. Perception of this fact allows the reader to question whether, as heteronormative conventions would impose, we should legitimately conclude that the poem is necessarily addressed to a woman.

centered (or U.S.-centered,[9] in the case of Mormon and Pentecostalist) practices. The latter function, as the saying goes in Portuguese, "para inglês ver," that is, as social manifestations suitable for display to foreigners and abroad.

Concomitantly, as I have mentioned above, Native American or First People practices, while not uniform throughout the Americas, demonstrate a striking continuity in terms of phenomena that Spanish and Portuguese invaders lumped together under the sin of sodomy and treated accordingly. Many of these practices are still found today among Native Americans, although perhaps often not untouched by the horrified reactions of explorers and missionaries that they elicited in an earlier age. The reader of Latin American culture within the parameters of European conventions—which include the elision of the unseemly,[10] as well as the enforced confirmation of unquestioned heteronormativity[11]—will have little occasion to confront sexuality in any of the multiple forms it takes in Latin American society. These forms range over the polydimensional continuums of Native American and Afro-American cultures as they intersect with hegemonic and, presumably, uniform/universal European traditions. Both in the translations of the Native American and the Afro-American cultures into Spanish and Portuguese and in their evocation by writers committed to their particularity, the scholar must be prepared to find systematic exceptions to Judeo-Christian heteronormativity and to account for the linguistic configurations of those exceptions and the universes of meaning they interpret. Any presumption of heteronormativity will only serve to blind the reader.

---

9. Bouchard notes the attraction of *candomblé* and the Yoruba Orisha religion to homosexuals (44). *Candomblé* and homosexuality is also studied by Trevisan. The anthropologist Luiz Mott has written extensively about what he identifies as gay culture in colonial Brazil, and his controversial hypothesis as to the possibility of the great slave rebel Zumbi dos Palmares being gay was a *cause célèbre* when he first formulated it in 1990. Nascimento argues that domination distorted Yoruban cultural values—which, one would add, would have been seen as "degenerate" (i.e., queer) by the slave traders—that Afrocentricity can seek now to recover for Brazilian culture (40–41). Lorando speaks of "'passive homosexuals,' or what Candomblé adherents call *adés*" (207). Santos and García use the term *adé* as a Brazilian translation of queer in their collection of research on queer culture in Brazil.

10. Witness what happens to classroom readings of the ending of Esteban Echeverría's "El matadero" (ca. 1840), where the story's less-than-subtle suggestion of anal rape of the Unitario is not very likely to be entertained. See Foster, "Towards Queering the Curriculum" and "Cultural Studies and Sexual Ideologies" on issues related to teaching queer-marked writing. Foster, "El estudio de los temas gay," is a survey of research in Spanish during the past quarter century (the gay of the title was imposed by the editors). We are lacking for Portuguese and Spanish the scholarship represented by Provencher and Spurlin for Queer English.

11. The lesbianism of Sor Juana Inés de la Cruz is also hardly likely to be a topic of class discussion. Ginway's discussion of a tradition of transgendering in Brazilian literature begins with Machado de Assis's 1884 story "As academias de Sião."

The presumption of heteronormativity is, however, the recurrent blinder to the ways in which a queer Portuguese or a queer Spanish may be operant long before an unquestioned adherence to the timeline of contemporary gay politics might imply. For example, two Brazilian women writers, Patrícia Galvão and Clarice Lispector (the former began writing in the 1920s, the latter in the 1940s), vie for a place of prominence in a working inventory of queer Portuguese. To be sure, there are specific lesbian references in Galvão's "proletarian novel" *Parque industrial* (Industrial Park; published under the pseudonym Mara Lobo in 1933), although considerably more interesting is the fragmentary style in which the novel is written and its creation of a virtually female-oriented narrative universe. Neither of these features is necessarily queer, although the creation of a female-oriented narrative universe is a respectable corrective to the masculinist-dominated one of the day, and to the systematic exclusion of Galvão from Brazil's literary record by a male-dominated literary academy (Foster, "The Feminization"). But there is a queering aspect to Galvão's rejection of academic prose, whether literary or otherwise, and *Parque industrial* stands in stark contrast, especially as a social-realist novel, to the journalistic norm prevalent in the genre in the 1930s. During those years other writers were experimenting with linguistic innovations that lend themselves to examination under the aegis of the queer—Mário de Andrade's *Gramatiquinha* (ca. 1922) was a major document in the linguistic discussions of the day—but literary social realism was expected to be written in the hegemonic register as exemplified by journalism: this was true even when that social hegemony was called into question by the sociopolitical thrust of the works themselves.

In the case of Clarice Lispector, the lesbian dimension of her life is perhaps a bit more available for scrutiny than any possibility with regard to Galvão.[12] Lispector spent close to the last decade of her life in the close company of Olga Borelli, although critical tact was resistant to seeing anything lesbian about this long cohabitation.[13] Of far greater importance is the female-oriented universe of Lispector's writings (this the object of important feminist analyses) and where that orientation opens up possibilities of non-heteronormative sexuality, such as the crux of the relationship of the two women in the story "A imitação da rosa" ("Imitation of the Rose") included in the 1960 collection

---

12. Although Norma Benguell's 1988 film on Galvão, *Eternamente Pagu*, does suggest, quite discretely, lesbian experiences with both the painter Tarsila do Amaral and the singer Elsie Houston.

13. Moser's masterful biography of Lispector makes only one passing comment on allegations of a lesbian identity for Lispector (18); he does not find it necessary to include this comment in his index.

Laços de família (Family Ties).[14] Much has been made of Lispector's use of Portuguese and her curious, fascinating decentering of syntax and vocabulary, as well as the various features of her literary language, in terms of her use of stream-of-consciousness, internal monologue, and ruptures with so-called realistic discourse. One of her greatest novels, *A paixão segundo G. H.* (1964; The Passion According to G. H.), turns on the emotional dislocations provoked by the female narrator's contemplation of the now abandoned room of her servant, and its meandering account is so complex that most readers seem actually to believe that the narrator partially consumes a cockroach, when close examination of the text reveals that nowhere is this explicitly stated.[15] The fissures in Lispector's prose defy the hegemonic norm that writing must be transparent—that is, that it must always comply with the linguistic version of natural theology and with perceived norms in terms of "the way things are supposed to be."

This essay has ranged over a wide variety of perspectives and cultural writings. In synthesis, I want to make it clear that, as interesting as the lives of writers may be, their sexuality—identitary, declared, in practice, by insinuation or attribution—is not a determining feature of their writing, no more than any biographical feature can, fallaciously, be taken to be creatively determinate. The analysis of a queer Portuguese or a queer Spanish must, rather, take into account complex issues of sociocultural context and linguistic creation. It must be attuned to the presence of hegemonic and heteronormative priorities and the degree to which a writer may develop a transgressive or deconstructive voice relative to them. Questioning the assumptions of those priorities, as imposed on writers by academic traditions and/or by critical protocols, is where the practice of queering begins. Perhaps there can be no institutional phenomenon such as "queer Portuguese" or "queer Spanish" in contraposition to the heterosexist norm. Rather, perhaps it is more a process of a particular consciousness, and perhaps, for literature, it might end up like the maps of the cartographers in Borges's homonymous story, "Los cartógrafos." It will remain to be seen if the practice of literature—or, more broadly, cultural production—can ever not be transgressive or deconstructive, as we as scholars examine texts, in a widening gyre, that refuse to conform to the business of life, sexual or otherwise, as it might be inevitably thought to unquestionably be.

What, then, I have attempted to do here is range across a wide variety of topics that question the stability of the sort of language sought after by nor-

---

14. Fitz refers to the repressed sexual passion of this story (91–95) and speaks of both homosexuality and lesbian desire (e.g., 172) with reference to other texts.

15. Moser (269) accepts the proposition that the narrator of *A paixão* does, in fact, eat the cockroach.

mative grammars and academic practices. Language in its daily use and, especially, in its poetic or affective use, goes against the grain of normativity, of all sorts of normativity, including heteronormativity. Perhaps Plato's exclusion of the poets from the ideal republic was grounded in the first identifiable perception that poetry—and, by extension, all creative art—is necessarily queer. This would suggest that poetry is perhaps the best place to begin an investigation of the queering of Spanish and Portuguese, especially in the case of writers about whom current research has demonstrated that queer issues played a part in their personal and artistic life: Gabriela Mistral and Mário de Andrade, for example. But it means also looking at writers whose artistic world is, in some ways, to use one of Jorge Luis Borges's favorite words, *unheimlich* (unhomelike—that is, otherworldly). Borges's own writing and, certainly, that of Clarice Lispector, both correspond to this description. Needless to say, a whole range of postmodern writers would come into play here, but I think especially of Manuel Puig or Marcelino Freire.

Early premodern scholarship (i.e., what we used to call the Golden Age) has begun to amass a significant amount of queer scholarship that has yet to reach the extent of premodern English scholarship on the topic (I think of Madhavi Menon's impressive collection of essays by a wide range of scholars, published in 2011 by Duke University Press under the title *Shakesqueer: A Queer Companion to the Complete Works of Shakespeare*). We need a "queer companion" for Portuguese and Spanish early premodern authors, as we do for the many contemporary authors I have mentioned for whom there is now a record of queer scholarship. And I would add other names that would begin with even those writers who are legendary paragons of heterosexism, such as Rubén Darío.

Much of the scholarship on queer issues in Spanish and Portuguese studies has been thematic in focus, whether it is related or not to known or speculative biographic details regarding authors. The proposals formulated in this essay call for the shift toward an examination of what is most materially evident in their writing, the language they use and worlds of meaning to which this language refers.

WORKS CITED

Altamiranda, Daniel. "Jorge Luis Borges." *Latin American Writers on Gay and Lesbian Themes: A Bio-critical Sourcebook*. Ed. David William Foster. Westport, CT: Westview, 1994. 72–83.

Bazán, Osvaldo. *Historia de la homosexualidad en la Argentina: de la conquista de América al siglo XXI*. Buenos Aires: Marea, 2004.

Bouchard, Jen Westmoreland. "Brazil." *The Greenwood Encyclopedia of LGBT Issues Worldwide*. Ed. Chuck Stewart. Santa Barbara, CA: Greenwood Press, an imprint of ABC-CLIO, 2010. 1:37–47.

Fitz, Earl E. *Sexuality and Being in the Poststructuralism Universe of Clarice Lispector: The Différance of Desire*. Austin: U of Texas P, 2001.

Foster, David William. "Cultural Studies and Sexual Ideologies." *ADFL Bulletin* 33.3 (2002): 20–24.

———. "El estudio de los temas gay en América Latina desde 1980." *Revista iberoamericana* 225 (2008): 923–41.

———. "The Feminization of Social Space in Patrícia Galvão's *Parque industrial*." *Brasil/Brazil* 19.33 (2005–06): 23–46.

———. "Towards Queering the Curriculum." *Hispanic Issues Online*. 2 pag. <http://spanport.cla.umn.edu/publications/HispanicIssues/hispanic-issues-online/Debates/Debates_Fall_ 2007.html>.

Fry, Peter. *Para inglês ver: identidade e política na cultura brasileira*. Rio de Janeiro: Zahar Editores, 1982.

Ginway, Mary Elizabeth. "Transgendering in Luso-Brazilian Speculative Fiction from Machado de Assis to the Present." *Luso-Brazilian Review* 47.1 (2010): 40–60.

Kulawick, Krzysztof. *Travestismo lingüístico: el enmascaramiento de la identidad sexual en la narrativa latinoamericana neobarroca*. Madrid: Iberoamericana; Frankfurt am Main: Vervuert, 2009.

Matory, J. Lorand. *Tradition, Transnationalism, and Matriarchy in the Afro-Brazilian Candomblé*. Princeton: Princeton UP, 2005.

Moraga, Cherríe. "Queer Aztlán: The Re-formation of the Chicano Tribe." *The Last Generation: Prose and Poetry*. By Cherríe Moraga. Boston: South End, 1993. 145–74.

Moser, Benjamin. *Why This World: A Biography of Clarice Lispector*. Oxford: Oxford UP, 2009.

Mott, Luiz. "Era Zumbi homosexual?" *Crônicas de um gay assumido*. By Luiz Mott. Rio de Janeiro: Editora Record, 2003. 155–63.

Nascimento, Elisa Larkin. *The Sorcery of Color: Identity, Race, and Gender in Brazil*. Philadelphia: Temple UP, 2007.

Rodríguez, Félix. *Diccionario gay-lésbico: vocabulario general y argot de la homosexualidad* . Madrid: Editorial Gredos, 2008.

Santos, Rick, and Wilton García, eds. *A escrita de adé: perspectivas teóricas dos estudos gays e lésbic@s no Brasil*. São Paulo: Xamã, 2002.

Spurlin, William J., ed. *Lesbian and Gay Studies and the Teaching of English: Positions, Pedagogies, and Cultural Politics*. Urbana: National Council of Teachers of English, distributed by ERIC Clearinghouse, 2000.

Trevisan, João Silvério. 1986. *Devassos no paraíso: a homossexualidade no Brasil, da colônia à atualidade*. Rio de Janeiro: Editora Record, 2002.

CHAPTER 4

Before Tordesilhas, and Beyond
The Politics of Native Agency across the Americas

TRACY DEVINE GUZMÁN

"IT WAS a monstrous discovery." So ruminates the entrepreneur, museum collector, and "Indian hobbyist" Adam Pell, one of the protagonists of Native North American writer D'Arcy McNickle's third and final novel, *Wind from an Enemy Sky*. Issued posthumously in the mid-1970s, McNickle's tale of the fictitious Little Elk people of the U.S. Northwest was written over the course of three decades, and was influenced not only by his literary imagination, but also by his many years of work as a civil servant for the Bureau of Indian Affairs, his training as an anthropologist, and his political activism on behalf of indigenous peoples across the Americas.

The "monstrosity" to which Adam Pell refers is one of his own making: as we witness through an intertwined narration of past and present events, the middle-aged entrepreneur has arrived at the Little Elk community to find its members on their proverbial knees. To his acute discomfort, if neither his repentance nor his sorrow, Pell learns that the combination of his "development" work and well-meaning but colonialist fondness for all things "Indian" has dealt the languishing Native population a near-fatal blow. His company has built a massive river dam on a sacred indigenous site to irrigate the fields of the white settlers who grow wheat on what was once Little Elk territory. In the aftermath of the 1887 Dawes Act, the 1898 Curtis Act, and the 1906 Burke Act—all legislation aimed at undoing, in different ways and at any price, the traditional use of Native lands and the traditional organization of Native life—

the Little Elk homelands have been divided up into individual plots, fenced off, and sold by the U.S. government in the name of modernization and progress.[1] As Bull, the Little Elk Chief (or "talker," in his language) laments: "They [. . .] killed the water [. . . and] I was afraid. How can a stream out of the mountains be killed? Will they [now] open up the earth and drop us in it? Will they take the sun out of the sky? It was bad for us when they came with guns. Now they will kill us in other ways" (3, 14).

The other forms of "killing" to which Bull refers are mostly spiritual, for Native life in his view is intimately tied to land and to a non-Weberian conception of sovereignty that is neither grounded in necessary violence nor infused with the imperialist, homogenizing imperative of national belonging that grounds the foundational logic of American settler states.[2] The Little Elk people, we learn, have been strengthened and resuscitated by the recent possibility of recuperating their long-lost medicine bundle—a traditional guarantor of shared strength and courage stolen from them by priests three decades earlier and handed over for a "small donation" to the Americana Institute—a New York City museum that Adam Pell happens to own (50). It was, as we come to discover, in the absence of that consecrated package and communal vessel of "all good things" (208) that collective suffering began and Little Elk life became virtually unbearable.[3]

Ultimately, the Little Elk's short-lived hope of recovering their sacred belongings will prove the root of their demise. Due to Pell's negligence, the precious bundle was long ago tossed into a dusty lumber room and forgotten for years, along with a clutter of broken furniture, abandoned exhibit pieces, and mangy stuffed animals. By the time the museum staff finally retrieves the sacred piece, mold and vermin have taken their toll: the bundle is utterly destroyed—barely recognizable by its yellowed, crumbling identification tag. Against a backdrop of profound misunderstanding, miscommunication, and an avalanche of catastrophic consequences that they provoke for the Little Elk people and the surrounding non-indigenous community, the fact of this

---

1. The Dawes or General Allotment Act gave the president authority to distribute Native lands to individuals and sell off "excess" land to non-Natives. The Curtis Act dissolved the governing authority of the Five Civilized Tribes prior to Oklahoma's statehood. The Burke Act allowed the Secretary of the Interior to remove allotted lands of "competent" Native peoples from trust, thus expediting the transfer of title and (in theory) the conferral of national citizenship. On the efforts to undo the damage to Native communities brought on by this legislation, see chapter 8 of Philp.

2. On indigeneity and the violence of dominant sovereignty, see Shaw. On Native conceptualizations of sovereignty, see Alfred; Alfred and Corntassel; and Barker's edited volume. On settler colonialism, see Wolfe and Tuhiwai Smith.

3. For twentieth-century "scientific" accounts of the medicine bundle, see Hanson and Thomas.

ruinous neglect is indeed the "monstrous discovery" that tears at the hearts of McNickle's tragically flawed characters (210).[4]

More monstrous than this rendering of early twentieth-century Native/non-Native relations, however, is our realization that the Little Elk community's battered and abandoned medicine bundle also stands in for indigenous peoples across the United States and the Americas. In Brazil and Peru—the other national contexts here under study—Native peoples were likewise turned over to republican and, at times, nominally democratic institutions that could not have bestowed upon "their" Indians more colonialist regimes of power. Bridging the so-called Indian problem[5] of these three countries are the national and transnational indigenist bodies headed by the (mostly) secular "missionaries" of their respective countries with regard to Native affairs: anthropologist bureaucrats like McNickle himself. Over the twentieth century, the U.S. Bureau of Indian Affairs, the Brazilian Serviço de Proteção aos Índios (SPI), and the Peruvian Instituto Indigenista functioned, with few exceptions, as assimilationist organizations that sought knowledge about the Native peoples under their tutelage in order to control them in more absolute terms.[6] Although the rhetoric of "protection" played out differently, and in distinctly local terms, it revealed in each context the dominant, assimilative impulse that has been targeted by Native political critique ever since.[7]

This neocolonialism would be simultaneously territorial, epistemological, ontological, biopolitical, spiritual, and linguistic. Through interwoven discourses of nationhood, national belonging, and nationalism—all channeled into state-sponsored de-Indianizing initiatives euphemistically labeled "schooling," but referenced in less formal discourse as "Indian improvement"—Native peoples across the Americas have been told where to live and what ways of being in and thinking about the world are authentically Indian enough. They have been informed which languages are sufficiently compatible with rational thought, and thus useful for progress and development. They have learned which spiritual beliefs and religious practices are appropriately civilized, and which are too backwards, even barbarous. And they have heard

---

4. For more on the relationship between McNickle's writing and life story, see Purdy (ed.) and Parker.

5. The long genesis of this term began with Peruvian socialist thinker José Carlos Mariátegui. See his famous 1928 essay by the same name ("El problema del indio").

6. Brazil's SPI was established in 1911 by a military engineer of indigenous descent named Cândido Mariana da Silva Rondon. The U.S. Office of Indian Affairs was established under the Department of War in 1824. It became a bureau of the Interior Department 123 years later, following the first meeting of the Instituto Indigenista Interamericano in Pátzcuaro, Mexico, in 1940. Peru's Institute Indigenista was established in 1946.

7. See Alfred and Alfred and Corntassel.

that they ought not to wear soccer jerseys, run businesses, drive nice cars, or even ride the bus if they wish to avoid being profiled as racial hucksters out to leech the state or otherwise exist in detriment to the non-indigenous poor.[8]

Critic Walter Mignolo long ago characterized such a rationale—the backbone of what sociologist Aníbal Quijano coined the "coloniality of power"[9]— as the "darker side" of Enlightenment thought—first of the Renaissance, then of Western modernity. Because, as Maori scholar Linda Tuhiwai Smith argues, many indigenous peoples worldwide have only recently begun to recover from the hegemonic influence of this rationale, the transnational task of decolonization is about controlling particular spaces, "bringing back into existence" a fragmented world (28), and "coming to know and understand theory and research from [Native] perspectives and for [Native] purposes" (39). One of the paradoxes, then, in the case of D'Arcy McNickle's depiction of Native North America in the aftermath of 1968—that global interrogation of some of the most nefarious legacies of colonialism—is that the institutions, organizations, and other bureaucratic entities deemed responsible for "protecting" Native lives and histories and showcasing Native cultures and cultural products in fact contributed greatly to their undoing. As with the Little Elk medicine bundle, such erasures resulted not only from ignorance and malfeasance but also, at times, from the very best of intentions.

When the ever-successful Adam Pell realizes after a long search that he holds responsibility for destroying the Little Elk's most treasured spiritual symbol, he offers as a replacement a priceless Inca figurine—a golden "Virgin of the Andes" seized during an earlier, adventurous outing to the Peruvian highlands. The omniscient narrator muses:

> It became [for Pell] a question of trying to determine what the Little Elk Indians had lost, and how they valued the loss. They had this notion that their water had been killed, but that, he felt, could be rationalized; they might even be brought to see it as a benefit. [. . .] [Then] he came full circle realizing that his original impulse to make amends by returning property he had no moral right to possess had come to nothing. He had entered into partnership with the government in taking what was not his, without compensating its proper owners. And now, as in the taking of the land, it was *ex post facto*. Sorry. My deep regrets. (214, 215)

---

8. For distinct versions of this narrative from Brazil, see, for example, Flores, Munduruku, and Potiguara.

9. The term coined by Peruvian Aníbal Quijano has been the source of recent controversy in the North American Academy. See Driscoll.

An archetype of U.S. ingenuity and individualism, the commanding Pell is accustomed to getting his way and thus shocked when his generous offer is rejected by destitute "Indians" in the name of kinship, a shared past, and communal spirituality—sources of value that money cannot buy and that he cannot understand. Thus we see how the failures of interpersonal and intercultural communication in McNickle's reading of the continuing encounter between Native and non-Native worlds exceed the complexities of language itself.

In *Wind from an Enemy Sky*, Native peoples' efforts toward decolonization and McNickle's representation of indigeneity more broadly are neither romanticized nor idealized, but they do summon the anti-imperialist and anticolonial struggles of the late twentieth century that foreground in the book the development of a global indigenous movement. At the same time, they mark the exclusion of indigenous peoples *as such* from many of those struggles—from organized movements for minority rights, workers' rights, students' rights, and women's rights, for instance; or from the rights-based discourse of national belonging typically associated with dominant notions of citizenship. In the United States, Native peoples were not granted citizenship until 1924, and in practice, many could not vote before the 1965 approval of the Voting Rights Act.[10] In Peru, the left-leaning administration of general Juan Velasco Alvarado, who came to power in a 1968 military coup, went as far as to remove the word "Indian" (*indio*) from official state discourse and replace it with the term *campesino* (peasant), thus disappearing nominal "Indians" from the national polity with the stroke of a pen. Finally, Native peoples in Brazil would not hold the rights of national citizenship until the ratification of the post-dictatorship Constitution of 1988. Prior to that date, they had to be legally emancipated from their condition of "Indianness" through civic education and other "de-Indianizing" measures in order to be recognized legally as Brazilian.[11]

Alongside the massive and massively controversial Belo Monte hydroelectric dam now under construction in the Amazonian state of Pará—"killing the water," as McNickle's tragic protagonist, Bull, would have put it—this second-tier or "tutorial" status is an enduring legacy of Brazil's century-old indigenist bureaucracy and the 1964–85 military government. That authoritarian regime, which began with the U.S.-backed ouster of democratically elected president João Goulart, intensified its grip on national society in December 1968 with the institution of the notorious Fifth Institutional Act (AI-5). In what amounted to an internal coup in the wake of growing social unrest,

---

10. For a chronology, see "Native American Citizenship," http://www.NebraskaStudies.org.

11. On these laws and the linguistic maneuvers related to "de-Indianization" in Peru and Brazil, see Devine Guzmán, "Indigenous Identity," and *Native and National in Brazil*.

President Artur da Costa e Silva dissolved the national congress and state legislatures, suspended *habeas corpus* rights, and limited even more rigorously the already circumscribed freedom of the press (Contreras).

It is this tumultuous context, then, that I wish to consider, alongside McNickle's interpretation of colonialist power, the contemporary critique offered by two fellow anthropologist-novelists: first, the Peruvian José María Arguedas, who self-identified as a "modern Quechua man" and claimed rootedness in indigenous Andean epistemologies despite the fact that he was born to a non-indigenous family; and second, Brazilian educator and politician Darcy Ribeiro, who laid no familial claim to indigeneity, but attested unwaveringly to his deep understanding of indigenous life and thought at home and abroad. Drawing on years of traditional ethnographic fieldwork, Ribeiro claimed the ability to appropriate an indigenous subject position at will, or, as he put it—and problematically so—"to see the Indian through the eyes of the Indian" (*Confissões* 155).

INDIGENIST MIRRORS

Though not completed until the 1970s, Ribeiro's first indigenist novel, *Maíra*, was drafted during the author's exile in Uruguay and political imprisonment in Rio de Janeiro in the early years of the Brazilian dictatorship. Arguedas's final novel, *El zorro de arriba y el zorro de abajo*, which was written as the author traveled from Chimbote to Lima and Santiago de Chile in the late 1960s, was published posthumously and in incomplete form in 1970—one year into the "revolution" of Velasco Alvarado, and just a few months after Arguedas took his own life. Marked by the chaotic era in which they were brought forth, these works, like McNickle's *Wind from an Enemy Sky*, situate indigenous peoples in the eye of the storm of a globalized modernity marked by the confluence of neo-imperialism, cultural conflict, and social disintegration. Each tale depicts the disruption of traditional, indigenous ways of being, thinking, and remembering through the violent introduction of international capital—an encounter that dominant nationalist discourses proposed would, in a positive (and positivist) vein, expedite the formation of productive, modern, and, most importantly, de-Indianized national subjects. In each case, the confrontation would be mediated (as reflected explicitly in McNickle's and Ribeiro's novels), by a state-run indigenist apparatus through which the diverse histories, distinct configurations of cultural power, and varying degrees of economic dependency of peoples identified as indigenous were subsumed under the blanket term "Indian." In Brazil and Peru, indigenist discourses *about* but rarely *by* Native peoples were reduced in dominant discourse to a common denominator of anti-imperialist nationalism whereby intellectuals like Arguedas and Ribeiro could adopt indigenous subalternity for themselves—mostly vis-à-vis the global North. In contrast, anti-imperialist critiques of U.S. Indian policy were, as in the case of the Salish-Kootenai tribal member, McNickle, driven largely by Native scholars and activists seeking to expose and close the gaps between purported democratic ideals and lived indigenous experience.

From similar contexts of social and political upheaval, then, Ribeiro, Arguedas, and McNickle interrogate the state-mediated elimination of Indianness by exposing the relationship between "Indian"-oriented projects of nation-building, anti-imperialist discourse, and intellectual self-positioning vis-à-vis subalternity through personal relationships with indigeneity. Though evident in Ribeiro's anthropological work, this self-positioning is particularly clear in *Maíra,* where as the creator of an imaginary world, the ethnographer appropriates indigenous voices freely and to his own ends. In *El zorro de arriba y el zorro de abajo,* on the other hand, Arguedas privileges the well-known autobiographical current of his fiction by interjecting four personal diaries into a fragmented and hyperracialized novel of sociocultural transformation. The result is a dark testimonial account wherein the author doubles as Native informant to serve as his own dejected interlocutor.

Intimately tied up in these deliberations over Indianness and indigeneity are divergent visions of how cultural metamorphosis does and ought to play out in traditional social formations confronting radical social and political change.[12] Responding to racist cultural universalism as a fatal discourse for those who will not or cannot conform to the idea of homogenous nationhood, Ribeiro and Arguedas, like McNickle, set themselves apart from indigenist discourses that posited Indianness as either hopelessly ephemeral or completely static, and pointed instead to the need for more subtle and complex ways of thinking about indigeneity and, in particular, the relationship between Native peoples and the nation-states in which they live.

FICTION AND AUTO-ETHNOGRAPHY

Ribeiro's anthropological training and work for Brazil's Serviço de Proteção aos Índios (SPI) began in the 1950s during the populist rule of Getúlio Vargas, who pushed the incorporation of "Indians" into national society as an "anti-racist" initiative to foster development and national unity. While Ribeiro

---

12. On the distinction between Indianness and indigeneity, see Devine Guzmán, *Native and National in Brazil,* especially the introduction and chapter 1.

repudiated such programmatic assimilation and condemned those who would subject Native peoples to its devastating effects, public opinion embraced the citizenship campaign as "humanitarian" and rallied behind the idea of a unified "Brazilian race" with little concern over the state's campaign for the cultural annihilation of surviving indigenous populations. As Ribeiro protested: "[State policy] meant abandoning them to their own luck without recognizing the civilizing avalanche that was about to overcome them with genocidal and ethnocidal furor"[13] (*Confissões* 153).

Ribeiro resigned from the SPI after a decade of ethnographic service due to ideological differences with the organization and what he considered its thinning moral fabric. He dabbled in indigenist fiction as a diversion from "more difficult theoretical work," but was disappointed by the minimal success of novels that earned the attention of academics rather than a popular audience (*Confissões* 515).[14] Seeking to expose nonspecialist readers to indigenous peoples and their thorny relationship with dominant national society, Ribeiro used *Maíra* to critique the state's indigenist apparatus while questioning widespread and widely accepted notions of peaceful and "democratic" miscegenation.

By depicting the state's deleterious intervention into relatively isolated indigenous communities in accordance with his earlier theory of "ethnic transfiguration"[15] and belief in the limits of transculturation, Ribeiro offered a fictionalized rendering of the encounter between precapitalist modes of thought and production and the burgeoning capitalist ethos of modernity. Having resided and worked in SPI "indigenous posts" for a decade, he had observed firsthand the workings of the state's assimilationist policies and come, mostly, to oppose them.[16] At the same time, he saw the posts not as de-

13. All translations are mine.

14. Ribeiro corresponded with writer and cartoonist Ziraldo (Alves Pinto) regarding his desire for a film version of *Maíra* to be directed by Ruy Guerra (Fundação Darcy Ribeiro).

15. Ribeiro's *Os índios e a civilização* (1970) was dedicated to the SPI founder whose progressive ideas, Ribeiro felt, had been perverted by decades of flawed indigenist practice. "Ethnic transfiguration" was driven by the indigenous encounter with "modern technology" that Ribeiro thought would eventually extinguish precapitalist forms of production. Change would be most intense when the community could not maintain traditional sociocultural structures while adopting an exogenous economic system. If the indigenous group could reformulate its cultural patrimony (and survive physical contact with non-Indians), the process of transfiguration would be gradual (254–93; 487–503).

16. After half a century of intervention, Ribeiro argued, state-backed indigenism could be credited with two accomplishments: (1) land-protection efforts had enabled some indigenous groups to maintain community-based economies rather than join regional workforces under the precarious conditions offered to other rural laborers; and (2) by creating artificial environments of indigenous/non-indigenous interaction, the SPI afforded "protected" groups opportunities to develop mechanisms for resisting assimilation (496).

Indianizing "citizen factories" (Luykx), but as sites of sociocultural negotiation where beliefs and practices were constantly challenged, defended, and reformulated. Ribeiro would later argue that programmatic efforts to undo indigeneity were both misguided and futile. The best possible Native/non-Native encounters, in contrast, were those enabling indigenous groups to maintain the cultural practices and social norms that could be reconciled with the capitalist imperative—those, in other words, through which the least amount of "ethnic transfiguration" would occur. An auspicious outcome of such contact would not be assimilation, then, but the reformulation of old ways of living to ensure survival in the present. "Tribal Indians," he argued, might lose specificity, but indigeneity would remain, nonetheless.

In each of the texts under study, the processes through which indigenous peoples encounter state-mediated neoliberalism are erratic and gruesome, marking the consolidation of an inherently violent geopolitical order. *Maíra* brings us to the banks of the Iparanã River, where in the deepest retreats of the Amazon rainforest, the fictional Mairum people are threatened with extinction on all fronts. Danger is posed by politicians, missionaries, the Catholic Church, the National Indian Foundation (FUNAI),[17] and the petty-capitalist *regatões*[18] who sell "trinkets and beads," as it were, to enrich themselves on the black market. Danger is even posed by do-gooders like the naïve protagonist, Alma ("soul"), who has fled a futile life of sex and drugs in Rio de Janeiro to seek redemption through service to the Natives. Also determined to become a nun, she heads to the remote mission of Nossa Senhora do Ó.

On her journey, Alma meets Isaías—an "ex-Indian," formerly known as Avá—who has abandoned many years of preparation for the priesthood to return to the Mairum community from which he was taken as a young boy by Italian missionaries. Rejected by the nuns with whom she had hoped to work, Alma accompanies Isaías on a long and perilous journey to his childhood home, where both lost souls seek renewed meaning for their confused, empty lives. The Mairuns receive the pair with joy and curiosity: Isaías is interrogated for detailed explanations of the "outside world," while Alma is poked, prodded, and scrutinized relentlessly by women and children who marvel over her hairy, white body (212–15). Vacillating from fascination to attraction to revulsion with regard to these experiences and the community as a whole, Alma serves as Ribeiro's ethnographic alter ego, constantly shifting her expectations of others and reformulating her view of a society that she still lacks the knowledge to understand. Through moments of blissful insight and painful

---

17. The military government established FUNAI in the late 1960s after dissolving the SPI.

18. Traveling salesmen who peddle national and international products and trade them for local goods.

confusion, she struggles to make some sense of her new home, but her efforts repeatedly fail. Ultimately, her burning desire to "live the everyday, little life of the Mairuns" (136) will never help her fit into a communal structure based on blood ties and familial relations.

Despite her inexorable foreignness, Alma adjusts more readily to Mairum life than her companion, Isaías, who suffers awkward loneliness and falls pathetically short of his former community's expectations for a new *tuxaua* (leader). Whereas Isaías is ill at ease in his own skin and highly critical of the Mairuns' lack of capitalist ambition, Alma relishes the isolation and "backwardness" of her adopted home and her new role as a conspicuous and sexually desirable newcomer. Her profound admiration for the community's autonomy from dominant society thus clashes with Isaías's desire to speed along Mairum "development" by channeling their enthusiasm for sport into a new agricultural business venture. Indignant over the suggestion, Alma retorts: "As far as I'm concerned, these Mairuns have already carried out the 'revolution in liberty.'[19] People here are neither rich nor poor; when nature is stingy, everyone thins out; when she's generous, everyone fattens up. No one is exploited. No one is boss. [. . .] They don't even fight. [. . .] Leave those people in peace, Isaías" (215).

Despite her enthusiasm for communal life and insistence that she "really [is] a Mairum" (248), Alma's attempt to go Native is finally undone by her desire to have an indigenous child: her plan to join the community by reenacting the Mairum creation myth of birthing twins[20] is foiled when she perishes during labor, along with the babies whose lives would have symbolized (at least for her) a felicitous union between indigenous and non-indigenous Brazil. Her celebration of Native life through sexual promiscuity is tragically incapable of propagating life, and thus fails to fulfill the Romantic promise of the white-Native "wilderness marriage" or to realize the "foundational" potential of its projected *mestiço* offspring.[21] In keeping with Ribeiro's anti-interventionist politics, our final vision of the Mairum community depicts an amorous encounter between two "authentic" Natives who have found one another after rejecting non-indigenous partners (Alma and Isaías). Pointing to relative isolationism and the sociocultural purity it engenders as the only way to ensure indigenous survival, Ribeiro excludes non-Mairuns (and his

---

19. *Revolución en libertad* was the slogan of Chilean President Eduardo Nicanor Frei Montalva (1964–70)—critic of Allende and, later, opponent of the Pinochet regime.

20. According to this myth, the twins, Maíra and Micura were born unto the Mairum people of their partnerless mother, Mosaingar (116–20).

21. Moacyr, son of José de Alencar's tragic heroine Iracema, from the 1865 novel of the same name, is perhaps the best-known case in the Brazilian literary tradition.

readers) entirely by penning the concluding conversation (an explicit sexual encounter) in the Guaraní-derived "Mairum language" (323). With this final gesture, Ribeiro reinserts himself into the novel—and into Brazil's national and indigenist communities, both targets of his critique—as an indispensable bridge between Native and non-Native worlds.

At the same time, however, Ribeiro's personal identification with his doomed heroine[22] reiterates the tendency for indigenist discourse to displace its Native object of study with the personal and political preoccupations of the indigenist at hand. Written when he was facing grave health problems alongside grim expectations for the future of indigenous Brazil, Ribeiro's anxiety over his mortality and the country's dark political horizon under the long shadow of dictatorship surfaced repeatedly as key subtexts of his auto-ethnographic preoccupations:

> What more could it want [. . .] this poor, insatiable heart of mine. [. . .] The glory to remain after me [. . .] galloping in the memories of the grandchildren of the children I never had. To go on. But how? I don't know. What I do know is my enormous envy of the lives in the death of my two friends, loved and snuffed out: Ernesto and Salvador. Oh the life that slips away in distraction, between the fingers of time [. . .]. We only remain [. . .] in the small corners of someone else's memory, on the eve of the long forgetting. (169–70)

A mere fragment of a narrative parenthesis wherein Ribeiro uses his own voice to comment on the fate of his characters, this declaration appears physically and ideologically at the center of the novel, hence pointing to the self-questioning and anti-imperialist agenda that grounded his indigenist projects.

INDIGENISM AND CAPITAL

Similarly traversing fiction and nonfiction, lived experience and ethnographic authority, Arguedas's *El zorro de arriba y el zorro de abajo* engages, from the context of political crisis in late 1960s Peru, processes of neocolonialism and sociocultural change akin to those depicted by Ribeiro's *Maíra* and McNickle's *Wind from an Enemy Sky*. The three texts reflect not only distinct understandings and uses of indigeneity in relation to national and nationalist indigenist discourses, but also the authors' parallel personal crises and diverging views on anthropological privilege—particularly, their own. For Ribeiro and McNickle,

---

22. Ribeiro declared his empathy with Alma in an unpublished 1986 interview: "Even Alma is [. . .] me" (Schleicher 24).

the anti-imperialist political struggles on the horizon tasked the ethnographer-as-policymaker with a crucial role in working for indigenous survival and future well-being. For Arguedas, obsessed with a market-driven transformation of indigenous life that threatened his lifelong efforts to open up ideological, cultural, and political spaces for Quechua-speaking peasants in a real and imagined Peruvian society, this hope had already approached its limits.

Seven years before taking his life, Arguedas published *Tupac Amaru kamaq taytanchisman* (*To Our Father and Creator, Túpac Amaru*),[23] an anti-imperialist manifesto that he wrote in Quechua and translated into Spanish. Though the "hymn-song" lashed out against the "armed and bloodthirsty Spaniard" and his heirs, more despicable for Arguedas was the "ex-Indian" who had turned against his own people: "My dear Father, [. . .] hear me: the heart of the masters is more fearsome, foul, inspires more hate. They have corrupted our own brothers, they have tainted their hearts, and with them, armed with weapons that even the devil of devils could not invent and craft, they kill us" (*Tupac Amaru* 19).[24] Alienated from spirituality and fanatical with power, such traitors would pose for Arguedas the foremost obstacle to resolving his country's "Indian problem." As he put it: "No incentive moves them more than rebellion, social climbing: [the desire] to stop being Indian, to become *mestizos* or masters (*señores*)" ("El indigenismo" 10).

In the early 1960s, however, Arguedas had expressed optimism that Peru's demographic transformation, impelled by the migration of highland peasants to the increasingly urbanized, *mestiza* coast, might begin to generate a more egalitarian national society. His ideal was not, as Mario Vargas Llosa argued, a hermetic, "utopian" world of pre-Columbian fiction, but one in which the democratic potential of human alterity might overpower racism and social exploitation in Peru, beginning with the capital city:

> We've arrived at the immense town of the masters and we are changing it. [. . .] We're united; we have congregated, town-by-town, name-by-name, and are squeezing this immense city that hated us, looked down on us like horse

---

23. The last Inca ruler, whose great-grandson (José Gabriel Condorcanqui) led the 1780 Túpac Amaru rebellion.

24. Arguedas was inspired, perhaps, by the following adolescent experience: "The most incomprehensibly cruel spectacle, which I witnessed for the first time, and in Lima, was a great parade of the Peruvian army. It was 1929, during the Leguía government [. . .]. While part of the crowd applauded, I had [. . .] to hold back my tears [. . .]. Not what we could call one "white" guy marched in the troop. The entire troop was Indian and black. And I knew [. . .] that those same people were the ones who shot at the Indians who, at the limits of desperation or rage, rose up [. . .] against the landholders who considered [. . . them] something less than dogs" ("Letter").

excrement. We must change it into a town of men who sing the hymns of the four regions of our world, [. . .] where the plague of evil never arrives. (*Tupac Amaru* 19–20)

Against this horizon of possible social transformation, Arguedas mapped his desire for Peru's future through and onto the double consciousness that he claimed in his writing voice. In keeping with his paean to Túpac Amaru, he hoped that the uneven integration of Hispanic and indigenous Peru might come to reflect what he considered the invaluable presence of the latter. Like Ribeiro, he relied on an anti-imperialist notion of indigeneity to uphold his projected fraternal community amid the solidarity-razing forces of global capital: "We believe Quechua will be the second language of Peru, and in the victory of the ideology that posits that the human being's march forward depends not on the ravenous confrontation of individualism, but [. . .] on the communal fraternity that stimulates creation as a good in-and-of itself, as well as for others" ("El indigenismo" 12). The vision of human solidarity, however, would not outlast the decade in which those words were written. Arguedas's Chimbote, absent any politically consequential sense of community, is filled instead with angst over the "plague of evil" that he associated with the increasingly market-driven transformation of human life.

Fleeing the abuse of highland landowners and in search of economic opportunity, Arguedas's peasants in *Los zorros* have descended on Peru's northern coast to join the exploitative fishmeal trade in the context of a profit-driven war on traditional Andean forms of life and thought. There, international capital wrings the lifeblood out of everything it touches, as fishermen, miners, prostitutes, roosters, guinea pigs, pelicans, anchovies, and even flies all die wretched, agonizing deaths. The mad prophet, Moncada, who bellows obscenities to strangers as he wanders the city carrying a cross on his shoulder, serves as a lucid voice of critique in the chaotic narrative. Juxtaposing the liberation theology of Chimbote's Yankee priests with the influx of U.S. mining interests, the madman likens foreign investment to a train that has run over an assemblage of vendible animals in the center of an open market:

> Life, death, the stench of fishmeal, the North American friar who doesn't pronounce Spanish properly. [. . .] Doesn't matter! They don't come to impose. Here they preach and risk their lives, gentlemen, among the stenches [. . .]. The rooster has died; the guinea pigs have died; the locomotive kills with innocence, my friends, just like the Yankees from Talara Tumbes Limited and the Pasco Hill Corporation. (55–56)

Faced with the locomotive of capitalism, highland peasants recently arrived to the malodorous fishing town react in a variety of ways to reveal Arguedas's once optimistic vision for Peru overcome by his difficulty in accepting or even making sense of his observations in Chimbote. Through their opposing views on capital, two provincial fishermen illustrate diverging paths for those struggling with and through the trials of Peruvian modernity. The young Asto, for example, is a recently arrived highlander who barely speaks Spanish, and yet rabidly disavows his non-Hispanic origins. Emboldened by his newfound (relative) prosperity and perception of a corresponding improvement in social status, he throws around cash and squanders his earnings on a light-skinned prostitute who refers to him cheekily as *vizcachita* (a highland rat) (39). Although his prowess makes him, in his mind, less Indian—"I white, fuck it, Argentine, fuck it. Who highlander now? [sic]" he brags (40)—Asto's arrogance is pathetic, and his degradation functions as a reproach to those who would readily discard Arguedas's Quechua world.

Arguedas constructs an alternative possibility for indigenous modernity, however, through the figure of Hilario Caullama, an Aymara union activist from Peru's eastern border with Bolivia. Unlike the frivolous Asto, whose ignorance has led him into the most defiled traps of capitalist culture, the literate Caullama is motivated by an acute social consciousness. He teaches migrants to read and embodies Arguedas's remaining hope that "work will one day defeat capital with [. . .] educashun [sic]" (96). Despite his anticapitalist ideology, Caullama's class-consciousness has not replaced his ethnic self-identification (the yet unrealized dream of the early twentieth-century Peruvian socialists), but rooted him in it more deeply. Persecuted and under threat for his undesirable political activity, he responds: "The Inca is by my side when we arrive to high seas. Atahualpa ain't dead. Tell [. . .] whatever sly, capitalist bloodsucker sent ya here like a fool. [. . .] The body-soul of the Inca is in the whole Cajamarca Valley, and from the cliffs of El Dorado, he tells the sea off, too. In time, [. . .] capital gonna surrender [sic]" (156–57).

Though he shares with highland migrants and North American immigrants a deficient knowledge of Spanish, Caullama's discourse is not one of ignorance, but of insight. Asto's materialism leads him to forsake his economic "inferiors," while the Aymara fisherman fashions an ethical relationship with modernity that prioritizes knowledge and social solidarity above the gratification of individual desire through the exploitation of others. Arguedas' anti-imperialist allegory emerges in Caullama's remark to one of the resident North American priests: "Why, Padre Cardozo, don't you stage your revolution in the United States, where it might actually be more necessary? [sic]" (157).

In this contrast between Asto, who is ridiculed for his desperation to de-Indianize, and Caullama, who draws on class-based and ethnic interests to navigate wave after wave of tradition-razing modernity, Arguedas's interrogation of the ideological and physical space for Native peoples in Peru resonates with the anti-imperialist anxieties of his personal narrative, as well as with those of McNickle and Ribeiro. Asto and Caullama are caricatured extremes, perhaps, of the future that Arguedas most feared versus the future that he once hoped might become, as expressed in his final diary, a new "historical cycle of human liberation" (198). And yet, if Caullama somehow embodied Arguedas's residual optimism regarding the prospects for the future of indigenous peoples and indigeneity in Peru and the Americas, the Aymara activist suggested an ideal with which the author, so deeply mired in personal crisis and the political and social upheavals of 1968, apparently failed to convince even himself.[25]

Like McNickle and Ribeiro, then, Arguedas positioned himself on the shifting borders between indigenous and non-indigenous worlds, portraying the economic and political forces of "de-Indianization," as well as the state's complicity in their triumph, as a matter of life and death—physical, cultural, and spiritual. In doing so, he interrogated the relationship between indigeneity—both as an abstract, analytical concept, and as lived experience—and the accelerated commodification of human existence that he saw pushing traditional and largely precapitalist sectors of American societies into the global marketplace. However, rather than seeking, like Ribeiro and McNickle, to prop up the crumbling walls of these putatively separate worlds, Arguedas sat down among the rubble and peered into the abyss, still clinging to the idea that the seemingly inevitable transformation of indigenous life might lead somehow to a more just society. On the eve of his death, he wrote with a conviction that reflected his confused, chaotic rendering of Chimbote: "What's happening to the borders of barbed wire [. . .]? How long will they last? Just like those who serve the gods of shadows, threats, and terror who erected and sharpened them [. . .], they weaken and corrode" (198). And yet, more than four decades later, Arguedas's once trodden desire begins to echo through the work of Peru's young people. At the conclusion of a 2010 meeting on indigenous media in Ayacucho, for example, participants published the following statement:

> The use of our Native language [. . .] is vital for the preservation of our culture, the transmission of knowledge, and the promise of our future genera-

---

25. For foundational contributions to the tremendous bibliography on Arguedas and Peruvian indigenism, see, for example, the work of Sara Castro Klarén, Antonio Cornejo Polar, Tomas Escajadillo, Martin Lienhard, Ángel Rama, and William Rowe.

tions. We agree that [. . .] the unity of our people, reciprocity, and solidarity will permit our visibility and the construction of plurinational, multilingual, and pluricultural states. The creation of modes of and spaces for indigenous communication is fundamental for projecting our worldview, traditions, and customs from our roots to the world. ("Declaración")

One cannot help but think that Arguedas—and Caullama—would be heartened by their words.

BEYOND IDENTITARIAN POLITICS

It was perhaps for their similar thinking about and experiences with Native life and thought that McNickle, Ribeiro, and Arguedas—one man indigenous, one not, one somewhere in between—found in the social sciences an insufficient means to represent the "indigenous question" of their respective times and places.[26] Because one central, if often unacknowledged, referent of indigenist discourse is the self, the authors' diverse engagements with indigeneity could not be circumscribed by professional, objective terms, and each man was compelled by a particular constellation of reasons to move between anthropology, self-referential fiction, and autobiography. And yet, the diversity and complexity of their articulations of indigenism also suggest that any fruitful engagement with indigenist politics cannot rest on the purported truth-value of identitarian claims, whether individual or collective, but instead must examine the relationships between those claims and the social, economic, and political contexts in which they are made, and—as Frederic Jameson taught us long ago—which also delimit their conditions of political possibility.[27]

Identification with Indianness has been used to explore the meaning of human life and existentialist "authentic existence;" to advance and critique nation-building projects of modernization and citizenship; and to adopt or align with subalternity as a means of deflecting or deflating dominant political, economic, and cultural regimes across the Americas. The self-positioning with regard to indigeneity by McNickle, Ribeiro, and Arguedas developed in each of these ways from varying degrees of personal and political commitment to reconciling Native ways of being, thinking, and remembering with national and regional discourses of "Indian protection" that were indelibly and

---

26. On the slippage between anthropology and fiction in Ribeiro and Arguedas (among others) in a Latin American context, see what Amy Fass Emery calls the "anthropological imagination."

27. See Jameson, *The Political Unconscious*.

ironically marked by the violence and erasures of global modernity. Dangerously and too frequently absent from such ambitions, however, has been the sustained and meaningful engagement with the expressed needs and interests of indigenous peoples. This was and is the tragic secret of the Little Elk medicine bundle; of the ongoing "killing" of the Xingu River; of the increasing commodification and commercialization of Machu Picchu; and of the enduring and uncritical celebration of Columbus Day. Year, after year, after year, it is always a monstrous discovery.

WORKS CITED

Alfred, Taiaiake. "Sovereignty." *Sovereignty Matters*. Ed. Joanne Barker. Lincoln: U of Nebraska P, 2005. 33–50.

Alfred, Taiaiake, and Jeff Corntassel. "Being Indigenous: Resurgences against Contemporary Colonialism." *Politics of Identity* 9 (2005): 597–614.

Arguedas, José María. "El indigenismo en el Perú." *Tlatoani* 18 (1967): 1–12. <http//:www.ciesas.edu.mx/Publicaciones/Clasicos/Index.html>.

———. "Letter." *Oiga* [Lima] 18 (July 1969): 15–16 .

———. *Tupac Amaru kamaq taytanchisman: haylli-taki; A nuestro padre creador Tupac Amaru; himno-canción*. Lima: Ediciones Salqantay, 1962.

———. *El zorro de arriba y el zorro de abajo*. Lima: Horizonte, 1971.

Barker, Joanne, ed. *Sovereignty Matters*. Lincoln: U of Nebraska P, 2005.

Contreras, Hélio. *AI-5: A opressão no Brasil*. Rio de Janeiro: Record, 2005.

"Declaración de Huamanga." Jornadas de Intercambio de Experiencias en Radio y Video Indígena. May 26–28, 2010. Text printed in: *Boletin Wayra* 58 (2010): 4–6.

Deloria, Philip J. *Playing Indian*. New Haven: Yale UP, 1998.

Devine Guzmán, Tracy. "Indigenous Identity and Identification in Peru." *Journal of Latin American Cultural Studies* 8.1 (1999): 63–74.

———. *Native and National in Brazil: Indigeneity after Independence*. Chapel Hill: U of North Carolina P, 2013.

Driscoll, Mark. "Looting the Theory Commons." *Postmodern Culture* 21.1 (2010). Web.

Fass Emery, Amy. *The Anthropological Imagination in Latin American Literature*. Columbia: U of Missouri P, 1996.

Flores, Lúcio Paiva. "Cultura e a ex-cultura." *Sol do pensamento*. Ed. Eliane Potiguara. São Paulo: Inbrapi/Grumin, 2005. 30–32.

Hanson, Jeffrey R. "Structure and Complexity of Medicine Bundle Systems of Selected Plains Indian Tribes." *The Plains Anthropologist* 25.89 (1980): 199–216.

Jameson, Frederic. *The Political Unconscious*. New York: Routledge, 2002.

Luykx, Aurolyn. *The Citizen Factory*. Albany: SUNY P, 1999.

McNickle, D'Arcy. *Wind from an Enemy Sky*. Albuquerque: U of New Mexico P, 1988.

Mignolo, Walter. *The Darker Side of the Renaissance*. Ann Arbor: U of Michigan P, 1997.

——. *The Darker Side of Western Modernity*. Durham: Duke UP, 2011.

Munduruku, Daniel. *Histórias de Índio*. São Paulo: Companhia das Letras, 1997.

Parker, Dorothy R. *Singing an Indian Song*. Lincoln: U of Nebraska P, 1992.

Philp, Kenneth. *John Collier's Crusade for Indian Reform*. Tucson: U of Arizona P, 1977.

Potiguara, Eliane. *Metade cara, metade mascara*. Rio de Janeiro: Global Editora, 2005.

Purdy, John Lloyd, ed. *The Legacy of D'Arcy McNickle*. Norman: U of Oklahoma P, 1996.

Ribeiro, Darcy. *Confissões*. São Paulo: Companhia das Letras, 1997.

——. *Maíra*. Rio de Janeiro: Círculo do Livro, 1977.

Schliecher, Britta. "Analisando nos romances *O Mulo* e *Maíra* do escritor brasileiro Darcy Ribeiro." Unpublished interview. 1986. (Fundação Darcy Ribeiro).

Shaw, Karena. *Indigeneity and Political Theory*. New York: Routledge, 2008.

Sommer, Doris. *Foundational Fictions*. Berkeley: U of California P, 1991.

Thomas, Sidney J. "A Sioux Medicine Bundle." *American Anthropologist* 43.3 (1941): 605–9.

Tuhiwai Smith, Linda. *Decolonizing Methodologies*. New York: Zed Books, 1999.

Vargas Llosa, Mario. *La utopía arcaica*. Mexico: Fondo de Cultura Económica, 1997.

Wolfe, Patrick. "Settler Colonialism and the Elimination of the Native." *Journal of Genocide Research* 8.4 (2006): 397–409.

CHAPTER 5

"Blister you all"

Sérgio Buarque de Holanda and the Calibanic Genealogy

PEDRO MEIRA MONTEIRO
TRANSLATED FROM PORTUGUESE BY JAMES IRBY

THIS CHAPTER is an attempt at situating Sérgio Buarque de Holanda's *Roots of Brazil* (1936) within a long line of thought, especially present in essays, that sees Latin America, or Ibero-America, as a civilizing "option" different from and *superior* to the one represented by the United States. However, I won't discuss *Roots of Brazil* directly. Instead, I will trace, in broad strokes, the curve of that Latin Americanist line of thought that envisions *another* kind of America, the other side to the mirror of America. My reflections will then lead up to the debate generated in Brazil when U.S. Latin Americanist scholar Richard Morse's study *O espelho de Próspero* (Prospero's Mirror) was published there in the late 1980s.

But where shall one begin? Perhaps with a short essay on Edgar Allan Poe in which Rubén Darío recalls his arrival in the United States at the port of New York at the end of the nineteenth century. There the poet sketches a misty, marvelous scene: "On a cold damp morning I came for the first time to the enormous country of the United States." One particular detail in this scene is worth noting: squeezed in between the vast extent of Long Island and the shape of Staten Island, even before the formidable skyline of Manhattan came into view, it was the beauty of it all, says Darío, that tempted "the pencil rather than the camera, due to the dim light" (17).

What do Latin American poets and essayists see when they glimpse that other America? What kind of terribly seductive mirror does it hold up to them? How do they imagine or intuit their *own* America, supposedly so different from North America? What is it that joins together such a diversity of intellectuals around a difference that, once postulated, turns them into demiurgical agents of national and regional discourse, privileged revealers of the secrets of an entire collectivity?

In this poet's provocative thoughts as he enters "enemy" territory, we can already hear, prefigured as it were, echoes of all the "Arielisms" that would come to mark so deeply the imagination of Latin America. That imagination, or rather that fantasy shaped by intellectuals about Latin America, was introduced by Darío even before Rodó, when, in the abovementioned essay on Poe, originally published in 1894, the Nicaraguan poet suggested that on the other side of the mirror it was Caliban who ruled:

"Those Cyclopes. . . ," says Groussac; "those fierce Calibans. . . ," writes Peladan. Was the strange Sar right to characterize in this way these men of North America? Caliban rules over the island of Manhattan, over San Francisco, over Boston, over Washington, over the entire country. He has managed to impose the rule of matter, ranging from its mysterious form created by Edison to the apotheosis of the pig in the overwhelming city of Chicago. Caliban there is soaked in whisky just as in Shakespeare's drama he was soaked in wine; he thrives and grows; and, no longer the slave of any Prospero, nor made to suffer by any spirit of the air, he fattens and reproduces himself; his name is Legion. (20)

Here we find established the main lines of a discourse about the divided territory of America. In supposing Europe split into the land on one side or the other of the Pyrenees, one ends up projecting an America that is also severed by a fundamental boundary, which replicates the broader nineteenth-century idea of the North/South civilizational division of the European continent. In this case, however, rather than a "Latin" America, what we have is an "Iberian" America, as Rodó would later call it.

These shadows cast upon North American civilization awaken Shakespeare's characters and make them speak of a world whose *newness*, however, is not restricted to Darío's present moment or to Rodó's. What's at issue is a question about the future—about the future of all nations, no less—at the precise moment when the South's eyes peer into an imaginary territory which, if we are to believe Darío, could only be circumscribed by the freedom granted to an exceptional pen. (On the "moral aristocracy" of fin-de-siècle intellectuals in both Spanish and Portuguese Americas, see Sarah Moody's chapter in this volume.)

We should remember that this Shakespearean reference has a history of its own. In an enlightening study, Chantal Zabus traces that "Calibanic genealogy" that leads to a critical and poetic recuperation of the savage, making it possible to suppose that, by an inversion of values (with Caliban supplanting Ariel and, moreover, subverting the powers of Prospero), a move of fundamental importance has been effected. The author of *Tempests After Shakespeare* associates such a move with the postcolonial imaginary that makes it possible to reread Shakespeare in the shadow of an old Calibanesque recuperation, which originates in Renan's *drame philosophique* entitled *Caliban, suite de* La Tempête, of 1878.

It's not at all accidental that it would be during the turbulent decade of the 1960s that a more or less ferocious critique of the United States would be rekindled in Latin America and the Caribbean by way of various reinterpretations of this Shakespearean legacy, such as those of Roberto Fernández Retamar, Aimé Césaire, and Frantz Fanon, which in turn can be added to the earlier arguments of ethnopsychiatry, with Dominique Mannoni and his well-known "Prospero complex" (Zabus 15–23).

But long before this deprivileging of Prospero, which would transform Caliban into a postcolonial hero—so palatable to the kind of theory now dominant in North American academia—it had been Ariel who had awakened the admiration of intellectuals living on the margins; in other words, those looking at the North from the South, or looking back at the South upon entering the North.

I don't propose to delve here into the genealogy of the concept of Latin America, which is often assumed to be an original product of French imperialist thought. I shall only recall how reactions against the corrupt world of the North may also lead to that *hispanismo* that Arcadio Díaz Quiñones, in his broad recontextualization of the turn of the nineteenth century, has associated with the Spanish-American war and its "silent referent" which is the United States. For this Puerto Rican critic, behind the quest for "fabulous fathers" who might compensate imaginarily for the threat posed by the North American invaders of 1898, there unfolds a Freudian "family romance," replacing the real fathers with "more grandiose persons" (Díaz Quiñones 131).

At any rate, it's with Rodó, but in his later *Mirador de Próspero* of 1913, that we can see the reduction of the concept of the Ibero-American and the definitive inclusion of Brazil in the mental perspectives of the continent:

> We South Americans do not need to speak of a Latin America whenever it is a question of legitimating our racial unity; we do not need to call ourselves Latin Americans in order to assume a broader name that will comprise us all, because we can call ourselves something else that signifies a greater unity

which is much more intimate and concrete: we can call ourselves "Ibero-Americans," grandchildren of that heroic and civilizing race which has only politically been fragmented into two European nations; and we could go even further and say that the same name of Hispano-Americans is fitting for the natives of Brazil. (qtd. in Díaz Quiñones 131–32)

This lineage that imaginarily coalesces in this more or less cosmic race is a long-standing one, which in the Brazilian context would include names such as those of Joaquim Nabuco and Manoel Bomfim, not to mention certain later essayists of the 1930s or the widespread anti-Americanism that has continued to shape the imagination of Brazilian intellectuals.

Neither is it fitting here to list the innumerable Hispanic American authors who, with greater or lesser solemnity, have treaded the path of this idealization of an America that is Hispanic or, more specifically, Iberian. I shall look only, within the limits of this chapter, at the idea of that "intimate unity" referred to by Rodó, which readers of Sérgio Buarque de Holanda will immediately associate with that incisive dictum found in *Roots of Brazil*: "Inside, we are still not American" (139).

The lack of that double referent—the American, and an America of our own—gives rise to a passionate quest, pervaded by the ambiguity of refuting an Other which is also, and perhaps unconsciously, an object of esteem. Just think, for example, of those marvels of ambivalence, of both love and unlove for the United States, that are the texts José Martí published in the Buenos Aires newspaper *La Nación*, especially those he wrote in the cyclopean city of New York.

The belief in an American race—that race about which, like Martí's readers, Sérgio Buarque de Holanda must have been thinking before he declared that this was an entity that had not *as yet* taken shape[1]—suggests the paradox, quite "Latin American" in flavor, of a collective unity to be based, in the final analysis, on the impurity of mixture and encounter. The most enthusiastic readers will see here a praise of hybridism, which is such fertile soil for the imagination and which Brazilians know so well, because they had the probable fortune of seeing it cultivated, starting in the 1930s, by someone of Gilberto Freyre's stature.

In any case, the more or less *mestizo* or more or less *moreno* civilization that took shape outside North America presupposes a unifying "intimacy" which intellectuals have been the first to be able to detect and savor (see,

---

1. That dictum ("Inside, we are still not American") appears in connection with the name of D. H. Lawrence—"one of the great poets of our time," Sérgio Buarque will say—in whose *Studies in Classic American Literature* the Brazilian writer will find the idea that "the blood is chemically reduced by the nerves, in American activity" (Holanda, *Roots* 139, 181).

apropos, Alfredo Bosi's chapter in the present volume). I think here of the final scene in Rodó's *Ariel,* where the master awakens hope in his disciples and then immediately withdraws. This gesture of withdrawal marks a "conquest of souls" thrown down as a challenge to a spiritual elite that will be the civilizing agent of the New World. The estheticizing aspect of this gesture did not escape the attention even of Unamuno (Castro 94).[2]

Rodó's call and solemn gesture reached, in 1920, a young man of seventeen who would write and publish, in the newspaper *Correio Paulistano,* an article entitled "Originalidade literária." In his first periodical text, Sérgio Buarque de Holanda would defend an "intellectual emancipation" which, for him, dispensed with any political emancipation. One of the authors immediately evoked by the young essayist is the Peruvian Francisco García Calderón, an *arielista* of the first rank, concerned, Holanda tells us, with the "complete spiritual emancipation of the New World, and, in particular, of the part dominated by the language of Cervantes" (Holanda, *O espírito e a letra* 35–41).[3]

A subsequent text that Sérgio Buarque, now eighteen, published in the *Revista do Brasil* in May 1920 is a review of *Ariel,* which also serves as an obituary for the recently deceased Rodó. This article is a veritable denunciation of the decadence of all those nations that kneel down before the grandeur and progress of exotic "races." Its author enthusiastically shares Rodó's diffuse reservations with regard to North Americans. "Yankee utilitarianism" is here the principal villain, and the young Brazilian never fails to associate it with the republican condition of the United States, clearly revealing his own monarchist ideals (Holanda, *O espírito e a letra* 42–46).

Rodó's elitism takes on, in Sérgio Buarque's review, a broad spirit that makes it possible to see in the United States "a tainted air of corruption emanating from the ruling classes which it is hard to find in Europe. Utilitarianism and the concern with making money, that *aura sacra fames,* have taken over the North Americans to the detriment of their intellectual spirit, their political morality and their own individual freedom" (43).

There's an enormous distance between the tone of these words and the critique of authoritarian thought that Sérgio Buarque would develop, sixteen years later, in *Roots of Brazil.* But it's worth noting what a strong impression the Latin Americanist cause had made upon this eighteen-year-old. And it's true that the cold, prosaic empiricism of the North Americans would reappear, though in an attenuated form, in the Weberian theses that provide a

---

2. See also, of course, Ángel Rama's classic *La ciudad letrada.*
3. On the young Holanda's Arielism, see Robert P. Newcomb's Nossa *and* Nuestra América.

framework for Sérgio Buarque's arguments in *Roots of Brazil*—a book that can be read as one long inquiry about a civilization that rejects the unfettered quest for efficiency and utility that would characterize the modern world and, especially, the great laboratory for civilization that was the United States.

Let's retain here the idea that a basic triangulation marks the imagination of the "Latin American" or of what, in the spectrum joining Sérgio Buarque de Holanda and Richard Morse, would be called *Ibero-American*. Let's see now how that triangle works.

In the realm of *hispanismo,* an imaginary reconstruction of Spanish roots provides an important compensation for the pride wounded in the war of 1898 and by the North American conquest of territories that were "Hispanic." Going even further back in time, *hispanismo* also functions as an antidote to the imperialism of the Monroe Doctrine. But Brazil too, considered within this broad American context, would have its own share in affirming an identity that, in the final analysis, reinforced the division of America into two parts. To put it more clearly, I don't think there can be any conceptualization or poetic imagination of origins, nor even any possible fantasy about a definitive severing of roots, without first postulating a third angle along which, as in a vertex (or even a vortex), the United States is projected with its constant threat to the integrity of that tumultuous world south of the Rio Grande.

In that same year of 1920, in a powerful invective against the United States published in the magazine *A Cigarra,* Sérgio Buarque de Holanda would react harshly to the "chimera of Monroism" which, according to him, was leading many of his compatriots to find, in the shadow of North America, a benevolent antidote to "all the attempts at colonization that European powers might see fit to make in the New World" (Holanda, "A Chimera do Monroismo").

It's amusing to see this young essayist so taken with that same European intellectual prowess which the Brazilian Modernists would treat so facetiously. Let's recall that, after the beginning of the 1920s in Brazil, Oswald de Andrade's "anthropophagous" reversal would allow Brazilian intellectuals to imagine they were devouring their own fathers and show that the real strength belonged not to the Europeans but rather to their *mestizo* descendants.

To summarize what I've set forth up to this point, I'll say that the inversion of the signs that associate Latin America either with the spiritual powers of Ariel or with a Caliban as reinterpreted by postcolonial struggles hardly conceals the fact that, in both cases, whether we are on the side of Ariel or that of Caliban, the antidote to "Anglo materialism" serves the same psychological purpose, which is to react against the seductive power of the monster of the North. This is what José Guilherme Merquior proposed, in a lapidary formulation, when, referring to the publication of *O espelho de Próspero* in Brazil, he suggested that "Morse's Calibanism vindicates, eighty years later, Rodó's Arielism" (Merquior 71).

Among the reactions to *O espelho de Próspero* upon its publication in Brazil, the harshest was that of Simon Schwartzman, who saw in Morse's book a "nostalgia for totality and for transcendence," as if it concealed a vicious "Sorelian millenarianism" and an idealized "lost millenarian essence" (187, 191–92).

However, before disqualifying Morse's thesis as a simple populist vestige, as if he were only seduced by the idea of an organic State, it's well to analyze what's at issue in the polemic generated by *O espelho de Próspero*. In a keen article, Mauricio Tenorio reconstructs the theoretical context from which the book must have arisen, claiming that when

> Morse speaks of a "different tradition," of the need to recognize in Latin America a "new ideology," he is simply echoing (and very much in tune) notes that have sounded from Lévi-Strauss and Eliade to Marcuse, Adorno, Foucault and Dumont. And one of the fundamental purposes of such echoes consists in a reevaluation of myth, a factor that gains importance as a form of knowledge and life, on the same level as scientific knowledge. (119–20)

Basically, Morse would be contributing to the "critique of modernity" found in an important segment of the social sciences and historiography that developed in the United States after the 1960s. However, it would not be as a simple "return" to a moment prior to modernization, but rather a recuperation of the role played by *myth* in the formation of collectivities, which suggests a closer relation to tradition. As Otávio Velho acutely observes, the secularization and desacralization of the world are forms of separation from that transcendent sphere that is always projected onto a *beyond* and is preserved there, on a level that at every moment threatens to return (96). In terms dear to Morse, which evoke Dumont and point to his later thought after *O espelho de Próspero*, it was the *holistic* character of neo-Iberian societies that compensated for North American *individualism*.[4]

Thinking in terms of an overall history of the social sciences in Latin America, one should recall that, beginning in the 1950s and 60s, there emerges a profound critique of modernism, or more precisely of its destructive effects,

---

4. See Morse, *New World Soundings*. Any detailed analysis of that redemptive view of Latin America should also take into account Morse's time as a student at Princeton University, where, as the historian himself recalls, Augusto Centeno "opened my eyes to García Lorca, San Juan de la Cruz, Ricardo Güiraldes" and where Américo Castro, "the great man of the Generation of '98 in Spain," also taught (Bomeny 130).

which the periphery, more than any other space, would understand. In other words, around the middle of the last century there is a turn that suddenly makes it possible to change the settings of analyses that had assumed that Latin American reality was inherently refractory to modernization. Reasserting the Latin Americanist imaginary, the continent gave itself over to the vertigo of an alternative project or to the dream of an autochthonous modernity. Either in the epic quests of revolutionaries or in the restrained fury of reformists, a different kind of modernity shined forth in many forms, even before Cuba attempted to embody the fantasy of a radical departure.

The possibility that the periphery might gain the status of a creative center corresponded fully to previous ideas concerning the most deep-seated modernist projects—projects that, especially in Brazil, focus on the mirage of a radical reversal of the relationship of *dependency,* a word that, not accidentally, gained such prestige in Latin America.

Perhaps the strongest metaphor used by Morse, who believes the "mirror" ought to be turned around (as in an *inverse teleology*), finds its origin in his bold preference—always somewhat quixotic, to be sure—for the models and proposals of a society supposedly deviant with regard to the traditional arrangements of Western modernity. Another West, another America, another Europe, even another geography, were proposed in order to picture an alternative future based on the belief in and preference for a singular past, which leads this historian's abundant imagination to formulate the paradox of a *promising past.*

To conclude, let's bring Sérgio Buarque de Holanda back into the picture. Obviously Sérgio Buarque isn't Richard Morse. *Roots of Brazil* is a much more ambiguous work, uneasy, moreover, with regard to an "Iberian" civilizational path. And yet, in both cases, *secularization* is the main theme.

The problem is perhaps that the "demythification of the world" turns literature, and along with it grand essays on national and regional interpretation, into a constant reconstruction of the *enigma* that secularization itself promises to unveil and do away with. I think here of Jorge Brioso's proposal which, focusing on Rubén Darío, aims to "recuperate the different settings in which Latin American modernist texts, even as they assume their profane and disenchanted condition, restore enigma, revelation and a sense of the sacred" (87).

How, then, can we explain *Roots of Brazil?* Where can we situate Sérgio Buarque de Holanda's book along that line that runs from secularization to a full reengagement with myth? If, on one hand, it's possible to imagine *Roots of Brazil* as a veritable "preface to modernity," as Antonio Candido recently told me, on the other hand, it's possible to contrast Sérgio Buarque's book with Richard Morse's lucubrations, in order to see to what degree, in *Roots of Brazil,* there is also the vision of a reenchanted world.

In concluding, I propose, then, a few questions: might it not be that, in examining the effects of secularization, Sérgio Buarque de Holanda's book ends up paradoxically raising Latin America to the category of an enigma? Might it not be interesting to connect the examination of neo-Thomism found in *O espelho de Próspero* to the continuation of a Catholic horizon in Brazilian political thought in *Roots of Brazil*? Doesn't this Counter-Reformationist horizon suggest, in fact, that political contracts require transcendence, that is, require all that lies beyond the individual? And finally, thinking in Weberian terms, doesn't this same *disenchantment* with the world make the impossible quest for *meaning* more anguished and urgent than ever?

The contrast between *O espelho de Próspero* and *Roots of Brazil* may remind us, finally, that the nature of Sérgio Buarque de Holanda's book isn't always "Apollonian."[5] This is a non-Apollonian character that, in his own Latin Americanist passion, Sérgio Buarque's North American counterpart Richard Morse may reveal in all its extent and breadth, by at last having plunged unrestrainedly into the continental truths of poets and novelists.

Perhaps it's now time to revisit *Roots of Brazil,* no longer in search of its internal coherence or admirable architecture, but rather to sound the dark depths that this luminous book conceals.[6]

WORKS CITED

Bomeny, Helena. "Saudades do Brasil de Richard Morse." *O código Morse: ensaios sobre Richard Morse.* Ed. Beatriz H. Domingues and Peter L. Blaseheim. Belo Horizonte: Editora UFMG, 2010. 119–39.

Brioso, Jorge. "De la desaparición de los oráculos y de la muerte y resurrección de los dioses: lo sagrado y lo profano en la obra de Rubén Darío." *Hacia una historia de las literaturas centroamericanas.* Vol. 2: *Tensiones de la modernidad: del modernismo al realismo.* Ed. Ricardo Roque Baldovinos and Valeria Grinberg Pla. Guatemala: F&G Editores, 2009.

Castro, Belén. Introducción. *Ariel.* By José Enrique Rodó. Madrid: Cátedra, 2004. 9–135.

Dantas, Luiz. Prefácio. *A queda do aventureiro: aventura, cordialidade e os novos tempos em* Raízes do Brasil. By Pedro Meira Monteiro. Campinas: Editora da Unicamp, 1999. 15–20.

Darío, Rubén. *Los raros.* Buenos Aires: Espasa-Calpe, 1952.

Díaz Quiñones, Arcadio. *Sobre los principios: los intelectuales caribeños y la tradición.* Quilmes: Universidad Nacional de Quilmes Editorial, 2006.

5. The use of Nietzschean categories for an understanding of *Roots of Brazil* was proposed by Luiz Dantas.

6. This chapter is an abridged version of my arguments developed in *Signo e desterro: Sérgio Buarque de Holanda e o Brasil* (Hucitec 2015), which will soon appear in English as *The Other Roots: Wandering Origins in* Roots of Brazil *and the Impasses of Modernity in Ibero-America* (University of Notre Dame Press, forthcoming in 2017).

Holanda, Sérgio Buarque de. "A Chimera do Monroismo." *A Cigarra* (1 Jul. 1920): n. pag.

———. *O espírito e a letra: estudos de crítica literária*. Ed. Antonio Arnoni Prado. São Paulo: Companhia das Letras, 1996.

———. *Roots of Brazil*. Transl. G. Harvey Summ. Notre Dame: Notre Dame UP, 2012.

Martí, José. *En los Estados Unidos: periodismo de 1881 a 1892*. Ed. Roberto Fernández Retamar and Pedro Pablo Rodríguez. Madrid: ALLCA XX, 2003.

Merquior, José Guilherme. "O outro Ocidente." *Presença* 15 (1990): 69–91.

Morse, Richard M. *O espelho de Próspero*. Trans. Paulo Neves. São Paulo: Companhia das Letras, 1988.

———. *New World Soundings: Culture and Ideology in the Americas*. Baltimore: Johns Hopkins UP, 1989.

Newcomb, Robert P. Nossa *and* Nuestra América: *Inter-American Dialogues*. West Lafayette: Purdue UP, 2012.

Rama, Ángel. *La ciudad letrada*. Hanover, NH: Ediciones del Norte, 2002.

Renan, Ernest. *Caliban, suite de La Tempête*. Paris: Calmann Lévy, 1878.

Schwartzman, Simon. "O espelho de Morse." *Novos Estudos Cebrap* 22 (1988): 185–92.

Velho, Otávio. "O espelho de Morse e outros espelhos." *Estudos Históricos* 2.3 (1989): 94–101.

Zabus, Chantal. *Tempests after Shakespeare*. New York: Palgrave, 2002.

PART II

WRITTEN FICTIONAL NARRATIVE

BRAZIL AND SPANISH-SPEAKING LATIN AMERICA

CHAPTER 6

The Literary Revenant in a Latin American Comparative Context

ROBERT MOSER

JUDITH A. PAYNE and Earl E. Fitz, in their work, *Ambiguity and Gender in the New Novel of Brazil and Spanish America,* propose that Brazil's relative sociopolitical unity, in contrast to Spanish America's political fragmentation during the nineteenth century, enabled Brazilian literature to evolve in a more cohesive fashion, absorb outside trends, and ultimately develop a stronger tradition of iconoclastic, experimental expression early on. Machado de Assis's groundbreaking use of metafiction, intertextuality, unreliable narrators, and gender deconstruction, as well as other Brazilian examples of atypically self-conscious narration in the latter half of the nineteenth century, set in motion, according to these critics, a cultivation of ontological, aesthetic, and especially gender-related "ambiguity" in Brazilian literature (2–3).

Arguably, it is the revenant that represents the literary figure of ambiguity par excellence. For this reason, a comparative consideration of the literary ghost, particularly in light of Brazilian literature's cultivation of the carnivalesque and *malandragem* (roguery), brings into focus some of the distinctive ways that Brazilian and Spanish American literary traditions have grappled with, expressed, and at times negated forms of ambiguity. By focusing on the expressive nuances and latent meanings ascribed to the revenant in both literary traditions, this study seeks to shed light upon not only the unique manifestations of this literary topos in Latin American fiction but also the region's converging and diverging means of relating to its past.

Despite what I have noted as the recurring presence of the carnivalesque *defunto* (deceased) in the works of Machado de Assis, Jorge Amado, and Érico Veríssimo, among other prominent Brazilian authors, it would be misleading to claim absolute uniqueness for the Brazilian figure of the dead or of death personified, as a figure endowed with a ludic, trickster, or carnivalesque quality.[1] Indeed, one can identify within this figure certain thanatological archetypes that are undoubtedly transcultural, such as the image of "laughing death," the "ghost as trickster," and "death as seducer." Carnival traditions intersecting with death and the dead are numerous and include (but of course are not limited to) the performance of symbolic burials, testaments, and reincarnations at Entroido festivals in rural Spain; the pre-Lenten ritualistic death and resurrection of the Dionysian Kouker figure in Bulgaria; the honoring of Supay, the spirit of the underground mines (later diabolized by the Catholic Church) during carnival in Oruro, Bolivia; the omnipresence of Gede, the bawdy, top-hat-wearing master of death and libido in Haiti's Vodou-infused carnival celebrations; and the bombastic Midnight Robber character in Trinidad's carnival who, through his "robber talk" and macabre garb, promises death and destruction to all.

A similarly ludic quality is expressed through the "joyful noise" of African American jazz funerals in New Orleans, intended to "cut the body loose" through dance, music, and humor; the festivities and tangible offerings to the dead surrounding Mexico's Día de los Muertos in which the image of death is routinely treated with humor, disdain, and familiarity; and the often erotic "Death and the Maiden" motif portrayed by North Renaissance artists such as German painter Hans Baldung Grien and Swiss painter Niklaus Manuel (Deutsch).

BRAZILIAN CARNIVAL AND THE DIALECTICS OF *MALANDRAGEM*

The trickster emerges as an important component of the Brazilian carnivalesque *defunto*'s personality as well. Moreover, Brazil's own street-wise trickster, the *malandro*, or rogue, is arguably the central protagonist in Brazilian carnival (DaMatta, *Carnivals* 208–9). The *malandro*'s sphere of activity in Brazilian society oscillates between the fringes of work, leisure, crime, and a bohemian lifestyle, and it is the *malandro*'s guile and adaptability that enable him to resist full integration into any particular social realm. The *malandro*'s

---

1. See Moser, *The Carnivalesque Defunto: Death and the Dead in Modern Brazilian Literature*.

ethos of *malandragem* is the focus of an essay by noted Brazilian critic Antonio Candido, who identifies it as a fundamental operating principle in the mid-nineteenth-century Brazilian novel *Memórias de um Sargento de Milícias* (Memoirs of a Militia Sergeant, 1852) by Manuel Antônio de Almeida and, by extension, within Brazilian society as a whole. According to Candido, the *malandro* operates between two distinct, yet ultimately permeable, social spheres—the world of order (work, family, civic and religious authority, financial and social stability) and the world of disorder (vagrancy, popular culture, festivities, and behavior otherwise deemed as immoral)—and, in so doing, exposes the frequently comic slippage of hierarchical forms into the realm of disorder, and vice versa. The flexibility inherent in these social (and corresponding moral) spheres, in the case of Brazil, is compared with American society's puritanical foundation, with its rigidly demarcated social, religious, racial, and moral spheres, as expressed most poignantly in Nathaniel Hawthorne's *Scarlet Letter* and the Salem witch trials (Candido 99).

Moreover, Candido stresses that the *malandro* in Almeida's novel springs less from erudite sources, such as the European picaresque tradition, than it does from both a universal trickster archetype and Brazilian popular culture (83). He also advances the notion of *malandragem* as a dialectic (with its *malandro* antihero) that forms part of a lineage unique to the formation of Brazilian literature, one that can be traced from Almeida's novel to modernist works such as *Serafim Ponte Grande* (1933), by Oswald de Andrade, and, most emblematically, *Macunaíma* (1928), by Mário de Andrade. In this respect, Candido concurs with Walnice Nogueira Galvão's following statement, which he quotes in his essay: "It is in this mode that Manuel Antônio de Almeida described the character Leonardo, which results in a *hero without any character*, or better, one who represents the fundamental traits of the stereotype of the Brazilian. Manuel Antônio de Almeida is the first to fix in literature the national character of the Brazilian, which then will have a long life in our literature [. . .] I believe that we meet in Leonardo the ancestor of *Macunaíma*" (102; emphasis in original).

To this deep tradition within Brazilian literature of the trickster or antihero, who simultaneously pushes the boundaries of order and disorder and promotes moral indeterminacy, one could arguably add Machado de Assis's Brás Cubas, João Grilo from Ariano Suassuna's play *Auto de Compadecida*, Vadinho and Quincas Berro Dágua from Jorge Amado's novels *Dona Flor e Seus Dois Maridos* and *A Morte e a Morte de Quincas Berro Dágua*, Luis Galvez from Márcio Souza's *Galvez, Imperador do Acre*, Max from Chico Buarque's *Ópera do Malandro*, and even, to some degree, Riobaldo from Guimarães Rosa's *Grande Sertão: Veredas*. Furthermore, carnivalization, masked characterizations, and inverted realities serve as key narrative features in an even broader range of Brazilian literature, by authors such as João do Rio, Augusto dos Anjos, Manuel Bandeira, Aníbal Machado, Lima Barreto, Roberto Drummond, Rubem Fonseca, Moacyr Scliar, Lygia Fagundes Telles, Silviano Santiago, João Ubaldo Ribeiro, and Sônia Coutinho, to name only a few.[2] In his article concerning the use of parody and carnivalization in Souza's *Galvez, O Imperador do Acre,* Luiz F. Valente echoes Candido's and Galvão's assertion of Brazilian fiction's pervasive carnivalesque tradition:

> In bringing back laughter to contemporary literature, Márcio Souza is upholding a truly national trait: the capability Brazilians have always had of laughing at themselves, that is, the paradoxical Brazilian ability of talking about serious issues in an outwardly non-serious way. But, more importantly, he is restoring a truly national literary tradition, which lay seemingly dormant in the dark years of the late 1960's and the 1970's: the carnivalesque tradition that is as old as Brazilian literature itself, going all the way back to Gregório de Matos and Manuel Antônio de Almeida, and culminating in Oswald de Andrade. (792)

Carnival, with its prevailing ethos of *malandragem,* is more than a tangential aspect of Brazilian social identity, as anthropologist Roberto DaMatta explains: "Carnival [. . .] is one of those perpetual institutions that has enabled Brazilians to sense and feel (more than abstractly conceive) their specific continuity as a distinct social and political entity through and over time" (*Carnivals* 15). As we shall see, the Brazilian *malandro* also flouts strictly held borders between life and death, particularly during those periods of licensed transgression that often characterize carnival. Before delving more deeply into the carnivalesque *defunto* as a Brazilian literary topos, let us first consider some underlying ways in which the *defunto* has been expressed within twentieth-century Spanish American literature.

---

2. For a list of specific works by these authors, in which carnivalization features prominently, see Moser (*Carnivalesque Defunto* 284, note 23). See also João Cezar de Castro Rocha's article "Dialética da marginalidade (Caracterização da cultura brasileira contemporânea)," in which he argues that Candido's "dialectic of malandroism" is being gradually substituted, in Brazilian contemporary cultural production, by a "dialectic of marginality," in which social injustices are being confronted rather than reconciled.

AN "ANCESTRAL IMPULSE" AND "AMERICAN BOOKS OF THE DEAD"

In her book *The Usable Past* Lois Parkinson Zamora begins her discussion of ghostly apparitions in the literature of the Americas (both North and South) by quoting Flannery O'Connor: "Ghosts can be very fierce and instructive" (76). With the intention, then, of exploring what it is that ghosts can teach us, as readers, Zamora outlines the full semantic and functional richness of this figure:

> Ghosts in American literature may serve as carriers of metaphysical truths, as visible or audible signs of atemporal, transhistorical Spirit. Or, they may carry historical burdens of tradition and collective memory: ghosts often act as correctives to the insularities of individuality, as links to lost families and communities, or as reminders of communal crimes, crises, and cruelties. They may suggest displacement and alienation or, alternatively, reunion and communion. [. . .] They may signal primal and primordial experience, the return of the repressed, or the externalization of internalized terrors. They are always double (here and not) and often duplicitous (where?). They mirror, complement, recover, supplant, cancel, and complete. Which is to say that literary ghosts are deeply metaphoric. They bring absence into presence, maintaining at once the "is" and the "is not" of metaphoric truth. (76–77)

Zamora then traces the multifarious trope of the ghost (in a very broad sense) through the works of Jorge Luis Borges, Gabriel García Márquez, Isabel Allende, Carlos Fuentes, Juan Rulfo, and Elena Garro, as well as North American writers such as Nathaniel Hawthorne, William Faulkner, Toni Morrison, and William Goyen, to name a few. She contrasts, for example, the "culturally specific" and historically repeating ghosts in García Márquez's fiction (such as the successive José Arcadios and Aurelianos, as well as Melquíades's ghost in *Cien Años de Soledad*) with the universalizing and archetypal "wraiths" (ones that embody "ideas, figures of philosophy or dream") expressed by Borges in his short stories "La muerte y la brújula" (Death and the Compass), "Las ruinas circulares" (The Circular Ruins), and "La otra muerte" (The Other Death) (81–84).

The predominant trait identified by Zamora in twentieth-century Spanish American literary ghosts, however, is what she describes as an "ancestral impulse" that seeks to recover lost, sacrificed, or oppressed oral and visual narratives, through a literary mode that transcends realism (123). Novels and short stories of this sort, which excavate ancestral presences and privilege local cultural knowledge over European sources, constitute for Zamora "American books of the dead, necrogeographies of the buried traces of indigenous cultural identity in a shared region of America" (79). To exemplify this idea, Zamora points to two Mexican novels in which the collective voices of the dead, inhabitants of towns long since deceased, serve as narrator: Elena Garro's *Los Recuerdos del porvenir* (Recollections of Things to Come, 1963) set during the post-revolutionary confusion of the Cristero rebellion in southern Mexico, and Juan Rulfo's *Pedro Páramo* (1955) set in Comala, a ghost town frozen in time, ostensibly set in Jalisco but, in fact, more mythically situated, as Zamora proposes, at the intersection of "Mexican Catholic and indigenous afterworlds" (100–101).

Mexican society has cultivated a deep and frequently festive relationship with the idea and figure of death that resonates with Brazil's own thanocratic traditions. The prominence of Mexico's Day of the Dead, with its profusion of *ofrendas,* sugary *calaveras,* public celebration of the deceased, and often ironic domestication of death is a well-recognized aspect of Mexican cultural identity. Arguably, the Mexican writer and poet most responsible for theorizing the Mexican connection to death, even in modern times, is Octavio Paz, who, in his essay "The Day of the Dead" in *The Labyrinth of Solitude* (1950), states: "The Mexican [. . .] is familiar with death, jokes about it, caresses it, sleeps with it, celebrates it; it is one of his favourite toys and his most steadfast love" (49). Claudio Lomnitz, in his comprehensive *Death and the Idea of Mexico,* argues that "the three great totems of Mexican national history" are "Guadalupe, (Benito) Juárez, and the playful skeleton" (43). According to Lomnitz, Mexico's intimate, ironic, and often lighthearted relationship to, and representation of, death contrasts sharply with other cases of a nationalized death, such as nineteenth-century Russia's romantic and tragic "sublimation of suffering," and late imperial Japan's "fearlessness before death," stemming as much from Buddhist belief as from the country's militarism at the time (20). Instead, the smiling face of death has become a national symbol in Mexico, one that has not only withstood modernity's broad denial of death but has become a common feature of everyday life there. Lomnitz traces the origins of this "nationalization of a playful familiarity with and proximity to Death itself" as far back as pre-Columbian Mesoamerican cosmology (with regard to death, the afterlife, and mortuary rituals), through the devastating holocaust of sixteenth-century Spanish conquest and the subsequent colonial administration of death by both church and state, to the impact of the Mexican Revolution (1910–20) and the modernist movement, which cultivated a broad, national familiarity with death (36). Paradoxically, macabre imagery and Day of the Dead festivities, celebrated in both traditional rural settings as well as the *paseos* of urban centers, flourished during the nineteenth century, precisely when enlightened rationalists in Mexico (as in Brazil), often inspired by positivism, were trying to rid the country of its "backwardness" and "superstition" (283). As Lomnitz observes, "Baroque Catholicism proved to be a tar baby for Mexican rationalists: the more they struggled against it, the more they were mired in it" (291).

Equally fascinating are the ways in which death became a template for Mexican modernist strategies of identification and cultural pride. Diego Rivera's mural *Day of the Dead—City Fiesta* at the Ministry of Education in Mexico City depicts a bustling urban fiesta in which every segment of Mexican society—the worker, peasant, revolutionary soldier, priest, student, capitalist, and the throng of popular masses—is represented as an active participant in the Day of the Dead, thereby suggesting a form of "national reconciliation in death" (Lomnitz 46). Similarly, the *mestizo* illustrator José Guadalupe Posada's satirical engravings of the Mexican upper class, in the guise of skeletons, during the progress-driven reign of Porfirio Díaz during the late nineteenth and early twentieth centuries, resonated with the modernists' affirmation of cultural *mestizaje*. Rivera's mural and the modernists' rediscovery (along with the French artist Jean Charlot) of Posada's illustrations acknowledged the viability of a Mexican "social pact," albeit an uneasy one shaped by cyclical historical conflict. Inherent in this pact, signed by death, was also the possibility of temporal and ethnic reconciliation, as Lomnitz indicates: "Thus Mexican attitudes toward death, as they are instantiated in the Days of the Dead, came to be paradigmatic examples not only of cultural *mestizaje* and its revolutionary potential but also the formula that would give voice to Mexico's singularity by way of an artistic expression that fused pre-Columbian and popular elements" (50).

It is the deadly weight of the past, and the impossibility of the future, that most characterizes Juan Rulfo's introspective *Pedro Páramo*. Comala is haunted not only by the lingering voices of the dead, but also by what Lomnitz calls "negative reciprocity," that is, a community founded on rape, murder, illegitimacy, and patriarchal authoritarianism, as embodied by the *cacique* Pedro Páramo (407). The return of Páramo's son, Juan Preciado, to Comala does not, in fact, bring reconciliation and forgiveness but rather further communal incorporation into the realm of the dead, which is frozen in time. Death does not bring about change in Comala. Instead, the novel suggests that there are forces from Mexico's past, such as its violent origins, religious conservatism, and rural patriarchy, which continue to hold their grip on the present. The murmurs of the dead that echo throughout Comala, as if rising from the ground itself (the word *páramo* refers to bleak highland terrain), are, to use Zamora's terminology, the subterranean traces of "ancestral presences" that bring with them "buried belief systems that still resonate in contemporary culture" (125).

Indeed, the list provided by Zamora of "boom" and "post-boom" Latin American writers whose work foregrounds "ancestral apparitions" and disinterred memories of what, as Fuentes put it, "the West sacrificed in other cultures," is particularly long and includes Miguel Ángel Asturias, Alejo Carpentier, José María Arguedas, Rosario Castellanos, Julio Cortázar, Carlos Fuentes, Luisa Valenzuela, Eduardo Galeano, Mario Vargas Llosa, and Isabel Allende.[3] Zamora also acknowledges those U.S. "minority" writers who similarly "give the earth voice" and listen to its indigenous, ancestral presences, namely William Goyen in his collection of short stories *Ghost and Flesh* (1952), Leslie Marmon Silko in her novel *Ceremony* (1977), Susan Power in her novel *The Grass Dancer* (1994), and Louise Erdrich in her novel *Tracks* (1988), among others.

It would undoubtedly be an exaggeration to claim that death in Brazil enjoys the same degree of prestige that it does in Mexico. The dancing skeleton and laughing skull, personifications of an ironic, domesticated death, do not appear in Brazil as they do in Mexico, where death has become a sign of national identity. Roberto DaMatta observes that Brazilians tend to cultivate strong, personal relations more with the dead than with death per se, though still not to the degree that Mexicans have celebrated this relationship (*A Casa e a Rua* 119). In fact, the social ritual in Brazil that most approximates Mexico's *Día de los Muertos*, in terms of its national scope and cultural currency, is arguably carnival. Indeed, it is the national vitality of carnival that partly explains why the *defunto* so frequently appears in Dionysian garb in Brazilian literature.

Moreover, Spain and Portugal's respective colonial endeavors in the New World were characterized by vastly different historical scenarios, circumstances, and approaches, despite their many parallels. To use Mexico as a point of comparison, important differences emerge with regard to the nature of the indigenous society conquered and assimilated (the highly developed civilizations of the Mayas and Aztecs in and around Mexico, in contrast to Brazil's partially sedentary and dispersed Tupi tribal groups and other diverse nomadic peoples); the respective systems of forced labor (Brazil's importation of large numbers of African slaves versus the Spanish use of forced indigenous labor through its *encomienda* system); and the significantly more centralized, structured colonial model employed by the Spanish (intended to repli-

---

3. For a list of specific titles by the aforementioned authors, see Zamora (123).

cate institutional forms of church and state in the New World), in contrast to Portugal's more decentralized colonial approach, characterized by immediate gains, an absentee crown, and a particularly weak presence of church hierarchy within the Brazilian colony.[4] This last factor is widely recognized as having contributed to the flourishing of unorthodox religious practices and values in colonial Brazil. One might speculate that the relative permeability of Brazilian religiosity, plus the contribution of African cosmologies, during colonial times would create the kind of conditions within which the carnivalesque *defunto* might appear as a modern literary manifestation of a colonial vestige.[5]

However, it would seem more likely, or at least more easily traceable, to return to the fundamental differences, in the case of Brazil and Mexico, between the most important collective social rituals of each society. Whereas for Brazilians carnival has signified a temporary moment of Dionysian subversion, a final indulgence of the flesh and libido prior to Lent, the festive celebrations of Mexico's Day of the Dead are endowed with a very specific restorative, totemic (rather than subversive) purpose, namely the reunion of the living with the dead, the distribution of offerings, and the restoration of communal ties and familial, national, and cultural allegiances. Whereas Brazilian carnival is intended, in theory, to "turn the world on its head" and imagine alternative social relations, the Day of the Dead reinforces ancestral relations and the reuniting of two worlds (that of the living and the dead) through celebration.

LATIN AMERICAN LITERATURE AND THE CARNIVALESQUE

To the extent that other parts of Spanish America (not including those Caribbean cultures whose histories of African slavery run more parallel to Brazil's) have developed diverse but comparable strategies and rituals for restoring and celebrating ties with their indigenous heritage, it is not surprising then that an "ancestral impulse" stands out as a salient feature of the literary ghost within these societies. Zamora's omission of Brazilian narratives within her "Latin American" framework for discussing the ghost, however, excludes a somewhat diverging manifestation of this literary topos—the carnivalesque

---

4. Key works of reference that discuss the differences between Portuguese and Spanish colonization of the Americas include Sérgio Buarque de Holanda's *Raízes do Brasil* (1936) and Lyle N. McAlister's *Spain and Portugal in the New World, 1492–1700* (1984).

5. While this question obviously requires further research, an exploration of African cosmological, narrative, and linguistic influences on the development of Brazilian literature (much in line with Henry Louis Gates's conceptualization of the Signifying Monkey and Eshu as major tropes in Afro-American literature) would be extremely valuable, particularly from a comparative perspective.

revenant, with its unbridled laughter, playful irreverence, and expressions of sensuality. Indeed, many of the defining qualities of Brazilian literary apparitions—Brás Cubas's whimsical narrative and moral ambiguity, Vadinho's *malandro* obscenity, Quincas Berro Dágua's bohemian carnality, and the subversive, mocking discourse of Érico Veríssimo's protesting *defuntos* in *Incidente em Antares*—are conspicuously absent in the Spanish American variant of the literary ghost.

A comparative perspective also reveals that Brazilian literature, most significantly in the case of Brás Cubas, is not unique within Latin America in its use of deceased narration as a rhetorical device. In fact, Sandra Messinger Cypress in her dissertation "The Dead Narrator in Modern Latin American Prose Fiction" (1968) calls attention to a fairly significant range of Latin American writers and works that, besides Machado de Assis and *Memórias Póstumas,* utilize posthumous narration, albeit in diverse manifestations. Examples of works narrated by a highly "self-conscious narrator," aware of both his own deceased state and narrative/literary voice, include the short story "El fusilado" (The Firing-Squad Victim) by the Mexican José Vasconcelos, and Machado's *Memórias Póstumas* (23). Recognition of deceased narration only comes to the reader of "El fusilado" halfway through the story, as it becomes evident that the man "about" to be executed by a firing squad is, in fact, recounting his past experience of the moment of death. The second category of deceased narration outlined by Cypress involves those prose works in which the narrator addresses the reader directly and from a posthumous position, but without any claim to the act of writing (86). These include the short story "El condenado" (The Condemned Man, 1951) and the novels *Anticipación a la muerte* (Anticipation of Death, 1939) and *La muerte de Pamilo* (The Death of Pamilo, 1964) by Mexican authors Juan José Arreola, José Rubén Romero, and Ernesto Ramos Meza, respectively; the short story "El espectro" (The Specter, 1921) by the Uruguayan Horacio Quiroga; and *Un muerto de mal criterio* (A Dead Man of Bad Judgement, 1926) by the Chilean Jenaro Prieto. Finally, Cypress addresses a third category in which deceased narration occurs not as a direct conversation with the reader, but as part of a dialogue with the narrator's own fictive world (166). Examples of this narrative voice (or voices) include Quiroga's short story "Más allá" (Further On, 1935), Rulfo's *Pedro Páramo,* the Uruguayan Enrique Amorim's *La desembocadura* (The Opening, 1958), and the Chilean María Luisa Bombal's *La amortajada* (The Shrouded Woman, 1938).

Despite the multitude of narrative positions, degrees of self-consciousness, thematic insights, and sociohistorical commentaries expressed by the many Spanish American deceased narrators examined by Cypress, it is notable that none possess the highly ironic, unreliable, Menippean whimsy of their Brazilian counterpart, Brás Cubas. In short, what is missing is the subversive, mocking, trickster element of the carnivalesque *defunto*.

The comparative framework outlined here is not intended to assert the total absence of a carnivalized literary ghost in the Spanish American tradition. It more than likely exists, or is expressed partially.[6] The point is that this figure does not emerge as a recurring, predominant topos in the way it occurs in modern Brazilian fiction. While the reasons for this difference may be difficult to identify with any absolute certainty, I have underscored the relative weight attributed to carnival (and its ethos of *malandragem*) in Brazilian culture, both as a national sign and ritual, and as an identifying literary mode characterized by playful subversion, syncretic ambiguity, and a dialectic of *malandragem*. In contrast to this mode, emblematic works of modern Spanish American literature have been characterized by a pertinacious and often consuming "ancestral impulse" that requires a creative reassessment of historical awareness, especially when confronted with the figure of the literary ghost.

Piers Armstrong makes some interesting comparative observations in *Third World Literary Fortunes* that shed further light upon this important distinction. He argues that Brazilian modernism, following the initial "revolutionary" rupture of the Week of Modern Art (1922) in São Paulo, is noteworthy for its "spirit of subjective individualism," as exemplified by Clarice Lispector, Guimarães Rosa, João Cabral de Melo Neto, and Carlos Drummond de Andrade, among other modern Brazilian writers (with some obvious exceptions such as Jorge Amado), for whom political convictions were secondary to their aesthetic goals (21). In contrast to this trend, Armstrong points to Spanish American modernism's "strong tendency of essentialism," (particularly during the "Boom" years but also dating as far back as the Nicaraguan Rubén Darío's turn-of-the-century innovations), characterized paradoxically by a greater cohesion among modernist intellectuals from various nations, by a more urgent sense of political purpose, and "above all by the sense of an historic mission to rewrite history" (21). This overarching ethos of political conscientization in Spanish American *modernismo* and in the writers of the Boom generation stems, according to Armstrong, from the region's history of "revolutionary moments," including the nineteenth-century independence movements and Simón Bolívar's dream of a pan-Hispanic Republic, as well as the Mexican Revolution, the Mexican-American War, the Spanish-American War, the Cuban Revolution, the oscillation between socialist experiments and brutal authoritarian regimes, and post–World War II resistance to

---

6. This is undoubtedly a fertile area for further research in a comparative Luso-Hispanic context.

neo-imperialist forces.⁷ One of the outcomes of these historical experiences is what Armstrong describes as a distinctive preoccupation among Boom writers with portraying "a polarized Utopian-dystopian duality in the perception of Latin America" (38).

Most importantly for our understanding of the underlying differences between the Brazilian carnivalesque *defunto* and the Spanish American "ancestral apparitions" is Armstrong's subsequent observation that, given these historical circumstances (to which we may add the initial destruction and fragmentation of highly developed indigenous civilizations during the Spanish *conquista*), "the Spanish American literary discourse of Latin American identity is consistently one of trauma" (40). Notwithstanding notable exceptions, such as Euclides da Cunha's *Os Sertões*, Graciliano Ramos's *Vidas Secas*, and a number of historical novels of social protest written following Brazil's 1964 military coup, it would appear true that this sense of acute, historical trauma is "conspicuously absent in the greater part of Brazilian writers" (40), relative to their Spanish American counterparts.⁸ In this regard, the Spanish American concern with ancestral apparitions has more in common with works such as Toni Morrison's *Beloved*, Louise Erdrich's *Tracks*, or Cristina García's *Dreaming in Cuban*—multiethnic literature in the United States in which the haunting figure of the ghost signals a collective history of oppression, marginalization, and unresolved trauma.⁹ A similar specificity, at least with regard to ethnicity, marginalization, and traumatic origins, cannot be claimed in the case of the Brazilian carnivalesque *defunto*.

The relatively greater focus of Spanish American literary discourse on ancestral trauma has, I believe, important repercussions for both the mode and the function of its literary ghosts. Saddled with the twin burdens of signaling the pain of past historical traumas, and of evoking the ancestral presence of buried indigenous, mythic voices, playfulness is largely emptied from the figure of the Spanish American literary ghost. In other words, the unen-

---

7. The involvement of many Spanish American writers, such as the Chilean Pablo Neruda and the Peruvian César Vallejo, in the Spanish Civil War also contributed greatly to a sense of socialist solidarity among this group of intellectuals (Armstrong 25).

8. This is not to say that trauma is not a concern of, or expressed by, modern Brazilian fiction (a clearly inaccurate statement), but rather that the form with which that trauma is represented differs from the Spanish American tendency. It is telling, for example, that one of the most unsettling literary depictions of the traumatic *anos duros* of the military dictatorship, Ivan Ângelo's *A Festa* (The Celebration, 1976), uses as its backdrop the gathering of wealthy individuals around a birthday celebration. See also Rubem Fonseca's *Feliz Ano Novo*, in which a New Year's Eve party is the backdrop for horrific acts of violence and retribution.

9. This notion of the ghost as a harbinger of the need to re-create ethnic identity is developed by Kathleen Brogan in her book *Cultural Haunting: Ghosts and Ethnicity in Recent American Literature*.

cumbered Dyonisian spirit finds little space or reception given this dual burden. In contrast, it is precisely this spirit of carnival subversion that serves as the *modus operandi* of the deceased reveler in modern Brazilian fiction.

WORKS CITED

Armstrong, Piers. *Third World Literary Fortunes: Brazilian Culture and Its International Reception.* Lewisburg: Bucknell UP, 1999.

Brogan, Kathleen. *Cultural Haunting: Ghosts and Ethnicity in Recent American Literature.* Charlottesville: UP of Virginia, 1998.

Candido, Antonio. "Dialectic of Malandroism." *On Literature and Society.* Trans. and ed. Howard S. Becker. Princeton: Princeton UP, 1995. 79–103.

Cypress, Sandra Messinger. "The Dead Narrator in Modern Latin American Prose Fiction: A Study in Point of View." Diss. U of Illinois, 1968.

DaMatta, Roberto. *Carnivals, Rogues, and Heroes: An Interpretation of the Brazilian Dilemma.* Notre Dame: U of Notre Dame P, 1991.

———. *A Casa e a Rua: Espaço, Cidadania, Mulher e Morte no Brasil.* São Paulo: Editora Brasiliense, 1985.

Gates, Henry Louis, Jr. *The Signifying Monkey: A Theory of Afro-American Literary Criticism.* New York: Oxford UP, 1988.

Lomnitz, Claudio. *Death and the Idea of Mexico.* New York: Zone Books, 2005.

Moser, Robert H. *The Carnivalesque Defunto: Death and the Dead in Modern Brazilian Literature.* Athens: Ohio UP, 2008.

Payne, Judith A., and Earl E. Fitz. *Ambiguity and Gender in the New Novel of Brazil and Spanish America: A Comparative Assessment.* Iowa City: U of Iowa P, 1993.

Paz, Octavio. *The Labyrinth of Solitude and Other Writings.* New York: Grove, 1991.

Rocha, João Cezar de Castro. "Dialética da marginalidade (Caracterização da cultura brasileira contemporânea)." *Caderno MAIS!, Folha de São Paulo,* 29 Feb. 2004.

Valente, Luiz F. "Parody and Carnivalization in the Novels of Márcio Souza." *Hispania* 70.4 (1987): 787–93.

Zamora, Lois Parkinson. *The Usable Past: The Imagination of History in Recent Fiction of the Americas.* Cambridge: Cambridge UP, 1997.

CHAPTER 7

Borges, Clarice, and the Development of Latin America's "New Narrative"

EARL E. FITZ

AS THE FIELD of inter-American literature continues to develop, and as Latin American literature continues to move it forward, comparative studies of Brazilian and Spanish American writers and texts will become more and more important to scholars who wish to engage with this exciting new discipline. And within the context of twentieth-century Latin American literary history and cultural production, few topics are as compelling as the appearance of the so-called New Narrative, a concept that, especially during the 1960s and 1970s, links the writers of North, Central, and South America as few other things can. But because even today the "New Narrative" is nearly always understood as defined by the "Nueva Narrativa Hispanoamericana" alone, that is, by the work of such Spanish American masters as Borges, Rulfo, Fuentes, Cortázar, Vargas Llosa, and García Márquez, what now demands inquiry is whether there was, in fact, another "New Narrative" emanating from Latin America, one deeply rooted in Brazilian narrative history and quite different from its better-known Spanish American cousin. If, as comparative Latin Americanists, we are willing to consider that this is so—that Latin America has actually produced not one but two theories of narrative—then we are forced to reconsider our standard thinking about the history of narrative development in Brazil and Spanish America.

In arguing that this is the case, I will make use of a dual focus: first, the year 1944, when two landmark narratives, Borges's *Ficciones* and Clarice

Lispector's *Perto do Coração Selvagem,* appeared, and second, 1880, when, in the *Revista Brasileira,* Machado de Assis's revolutionary *Memórias Póstumas de Brás Cubas* burst upon the scene. I proceed in this fashion because I seek to demonstrate that while Borges's "fictions" break dramatically from a formally staid and hidebound tradition of fiction-writing, the Brazilian texts are directly connected to a well-established tradition of innovative narrative. While, to be sure, formally innovative texts were written in Spanish America during the early years of the twentieth century, these, along with Alejandro Tapia y Rivera's 1872 novel, *Póstumo el transmigrado,* remained discrete islands of change in an otherwise very placid narrative sea. In other words, while Borges's *Ficciones* are largely sui generis, Lispector's novel is the logical product of a very coherent, very cohesive national literature and of a long-standing tradition of experimental fiction, one that also featured a new vision of women as literary creators and as citizens in the Brazil of the future. From this, we can conclude that Latin American literature's original "New Narrative"—the Brazilian variant—dates from 1880, some fifty to sixty years before the better-known Spanish American "nueva narrativa."

Borges's "ficciones" are virtually devoid of women, and as such, all but demand consideration from the perspective of gender. These cerebral and deracinated short narratives offer themselves up as fascinating problems in stylistic and structural analysis, but they render women invisible, essentially nonentities. Only the later, and quite different "La intrusa" features a more substantive role for a female character, and even then in a distinctly problematic fashion. The Borges texts do, however, feature a wide variety of male characters, some fanciful or "fantastic" and some historically believable, though very few of these are the "flesh-and-blood" characters of traditional narrative realism. The oddity, with respect to gender in the *Ficciones,* has to do with the overwhelming preponderance of men and Borges's creation of a very male-oriented world. While some nine or ten women are mentioned in the *Ficciones,* none ever becomes what we think of as a protagonist or even a character with a major role to play.

The simple fact that women are largely absent from Borges's texts also calls attention to the binary, either/or world so closely associated with structuralism, one in which, as far as the *Ficciones* are concerned, maleness is the norm and femaleness is the essentially superfluous "Other," a kind of being that has no place in the hierarchical scheme of things. It is not that women have no value in the *Ficciones,* but that their value is not equal to, or commensurate with, that of the male figures. In "Tema del traidor y del héroe," for example, the task of Calpurnia, Caesar's wife, is to establish a historical parallel with what happens to the narrative's male protagonist and his struggle with "some secret *shape* of time"—again the importance of form or structure—"conceived by repeating lines" (*Collected Fictions* 144; my emphasis). Although a few women do play supporting roles in the "fictions," they are, in effect, "invisible," rather in the mode of Ralph Ellison's *Invisible Man,* someone who is "there" but is neither "seen" nor valorized within the reigning structure. Women, to put it more succinctly, have no agency in Borges's *Ficciones.* Perhaps the most disturbing issue raised here is that in this world, women have no intellectual role or standing. There is no female Pierre Menard, no female Erik Lönnrot, and no female Juan Dahlmann.

Standing in sharp contrast to the male-dominated, if not necessarily masculine, world of Borges's *Ficciones,* Clarice Lispector presents herself, in *Perto do Coração Selvagem,* as a woman writing about women in a male-dominated culture. But is the real issue in Lispector's novel male domination? Or is it, more fundamentally, an interrogation of any system or structure that restricts a person's freedom, male or female? In other words, do the problems we now think of as logocentrism and phallogocentrism repress and warp not only women but men as well? The peculiar nature of Lispector's tale leads one to think that this is the case. While Lispector's female characters (again in contrast to Borges) are her most interesting and most challenging, the main male character of the novel, Otávio, is both complex and intriguing because he illustrates the harm done to both men and women by "either/or" structuralist thinking. With its privileging of *logos* and its (for everyone) imprisoning slide into a pernicious phallogocentrism, this kind of binary-dependent thinking is itself shored up by a spurious though rigidly held distinction between "being male" and "being female," two ontological modes that societies that were built on structuralist principles judge to be mutually exclusive.

In discussions of the novels of the Spanish American "boom" during the 1960s, only Elena Garro's *Los recuerdos del porvenir* (1963) is routinely mentioned, whereas in Brazil during roughly the same period the reader is treated to a plethora of marvelous women writers, including Rachel de Queiroz, Lygia Fagundes Telles, Dinah Silveira de Queiroz, Lya Luft, and Nélida Piñon, all of whom owe an enormous debt to Lispector. Why were so few women involved as writers in the New Novel of Spanish America? Why this disparity in numbers? In the nineteenth century, Spanish American literature made use of women as important characters, as we see in such novels as Lizardi's *La Quijotita y su prima* (1818), Gertrudis Goméz de Avellaneda's *Sab* (1841), Mármol's *Amalia* (1852), Mera's *Cumandá* (1871), and Tapia's *La cuarterona* (1878), but the women who appear in these works are of a very different sort than those who appear in such canonical Brazilian texts as Macedo's *A Moreninha* (1844),

Alencar's *Iracema* (1865) and *Senhora* (1875), Assis's *Memórias Póstumas de Brás Cubas,* and Azevedo's *O Cortiço* (1891). With respect to the development of women as characters, and to their importance to the emergence of the "new Brazil" during the second half of the nineteenth century, something different was clearly happening in Brazilian narrative. It is therefore possible to argue that nineteenth-century Brazilian letters can boast of a narrative tradition that stressed innovation and experimentation in form and that consistently included strong women, not (in the beginning) necessarily as writers, but at least as characters (developed by male writers) who were consistently portrayed in ways that were, to greater and lesser degrees, complex, empowering, and intelligent.[1]

It is this tradition that produces *Perto do Coração Selvagem.* Besides the novel's protagonist, Joana—whom we meet in four different states of existence: as a little girl, an adolescent going through puberty, a married woman, and a woman freeing herself from an unhappy marriage—Lispector also gives us Joana's memorable aunt, a woman brilliantly (and wryly) personified by her ample breasts. This nameless older woman, gendered by the values of an earlier generation and whose identity here is comically, and derisively, body-based, serves as a foil for Joana, who abhors all that her *tia* represents. Narrating indirectly, from within Joana's turbulent mind, Lispector writes of the young Joana's first encounter with her buxom relative: "Before she could move in self-defence, Joana found herself being buried between those two mounds of soft, warm flesh which quivered with every sob" (*Near* 33). Almost immediately, Lispector follows this distinctly negative reception of the aunt, her body, and all it signifies with two more, equally negative responses: "The cleavage between the aunt's breasts was deep. She could have put her hand in these as if she were dipping into a bag and pulling out some surprise, an animal, a casket, whatever [. . .] Those breasts could bury someone! [. . .] Her aunt's breasts were in danger of spilling over her, melted into fat" (34). By presenting the aunt's breasts not as life-sustaining, or as objects of desire and Eros, but as suffocating masses of flesh likely to overwhelm and entomb a person, Joana inverts conventional structures of meaning and forces the reader to consider gender as a volatile construct, a system of situational values rather

---

1. One thinks, again, of Joaquim Manuel de Macedo's *A Moreninha* (1844), a text widely regarded as Brazil's first formal novel, but also of José de Alencar's *Iracema* (1865) and *Senhora* (1875), Aluísio Azevedo's *O Cortiço* (1890), Júlia Lopes de Almeida's *A Família Medeiros* (1892), and Machado de Assis's *Memórias Póstumas de Brás Cubas* (1880), *Quincas Borba* (1891), and *Dom Casmurro* (1899/1900). Twentieth-century Brazilian literature continues with this tradition of strong women writers and characters.

than a presentation of some supposedly immutable truth to which Joana must adhere.

Further complicating matters, the motif of female breasts returns later in the narrative to distinguish between Lídia, Otávio's former betrothed (and, after marrying Joana, his lover), and Joana, now in the midst of her physical and psychological transformation as a woman and a freedom-seeking human being, someone who is, in the words of James Joyce, "alone" and "unheeded, happy and near to the wild heart of life" (Lispector, *Perto*, epigraph to part 1). Different from the experience she'd had with her aunt, Joana's relationship with Lídia seems at least partially homoerotic, with Joana being both attracted to and repelled by her husband's now pregnant lover. Then, of Otávio's attraction to Lídia, Joana thinks to herself that he "cannot look at a woman with an ample bosom without wanting to rest his head there" (133), though Joana herself, in a destabilizing fusion of the motherly and the erotic, knows that she, too, would like a woman "with large breasts" to bathe her and put her to bed (137). It is not merely that Lispector has replaced the phallus with female breasts as the prime signifier; she also shows that, as signifiers, these same breasts are semantically polyvalent. As powerful but nonstable signs they elicit a wide range of responses and function, in the course of the narrative, as floating signifiers, which (as Joana demonstrates) are themselves subject to constant fluctuations of meaning.

Following in the liberating wake of Machado de Assis, Clarice Lispector will make it possible for women to write in Brazil as creative equals, that is, to possess and deploy language. In a scene ripe with symbolism, for example, Joana brazenly steals a book; she takes the book, she declares to an astonished onlooker (and to the similarly astonished reader), simply because she wants to. Thus, with the appearance of *Perto do Coração Selvagem* in 1944, Brazil's well-established tradition of formally and thematically "transgressive" narrative (begun so brilliantly with Machado de Assis and the *Memórias Póstumas de Brás Cubas* in 1880) is given new, largely female-centric life, as will also be the case in the work of such writers as Nélida Piñon, Sônia Coutinho, Márcia Denser, Lya Luft, Marilene Felinto, and Regina Rheda, among many others. Incidentally, this list includes a wide variety of male writers as well, including Domingos Olímpio, Oswald de Andrade, and João Guimarães Rosa.

In contrast to Lispector and her literary progeny, Borges engendered a generation of innovative male novelists (the giants of the "Boom" period, i.e., Rulfo, Fuentes, García Márquez, Donoso, Vargas Llosa, Cortázar, et al.) but virtually no female novelists, with the aforementioned Elena Garro being the main exception. With respect to the question of influence on later generations of writers, then, the difference between Borges's impact on the development of

Spanish American narrative and that of Machado and Lispector on Brazilian narrative could hardly be more striking.

But if, in Brazil, Machado had by 1880 freed narrative from the (for him) suffocating strictures of realism with the completion of the *Memórias Póstumas de Brás Cubas,* he does so primarily by offering a pre-Saussurean view of the relationship between language and reality and between text and reader. The proof lies in the critical conclusions reached by Machado between 1878 and 1879, the years that separate his early phase from his more famous mature period. In 1878, for example, in his critique of Portuguese novelist Eça de Queirós, Machado offers the following advice to Brazilian writers and readers: "Let us turn our eyes once again to reality, but let us exclude Realism, so as to not sacrifice aesthetic truth" (913). Continuing this line of thought, he declares a short time later (and on the eve of *Memórias Póstumas de Brás Cubas*) that, "reality is good [. . .] it is realism that is good for nothing" ("A Nova Geração" 830).[2] The radically New Narrative theory that Machado lays out here, that literary art is an exercise in verisimilitude and a self-referential structure of linguistic signs[3] that do not depend on any external reality for their efficacy and meaning, is remarkably similar to that advanced much later by the eminent critic René Wellek, when, in 1963, he wrote that "the theory of realism is ultimately bad aesthetics because all art is 'making' and is a world in itself of illusion and symbolic forms" (255). This perspective—so transformative in its impact on the ways that modern narrative will be understood and practiced—was definitely put into play by Borges in the 1930s, but its earliest appearance in the Americas comes in Machado's post-1880 novels and short stories.

Reading the *Ficciones* against *Perto do Coração Selvagem,* one is immediately struck by how, in Borges's text, we are pulled along by the power of the many interconnecting structures that constitute his narratives (those of "La biblioteca de Babel," for example), whereas in Lispector's more opaque, semantically fluid world the reader's attention is drawn to what is for the Brazilian author the slippery, mercurial nature of each linguistic sign and its ability to create a cohesive subject. Both Borges and Lispector reject realism (as Machado did before them) and demonstrate that narrative verisimilitude is an order of mimesis very distinct from painting and sculpture. In rejecting realist norms in favor of the ambiguities and uncertainties of reality, Machado effectively discovers what Barthes, Derrida, Kristeva, and others will later call

---

2. Translations of Machado de Assis's criticism are the editors' own.

3. This very issue, *verossimilhança,* appears, directly or indirectly, as a fundamental concern in all of Machado's post-1880 novels and in many of his short stories. Indeed, the entire plot of *Dom Casmurro* turns upon it.

the free play of signs that characterizes all language use, a free play, moreover, in which the reader must accept a new responsibility for active engagement with textual meaning, understood as the interaction of its signs and signifiers. Machado's insistence on the importance of the reader's role in literary activity predates by some fifty to sixty years a similar argument made (more famously) by Borges in the 1939 story, "Pierre Menard, autor del Quijote": "Menard has (perhaps unwittingly) enriched the slow and rudimentary art of reading by means of a new technique—the technique of deliberate anachronism and fallacious attribution" (*Collected Fictions* 95). Terming this emphasis on reading "one of the basic tenets of Borges' poetics," Monegal contends that, for Borges, it is the reading of a text, and not its writing, that brings it to life and that allows it to grow, develop, and expand in terms of its range of meanings and its levels of applicability (77; 77–78).

But, in our newly comparative history of Latin American narrative, we know that it is Brazil's Machado de Assis, who, through the constant hectoring of his reader by his dead but nonetheless loquacious narrator, Brás Cubas, first makes this important point, insisting in *Memórias Póstumas de Brás Cubas* on the creation of a "new reader" for his "New Narrative." As a result of the impact of Machado's 1880 novel, the text that is aware of itself, that is conscious of its own making, its own artifice, and that is acutely sensitive to the reader's role in its consumption and in the creation of its significance becomes a staple of Brazilian narrative, and, as a fledgling writer in 1944, Lispector was steeped in it.

Thematically speaking, Lispector's narrative takes the rather esoteric philosophical problem of the reader's role in the literary text and develops it as the active ingredient in the construction of the protagonist's identity. It is impossible to think of Joana except in terms of her role as a function of the ebb and flow of language. We do not see this in Borges's *Ficciones*, where, though they most certainly deal with the nature of structure and language, the narratives reflect the power of structure (working in concert with our desire to find or create structure) to control our thinking. Further, they tend to hew toward the cerebral, analytical side of things, eschewing the messy, desire-based, bodily driven functions of human life that Lispector cultivates. For Lispector, language, in all its anarchic and creative glory, can fairly be said to be the primary subject. But unlike the *Ficciones,* which are rather otherworldly (even when dealing with topics we seem to recognize), Lispector's work, beginning with *Perto do Coração Selvagem,* puts a human face on the defining characteristics of poststructuralism. Joana, one might say, is Western literature's first poststructural protagonist. She develops in a tangled, often inconsistent, and ever-mutating frame of reference, and stands in sharp contrast to Eric Lönnrot, the "reasoning machine" (*Collected Fictions* 147) who uses the perfect, eternal, and unvarying structures of axiomatic geometric truth to solve his case. What sets Lönnrot and Joana apart, then, is essentially what distinguishes structuralism from poststructuralism.

When John Sturrock wrote, in a reference to "The Library of Babel," that it was "the bad dream of a Structuralist" (xviii), he was not merely making an acute observation about a particular text. Rather, he was getting at something very fundamental to, and distinctive of, Borges's *Ficciones*—and to Borges's thinking about the nature of narrative at the time of their composition. So important was Borges to the French structuralists that one can speculate whether he might have had a direct influence on Roland Barthes, whose essay "The Structural Activity" defines structure in terms of its status as "artifice," a key term for Borges and the title ("Artificios") of the second half of the *Ficciones*. Nor is it of idle interest that the eminent structuralist critic Gérard Genette wrote in 1964 one of the earliest and most influential essays, "La littérature selon Borges," on the new nature of Borges's *Ficciones*, which had been translated into French in the 1950s. This essay, and others like it, firmly established Borges as the darling of the French structuralists (see, for example, Foucault's discussion of Borges in *Les Mots et les choses*), as the writer whose texts most fully exemplified the kind of creative writing the structuralist theoreticians had been seeking.

For the structuralists, meaning is determined by the *systèm*, the specific linguistic structure in which words *qua* linguistic signs occur, and not by the traditional techniques of narrative realism. That Borges had thought all this through as early as the 1930s is strongly indicated by the publication, in the magazine *Discusión*, of two key essays that, when read together, lay out the basics of a new and profoundly antirealistic narrative poetics. The essays in question, "La postulación de la realidad" and "El arte narrativo y la magia," both appearing in 1932, take up the ancient and hoary issue of verisimilitude. For Borges, as Monegal contends, "verisimilitude is not what conforms to the real, or what a certain literary period or a certain genre claims to be the real. [. . .] Verisimilitude has less to do with reality than with the conventions of a certain culture about how to portray reality" (248). These are points Machado de Assis had made some fifty years earlier. Arguing for the aesthetic superiority of a new kind of narrative fiction, one dominated by the dictates of magic rather than by the dictates of realism, Borges concludes that "in magical narratives everything is relevant; there are no loose ends. A perfect structure forces every part to correspond to the whole," with "causality," and not our traditional notions of "reality" and its representation, emerging, finally, as the prime element in this dramatically new "teleology of narrative" (Monegal 248).

Approached most productively from the perspective of *l'écriture,* Lispector's novel exemplifies not the quest for a "perfect structure" but "textuality," the equally radical idea that all language use involves destabilizing play, and is an open-ended process of signification and erasure that resists all attempts at closure. For Lispector, this process is manifested most clearly, à la Kristeva, in her disruptive syntax. The primary distinction between Borges's *Ficciones* and Lispector's *Perto do Coração Selvagem* thus reveals itself as a matter concerning the true nature of Saussure's linguistic sign. Is it stable, existing in a one-to-one relationship, like the two sides of a single sheet of paper, or as the Swiss linguist himself describes it, as a function of syntax? Is it always in flux, changing its meanings and implications as it expands and contracts in a never-ending semantic exchange between the author, the text (that is, other signs), and the reader? By concentrating on the protean nature of the sign, rather than on the larger, and more stable structure in which it occurs, Lispector cultivates precisely that quality of structuralism (the supposed stability of the linguistic sign) that Derrida would later point to as its essential error, the weakness that poststructuralism sought to explore. Beginning in 1944 with *Perto do Coração Selvagem,* the Brazilian writer begins to create a kind of writing that would exult in what Derrida would come to call *différance* and, later still, Hélène Cixous (referring specifically to Lispector's *Água Viva*) would celebrate as the purest, most prototypical form of *l'écriture féminine* (Conley vii), a pronouncement that would never be made about the *Ficciones.*

The aporia, tensions, and conflicts that exist within Joana provide the erotic *frisson* that we feel in reading Lispector's *Perto do Coração Selvagem.* So utterly is Joana's characterization achieved by semantic free play, by *plaisir* (of both Barthesian "texte" and body), and by *supplément,* that her adult coming-into-being is depicted, in its progressive development, by three intensely lyrical scenes that seem to involve both language use and masturbation, with the moment of orgasm serving as the fusion of language and being that Joana is so ardently seeking. Of the three,[4] the first is the most dramatic in terms of its importance to Joana's process of self-realization and thus to the novel's development:

---

4. The second of these scenes, even more self-affirming than the first and taking place in the presence of a sleeping Otávio, occurs in part 2 of the novel at the end of the chapter entitled "O Encontro de Otávio." The third scene, depicting a newly confident Joana, is found toward the end of "A Partida dos Homens," just before she is about to set out on her voyage of self-discovery that, without ending it, brings the narrative to a close.

> At night, between the sheets, the slightest movement or unexpected thought awakened her to herself. Mildly surprised, she opened her eyes wide, perceived her own body plunged into reassuring contentment. She wasn't suffering, but where was she?
>
> – Joana . . . Joana . . . she softly called to herself. And her body scarcely responded, quietly echoing: Joana. (*Near* 92)

This line of interpretation gains additional credence when one considers that Lispector herself once referred to her own *écriture* as resembling "un orgasme" (Varin 70). Already in the distinctly gynocentric *Perto do Coração Selvagem*, we see how the "signifier floats away from the signified, *jouissance* dissolves meaning, the semiotic disrupts the symbolic, *différance* inserts a gap between signifier and signified, and power disorganises established knowledge" (Selden 102).

We can, in conclusion, argue that our modern Latin American "New Narrative" actually has two great taproots, each of which epitomizes the kinds of writing associated with the two dominant literary theories of the twentieth century, structuralism and poststructuralism. This conclusion is of tremendous importance for the development of inter-American literature as an emergent new discipline and for the acceptance of Spanish American and Brazilian literature on the world stage. It instantly elevates our writers from the status of mere imitators to that of initiators, and shows them to be true pioneers with respect to the relationship between language and reality, the nature of literary representation, and in the production and consumption of narrative fiction. This is an argument that comparative Latin Americanists can, and should, make as they integrate their authors, texts, and literary histories with other writers in the Americas and around the globe.

WORKS CITED

Assis, Joaquim Maria Machado de. "A Nova Geração." *Obra Completa*. Vol. 3: 809–36.

———. "Eça de Queirós: *O Primo Basílio*." *Obra Completa*. Vol. 3: 903–13.

Borges, Jorge Luis. *Collected Fictions*. Trans. Andrew Hurley. New York: Penguin, 1998.

———. *Ficciones*. Buenos Aires: Emecé Editores, 1956.

Conley, Verena Andermatt. "Introduction." *Reading with Clarice Lispector*. By Hélène Cixous. Ed., trans., and intro. Verena Andermatt Conley. Minneapolis: U of Minnesota P, 1990. vii–xviii.

Lispector, Clarice. *Near to the Wild Heart*. Trans. Giovanni Pontiero. New York: New Directions. 1990.

———. *Perto do Coração Selvagem*. Rio de Janeiro: Rocco, 1998.

Monegal, Emir Rodríguez. *Jorge Luis Borges: A Literary Biography.* New York: Dutton, 1978.

Selden, Raman. *A Reader's Guide to Contemporary Literary Theory.* Lexington: U of Kentucky P, 1985.

Sturrock, John. "Introduction." *Ficciones.* New York: Knopf and Everyman's Library, 1993. xi–xxiv.

Varin, Claire. *Langues de feu: essais sur Clarice Lispector.* Québec: Éditions Trois, 1990.

Wellek, René. "Realism in Literary Scholarship." *Concepts of Criticism.* Intro. Stephen G. Nichols. New Haven: Yale UP, 1963. 222–55.

CHAPTER 8

Mapping Citizenship in Luiz Ruffato's *Inferno provisório* and Guillermo Saccomanno's *El pibe*

LEILA LEHNEN

WHAT IS the correlation between city and citizenship? In their introduction to the collection *Cities and Citizenship* Arjun Appadurai and James Holston focalize the link between the configuration of citizenship, which has become increasingly synonymous with the allocation of rights (Yashar), and urban space.[1] Appadurai and Holston identify the urban sphere as a "strategic arena for the development of citizenship" (2). Urban spaces, especially those that are propitious for civic gatherings, are good *fora* for demanding various types of rights.

However, the city is not only a place for the development of citizenship. Its geography is also pockmarked by sectors of material and symbolic disenfranchisement (Caldeira).[2] In these shadow zones, social, civil, political, and cultural agency[3] are weakened or disappear altogether. *Favelas, villas miserias, barriadas,* and *poblaciones*—terms that refer to shantytowns or marginal neighborhoods in Latin American cities—are prototypical territories of

---

1. I am using the term "citizenship" in its liberal permutation here. This model presupposes equality and individual freedom and perceives the state as a guarantor of individual rights.

2. For other works dealing with urban segregation, see Harvey, Ventura, Sassen, Kowarick (*A espoliação*), Rotker and Goldman, Roitman, Davis, Aboy, Ortega-Alcázar, Vidal-Koppman, Campesi, and Soja, among others.

3. T. H. Marshall identifies three spheres of citizenship: social (rights such as access to health care, social security, education), political (such as voting rights), and civil rights (as for example right to judicial redress, to association). To these one can also add cultural rights, which include the rights to language, artistic expression, and religion, for example.

exclusion, locales where differentiated citizenship (Holston) becomes glaringly evident. Anthropologist James Holston defines differentiated citizenship as a form of "citizenship that manages social differences by legalizing them in ways that legitimate and reproduce inequality" (3–4). This is to say, differentiated citizenship justifies socioeconomic disparities through legal means. Differentiated citizenship is a by-product of what Holston calls "disjunctive democracies," electoral democracies that nevertheless have an uneven distribution of social, civil, and, at times, political rights.

Between the enclaves of privilege and the exclaves of disenfranchisement, in-between spaces exist where citizens at the same time possess a measure of power and are marginalized. In these arenas, substantive (i.e., enacted) citizenship is under continual (re)negotiation. These localities are the setting for Brazilian Luiz Ruffato's and Argentinian Guillermo Saccomanno's renderings of urban proletarian life.[4] In their novels *Inferno provisório* (*Provisional Hell*, 2005–11)[5] and *El pibe* (*The Kid*, 2006), Ruffato and Saccomanno transform the working classes into unlikely protagonists of the nation.[6]

This essay examines the conjunction between urban space and the constitution/erosion of citizenship in selected narrative fragments from *Inferno provisório* and in *El pibe*. In both Ruffato's and Saccomanno's texts the city becomes the epicenter of the working classes' social aspirations. It is where citizenship materializes (in the form of steady jobs, homeownership, public education, and communal spaces). Nonetheless, their narratives also reveal the precariousness of the working classes' social citizenship[7]—a result of Brazil's and Argentina's disjunctive formulation of social, civil, and political rights.[8] *Inferno provisório* and *El pibe* reveal, at the fictional level, the dynamic

---

4. The Latin American proletarian novel does not originate with Ruffato and Saccomano. In Brazil, one can cite Aluísio de Azevedo's *O cortiço* (1890) and Patrícia Galvão's *Parque industrial* (1933). In Argentina, one can cite the works of Manuel Puig and Oswaldo Soriano, among others. More recently, Sergio Bizzio also thematized the Argentine working classes in *Rabia* (2004). In Brazil, Fernando Bonassi, similar to Luiz Ruffato, also hones in on the erosion of citizenship experienced by the urban working classes.

5. *Inferno provisório* encompasses five books: *Mamma son tanto felice* (2005), *O mundo inimigo* (2005), *Vista parcial da noite* (2006), *O livro das impossibilidades* (2008), and *Domingos sem Deus* (2011). All five volumes of *Inferno provisório* are a collection of narratives that can be read separately, as if they were short stories, or as part of a larger narrative (a novel).

6. In this sense, Ruffato's and Saccomano's fictions represent the transformation of the traditionally bourgeoisie genre of the novel (Ruffato, Interview with Heloísa Buarque de Holanda).

7. Social citizenship is a concept introduced by T. H. Marshall in his essay "Citizenship and Social Class." It implies welfare rights, though not the abolishment of social classes, i.e., of social differentiation. Among welfare rights one can include rights to education, health care, social security, among others.

8. For a discussion on disjunctive citizenship in Brazil, see Holston, Dagnino. About citizenship in Argentina, see March and Stanley.

process of citizenship, its unequal implementation, and how the material and imaginary urban cartography reflects and reinforces these disjunctures and transformations of citizenship. The working-class neighborhoods depicted in Ruffato's and Saccomanno's texts are thus frontier zones of citizenship, places where the markers of national belonging co-exist with the signposts of socio-economic exclusion. The two authors highlight the importance of the urban space in proletarian social life. *Inferno provisório* and *El pibe* show the destabilizing impact of the differentiated allocation of such rights on said social segments. At the same time, these texts also propose literature as a mode of what James Holston calls "insurgent citizenship," processes of civil, political, and cultural resistance to disenfranchisement that aim at regaining agency.

Ruffato and Saccomanno's emphasis on proletarian characters dovetails with an increasing attention in contemporary Latin American literature to both the formulation and the enactment of citizenship in the aftermath of the democratic transitions of the 1980s (1983 in Argentina, 1985 in Brazil) and to marginalized social sectors within—and as part of—the nation. There is doubtless a certain voyeurism of the abject in some of this literary and cultural production, with its often neonaturalist depictions of violence and poverty. This is especially the case in Brazilian cinematic and, to a lesser degree, literary production.[9] In contrast, Ruffato's series of interrelated narratives and Saccomanno's novel eschew this hypernaturalist timbre. Instead, they suggest structural violence by describing quotidian iniquities: for instance, the father who must borrow money to buy medicine for his son (*El pibe* 95), or oppressive factory labor (*Inferno provisório*). Differentiated citizenship in *Inferno provisório* and *El pibe* not only relates to material poverty but also refers to curtailed existential horizons, to the gradual crumbling of the hopes, life expectations, and dreams of the novels' characters. In this respect, Ruffato's and Saccomanno's texts reflect a shift in how citizenship is defined in Latin American literature.

Traditionally, citizenship implies belonging to a certain body politic and having access to a set of rights and obligations towards the community, especially within the currently prevalent liberal tradition of citizenship. Since T. H. Marshall's influential 1950 essay, citizenship has been commonly defined in the academic literature by access to social, political, and civil rights. Examples include access to healthcare and education (social), and rights to representation (political) and due process (civil). Increasingly, however, citizenship is understood to also encompass a cultural dimension, which includes the

---

9. Cinematic examples include *Cidade de Deus*, *Tropa de elite* I and II, and *Última parada 174*. In literary production, one can cite the works of Patrícia Melo and Ana Paula Maia's *Entre rinhas de cachorros e porcos abatidos* and *O trabalho sujo dos outros* (2009).

right to self-articulation. Literature can become a venue through which traditionally disempowered groups can gain visibility and voice their concerns and demands for social improvement. In other words, literature, as a mode of self-articulation, can become both a tool and an expression of citizenship.

Ruffato and Saccomanno propose literature as a mode to engage with the social conditions that generate and perpetuate inequity. Whereas Luiz Ruffato speaks about the "Igreja do livro transformador" (Interview, Eliane Brum) and has indicated that he perceives literature as a tool for social transformation, Saccomanno sees in literature a partial chronicle of specific sociopolitical conditions. He claims that although he is not a "historian; I am a writer. But it is evident that the fiction is often able to broach political and social phenomena better than historical texts" (Interview, *Clarín*).[10] *El pibe,* similarly to Ruffato's *Inferno provisório,* draws on autobiographical material to foreground Argentina's proletariat. Books (i.e., literature) are described by the novel's young protagonist as "medios para un cambio de consciencia, una 'superación'" (*El pibe* 147). The literary text, which is inspired by the conditions that generate differentiated citizenship, serves to critique and surmount these conditions symbolically. Not only can literature advance social consciousness, it can also be an instrument of social advancement. Literary initiatives, such as neighborhood soirées and testimonial literature, work to empower traditionally underrepresented social groups.

This essay does not suggest that the texts analyzed here effect direct social change. Rather, it uses Ruffato's and Saccomanno's fictionalized representations of the Brazilian and Argentine working classes, respectively, as examples of literary artifacts that trace a genealogy of differentiated citizenship and, by doing this, instigate reflection about the real-life consequences of this configuration. Beyond this, *Inferno provisório* and *El pibe* delineate strategies of insurgent citizenship (albeit not unproblematic ones), specifically homeownership—achieved through autoconstruction—and education. Finally Ruffato's and Saccomanno's texts also propose (fictional) writing itself as an insurgent exercise. *Inferno provisório* and *El pibe* thus describe a circular movement with literary production as the starting and ending points of insurgent (cultural) practice.

WORKING WITHIN PROVISIONAL HELLS: LUIZ RUFFATO'S *INFERNO PROVISÓRIO*

Luiz Ruffato's *Inferno provisório* is paradigmatic of the social engagement that transpires in what I call a "literature of disenchantment," which describes texts

---

10. "Historiador; soy escritor. Pero es evidente que la narrativa muchas veces da cuenta de los fenómenos políticos y sociales mejor que los textos históricos." This and all translations mine.

that at the same time denounce adverse social circumstances and broach the difficulty—or impossibility—of transforming these conditions.[11] *Inferno provisório* illustrates the transformation of Brazil from an agrarian to an industrialized, and finally, a globalized (in the neoliberal sense) nation and the accompanying erosion of the working classes' social citizenship. The books, written as a series of interrelated, but not always overtly connected narratives, focus on the effects of differentiated citizenship on the everyday existence of working-class men and women.

Spanning approximately five decades in recent Brazilian history, *Inferno provisório* has five volumes. All five tomes concentrate on the history of the Brazilian proletariat from the 1950s to the present,[12] depicting how modernization, postindustrialization, and accompanying haphazard urbanization impacted social citizenship within these classes. In this essay, I will examine volumes 1 through 4 of *Inferno provisório*.

The setting of *Inferno provisório* is mainly Ruffato's hometown of Cataguases, in the southeast of Minas Gerais. Taken together, the first four tomes draw a complex map of the city, which includes its central areas, and its rural and metropolitan outskirts, and extends to larger conurbations, such as Rio de Janeiro, Santos, and São Paulo. These regions are linked to each other by the physical movements of the books' characters, and by the figurative traffic of dreams and disappointments that circulates between the various spaces. Thus, the symbolic valence of each terrain (city and country) is ambivalent, pregnant with both hope and disenchantment. On one hand, the urban perimeter represents socioeconomic progress, but also the negation of these aspirations. On the other hand, the countryside emblematizes both socioeconomic stagnation and an idealized past.

The cycle's first volume, *Mamma son tanto felice*, narrates the migration from rural areas into smaller urbanizations such as Rodeiro, Ubá, and Muriaré, which surround Cataguases proper. In the second volume, *O mundo inimigo*, the characters have moved from the small towns around Cataguases to the metropolitan perimeter. They inhabit the city's despondent central terrains, symbolized by the *Beco do Zé Pinto*, a lower-income settlement where large portions of the narratives take place. *Vista parcial da noite* traces the trajectory from the poor urban center into the urban periphery, as the working classes seek social ascension through homeownership. They move into the low-income housing projects that emerge on the city's outskirts. Nonetheless, the migration from city center to the periphery ultimately does not offer the

---

11. Guillermo Saccomanno's most recent novel, *El oficinista* (2010), fits this thematic mold. In this text, an oppressed office worker experiences the collapse of his already precarious *Lebenswelt*.

12. The fourth tome, *O livro das impossibilidades*, ends at the turn of the millennium.

possibility of social ascension. Finally, in *O livro das impossibildades,* the characters leave Cataguases and its periphery, looking for better socioeconomic opportunities in larger metropolitan centers such as Rio de Janeiro and Santos, where they settle in impoverished and/or industrial neighborhoods on the urban outskirts, reproducing the sociogeographic pattern that led to their initial emigration.

Violence, or rather different modalities of violence, both private and public, a manifestation of social disenfranchisement, is a recurrent theme in all five tomes of *Inferno provisório* and establishes the symbolic coordinates of the books' cartography. Often aggression transfers from one locale into another, pursuing the characters like a shadow. Paradigmatic is the narrative "A expiação" (from *Mamma son tanto felice*). In this story, one form of brutality leads to a cycle of violence that haunts several of its characters and scars two generations in two different spaces.

"A expiação" is divided into three parts: "Ritual," "Fim," and "Tocaia." Each segment relates different moments of a tragedy: the supposed murder of the character Orlando Spinelli by his "adoptive son," Badeco. Here I will only focus on the last segment of "A Expiação," "Fim." "Fim," interwoven between "Ritual" and "Tocaia," presents Badeco many years after his escape from the scene of the involuntary murder of his stepfather and the ensuing vengeance on behalf of Spinelli by his family. Escaping to São Paulo, he takes on the alias Jair. We encounter Jair on his deathbed. "Fim" has two parallel timelines: the story fluctuates between the protagonist's current death throes and his remembrances of life after he arrives in São Paulo. As in other segments of *Inferno provisório,* different typefaces indicate the two temporalities. Italics signal the past, and standard font type indicates the present. Using italics to signal the discourse of memory, Ruffato imbues reminiscence with a fluidity that vanishes in the lived moment, highlighting the notion of truncation, that is, of ending.

Initially the city represents an escape from arbitrary violence for Badeco/Jair, a domain where a perhaps rudimentary pursuit of citizenship is possible. Repeating the trajectory of countless rural migrants, Badeco/Jair gradually achieves the privileges of working-class status.[13] His social mobility parallels the progress of the urbanization of the metropolitan periphery,[14] the locales that James Holston has identified as being the primary sites of both disjunctive and insurgent citizenship. Material and symbolic signposts such as a full-

---

13. Holston notes that the movement of migrants to the urban periphery is motivated by the desire for homeownership, and for the independence and security that such property connotes (*Insurgent* 174).

14. As the periphery urbanizes, it also receives services such as running water and electricity, as well as schools, community centers, etc., services and spaces that address the needs of citizens for basic comfort and community.

time job, marriage, and homeownership reveal the piecemeal growth of social citizenship that parallels the development of the urban space, and, more concretely, the insertion of its peripheral terrains into the geographic and social mapping of the official *urbe*.[15] Homeownership in particular can signify not only social improvement but also advancement through the enactment of values such as entrepreneurship and material as well as social responsibility within the community (*Insurgent* 173).

Landed property ownership is of fundamental importance in the execution and (self) perception of citizenship (*Insurgent* 171).[16] "Fim" links the transformation of the family, whose very growth is an index of augmented financial stability, with the expansion of the home via autoconstruction of individual homes and the transformation of the peripheral landscape in which the family resides: "*And the children and progress came: Josué and electricity, sewage and running water; Jairzinho, pavement and an addition with two more rooms; Orlando, supermarkets and stores and another floor with a bathroom; Ruth, a health clinic and a room for herself*" (*Mamma* 94).[17] Domestic expansion is synonymous not only with private "advancement" but also with the "progress" of the public sphere through the periphery's increased urbanization. However, as Holston elucidates, a centrifugal urban evolvement does not necessarily correlate with the continual betterment of social and civil rights for the inhabitants of the urban periphery. Following the mold of disjunctive citizenship, peripheral expansion is often fraught with ongoing disparities, such as, for example, an inadequate (public) school system, a lack of public spaces and suitable public transportation, open sewers, and high crime rates, among other indicators.

The dichotomy between spatial evolution and social and, by extension, familial involution becomes the drama that unfurls in "Fim." Exigency contaminates the working-class idyll, claiming two of Badeco/Jair's sons, who get involved with drug-related criminality. The violence that bit-by-bit envelops the two young men literally penetrates the domestic haven, tainting all of its residents and transforming the house into a microcosm of the larger community:

---

15. James Holston observes that the development of the periphery via autoconstruction is paradoxical. He asserts that "settling the periphery to build a house of one's own is itself a spatial paradox: each instance of autoconstruction reproduces the periphery, pushing its leading edge farther into the hinterland; but in so doing, it brings the center and its promise of a different future that much closer to the individual house builder. Furthermore, as each autoconstructing family develops, the entire neighborhood evolves" (*Insurgent* 166).

16. See also Kowarick (*A espoliação*), Silva, and Rohe.

17. "*E os filhos e o progresso foram chegando: Josué, luz elétrica e rede de esgoto e água; Jairzinho, asfalto e um puxado com mais dois quartos; Orlando, supermercados e lojas e mais um andar com banheiro; Ruth, posto médico e um quarto só para ela.*"

(It seemed as if Ruth, the youngest of the children, would continue her studies. A good, intelligent girl . . . But things started going awry, her brothers got involved with the neighborhood's bad elements, the bandits, then came the fights, the confusion, the comings and goings day in, day out, the mother had a heart attack, sleepless nights, a dreadful sorrow. . . .) (*Mamma* 96)[18]

The transformative potential epitomized by the security of landed property—which fuels social aspirations (the continuation of education, in this case) is truncated by the social violence (a result of income disparity and curtailed possibilities for social ascension) that ultimately erupts into the private sphere. "Fim" thus signals the ending of one story (namely "A Expiação") but portends the tales of migration and social crises that constitute the kernel of *Inferno provisório*.

GROWING UP WORKING CLASS

Published in 2006, Guillermo Saccomanno's short novel *El pibe* also concentrates on proletarian spaces. Though the novel makes occasional excursions into the larger city of Buenos Aires, its primary stages are the working-class *porteño* neighborhoods of Mataderos and Floresta. *El pibe* is set primarily in the mid-1950s, during the second presidency (1952–55) of Juan Domingo Perón, whose figure looms in the background as a symbol of repressive-paternalistic authority. National history and politics are communicated through the individual stories of the *barrios*' inhabitants: for instance, the protagonist's anti-Peronist father, who witnesses the June 1955 bombing of the Plaza de Mayo (72), and the neighborhood children whose slingshot battles foreshadow their militant youth (102). As a result, the protagonist's urban vicinity becomes a microcosm of working-class Argentina.

The narrative, written in the first person, focuses on the protagonist's childhood and develops primarily between the two urban terrains of Mataderos and Floresta. Mataderos is depicted as a frontier land between city and country, between legality and transgression ("Upon entering Mataderos, one comes across little farms and pastures, the neighborhood is an assembly of homes inhabited by immigrants, *criollos* and shady characters" [15]).[19] In contrast, Flo-

---

18. (*Ruth, a caçula, parecia que ia levar adiante os estudos. Menina boa, inteligente. . .Mas as coisas começaram a andar erradas, os irmãos se meteram com a bandidagem do bairro, com os maus elementos, veio a brigalhada, a confusão, o entra-e-sai dia e noite, a mãe teve um ataque de nervos, noites em branco, uma tristeza danada. . .*).

19. "Adentrándose en Mataderos, se atraviesan quintas y potreros, el barrio es un caserío habitado por los inmigrantes, los criollos y el malevaje."

resta, separated from Mataderos by a stream, has petit bourgeois aspirations that are nonetheless invalidated by its residents' social status (they are mainly blue-collar workers and artisans) and by the precariousness of the public infrastructure in both neighborhoods. Their unpaved streets and shared proximity to the Lisandro de la Torre slaughterhouse indicate a lack of public investment in these urban areas. The description of muddy streets and stagnant pools of water in the two neighborhoods signifies how the effects of differentiated citizenship mark the cityscape in the form of inadequate public infrastructure.

In contrast to the modest homes and streets of Floresta and Mataderos is the recently founded Ciudad Evita (1947). Here live those who, thanks to their affiliation with the Peronist party, have ascended to the ranks of the petit bourgeoisie. Unlike the peripheral districts where the narrator spends his childhood, Ciudad Evita intimates order: "The streets are still unpaved, but the brand new little chalets, with their shingled roofs and their gardens[,] impart the neighborhood a respectable air of prosperity" (121).[20] Ciudad Evita emblematizes the model of disjunctive democracy that fosters differentiated citizenship. While Perón expanded the working classes' social rights (such as pension and healthcare benefits), many political and civil rights were curtailed during his time in power. Social rights were also attained mainly through a system of patronage that presupposed Peronist loyalty. Thus, the narrator's relatives are able to buy their home in Ciudad Evita thanks to their involvement in the party's Unidad Básica.[21] In contrast, social rights are denied to those who oppose the regime, threatening them with indigence (70). The novel suggests that differential social—as well as political and civic—rights are not specific to Perón's presidency, but would continue to be part of the national panorama in Argentina for several more decades.

As the narrative epicenter of Saccomanno's novel, Mataderos and its surrounding areas are not only the stages on which the story's events take place but also a character in the account. Its daily routines, the texture and rhythms of its streets, become an integral part of the storyline. Not coincidentally, *El pibe* opens with a description of the neighborhood, inverting the traditional establishing shot used in film through the reproduction of the (reverse) zoom that moves from detail (cattle trucks carrying their cargo to the frigorífico Lisandro de la Torre) to the larger environs:

> Crossing Directorio northbound, the pavement begins, contrary to the pockmarked dirt roads in our neighborhood. On that side, one is more middle class than here, just one block south, where the stench from the cattle, the

---

20. "Las calles todavía son de tierra, pero los chalecitos nuevos, con sus techos de tejas y sus jardines le otorgan un respetable aire de prosperidad."
21. Social and educational associations affiliated with the Peronist party.

pestilence from the processing plants and the stagnant water in the ditches make the air dense. Here the middle class declines into a Peronist proletariat with petit bourgeois aspirations. (13)[22]

The narrative gaze maps the city literally, but also symbolically, creating a social topography of sorts that remits the reader to the time of the narrative, the mid-1950s and early 1960s. Characters that signify the period, such as the narrator's anarchist great-uncle, the uncle who is a prodigal accordion player, and several immigrant figures (the beautiful Italian neighbor, the Portuguese baker, the Japanese dry cleaner), reinforce the novel's periodization. At the same time, the description of the cattle trucks at the beginning of the novel resonates with Argentina's literary past. The opening scenes of cattle waiting to be slaughtered alludes to Estebán Echevarría's short story *El matadero* (1839/1871), which concerns the conflicts between *federales* and *unitarios* during the presidency of Juan Manuel de Rosas (1835–52). Finally, the image is also a metaphor of the lack of agency experienced by several of the *barrios'* inhabitants, who seem trapped within their social condition/ing.

Though the narrator draws a correlation between the cattle awaiting slaughter and the residents of Mataderos and Floresta (26), *El pibe* does propose strategies of resistance. Specifically, Saccomanno's novel implies that homeownership, education, and writing are means of insurgent citizenship. Similar to Ruffato's *Inferno provisório*, homeownership is synonymous with respectability, and signifies socioeconomic ascension. In *El pibe*, this is emblematized by the Motorman's story. The Motorman is the narrator's deceased paternal grandfather, who worked as a train conductor. An Italian immigrant, he exemplifies empowerment through labor and the gradual autoconstruction of his home (36). For the Italian immigrant, homeownership connotes a transformation in the configuration of citizenship; it signifies that he has become an integral member of the (national) community. Referring to the importance of homeownership for the Brazilian working classes, sociologist Lúcio Kowarick maintains that owning (and building) a residence points to the shift of citizenship from the public to the private sphere. Through homeownership the subject becomes what Kowarick terms a "private citizen" (*A espoliação* 94). Though Kowarick specifically references the Brazilian context, one can argue that the material security that homeownership signifies transcends national

---

22. "Cruzando Directorio hacia el norte, empieza el empedrado, a diferencia de nuestras calles, que son de tierra y tienen zanjas. De aquel lado, se es más de clase media que acá, apenas una cuadra más al sur, donde el hedor del Ganado, las pestilencia de las curtiembres y el agua estancada de las zanjas enrarecen el aire, que todavía es de campo. Acá la clase media decae en un proletariado peronista con ínfulas de pequeña burguesía."

borders. Moreover, as indicated by Kowarick, homeownership also suggests insertion into a community, the strengthening of social ties.

Similarly to the characters of "Fim," for the Motorman, the expansion and improvement of the home theoretically provides a way out of the socioeconomic constraints that limit him and his family in the present. The home denotes stability. It is thus significant that for the Motorman, it should be made of bricks (37), a material that symbolizes solidity. However, after his death, the house that the Motorman literally constructed brick by brick falls into disrepair. Its disorder reflects the disarray of the current inhabitants, the Motorman's three younger sons. None of the three men has the same work ethic as their father or older brother, the narrator-protagonist's father. Rather, they fall prey to alcoholism and gambling and work in low-paying jobs that do not have the social prestige of a train conductor. If during the Motorman's lifetime the house was kept in perfect order, after his death and his sons' gradual social descent, the domicile becomes neglected (131–32). Neglect signifies a gradual retreat from the ideal of full-fledged citizenship, connoting the progressive advance of the three brothers into the realm of transgression. Indeed, later in the narrative, one of the brothers ends up in jail and the two others die of alcoholism.

Beyond homeownership, the novel also intimates that education also can serve as a tool to counter social disenfranchisement. Although he has little money, the narrator's father regularly invests some of his salary in books. For him, books are an instrument to achieve social improvement (147). In this sense, books signify both expenditure and income—symbolic earnings, but also, occasionally, hard cash. Thus, for example, at the end of the month, when there is no money left, the father must sell his beloved books (153). Nonetheless, selling his books demeans the father, for whom education is empowerment. By hawking his books, he is giving up part of his (real and imagined) agency. Disenfranchisement is highlighted in the description of the transaction's aftermath. After leaving the bookstore, father and son walk down Corrientes Avenue, one of Buenos Aires' main thoroughfares, known for its entertainment venues. It is a Saturday night and the street is bustling with life. However, the narrator remarks that he and his father are excluded from the merriment surrounding them (154). Despite the characters' aspirations and efforts at social improvement, *El pibe* makes it clear that the working class leads a precarious existence, teetering on the verge of poverty. As a result, working-class characters must develop varying strategies to cope with the effects of disjunctive citizenship. For the father, political militancy develops as his first coping strategy, seconded by education. Later, writing is his antidote against forgetting both personal stories and national history. Without memory—that is, without writing—agency is not possible. This becomes particularly evident in the book's ending. Set in the aftermath of the 1976 military coup de état, Buenos Aires has been transformed into a dangerous terrain, from which citizenship has effectively been erased due to the state of exception (Agamben):

> One morning (after the 1976 coup), while my father waits for the bus, a green Falcon brakes in front of the stop. Four men kidnap a young woman. My father struggles with them. One of the men hits him with a revolver. While they force her into a car, the woman shouts out a phone number. My father returns home crying. He forgot the number. (155)[23]

Jumping forward in time (from the 1960s to the mid-1970s), the narrative voice establishes a continuum of political and civil disenfranchisement. It is suggested that memory can help counteract this disempowerment, and that memory is made possible through writing.

For the father—and, by extension, the son, whose story we are reading—literature supplies a remedy of sorts against subjugation. Writing and, more specifically, literature serve both to comprehend better and to transcend Mataderos's and Floresta's suffocating social milieu. The father writes a novel, which, it is intimated, is completed by the son, whose narrative we read. The chronicle of everyday working-class life salvages the narrative of proletarian existence from the anonymity to which it generally is condemned.

Saccomanno's text proposes writing as a means of agency not only for the characters of *El pibe* but also for the readers who read their stories. And as we read these stories, we partake in this act of retrieving the stories of said social segment. Writing (and reading), which emerges within the cracks of disjunctive citizenship, becomes an expression of what Holston denominates "insurgent citizenship," a reclaiming of power from within marginal spaces. In this framework, the child's voice that resonates in *El pibe* and that will transmute into an adult voice is emblematic of hope as it provides an arena for the memory of the working classes.

In comparison, the subjects of Ruffato's narratives are mostly trapped in existences that vary from mediocre to miserable, and several struggle to transcend not only their geographic space (by repeating the trajectory of countless migrants from rural, small, and midsize towns into the larger conurbations of

---

23. "Una mañana (después del golpe de 76), mientras mi padre espera un colectivo, un Falcon verde frena en la parada. Cuatro tipos secuestran a una chica. Mi padre forceja con ellos. Uno de los tipos lo golpea con una pistola. Mientras la cargan en el auto, la chica grita un teléfono. Mi padre vuelve a casa llorando. Olvidó el número."

southeastern Brazil) but also their social conditions. However, even though disenchantment saturates the stories of *Inferno provisório,* the cycle's title also alludes to the possibility of redemption—perhaps also through the voicing of disjunctive citizenship, an insurgent consciousness can be forged.

That literature has become an important arena for (at least symbolically) retrieving social and cultural citizenship in Latin America is made evident through the recent popularity of marginal writers such as the *paulista* author Reginaldo Ferreira da Silva (Ferréz) and the Argentine Washington Cucurto, who depict life at the socioeconomic borders. Ferréz and Cucurto both recycle and challenge prevailing stereotypes about low-income urban communities, as for example the purported widespread criminality that exists in these communities. As such these authors, similarly to Ruffato and Saccomanno, employ writing as a form of insurgent agency that serves to make the reader aware of the problems faced by impoverished citizens while also addressing and interrogating the middle-class reader's prejudices about these subjects.

Beyond these writers, cooperative publishing initiatives such as Eloísa Cartonera, founded in 2003 by Cucurto and the artist Javier Barilaro in Buenos Aires, and its Brazilian counterpart, Dulcinéia Catadora, created in 2007 by the artist Lucia Rosa and by Peterson Emboava, the son of paper collectors (with the support of Eloísa Cartonera), are also playing a part in the contestation of differentiated citizenship. Both ventures publish books by known and emerging writers on reclaimed cardboard, which they buy from local paper collectors at higher prices than these materials would normally fetch. The books are adorned with work from local artists, often members of disadvantaged communities. Both cooperatives aim to value the work of paper collectors, foster new literary and artistic talent, especially that from economically disenfranchised communities, and encourage social consciousness through culture.

Finally, cultural initiatives with a social bent are increasingly going mainstream, thus reaching a wider audience. After printing his first novel, *Capão Pecado,* in 2000 with the smaller, alternative press Labortexto Editorial, Ferrréz reissued this book with the well-established publishing house Objetiva in 2003. Cucurto, on the other hand, has also distributed several of his works with Emecé that, similar to Objetiva, is also commercial publisher. And his novel *Cosa de negros* (2003) was translated into Portuguese and came out with Rocco in 2007. Furthermore, both Eloísa Cartonera and Dulcinéia Catadora have built an international reputation and achieved commercial success. Eloísa Cartonera, the first of this type of venture, has spawned similar initiatives not only in other Argentine cities but also throughout Latin America. Beyond Dulcinéia Catadora, other *cartonera* projects can be found in Chile (Animita Cartonera), Peru (Sarita Cartonera), Bolivia (Madágora Cartonera and Yerbamala Cartonera), Paraguay (Yiyi Jambo and Felicita Cartonera), and Mexico (La Cartonera and Santa Muerte Cartonera). Dulcinéia Catadora has recently opened an exposition, entitled "O Abrigo e o Terreno" (Shelter and Land), in the Museu de Arte do Rio de Janeiro. It is also attempting to spread its model to other communities in São Paulo.

Similar to the novels analyzed in this essay, the above-cited marginal literary expressions and enterprises are phenomena that point towards a (re)conceptualization of culture as a tool of insurgent citizenship that employs the elements of social disempowerment (i.e., tales of socioeconomic marginalization and paper debris, collected by an informal and socioeconomically disenfranchised workforce respectively) to reclaim a measure of social, economic, and symbolic agency.

WORKS CITED

Aboy, Rosa. *"Ellos y nosotros": Fronteras sociales en los años del primer peronismo.* Ecole des hautes études en sciences sociales, 2008.

Agamben, Giorgio. *State of Exception.* Trans. Kevin Attel. Chicago: U of Chicago P, 2005.

Appadurai, Arjun, and James Holston. "Introduction: Cities and Citizenship." *Cities and Citizenship.* Ed. James Holston. Durham: Duke UP, 1999. 1–20.

Caldeira, Teresa P. R. *City of Walls: Crime, Segregation, and Citizenship in São Paulo.* Berkeley: U of California P, 2000.

Campesi, Giuseppe. "Policing, Urban Poverty and Insecurity in Latin America." *Theoretical Criminology* 14.4 (2010): 447–71.

Cucurto, Washington. *Coisa de negros.* Rio de Janeiro: Rocco, 2007.

———. *Cosa de negros.* Argentina: Interzona, 2003.

Dagnino, Evelina. "Citizenship: A Perverse Confluence." *Development in Practice* 17.4–5 (2007): 549–56.

Davis, Mike. *Planet of Slums.* London: Verso, 2006.

Ferréz. *Manual prático do ódio.* Rio de Janeiro: Objetiva, 2003.

Harvey, David. *The Urban Experience.* Oxford: Blackwell, 1989.

Holston, James. *Insurgent Citizenship: Disjunctions of Democracy and Modernity in Brazil.* Princeton: Princeton UP, 2008.

Kowarick, Lúcio. *Escritos urbanos.* São Paulo: Editora 34, 2000.

———. *A espoliação urbana.* Rio de Janeiro, RJ: Editora Paz e Terra, 1980.

March, Carlos. "Participation and Democracy: The Case of Argentina." *Citizenship in Latin America.* Ed. Joseph S. Tulchin and Meg Ruthenburg. Boulder, CO: Lynne Rienner, 2007. 219–34.

Marshall, T. H. *Citizenship and Social Class, and Other Essays.* Cambridge: Cambridge UP, 1950.

Ortega-Alcázar, Iliana. "Five Windows into Latin American Cities: Current Research from Brazil, Argentina, Chile, and Mexico." *Space and Culture* 12.4 (2009): 435–41.

Rohe, William, S. Van Zandt, and George McCarthy. "Home Ownership and Access to Opportunity." *Housing Studies* 17.1 (2002): 51–61.

Roitman, Sonia. "Who Segregates Whom? The Analysis of a Gated Community in Mendoza, Argentina." *Housing Studies* 20.2 (2005): 303–21.

Rotker, Susana, and Katherine Goldman. *Citizens of Fear: Urban Violence in Latin America*. New Brunswick: Rutgers UP, 2002.

Ruffato, Luiz. Interview by Eliane Brum. "A igreja do livro transformador. O escritor Luiz Ruffato conta como foi salvo pela literatura. Entrevista com Luiz Ruffato." *Época* 31 (Jan. 2011). Web. 24 Feb. 2011.

———. Interview by Heloísa Buarque de Holanda and Ana Ligia Matos. "Literatura com um projeto." *Revista Z* 4.1 (2006). Web. 11 Feb. 2010.

———. *Mamma, son tanto felice*. Rio de Janeiro: Record, 2005.

Saccomanno, Guillermo. Interview by Flavia Costa. "La patria de los rencores." *Clarín* (2003). Web. Feb. 2011.

———. *El pibe*. Buenos Aires: Planeta, 2006.

Sassen, Saskia. *Cities in a World Economy*. Thousand Oaks, CA: Pine Forge, 2000.

Silva, Ana A. *Moradia e cidadania: Um debate em movimento*. São Paulo, SP: Pólis, 1994.

Soja, Edward W. *Seeking Spatial Justice*. Minneapolis: U of Minnesota P, 2010.

Stanley, Ruth. "'Living in a Jungle': State Violence and Perceptions of Democracy in Buenos Aires." *Violent Democracies in Latin America*. Eds. Enrique Desmond Arias and Daniel Goldstein. Durham: Duke UP, 2010. 133–60.

Ventura, Zuenir. *Cidade partida*. São Paulo, Brazil: Companhia das Letras, 1994.

Vidal-Koppmann, Sonia. "Fragmentación socio-espacial en la periferia de la región metropolitana de Buenos Aires." *Journal of Latin American Geography* 8.1 (2009): 79–97.

Yashar, Deborah J. "Citizenship Regimes, the State, and Ethnic Cleavages." *Citizenship in Latin America*. Eds. Joseph S. Tulchin and Meg Ruthenburg. Boulder, CO: Lynne Rienner, 2007. 59–74.

PART III

LUSO-HISPANIC POETRY, MUSIC, AND EXPRESSIVE CULTURE

CHAPTER 9

The *Parábola* of the Latin American Avant-Gardes

ALFREDO BOSI
TRANSLATED BY ROBERT PATRICK NEWCOMB

I Saw the World. It Began in Recife.[1]
—Title of a painting by Cícero Dias, shown in the "Revolutionary Salon,"[2] 1931

IF WE CONSIDER our literary avant-garde movements from a purely synchronic perspective, that is, if we view them as a *cultural system* that can be defined spatially and temporally, they suggest the form of a mosaic of paradoxes. They resist the historian's attempts to describe them synthetically, with the search for common elements blocked at every turn by contrasting judgments and positions. The contemporary reader, if interested in detecting the character of this continent-wide avant-garde movement, the *quid* that allows us to distinguish it from its European counterpart, may look to the defects embodied in opposing tendencies that, in many cases, were pushed to the extremes: our avant-garde movements were marked by both *excesses of imitation* and *excesses of originality*.

Those who insist on this synchronic approach are confronted, at times in the same group or journal, with manifestos in which cosmopolitan modernity (which risks shifting from modernity to a parody thereof, and which employs a Babel of recently imported signs evocative of technology)[3] stands side by side with the heart-felt exigencies of national, or even ethnic identity, the latter

---

Originally dated January 1991 and published as "A Parábola das Vanguardas Latino-Americanas," in *Vanguardas Latino-Americanas: Polêmicas, Manifestos e Textos Críticos*.
   1. *Eu Vi o Mundo, Ele Começava em Recife*
   2. "Salão Revolucionário"
   3. [. . .] *até à fronteira do modernoso e do modernóide com toda a sua babel de signos tomados a um cenário técnico recém-importado* [. . .]. In cases in which I have taken greater

coupled with denunciations of the imperialism that from the first has decimated the peoples of Latin America.

In this way, within the same current—for instance, the Brazilian modernists during their most combative phase (from 1922 to 1930, approximately)—aesthetic values *and* nationalist protests impose themselves on the researcher who attempts to be both analytical and free of bias. The historian is ultimately compelled to adopt a language composed of terms that are semantically contradictory though syntactically acceptable: "modernism was cosmopolitan and nationalistic"; "avant-garde movements sought inspiration in the *-isms* of Paris *as well as* in indigenous myths and Afro-Antillean rites"; or even "Latin American art of the 1920s was *not only* absolutely pure, *but also* radically engaged."

This static reading tends to collapse under the weight of the antinomies it attempts to aggregate. The avant-garde movements were not compact like a rock crystal, nor did they form a cohesive system in which each facet reflected the uniform structure of the whole. The avant-gardes should be considered within the flux of time, a temporal movement that describes a parabola that passes through diverse points or moments.

However, a vision of the avant-garde movements that aspires to comprehend their differing modes and rhythms should not obscure the image of another unity, one marked by suffering and necessarily by contradiction: the unity of an overarching social process which gave birth to our avant-garde movements. The differences between a movement *a* and a movement *b*, or between varying positions within the same movement, only become plainly intelligible when understood in the context of the *colonial condition*,[4] a historical phenomenon of long duration in which prestigious metropolitan models, and the fumbling search for origins and an original identity, maintain a structural relationship of conjunction and mutual tension.

In the most vigorous writers, whose complex internal lives allowed them to wrest themselves free from a language of order, it is the search for a simultaneously universal and personal form of expression that guides their poetics and their aesthetic achievements. For example, the apparently abrupt transitions one notes in certain passages from Mário de Andrade and Borges are the products of aesthetic and ideological forces operating beyond the pendulous oscillations of avant-garde fashion. This said, since nothing occurs outside of history (understood in its totality, that is, in its public and private dimensions), the choices made by these two artists, so distinct from one another,

---

than usual license or when there exist less-than-ideal options for the translation of a phrase, I provide the original version of the relevant phrase in a footnote.—Trans.

4. For Bosi's discussion of the colonial condition, see his classic 1992 study *Dialética da Colonização*.—Trans.

are inscribed within a dialectic defined by *reproduction of the other* and *self-discovery*, which moves through all colonial or dependent cultures.

This dialectic's twin poles, observed within a short period (the 1920s through the end of the 1930s), appear reversible: one term, whether cosmopolitanism or nationalism, need not necessarily precede the other; either one can be said to occupy the first position, given their complementarity as two aspects of the same process.

To blaze a path through the most advanced international artistic currents, and to then draw on the treasures of popular indigenous-luso-black culture—this was the task of Mário de Andrade, founder of *desvairismo* (hallucinationism) and, a few years thereafter, a participant in the struggle to build up a national literature. Following the same path, but moving in the opposite direction, was Jorge Luis Borges, first the young poet of *porteño* magic, and later, the most cosmopolitan of Spanish American writers. Might the avant-garde be a bridge with traffic running in two directions?

The polarizing tendencies of the avant-garde groups, likewise the changes in direction of individual participants, are the products of a condition of dependency that is multidirectional. Otherwise these positions and movements cannot be explained. Or, rather, they are misleadingly described when attributed exclusively to the presumed inconsistency of peripheral cultural formations.

We may note the richness of some of these trajectories, for instance, those traveled by Vallejo, Mário de Andrade, Oswald de Andrade, Carpentier, and Mariátegui. And we may consider certain polemical concepts (such as Mário's "pragmatic nationalism" and "critical nationalism," Oswald's "cannibalism," Mariátegui's "incomplete nation" and "sketched-out nation,"[5] or, from another perspective, Asturias's "magical realism" and Carpentier's "marvelous real") in order to recognize in these adventures of thought and fantasy the workings of an internal logic and the expression of a hunger for truth.

Both of the directional movements mentioned above (from the incorporation of the other to the search for identity, and vice versa) require an intellectual effort that aspires to uncover an underlying meaning in the history of the avant-garde movements and in the cultural production that followed in the wake of the avant-garde, over the course of the 1930s.

In Borges and in the efforts of the intellectuals of our America to avoid the pitfalls of provincialism we see the motivating force that gave rise to these verses by Argentina's Oliverio Girondo, the brilliant literary experimenter of the 1920s and the author of the nationally evocative *Campo nuestro* (*Our Countryside*, 1946):

---

5. *esboço de nação*

Never permit, country, that our
thirst for horizons and movement be quenched[6]

The *pampa* is origin, but not determining meaning. It is wellspring, but not limit. It provides inaugural images, but does not contain the definitive word. Here *Campo nuestro* should be understood figuratively: it is a metonym for all of the landscapes that inspire regional-universal poetry. Poetry drinks at the well of memory and sight, but the poet modulates his verse to fit the imagination's curious notation, into which flow both the accumulated perceptions of our days and the dreams of a life not constrained by fixed borders. In fashioning the truth of poetry (and this is the lesson of another avant-garde, which dates from the pre-Romantics), the real, the unreal, and the fluctuating space between the real and unreal, which we call *the possible,* make equally legitimate contributions.

I will draw on an example taken from another regional context to illustrate the movement toward universalization.

Alejo Carpentier's early novel *¡Ecué-Yamba-O!,* from 1933, is the author's exercise in singular attention to Afro-Cuban rites. It can also be understood as the subterranean pre-history of a wide-ranging narrative project in which the "particular"—where God lives, in Warburg's fine formulation—offers Carpentier the most fruitful means for describing the enigmatic face of the universal.

"We must take *our things, our men* and project them onto events of universal significance so that the American setting ceases to be exotic."[7] These are the words of the author of *El siglo de las luces* (Explosion in a Cathedral) and *El recurso del método* (Reasons of State), works that weave together the delicate strands that connect pre-Columbian myths to the history of the West and, conversely, the Latin American past to universal myths. And if we dig down to the sources of Carpentier's thought and poetics, we find the same ideas that animated the most expressive of Cuba's avant-garde journals, *Revista de Avance,* perhaps the first journal to publish the island's so-called black poetry. We should recall that it was the journal's editor, Jorge Mañach, who in 1928 published his *Indignación del Choteo* (Inquiry into "el choteo"), an essay in which he proposed to sketch out *cubanidad*. Taken as a whole, Alejo Carpentier's work marks the movement from *campo nuestro* (our countryside) to *nuestra sed de horizonte y de galope* (our thirst for horizons and movement), as mentioned by the avant-garde writer Girondo.

Let us now turn to another movement described by the parabola: that which ostensibly breaks with the past and attacks academic conventions,

---

6. "Nunca permitas, campo, que se agote / Nuestra sed de horizonte y de galope"

7. "Hay que tomar *nuestras cosas, nuestros hombres* y proyectarlos en los acontecimientos universales para que el escenario americano deje de ser una cosa exótica."

denouncing them as "realist" or "slavish copies." Here we find the core of all of the formally innovative avant-garde movements: the championing of a "new" or "modern spirit," which unites futurists and *ultraístas*, creationists and Dadaists, *desvairistas* and Stridentists. But what, we might ask, did these tendencies absorb from contemporaneous European movements?

They absorbed the fundamental idea of *the autonomy of the aesthetic sphere*, a radical idea that is the product of post-Romantic modernity. According to sociologically inclined interpretations (whether Marxist or Weberian), the aesthetic avant-gardes represent the spearhead of the modern process by which art becomes "autonomous," in that these movements are analogous to an increasingly acute division of labor and to the technical specialization which occurs in advanced industrial societies.

This thesis, which is tied down by determinism,[8] was contextualized by Leon Trotsky in his interpretation of futurism. He observed that the futurists' most strident idealizations of technology did not issue from countries in which industry had become dominant (the United States, Great Britain, and Germany). Rather, they were made by writers from less developed nations, like the Russia of the cubist-futurists, and Italy, the homeland of Marinetti.[9]

The texts of the formally innovative avant-gardes, then, were not produced in mechanical fashion by economic progress. Instead, they found fertile ground in the periphery, or, rather, in a particular periphery in which an ardent desire for the new was stronger than the objective conditions of modernity.

Certain Mexican, Argentine, and Brazilian journals and manifestos from the 1920s bear out Trotsky's thesis, which should be understood dialectically, given that some of the most lucid avant-garde writers of the same period, like Vallejo, Mariátegui, and Mário de Andrade, rejected Marinetti's mythology of the machine and, to a greater degree, the traces of fascist rhetoric contained in his work. The reproduction of the other in dependent countries is neither always nor invariably blind, nor is the possession of a critical faculty the privilege of those who have finished first in the race toward revolutionary technical change and imperial hegemony.

I believe that the basic point to consider with regard to the question of the "transplantation" of aesthetic currents is that we must determine the *significance* for Latin American art of the avant-garde's renewed contact with European culture during the first quarter of the twentieth century.

---

8. *que se escora no travejamento de nexos deterministas*

9. Trotsky states: "The backward countries which were without any special degree of spiritual culture, reflected in their ideology the achievements of the advanced countries more brilliantly and strongly [. . .] In the same way, Futurism obtained its most brilliant expression, not in America and not in Germany, but in Italy and in Russia" (126–27).

The retrospective view that we are afforded now, seventy years removed from the emergence of the avant-garde, favors the discarding of the superfluous and the preservation of what is essential.

Granted, we did not invent the theory of the autonomy of art, but we were able to develop its most potentially productive general precept: the principle of freedom, understood in both its constructive and expressive dimensions.

Aesthetic freedom is the *a priori* of all literary avant-gardes. A sense of freedom allows, on one hand, for playful actions in the present moment that work toward the creation and combination of forms. On the other hand, it broadens the subjective terrain, by achieving a higher degree of critical consciousness (the cornerstone of modernity), through the only apparently contradictory action of opening writing to those affective pulsations that prevailing standards tend to censure.

To form freely, to think freely, to express freely: this is the truly radical legacy of the "new spirit" that the Latin American avant-gardes introduced to their respective national contexts.

This does not amount to a case of borrowing of-the-minute themes and terms, that is, a case in which elements of only passing importance are imported. Rather, this is the activation of a principle that affirms itself in the negativity of its action. In the same way, ethical freedom does not bring with it readily applicable moral content (except when farcical), but rather clears the terrain of oppressive elements and false attitudes, leaving the conscience free to choose and judge ways of acting as it sees fit.

Freedom allows the "thirst for horizons and movement" to be satisfied where and when one wishes. As such, it must first break with objectionable affirmations[10] and ossified conventions. Then, or in the course of the struggle, the writer will confront his subject, and he will be pushed back to his own vital and socially significant experiences. Freedom, then, will demarcate new terms and limits, and will require the right tone, the proper perspective. And the modernist will give himself over to a modernity that transcends fashion.

The landscape, which tightly binds freedom and action, was utilized by those poets and writers who moved along the parabola toward the proclamation of liberating ideas in their "fumbling search for identity," which, as we saw pages earlier, is one of the poles of literary expression under the colonial condition.

The breaks having been removed, it was a time of departure—but for where? To the terrain of social history, to the terrain of subjective history. César Vallejo, Mário de Andrade, Oswald de Andrade, José Carlos Mariátegui, Leopoldo Marechal: these are names that give exemplary definition to

---

10. *má positividade*

this journey. What was it that gave them intimate knowledge of Italian and Russian futurism, of German expressionism, of French surrealism? It was the desire for new intellectual and artistic experience, which immediately shielded them from the half-naturalistic, half-Parnassian clichés of the *belle époque*, and threw them into the search for the Brazilian, Peruvian, or Argentine "character" or "non-character." This was an adventure pregnant with aesthetic significance as well as one that was eminently social and political.

If our discourse remains faithful to its dialectical inspiration (through which repetition and difference call upon and clarify each other), we may qualify the dualisms that so often mark our scholarly language when it adopts the severe tone of a polemic: avant-gardes of pure art *versus* avant-gardes of engaged art; the aesthetic option *versus* the ideological option, and so on. The movement along the parabola that we are trying to describe here does not allow our thought to become stranded among the oppositions put forth by dated attitudes. What interests the historian is to see whether and when there exists the potential for movement between the poles—a potential that is imminent to the tension between them.

The new literature's initial rejection of already exhausted styles gave it the strength to take on the cognitive and expressive work entailed in all symbolic actions. In the wake of *Macunaíma, Memórias Sentimentais de João Miramar* (Sentimental Memoirs of João Miramar), *Siete ensayos de interpretación de la realidad peruana* (Seven Interpretive Essays on Peruvian Reality), and *Adán Buenosayres* (which Marechal began writing around 1930), it does not seem necessary to separate, as if geometrically, the assimilation of the principle of formal liberty from anthropological self-examination, since these tendencies coexist with one another, and, indeed, were present in intertwined form in the most creative productions that followed the avant-garde manifestos.

There came a moment in which the Latin American artist, impelled by his knowledge of the other, looked upon himself and saw the human, and therefore universal, face in his own songs and myths, in his everyday passions and in figures of memory.

Research into one's own culture achieved varying degrees of originality relative to contemporaneous developments in European literature. Here, it is the notable diversity of Latin American social formations and paces of development that account for differences within post-avant-garde literature, as well as its ideological and artistic results.

Cultures containing dense and significant non-European layers gave birth to a sort of "marked" literature that contrasted with metropolitan literatures. This was the case of the Quechua Peru of Ciro Alegría and José María Arguedas, of the Aztec and *mestizo* Mexico of Agustín Yáñez and Juan Rulfo, of the *maya-quiché* Guatemala of Asturias, of the Guarani Paraguay of the early Roa Bastos, of the black Cuba of Nicolás Guillén, of the *mestizo* Puerto Rico of Luis Palés Matos, of the mulatto Antilles of Carpentier, Jean Price Mars, and Aimé Césaire. This is the partial case of the black and mulatto Brazilian Northeast of Jorge de Lima. All of these benefited from the gust of freedom that blew in on the wind during the 1920s. The *sertão* of Minas Gerais (Portuguese, black, and *caboclo*) described in *Sagarana*, Guimarães Rosas's first collection of novellas, does not lie completely outside of this grouping, though it does remit to a peculiarly Brazilian context in which Portuguese retained its hegemony during the process of linguistic miscegenation.

In these and in other contexts we see the outlines of what I term a *vanguardia enraizada* (rooted avant-garde),[11] an aesthetic project that finds in its own habitat the materials, themes, certain forms, and, principally, the *ethos* that give form to the work of creation.

We may cite examples from other art forms, such as music and painting, in giving definition to this term. Heitor Villa-Lobos's *Bachianas Brasileiras* (Brazilian Bachianas) and the Mexican Carlos Chávez's *Sinfonía India* (Indian Symphony), both composed during the 1930s, are brilliant musical syntheses, modern, postimpressionistic interpretations of autochthonous timbres, rhythms, and musical phrases. Once again, liberty and choice stand side by side.

Critics have already noted how successfully the Mexican muralists—Siqueiros, Rivera, and Orozco—fused themes taken from national history with formal elements suggestive of cubism and expressionism. As early as his "Tres llamamientos de orientación actual a los pintores y escultores de la nueva generación americana" (A New Direction for the New Generation of American Painters and Sculptors, 1921), David Alfaro Siqueiros had affirmed *"the preponderance of the constructive spirit over the decorative or analytical"* (an idea taken from Cézanne) and called for "an understanding of the admirable human context of *Negro Art* and *Primitive Art* in general." In this vein, Siqueiros insisted:

> We must come closer to the work of the ancient settlers of our valleys, the Indian painters and sculptors (*Mayas, Aztecs, Incas,* etc.); our physical proximity to them will help us to absorb the constructive vigour of their work, in which there is evident knowledge of the elements of nature, and these things can be our point of departure. We must adopt their synthetic energy.[12]

---

11. See Bosi, "A Vanguarda Enraizada (O Marxismo Vivo de Mariátegui)."—Trans.

12. See *Art and Revolution* 21–22. There is, in this appeal by the great Mexican artist, a perspicacity and a balance of positions that the dogmatic tone of Siqueiros's and Rivera's decla-

The metaphor of rootedness risks sounding naturalistic, and for this reason we should clarify its meaning to avoid potential misunderstandings. I understand the word as alluding to the idea of cultural and existential context. This sphere encompasses the most prosaic of quotidian perceptions—the tightened web[13] of necessity—as well as its opposite, the polysemous figures of the imagination. These figures are subject to the ambivalence of symbolic forms, for though they are the products of desire, they aspire to the status of "mental object" and "precise fantasy," to draw on Leonardo's terminology for art.

A writer can "root himself" in a number of ways. He may feel and communicate his great pleasure in describing the most humble surface elements of his environment, and in doing so achieve a truthful and vital neorealism. But he may also, depending on his calling, plumb the mythical depths of his youth and discover in the labyrinths of memory the archetypes of love and death, of hope and fear, of struggle and resignation—feelings that are proper to narratives from all latitudes. *Leyendas de Guatemala* (Legends of Guatemala), *Hombres de maíz* (Men of Maize), *Vidas Secas* (Barren Lives), *Fogo Morto* (Dead Fire), *Sagarana, El reino de este mundo* (The Kingdom of this World), *Los ríos profundos* (Deep Rivers): oh, how they can be mined for particular and universal truths!

Their narrators inherited from the intellectual revolution of the interwar years the idea that the spirit should venture where it pleases. And for this reason, they ignored strictures imposed by schools and groups, resolutely attending to materials taken from their own lives and thoughts.

Comparing their achievements in terms of novelistic structure and style with the old regionalisms of their respective literatures, we can see how thoroughly, and in various respects, the avant-garde cleared the narrative terrain: the representation of space, the sense of time, the oral quality of dialogues, the authenticity of tone, and the crafting of point of view.

In Asturias's Guatemalan legends, familiar landscapes are given the magical aura of strange places seen as if for the first time. Here is a felicitous case in which contact with surrealism stimulated in the narrator-poet a desire to uncover what is potentially mysterious in the relationships between human beings, between men and women, and between man and nature.

In Graciliano Ramos's incisive prose the ruinous depravation of the life of the *sertanejo* (inhabitant of the backlands) of the Brazilian Northeast is analyzed without folkloric condescension or bourgeois prejudices.

---

rations sometimes worked to obscure. This dogmatism, in my opinion, has undercut muralism's critical fortunes. For a reading that is both sympathetic and lucid, see Luis Cardoza y Aragón.

13. *a rede apertada*

And the words of the Peruvian peasant, even when conveyed in Argueda's clear Spanish, are marked by accents and syntactic modulations that only an affectionate closeness to the Quechua language could have inspired.

Dedication to the ethical coincided with the search for a language in which truth and beauty would find the correct path.

The literature of the 1930s and 1940s created a new image (dense, dramatic, and challenging) of areas of the continent in which centuries of domination left—and continue to leave—deep marks: the northeastern *sertão*, the black Antilles, the highland villages of Central America and Peru.

Anthropological and historical studies of the diverse ethnic and social formations of Latin America moved in lockstep with the aforementioned literary production, and were sensitive to issues of artistry and literary composition.

In Cuba, Fernando Ortiz, a valiant researcher of popular traditions (music, dance, *santería*, etc.) and the Afro-Antillean economy, inspired and accompanied Nicolás Guillén during the initial stages of his composition of his *poesía mulata* (mulatto poetry) and supported the young Alejo Carpentier's efforts to delve into the secrets of the local past.

In Peru, a well-developed line of research into the Incan and pre-Incan civilizations, which brought together the ethnologists Julio Tello and Castro Pozo, the essayist Mariátegui, and the painter José Sabogal, had profound repercussions for José María Arguedas's narrative work and political ideas.

In Mexico, José Vasconcelos, the mind behind *La raza cósmica* (The Cosmic Race), in his capacity as Minister of Education, gave long-term support to the muralists Rivera, Siqueiros, and Orozco.

In Brazil, the influential social anthropologist Gilberto Freyre inspired José Lins do Rego to adopt narrative forms that utilized oral tradition to capture his childhood experience as a plantation boy in the state of Paraíba.

Layered individual and group memories, as expressed in novelistic writing and anthropological research, worked to differentiate a conventional and naturalistic treatment of these social formations from an affective and often politically engaged reconstruction of the day-to-day experience of these formations.

One other achievement that is absolutely worthy of note, and that is common to intellectuals as distinct from one another as Ortiz, Mariátegui, and Gilberto Freyre, is the overcoming of the idea of *race*. During these years of the pre-Nazi period, the Latin American intelligentsia made an irreversible qualitative leap. As is well known, the same did not occur in the case of José Vasconcelos, a notable public figure, but also a confused mixer of Darwinism, Nietzsche, and the most extreme nationalism.

The same principle of aesthetic liberation that preceded the rediscovery of a popular ethos and of social conditions on the continent was also active in novelists and poets attracted to the particularities of inter- and intrasubjective reality. Utilizing tools that entailed a high degree of analytical rigor (such as internal monologue and the shifting of narrative focus), these writers expanded the boundaries of psychological realism so as to encompass dreams, delirium, and a cruel hyperawareness of modern urban anomie and alienation.

This literature, forged from the urbanite's achievement of self-knowledge, lies somewhere between "objective" and "expressionistic." It too can be considered "rooted," given that history's contradictions fashion an internal, lived, and imagined object that is as real as those wrought from collective destinies.

I am thinking of the Buenos Aires and the Santa María—simultaneously imagined and real, a closed-off purgatory of souls and a place with an absolutely familiar geography—which appear in Juan Carlos Onetti's short stories and in his tortured *Tierra de nadie* (No Man's Land). I am thinking of the nightmarish Porto Alegre of Dionélio Machado's *Os Ratos* (The Rats). And there is certainly much that we can find in the veins opened by the author's experience of a changing city in Mário de Andrade's short stories and in his "Meditação sobre o Tietê" (Meditation on the Tietê), so profoundly evocative of São Paulo. This is also true of Carlos Drummond de Andrade's poetry and Marques Rebelo's short stories and novels—perplexed and ironic filters of day-to-day life in Rio de Janeiro.

Examples can merely indicate, and may be complemented. For example: Latin American criticism has yet to map the paths, some of them winding and unexpected, taken by surrealism in the development of our poetry during the 1930s and 1940s.

Murilo Mendes, Jorge de Lima, César Moro, a certain Neruda, the young Octavio Paz, Xavier Villarrutia, and Lezama Lima await a collective reading that accounts for the interweaving of the avant-garde and belief (religious or immanent) as manifested in the Orphic powers of image and poetry.

What matters, ultimately, is that we contemplate the variety of paths—some taken during daylight, others nocturnal, some traveled in groups, others alone—that the avant-garde cleared for the Latin American writers who were associated with it or who came in its immediate wake. Its destiny as a bridge seems to me to also be its greatest promise: a promise of wide-open freedom to choose this or that concrete option. But it is not just a bridge; it is also a pier from which one departs, a runway from which one takes off, a free space that allows the writer to leap over the barriers that separate the territory already charted from the horizon he hopes to reach.

But the opposite may also occur: the avant-garde, instead of permitting movement, may also appropriate new forms and exalt in itself, abstractly. Instead of bridges, it may build windmills of letters and houses of cards.

WORKS CITED

Belluzzo, Ana Maria de Moreas, ed. *Modernidade: Vanguardas Artísticas na América Latina.* São Paulo: Memorial da América Latina / Unesp, 1990.

Bosi, Alfredo. *Dialética da Colonização.* 4th ed. 8th printing. São Paulo: Companhia das Letras, 1992.

———. "A Parábola das Vanguardas Latino-Americanas." *Vanguardas Latino-Americanas: Polêmicas, Manifestos e Textos Críticos.* Ed. Jorge Schwartz. São Paulo: EDUSP; Iluminuras, FADESP, 1995. 19–28.

———. "A Vanguarda Enraizada (O Marxismo Vivo de Mariátegui)." *Estudos Avançados* 8 (Jan.–Apr. 1990): 50–61.

Cardoza y Aragón, Luis. "El humanismo y la pintura mural mexicana." *Casa de las Américas* 161, Havana (Mar.–Apr. 1987): 101–7.

Siqueiros, David Alfaro. *Art and Revolution.* Trans. Sylvia Calles. London: Lawrence and Wishart, 1975.

Trotsky, Leon. *Literature and Revolution.* New York: Russell & Russell, 1957.

CHAPTER 10

Brazilian Symbolism and Hispanic American *Modernismo*

Resonance across the Luso-Hispanic Divide

SARAH MOODY

> *Eu quero em rude verso altivo adamastórico,*
> *vermelho, colossal, d'estrépito, gongórico,*
> *castrar-vos como um touro—ouvindo-vos urrar!*
> —João da Cruz e Sousa, "Escravocratas"[1]

A SHIFT occurred in poetry around the dawn of the twentieth century, when many poets came to believe they had exhausted the possibilities of metrical regularity, and the battle cry of "Freedom!" increasingly inspired their work. As science and industry grew in importance, making the world seem ever more objective and regularized, the poets' traditional specialization in the subjective lost its social prestige. After all, what use was a poet, when society purported to need "order and progress"?[2] Some poets advocated a return to themes of enchantment, mystery, and beauty that had been developed during romanticism; in Latin America, as elsewhere around the world, some found inspiration in the work of French symbolists, who emphasized the importance of individual experience and evocative, fluid verse. The continent echoed with the explorations of both phonic regularity and rhythmic breaks. Though contact between the Hispanic American *modernistas* and the Brazilian symbolists was limited, the two groups share certain characteristics due in part to their common inspiration in the tradition of French symbolism. A focus on subjectivity as poetry's defining element, as well as an insistence on verse's musicality and a sense of frustration with rationalism, stand out as important

---

1. "I want with coarse, haughty, monstrous verse, / vermillion, colossal, thunderous, Gongoresque, / to castrate you like a bull—hearing you roar!" (João da Cruz e Sousa, "Enslavers" 145). Unless otherwise noted in the bibliography, all translations of quotations are my own.

2. The values of "ordem e progresso" (order and progress) were enshrined in the 1889 Brazilian flag, still in use today.

commonalities between Brazilian symbolism and Hispanic American modernism.[3] Drawing on local romantic traditions, the symbolists and *modernistas* favored spirituality and aestheticism over a realist mode, often considering the minutest details of a poem as symbolic of a cosmic order to which the poet has special access.[4]

In Hispanic America as in Brazil, many poets rejected the period's increasing emphasis on the values of positivism, such as the "ordem e progresso" of the 1889 Brazilian flag, using their verse to distance themselves from what they saw as a prevailing obsession with material progress. Modernists including Rubén Darío, Manuel Gutiérrez Nájera, and José Martí wrote for the mainstream media as chroniclers and foreign correspondents, but set their poetry aside as a protected, almost sacred realm of the self.[5] Darío famously insisted on the individuality of poetic style, advising fellow poets not to follow any models, but rather to develop their own personal voice: "My literature is *mine* in me; he who slavishly follows my footsteps will lose his personal treasure" (762; emphasis in original). Brazilian symbolist poets also cultivated a subjective approach to verse and considered it a realm of purity that should be protected from the contamination of commercialism and objectivism, and this approach formed the foundation of what Brito Broca called the symbolists' "moral aristocracy" (128). Despite these many similarities between the two groups, the *modernistas* of the Spanish-speaking Americas are today quite well known, beginning with Rubén Darío as the "father" of that movement, but the Brazilian symbolists have been nearly lost to literary history. This essay seeks to consider why this is the case.

---

3. In the rest of the essay, I refer to Hispanic American *modernistas*—particularly Rubén Darío and José Asunción Silva, but more broadly their pan-Hispanic cohort—as simply modernists. This should not be confused with reference to the Brazilian modernists, whose innovations occurred later, especially beginning with the *Semana de Arte Moderna* of 1922, and were more akin to their contemporaries, the so-called avant-garde groups of Hispanic America.

4. For more information on modernismo's connections to romanticism, see Jrade.

5. Julio Ramos has written about the day jobs of many modernist poets, who produced chronicles for mainstream newspapers. Ramos argues that poetry's juxtaposition with remunerated, journalistic writing pushed poetry toward associations with home, privacy, and an authentically individual aesthetic (83–85). Jrade also notes the increasing spiritual weight of poetry in this period, referring to poetry when she writes, "the Modernist author deals with feelings of fragmentation and alienation by attempting to rediscover a sense of belonging and 'wholeness'" (4); "the poet's art was becoming an 'evocative magic,' a sacred function [. . .] The centrality to Modernism of this search for unity comes to the fore in Darío's poetry" (8–9). Similarly, according to Susana Rotker, "the modernists believed in poetic form as an instrument of revelation, an important distinction from the pursuit of art for art's sake. For the modernists, the contemplation of beauty taught one to appreciate and care for the cosmic totality, instilling a sort of profane religiosity and dedication to what Darío called the 'rhythm of the immense celestial mechanism'" (21).

Because Brazilian symbolism is less widely understood than other movements in the literary history of Brazil, such as romanticism and *modernismo,* an introduction to the movement's development seems worthwhile. The 1880s in that country saw the growing prestige of the Parnassian group, followed by their professionalization and institutionalization in the 1890s.[6] Slavery was abolished in 1888, and the Republic declared in 1889, marking the entry of Brazil into a sort of political modernity; meanwhile, as positivism and scientific discourse became increasingly important, the symbolists "sought to reaffirm the realm of the spiritual" (Aguiar 13). João da Cruz e Sousa was the best-known and most influential Brazilian symbolist, and his twin publications of 1893, *Missal* and *Bróqueis,* marked a moment of aesthetic consolidation for the style, which was also advanced by other poets, including Alphonsus de Guimaraens, Emiliano Perneta, and Virgílio Várzea. In Cruz e Sousa's verse, musicality and vague mists of inspiration join a decadentist interest in insanity and eroticism. Flávio Aguiar highlights the poet's "strategies to seduce and enchant the reader with strangeness, difficulty, richness of expression, as if to make vibrate the powers of language liberated by dreams and by disengagement from the world of raw, objective reality" (16). Of little social prestige, however, the participants in symbolism led difficult lives shaped by poverty, disease, and rejection.

Focusing on the 1890s, this essay will explore one specific shared interest among Hispanic American modernists and Brazilian symbolists, namely that of metrical innovation as a vehicle for modernizing their languages' poetic possibilities, while at the same time contextualizing those changes within a social framework. We will see that, like the modernists (especially Rubén Darío and José Asunción Silva), Brazilian symbolists (focusing here on João da Cruz e Sousa) brought significant rhythmic innovation to the poetic tradition. In both groups, experimentation led to the incorporation of new rhythms and verse styles, including free verse and poetic prose, as well as metrical schemes adapted from foreign languages such as French and English. Though its limited scope does not allow an exhaustive treatment of the subject, this essay brings together critical discourse on these two traditions, highlighting formal correspondences as well as social similarities and differences, with the objective of inspiring further investigation in this area.

The Colombian José Asunción Silva offers one example of the metrical innovation wrought in Spanish-language verse during modernism, particularly in the form of polymetric verse. His most famous poem, "Nocturno"—

---

6. This is apparent, for instance, in their effort to form the Academia Brasileira de Letras in 1897 (see El Far) and in the diplomatic or municipal positions given to poets including Olavo Bilac, Alberto de Oliveira, and Raimundo Correia.

one of the best-known poems in Spanish from any period—arranges verses of four, six, eight, twelve, and twenty-four syllables randomly, though almost always in four-syllable phrases.[7] The poem's sense of circular melancholy stems from irregular, assonant rhyme, and frequent repetition amplifies the phonic echoes that create a chantlike effect. First published in 1894 in the Cartagena journal *Lectura para todos*, "Nocturno" is probably the most rhythmically innovative Spanish verse of its decade. Alberto Acereda is right to note that "Nocturno" is not an example of free verse because it contains rhyme ("Revisión" 113),[8] but the irregularity of that rhyme and the random arrangement of differing verse lengths represents undeniable originality, particularly given the strong rhythm created in the poem.

Setting aside the early and influential but perhaps isolated example of Silva's "Nocturno," the greatest innovator of Spanish-language verse in this period was clearly Rubén Darío. His *Prosas profanas,* of 1896 and 1901, builds

---

7. I transcribe the poem's first stanza as an example of its metrical schema:

> Una noche,
> una noche toda llena de murmullos, de perfumes y de músicas de älas,
> una noche
> en que ardían en la sombra nupcial y húmeda las luciérnagas fantásticas,
> a mi lado, lentamente, contra mí ceñida toda, muda y pálida,
> como si un presentimiento de amarguras infinitas,
> hasta el más secreto fondo de las fibras te agitara,
> por la senda que atraviesa la llanura florecida
>   caminabas.
>   Y la luna llena
> por los cielos azulosos, infinitos y profundos esparcía su luz blanca,
>   y tu sombra
>   fina y lánguida,
>   y mi sombra
> por los rayos de la luna proyectadas,
>   sobre las arenas tristes
>   de la senda se juntaban.
>   Y eran una
>   y eran una
>   y eran una sola sombra larga
>   y eran una sola sombra larga
>   y eran una sola sombra larga . . . (204–5; ellipsis in original)

8. I am using Acereda's definition of modern free verse as "that verse with total freedom, permitting any combination without regard for pre-established rhyme or rhythm. Even (and this is rarer) without rhythm, although in these verses normally a phonic, syntactic, or semantic configuration prevails." Acereda points out that his own definition does not include blank verse (*verso blanco* or *suelto*), though in the 1890s the definition of *verso libre* was flexible and included these styles as well ("Música" 81). In contrast, a prose poem does not include the line breaks of free verse, but it does have the prominent use of metaphor and heightened sensitivity to sound and rhythm that we associate with poetry.

its poems with verses of at least nine different syllabic counts, and employs free verse, polymetric verse, and poetic prose as well. Calling Darío the "magician of rhythm," Isabel Paraíso argues that the Nicaraguan poet was the "first great disseminator" of free verse in Spanish; for Paraíso, *Prosas profanas* "founded the most innovative forms of free verse" (102), while *Cantos de vida y esperanza,* of 1905, shows his deeper immersion in the style (112). Acereda maintains that "El país del sol," probably written in 1893, "inaugurates in Spanish poetry a type of prose poem that later would be taken up by many, including Juan Ramón Jiménez" ("Música" 84);[9] he points to "God Save the Queen," "Heraldos," and "Friso" as examples of Darío's free verse from the period of *Prosas profanas*.[10] Darío continued to explore free verse in *Cantos de vida y esperanza* (see "Salutación del optimista" and "¡Aleluya!") and in *El canto errante,* of 1907 (for example, in "Salutación al Águila" and "Árbol feliz"). Noé Jitrik observes this emphasis on the musicality and rhythm of verse in modernism as a whole, arguing that rhythm was the shaping force for the period's innovations in poetry, and that the system that defines modernist verse depends on an "ideology of sonority" (19).

Darío's verse refers to the poetic process with a frequency that borders on obsession, and the poems in *Prosas profanas* are arranged in an order that suggests an evolving interest in rhythmic regularity and freedom. If the volume's earliest poems flaunt the poet's skill with his trademark alexandrine verse, which he helped to develop and circulate in the Spanish language, some poems from the middle sections of *Prosas profanas* explore freer metrics (including, for example, "La página blanca" and "Heraldos"). The final poem of the volume, "Yo persigo una forma . . . ," makes a show of its metrical chal-

---

9. In "El país del sol," Darío offsets a refrain after each paragraph of poetic prose. I transcribe the first such paragraph and verse.

> Junto al negro palacio del rey de la isla de Hierro—(oh cruel, horrible destierro!)—, ¿cómo que tú, hermana armoniosa, haces cantar al cielo gris tu pajarera de ruiseñores, tu formidable caja musical? ¿No te entristece recordar la primavera en que oíste a un pájaro divino y tornasol *en el país del sol*? (788; emphasis in original)

10. In "Heraldos," one or more women's names compose the first verse of each stanza, followed in the second verse by a description of the women's announcers. Despite this repetitive structure, the verse lengths vary considerably, from two to fourteen syllables. I transcribe the first three stanzas:

> ¡Helena!
> La anuncia el blancor de un cisne.
>
> ¡Makheda!
> La anuncia un pavo real.
>
> ¡Ifigenia, Electra, Catalina!
> Anúncialas un caballero con un hacha. (792)

lenges and triumphs with its use of poetic license, with a hiatus in the ninth verse. In addition, the poem's proparoxytone and oxytone words at the end of initial hemistiches force an awkwardness in its regularity just as the poetic voice discusses its desperate but failed attempt to achieve perfect form.[11] The sum effect of this poem, and the closing note of *Prosas profanas* as a whole, is a sense that regularity alone is not enough, that perfection—and indeed any absolute, even one of beauty—is a false promise. Though Darío's poetry after *Cantos de vida y esperanza* did not linger on free verse, it also did not praise form for its own sake, as it can be said to do in *Prosas profanas*. His work gradually took on, rather, a greater interest in sociopolitical and historical concerns, as seen for instance in the anti-U.S. sentiment of "Oda a Roosevelt."

These observations regarding Hispanic American modernism are well known. If the innovations and aesthetic importance of modernists around the turn of the twentieth century are widely accepted, however, the same cannot be said of Brazilian literature of the period. Called *pós-Romantismo* and *pré-Modernismo*, among even less flattering names,[12] the period is sandwiched in Brazilian literary history between the major movements of romanticism and modernism, whose recognized and lasting importance contrasts with its own, supposedly transitional status. The inadequacy of these labels has even inspired José Paulo Paes to call Brazilian literature between 1890 and 1920 *art nouveau*, due to its frequent recourse to ornamentalism (65). The prevailing theory seems to be that while Hispanic American *modernistas* developed a watershed movement that brought about significant aesthetic and social changes in the literary field, Brazilian literature of the same period was dominated by the increasingly ossified dogmas of the Parnassian school and the vestiges of romanticism, which it would not cast off until the arrival of Brazilian modernism and the *Semana de Arte Moderna*, its moment of true innovation. And yet, the work of many Brazilian poets resonates with the famous innovations also seen in Spanish.

---

11. I transcribe the first and third stanzas of the poem. The moments of poetic license, and the rhythmic awkwardness that question the very idea of regularity, are in the third stanza:

> Yo persigo una forma que no encuentra mi estilo
> botón de pensamiento que busca ser la rosa;
> se anuncia con un beso que en mis labios se posa
> al abrazo imposible de la Venus de Milo. [...]

> Y no hallo sino la palabra que huye,
> la iniciación melódica que de la flauta fluye
> y la barca del sueño que en el espacio boga; [...]. (856)

12. Accusations of "nefelibatismo" (roughly, having one's head in the clouds) and artistic "neurastenia" (or hysteria, with its gendered connotations) were rampant in this period, but in Brazil they were most frequently leveled against the symbolists.

Despite affirming that "only a minority of our Symbolist poets contributed substantially to the establishment of new metrical patterns" (643), Sânzio de Azevedo explores the groundbreaking work of that minority, concluding that "what is clear is that it was the Symbolist poets [. . .] who rose up, consciously and obstinately, against the rigid canons of the dominant versification" (644). Azevedo's helpful essay studies Alphonsus de Guimaraens's tripartite alexandrines and polymetric verse, and Emiliano Perneta's trimeter and irregular decasyllables, adding that Mário Pederneiras and Dario Veloso similarly paved the way for free verse with their polymetric verse and variable silvas;[13] these poets maintained rhyme and thus did not venture into truly free verse, in spite of Pederneiras's fame for having done so (641–42). Their modifications of the alexandrine verse, and such experimentation as free verse and polymetric verse, recall the explorations of rhythm then occurring in other parts of Latin America. In the case of João da Cruz e Sousa, arguably the most important Brazilian symbolist, Azevedo studies an interest in proparoxytone words and some fourteen-syllable alexandrine verses, which follow the Spanish style rather than the twelve-syllable alexandrine then favored in French and Portuguese;[14] otherwise, however, Azevedo emphasizes Cruz e Sousa's metrical conservatism.

A recent book by Jefferson Agostini Mello sees more formal innovation in Cruz e Sousa's work. This study of *Missal* (1893), a volume of prose poems, reminds us that this form had not previously been developed in depth in Brazil (19). Along with its verse-based and more-studied partner volume,

---

13. An essay by Antonio Secchin is illuminating with regard to Pederneiras and metrical innovation. He describes the poet as more a "divulgador" (a spreader of the word) than a creator of free verse. As earlier precedent, Secchin mentions Alberto Ramos's *Poemas do mar do norte* (1898) and A. Guerra Duval's *Palavras que o vento leva* (1900). Moreover, Pederneiras's "free verse" could also be considered polymetric verse. As an example, Secchin quotes part of "Terra carioca" (from *Histórias do meu casal*, 1907):

>   Mas hoje a tua vida interna
>   Sob a vassalagem
>   Desta agitada estética moderna,
>   Vai-se movendo e transformando tanto
>   Que muito breve perderás o encanto
>   Da primitiva plástica selvagem. (Pederneiras, cited in Secchin xx–xxi)

Secchin concludes that, rather than free verse, this passage shows "a continuation of older styles under a façade of the modern" (xxi).

14. He cites, for example, from "O final do Guarani" (1883):

>   Ceci—é a virgem loira das brancas harmonias,
>   A doce flor azul dos sonhos cor-de-rosa,
>   Peri—o índio ousado das bruscas fantasias,
>   O tigre dos sertões—de alma luminosa. (Cruz e Sousa, cited in Azevedo 633)

Bróqueis, also by Cruz e Sousa and published in 1893, *Missal* marks a foundational moment for Brazilian symbolism. Much previous scholarship of Cruz e Sousa's work has focused on social factors such as the poet's race, but Agostini Mello is careful to link these to poetic form, arguing that *Missal* is the "poetic internalization of a precarious social reality" (181). For Agostini Mello, the unfinished quality of prose poetry is the most important formal issue in *Missal*. While Davi Arrigucci also notes Cruz e Sousa's "negation of perfect form, by way of ugliness," which he links to the poet's suffering in relation to the impossible goal of transcendence (169),[15] Agostini Mello attributes the poet's interest in fragmentation and mixture not to a transcendental struggle but rather to social strife. *Missal,* he writes, "presents a sharp and problematizing vision of turn-of-the-century Brazilian reality":

> Due to the mixture, in most cases without polishing, of literary, artistic, theoretical and historical forms and contents, [. . .] with new contents and forms received from Europe, *Missal* obliquely projects, in its whole and in its parts, a country in pieces, which had just gone through one more of its pseudo-revolutions. (Mello 28)

The life of Cruz e Sousa provides an illustrative if extreme example of the social difficulties that conditioned the options of many Brazilian symbolists. Black, the son of freed slaves, and an outsider to the cultural scene of Rio de Janeiro, because he was from the southern state of Santa Catarina, Cruz e Sousa had been educated by his parents' former owner but nonetheless suffered greatly in his brief life: his four children died very young of tuberculosis, which later killed the poet as well at the age of thirty-six. His race was especially important in defining his social possibilities. Even the poet himself shared mainstream beliefs of the period that Africanness was related to laziness and sensuality;[16] however, as Alfredo Bosi notes, these prejudices operate in tandem with another set of associations, in which a poet represents

---

15. Arrigucci's study of the relationship between poetic form and Cruz e Sousa's social status focuses on the heightened individual subjectivity of the poet's work. Expanding on the ideas of Roger Bastide, he notes that the dramatic hallucination that defines Cruz e Sousa's work functions as "an image of his own process of alienation" (179) and argues that, for this poet, "the poem is a symbol of an absent reality, impossible to name except with that agitated world of enigmatic interiority, projected as a *vision*" (180; emphasis in original).

16. Scholars have discussed the difference between Brazilian and French symbolisms principally as one of references: each group ostensibly wrote about its own context but followed similar forms, with race and the notion of Brazilian *saudade* as the most frequently cited referential differences. In Massaud Moisés's summary, "the cliché of *saudade* was considered enough to establish the difference between French and Brazilian poets [. . .] In addition to sentimentality and love lyricism, this circumstance helps to define the Brazilian shape of our Symbolist

idealism and "the freest and most exalted individuality [*mais livre e sublimada individuação*] dug from the Hugoean and Symbolist mines" ("Poesia" 175). Cruz e Sousa thus represented two radically different social roles for the period: as an Afro-Brazilian, he was denigrated by prejudicial pseudoscience that viewed his race as negatively deterministic of his intellect, while his identification as a poet marked him with a "double conception of the poet as a prophet of humanity and a demiurge of form" (Bosi, "Poesia" 173). For Bosi, the result is Cruz e Sousa's "poetically counter-ideological language" ("Poesia" 174), a characteristic that is necessarily related to his aesthetic innovations: "In various texts of *Evocações,* the figure of the *poeta maldito* shifted from the tension of artist versus bourgeois, apparent in Baudelaire and in Verlaine (in the Verlaine who paved the way for Rimbaud [*no Verlaine revelador de Rimbaud*]), towards the tension of Africa versus civilization or, broadly, Africa versus universal history" (Bosi, "Poesia" 179). In this formulation, then, race is the foundation for a new, Brazilian element added to the adapted aesthetic of French symbolism.[17]

The opposition between symbolism and Parnassianism tends to define critical approaches to turn-of-the-century Brazilian poetry, be the critics supportive or skeptical of said difference. The battle of the schools continues to dominate critical thought, but scholars' emphasis on the social circumstances of the symbolists, and the social themes of their work (such as race), dates back to firsthand observers of the period. In Brito Broca's telling, the social difference between the two groups was at least as important as aesthetic differences: "The Parnassians, though many really were bohemians, in most cases [...] fought arduously for their livelihood and were ready to write sonnets for order, as long as this brought them economic advantages" (127–28); they cultivated an "objective" poetry based on carefully constructed forms, which they believed anyone with sufficient patience could craft. Meanwhile, against this seemingly bourgeois approach, the symbolists endeavored to return to poetry some of the romantic enchantment that the Parnassians had brushed aside. For the symbolists, the poet was part of a "moral aristocracy" and "would

---

poetry" (*História* 264). Similarly, race has been approached as an essential, inescapable difference from Europe (see Bastide).

17. Bosi further points out that Cruz e Sousa's marginal social status was a part of his poetic persona and a factor in his somewhat iconoclastic critique of mainstream culture. In this the poet contrasted with the period's other nonwhite writers of cultural importance, including the novelist Machado de Assis, whose critiques were less direct and more ironic: "In his aversion to conventional norms, [what he called] 'the decrepit Convention with a capital letter,' the poet [Cruz e Sousa] includes all the dilettantes of literary life, the *belle époque* that was taking off in Rio during the end of the nineteenth century. He makes clear that he's not mixed up with the 'well-educated egotism' of false rebels" ("Poesia" 176).

remain intangible in his elevated spiritual category, above all the smallness of the world" (Broca 128). This focus on the differences between symbolists and Parnassians has been undermined more recently; Moisés, for example, reminds us that, "the Symbolist poets did not free themselves entirely from the Parnassian preoccupation with perfect and polished forms, beginning with the cult of the sonnet. Far, nevertheless, from giving in to formalism per se, they ended up attributing new characteristics to it, in order to adapt it to their pet purposes" (*História* 264). This recent tendency to question the perhaps superficial divisions among the period's socio-aesthetic groups is valuable, and critical discourse would benefit from bridging even broader divides, that is, by further interrogating Brazilian symbolism—and Parnassianism too, for that matter—in dialogue with innovations then occurring elsewhere in Latin America.

Despite the posturing and factionalism of these two groups, aesthetic differences tend to be more individualized, rather than to correlate clearly with one group or another. This is not to say, however, that the Parnassian-versus-symbolist debate is without meaning to scholars today, because it is clear that the writers' social circumstances had significant effects on the circulation of their work. Following a period of bohemianism in the 1880s, many Parnassians gained the sort of recognition that alleviated much of their economic hardship: Olavo Bilac, Alberto de Oliveira, and Raimundo Correia achieved one mark of social legitimacy as writers when they occupied seats in the Brazilian Academy of Letters after that institution's founding in 1896, and they also enjoyed some economic stability due to their appointment to governmental posts. Their symbolist rivals, meanwhile, continued to struggle economically and were excluded from these mechanisms of social legitimacy.[18] While for these reasons it is important to acknowledge the social spectrum represented by the poets of turn-of-the-century Brazil, this information should not eclipse a critical discussion of the aesthetic particularities of their work.

The modernists of Hispanic America, represented here by Rubén Darío and the José Asunción Silva of "Nocturno," carried out a profound modernization of Spanish and its rhythms and meters. The innovations of the Brazilian symbolists were likewise significant in Portuguese, but in their case social factors including race drew a large portion of the critical attention paid to their work, both during the period of their activity and in subsequent decades. Though some of the modernists were also vilified for their race—Miguel de

---

18. See, for example, El Far: "Olavo Bilac, Guimarães Passos and Pedro Rabelo, known for their refined poems and chronicles in *carioca* newspapers, went so far as to write, under pseudonyms, texts-to-order of low quality and pornographic stories, in the attempt to alleviate their constant financial difficulties" (16).

Unamuno famously scorned Darío, for example, for the latter's mixed heritage[19]—in their case the issue does not usually overshadow discussions of the group's aesthetic importance. It would seem that the very race-sensitive climate that shaped the symbolists' original reception has continued to figure prominently in more current perceptions of the movement, limiting the attention paid to the group's important contributions to the modernization of Portuguese-language verse. The irony, of course, is that social factors contributed to the symbolists' approach to form: in rejecting a "Parnassian" interest in perfect forms, they sought a higher sort of perfection, a spiritual one in which the vessels of poetry—the metrical form, the poet's racialized body— are secondary, after the perfection of the symbol (the idea, the concept, and the spiritual valence of these).

This essay has indicated a field of shared innovation across national and linguistic divides in Latin America, arguing that the Brazilian symbolists and Hispanic American modernists bear more similarities than have previously been noted. Formal innovations in both groups pushed the limits of what was rhythmically possible in their respective languages, as they redefined the role of the poet in society and expanded the possibilities of poetry, for example by delving into prose poetry and free verse. Though the social realities that constrained the possibilities of Brazilian symbolists like Cruz e Sousa should not be overlooked, this essay has proposed that a formal analysis of their work can help us to understand their poetic aspirations and methods. Moreover, we have seen that a critical interest in social factors (especially race) has—in Cruz e Sousa's time as well as since then—limited the circulation of his poetics. If the poet saw his verse as a weapon for his vindication, as is suggested in the epigraph above ("Escravocratas"), then deepening our study of his poetics will teach us not only about his aesthetic innovation but also about his incisive social critique. For Cruz e Sousa, the symbol and the structured sound of poetry were tools for inspiration and for protest, for social critique as well as for aesthetic proposals. The poet was brilliant but felt unheard. Considering Brazilian symbolism in comparison to Hispanic American modernism, which can teach us to better read the innovative forms of that movement, can help us to understand the sense of rage that occasionally comes through in his verse. Rich areas of potential for future investigation include, among other subjects, the direct connections between symbolists and modernists, such as Ricardo

---

19. It appears that the grain of truth in this story became inflated, but the anecdote became famous nonetheless. In an article written upon Darío's death, Unamuno clarified the regrettable circumstance: "With this tongue that the Devil has given us men of letters, I said once, before a fellow man of the quill, that Rubén's feathers—those of the Indian—were visible beneath his hat; and the man who heard me say this, being neither dumb nor lazy, spread the news, which traveled to Darío's ears" (Unamuno, cited in Mallo 63).

Jaimes Freyre's knowledge of Cruz e Sousa, the topic of his address before the *Ateneo de Buenos Aires*; the groups' indirect contact via magazine subscriptions, correspondence, and other modes of textual circulation; and comparative studies of specific themes across the work of various poets (for example, the conceptual importance of whiteness in Manuel Gutiérrez Nájera and Cruz e Sousa would provide material for a fascinating study).[20] Beyond identifying similarities and differences across national borders, the goal should be to trace the networks of contagion and exchange by which ideas and forms travel, develop, and build up as they simultaneously reach beyond national, regional, or linguistic traditions.

WORKS CITED

Acereda, Alberto. "Juan Ramón Jiménez y el verso libre en la poesía española: Del simbolismo francés a *Diario de un reciencasado.*" *Estudios humanísticos. Filología* 17 (1995): 11–27.

———. "Música de las ideas y música del verbo. Versolibrismo dariano." *Revista Anthropos: Huellas del conocimiento* 170–71 (1997): 81–89.

———. "Revisión, inicio y presencia del verso libre en el modernismo hispánico: El caso de José Martí." *Anuario del Centro de Estudios Martianos* 18 (1995–96): 105–23.

Aguiar, Flávio. "A secreta malícia." Introduction, *Os melhores poemas de Cruz e Sousa.* João da Cruz e Sousa. São Paulo: Global, 2001.

Arrigucci, Davi, Jr. "A Noite de Cruz e Sousa." *Outros Achados e Perdidos.* São Paulo: Companhia das Letras, 1999. 165–84.

Azevedo, Sânzio de. "Desarticulação rítmica e irregularidades métricas no simbolismo brasileiro." *Revista de Cultura Vozes* 71 (1977): 631–44.

Bastide, Roger. "Quatro estudos sobre Cruz e Sousa." *A Poesia Afro-Brasileira.* São Paulo: Martins, 1943. 157–89.

Bosi, Alfredo. "Poesia *versus* racismo." *Literatura e Resistência.* São Paulo: Companhia Das Letras, 2002. 163–85.

———. *O Pré-Modernismo.* São Paulo: Editora Cultrix, 1969.

Broca, Brito. *A vida literária no Brasil—1900.* [Rio de Janeiro]: Ministério da Educação e Cultura, Serviço de Documentação, 1956.

Darío, Rubén. *Obras completas.* Vol. V. Madrid: Afrodisio Aguado, 1953.

El Far, Alessandra. *A Encenação da Imortalidade: Uma análise da Academia Brasileira de Letras nos primeiros anos da República (1897–1924).* Rio de Janeiro: Editora FGV, 2000.

Jitrik, Noé. *Las contradicciones del modernismo: Productividad poética y situación sociológica.* México: Colegio de México, [Centro de Estudios Lingüísticos y Literarios], 1978.

Jrade, Cathy Login. *Rubén Darío and the Romantic Search for Unity: The Modernist Recourse to Esoteric Tradition.* Austin: U of Texas P, 1983.

---

20. Robert Moser's study on the literary revenant in the Brazilian and Spanish American traditions, included in this volume, is an excellent example of theme-based comparative work.

Macambira, José Rebouças. *Estrutura Musical do Verso e da Prosa*. Fortaleza: Secretaria de Cultura e Desporto, 1983.

Mallo, Jerónimo. "Las relaciones personales y literarias entre Darío y Unamuno." *Revista Iberoamericana* 9.17 (1945): 61–72.

Mello, Jefferson Agostini. *Um Poeta Simbolista na República Velha: Literatura e Sociedade em Missal de Cruz e Sousa*. Florianópolis: Editora da UFSC, 2008.

Moisés, Massaud. "Brazilian Poetry from 1878 to 1902." *The Cambridge History of Latin American Literature*. Vol. 3. Eds. Roberto González Echevarría and Enrique Pupo-Walker. Cambridge: Cambridge UP, 1996. 83–104.

———. *História da Literatura Brasileira*. Vol. 2. São Paulo: Editora Cultrix, 2001.

———. *O Simbolismo (1893–1902)*. São Paulo: Editora Cultrix, 1969.

Paes, José Paulo. "O Art-Nouveau na Literatura Brasileira." *Gregos e Baianos*. São Paulo: Brasiliense, 1985. 64–80.

Paraíso de Leal, Isabel. *El verso libre hispánico: Orígenes y corrientes*. Madrid: Editorial Gredos, 1985.

Peixoto, Marta. "Brazilian Poetry from 1900 to 1922." *The Cambridge History of Latin American Literature*. Vol. 3. Eds. Roberto González Echevarría and Enrique Pupo-Walker. Cambridge: Cambridge UP, 1996. 233–45.

Ramos, Julio. *Divergent Modernities: Culture and Politics in Nineteenth-Century Latin America*. Translated by John D. Blanco. Durham and London: Duke UP, 2001.

Rotker, Susana. *The American Chronicles of José Martí: Journalism and Modernity in Spanish America*. Trans. Jennifer French and Katherine Semler. Hanover and London: UP of New England, 2000.

Secchin, Antonio Carlos. "Mário Pederneiras: às margens plácidas da modernidade." *Mário Pederneiras: poesía reunida*. Mário Pederneiras. Rio de Janeiro: Academia Brasileira de Letras, 2004. xiiv–xxvi.

Silva, José Asunción. *Poesía. De sobremesa*. Ed. Remedios Mataix. Madrid: Cátedra, 2006.

Sousa, João da Cruz e. *Os melhores poemas de Cruz e Sousa*. Ed. Flávio Wolf de Aguiar. São Paulo: Global, 2001.

Weber, Eugen. *France, Fin de Siècle*. Cambridge, MA, and London: Belknap P of Harvard UP, 1986.

CHAPTER 11

Shared Passages

Spanish American–Brazilian Links in Contemporary Poetry

CHARLES A. PERRONE

> *Albañiles / del Brasil, golpead la frontera /*
> *pescadores, llorad de noche / sobre las aguas litorales.*[1]

IN THE realm of lyric, no happening better expresses the transatlantic, transamerican, and transcendent spirits of the present volume than Tordesilhas—Festival Iberoamericano de Poesia Contemporânea, imagined by its organizers as "a literary event that seeks to present and to discuss recent production of poetry in Latin America and the Iberian Peninsula." The guiding deconstructing proposal, "Desconstruindo a Linha de Tordesilhas," expresses the search for new dialogues and agreements between Portuguese-language and Spanish-language poets in those countries.[2] Such transnational and ecumenical intentions have become increasingly evident in like gatherings since about 1990. Multilateral Old and New World relationships and exchanges have been the focus of public celebrations and colloquia, both academic and civilian, throughout the Americas—Brazil, Spanish America, the Caribbean, and North America—whether focused on the hemisphere as a whole or specifically on Luso-Hispanic literary relations.[3] Tracking and interpreting activity of this

---

1. Pablo Neruda, *Canto General I* (Buenos Aires: Losada, 1955), 194. [Carpenters of Brazil / strike ye the frontier / fishermen, weep ye at night / over the waters of the shore.]

2. São Paulo, November 2007. See statements and program at: <http://www.revistazunai.com/materias_especiais/festival_tordesilhas/index.htm>. A follow-up event was held in 2011 in Lisbon.

3. Two examples since the turn of the decade are the symposium "Poetry of the Americas," Department of Comparative Literature, Princeton University (April 2010), and Simpoesia (Simpósio de Poesia Contemporânea) in São Paulo (June 2009), which brought together poets from North and South America, as well as Iberia.

sort was one of the aims of "*Banda Hispânica*: Spanish American–Brazilian Links in Lyric and Landings," chapter 5 of my *Brazil, Lyric, and the Americas*, a segment that examines source affinities, historical conflicts, early attempts at cultural rapprochement, key modern scriptural relationships, select aspects of the poetry of song, and editorial diplomacy. Since the appearance of that study, fresh relevant material has come to light to add to the demonstration of this lively phenomenon-in-progress. Significant contributions have been made in theory/criticism and the creative domains alike, especially with regard to musically inspired verse and to Afro-diasporic poetry that traverses political divides and ponders shared heritage.

Different kinds of contemporary letters and their connections in the extreme Western hemisphere (the Americas) can be grasped via comparative approaches known variously as Inter-American literature (Earl Fitz), New World studies (Roland Greene), and, most germane to the genre of lyric, transamerican poetics. All consider commonalities and, to varying degrees, interrogate perimeters, provinces, and mutations in space. Transamerican inquiry posits attitudes and practices that cross national boundaries, as well as artistic efforts to surpass conventional limits of languages and geography. Related poematic practice and critical response may involve textual interrelations, hemispheric consciousness, neo-millennial responses to multicultural imperatives, and even culturally expressive effects of neoliberal policies. Such interests often imply, in addition to literature per se, recourses to the fine arts and discursive genres of popular culture: comics, film, jazz, rock music, and touristic propaganda. These may originate in Brazil, in neighboring Hispanic nations, or, more forcefully—given the widespread influence of U.S. media—in the United States. Symptomatic uses of the hemispheric and the nonliterary in recent Brazilian poetry entail input from the realms of mass media, mostly electronic, as well as gestures of outreach, toward North, Central, and South America. Organizing tropes of *Brazil, Lyric, and the Americas* include *interface* (in connotations ranging from technological commonalities to intellectual exchange), *invention* (as both discovery and artistic contrivance), and *insularity* (the literal geographical configuration of the island and the cultural sense of isolation or separation). The open seas figure plentifully in the periplus of epical verse in the Americas, and one of the ways Brazilian poets have both pondered Old World sources and dialogued with Latin America is via new modalities of (quasi-)epical poetry.[4] Modern musical phenomena bring countries together almost like maritime routes.

---

4. Chapter 4 of *Brazil, Lyric, and the Americas* concerns neo-epical works, including *Toda a América*, by Ronald de Carvalho (1926), which also had a bilingual Spanish-Portuguese edition.

In the critical arena at the turn of the second decade of the new millennium, *PMLA* featured an updated synthesis of Hemispheric American studies (Bauer), an appellation in which the absence of terms such as *literature* and *poetics* indicates greater concern with historical and culturalist factors. For their part, Spitta and Zamora employ the muralism of Diego Rivera as a point of departure to argue for the expansion of comparativist horizons in *Comparative Literature*. While the referents "Brazil" and "poetry" do appear at least once in both accounts, acute biases toward the Anglophone, Hispanism, and narrative are undeniable, and the relative lack of attention to the Afro-American should also be noted. A more motivated site of intersection and confluence emerges in Justin Read's *Modern Poetics and Hemispheric American Cultural Studies*, which asks, "why is poetry necessary to understanding the Americas as temporal, spatial, and historico-cultural contexts?" (xiii). He notes how U.S.-centric New World studies have progressed positively and how Latin Americanism too has surpassed a certain insularity that characterized it into the late twentieth century. For Read, migration, translation (literal and figurative), and transculturation are bases to assert American identity and voice. His chapters ponder revealing aspects of modernists in the Americas: Ezra Pound and William Carlos Williams in the North, and Vicente Huidobro and Mário de Andrade in the South. The theoretical crux of Read's argument is the belief that the only way to study national cultures hemispherically is to examine the intercultural collisions both *between* American nations and *within* them. Indeed, one can scarcely argue against relational complexity, especially as the economy of lyric evolves in an age of accelerated technology and globalization, which has aesthetic roots in the 1920s. After all, the Jazz Age and the Internet do prove to overlap in meaningful ways in the arts.

If Read's study in poetics is a welcome advance in inter-American thought, an additional ideal exemplification of border- and genre-crossing transamericanity in lyric is *Noite Nula*, by Carlos Felipe Moisés. This established poet and professor from São Paulo explores open subjectivities in a series of twenty titles (several with multiple sections) that articulate outreach as much as introspection. About a third of the poems build poetic spaces and moods driven by only vaguely circumscribed creative experience, while an equally large subset of poems is inspired by and specifically addressed to great names in African American jazz and blues: Leadbelly, John Coltrane, Billie Holiday, Charlie Parker, and others. Complementary poems contemplate important U.S. figures in other areas of expressive culture (sport, film, dance, art), while literary intertextuality—a hallmark of transamerican endeavors—occurs in a poem entitled "Gertrude Stein." The longest piece in *Noite Nula* is the four-part titular poem, built upon polyvalent nocturnal imagery. Therein, use of the colonial term *el-rei* recalls the historical nexus of the Spanish and Portuguese monarchies and languages. And precisely at the center of the sequence of poems is an homage to the icon of tango, Carlos Gardel. Thus, *Noite Nula* participates forcefully in the surprisingly prominent inter-American vein of Brazilian poetry inspired by the music-making (mostly Afro-American) of the United States, and of Spanish America.

Dynamic illustrations of musico-poetic encounters reside in the repertories of Edimilson de Almeida Pereira (EAP; Juiz de Fora, Minas Gerais, 1963), whose writings further link Brazil to the other Americas via themes and behavioral manifestations of the African Diaspora, a source of unabated inspiration for him. In his extensive bibliography, four collections of poems obtain most significantly in the context of the present study: *Zeosório Blues*, overtly and purposefully tied to U.S. popular music; *Caderno de retorno* (Return Notebook), a multilingual lyrical epic sequence; *Signo cimarrón* (Maroon Sign), written in Spanish with the legacies of slavery and resistance patently in mind; and *Variaciones de un libro de sirenas* (Variations of a Book of Sirens), also in Spanish and with its own varied epical residues. Poetic articulations of common backgrounds and foregrounds in the dramas of the African-Latin-American Diaspora are central here. There have been numerous cases of diasporically tinged transamericanity in Brazilian poetry since the 1960s, but none quite as compelling as that of the poet-critic-anthropologist EAP. A prolific scholar, he mixes fieldwork into his creative endeavors, recovering and rewriting Afro-Brazilian memory in lyric.[5] His diasporic awareness embraces the sacred and the secular, as well as situations of rural folk culture and urban environs, and the local as part of the whole American hemisphere. *Zeosório Blues* serves as a springboard, a conceptual point of departure for us to grasp his oeuvre as a whole (Cruz, "Canto-poema"). In an extended "reaction poem," an effusive Ronaldo Augusto indicates the collection's breadth and clout: ". . . *zeosório* polyvalent / hermetic & pop / the very title accounts / for that dialectic . . . its radio-lunch pail / overturns the whole world . . . soul nothingness . . . familiarity of music kept quiet . . ."[6] The lines of EAP's "Orfeu" (70–76), in particular, celebrate Afro-descendant musicality and genius in wider perspective. Ostensibly a *carnaval* poem, it is also a platform to invoke "spirituals . . . aimé césaire . . . os negros os mexicanos / os amarelos" [blacks, mexicans / yellows], as well as the dramatis personae of samba schools. Men-

---

5. On varieties of black poetry in Brazil, in rural folklore and literature, see the forty-two studies in Pereira, *Um tigre na floresta*.

6. ". . . *zeosório* multivalente / hermético & pop / o título mesmo já dá conta / dessa dialética . . . seu rádio-marmita / tresanda todo o mundo . . . soul la nada . . . familiaridade de música calada . . ."

tion of the renowned Francophone Caribbean author Césaire allows citation of "as ilhas," the islands of a recurring insular motif. Yet the geo-metaphorical crux of the collection is the word of multiple connotations, *esquina* (corner), in "Fábulas" (Fables, Tales) (164):

> A corner is not a part of the street, nor an elbow of a knife
> Nor a cavern where one hides, if pursued
> Nor a soft spot for the love of those with no bed
> Neither a church nor a theater, even if there so many represent. A corner is not a bar nor a fair nor an arrow indicating a detour. More than a place it is the recitation of a passage.[7]

Barbosa (21–22) explains her adoption of the closing expression of the poem as the title of her ambitious critical study: the phrase suggests "both the contours of a language reinvented by poetic playfulness and the epistemological and ontological unfolding of the textual play." The words *recitation* and *passage* further suggest poetic reading, recitation, narration and referencing, as well as lines in books, movement, corridors, transition, communication links, sectional switches in music, and travel tickets. One could surely add a crucial echo via the English term *middle passage,* the slave-bearing leg of the transatlantic triangle of trade from Africa to the Americas to Europe. Academic translations, in fact, include *passagem trans-atlântica* and *passagem do meio.* In EAP's many poems with diasporic substance, allusions are made to the infamous slave-ship voyages, though without explicit references.[8] Yet the cultural expressions of forced migrants and their descendants are a backbone of his gregarious repertory, which refers to black communities in the Portuguese, French, English, and Hispanic Americas.

Before writing two collections in the language of Nicolás Guillén, EAP incorporated numerous passages in Spanish, as well as in Caribbean French, into *Caderno de retorno.*[9] This (relatively short) lyrical epic concerns and

---

7.
   Esquina não é parte da rua, nem cotovelo de faca.
   Nem caverna onde um se esconde, se perseguido.
   Nem macio para o amor de quem não tem leito.
   Nem igreja ou teatro, mesmo que aí tantos representem. Esquina não é bar nem feira nem seta indicando desvio. Mais que um lugar é a recitação da passagem.

8. Barbosa (77–78) analyzes "Anti-ode marítima," which considers with powerful irony the names of commercial ships that also transported slaves on return trips from Angola.

9. In Pereira, *As coisas arcas* (194–241). For in-depth, wide-ranging analysis, see Barbosa (121–43).

lends nuanced poetic form to the African Diaspora, with its striking stylistic diversity, thus confirming the validity of Read's emphasis on migration, translation, and transculturation. A Southern Cone colleague of EAP's perceives in the poet's textual codification in *Caderno de retorno* certain unifying elements: *el desplazamiento* (movement and displacement) as confrontation and as constant passage of the self in dialogue with Others from a perspective that undermines dominant discourses. By operating within a "complex web of national, cultural and intellectual traditions, the author gradually opened up to a multiplicity of voices and, in this way, to an original poetics of transnationality" (Carrizo 8). EAP questioned hybridity and *mestizaje* (mixed bloodlines) as the only horizon of cognitive probability by recreating Brazilian Portuguese and the problematics of the African Diaspora via disruptive invocations of French and varieties of Spanish, resistant and marginal, and by bringing all this together in a new territory without demarcation (Carrizo 8). One line toward the end of the expansive poem is rightly highlighted as an encapsulation of the historico-poetic adventure: "What belongs to us all so we might recognize ourselves / as neighbors in the same boat?"[10]

Multiple acts of recognition and recognizance occur in the forty poems of *Signo cimarrón*. The scope of the title is wide indeed. The original meaning of *cimarrón* suggested wildness, savagery, remoteness (*cima* = mountain top), as with escaped domesticated animals. That sense was extended to designate fugitives, runaway slaves in Cuba and other New World colonies, giving rise to the English word *maroon* (and not vice versa, as some have indicated). Given that the "*cimarrón* is, by antonomasia, the principal figure of the struggle for justice and liberty in the world of the Americas" (Luis 8), the set of poems by EAP takes on a continental mantel of resistance and counterdiscourse. But beyond these inexorable sociopolitical and historical associations, EAP's deployment of the axial term invokes the poetic function of language and what amounts to a linguistic imperative. As confirmed in the poem "Signo," the two words that give the book in question its title operate to suggest plurisignificational presences, ambiguities, and slippery referents. The tandem is used "to indicate the movement of the sign and to elaborate upon its versatility and mobility [. . .] The mutating sign brings with it centripetal and centrifugal forces that de-center meanings" (Barbosa 104). The actual *cimarrón* lyricized becomes "a sign, a signal, a look, a gesture, a word, but also letters, writing, the poem, it is the fugacious image that by its very nature hides and lives in the margins to appear later and dismantle the center" (Luis 13). Thus, EAP engages both the shame of slavery in sister Hispanic nations and their

---

10. "O que é de todos para que nos reconheçamos / vizinhos de um mesmo navio?" (239).

very language, its instrument of expression, in order to interrogate them and their situated appearances. In its "double inscription"—the maroon theme and the poet's opting for Spanish—the book presents "a declaration of intentions, of a tenacious and necessary task" (Carrizo 11), as in the opening salvo "Indicios" (Indications), which declares that "the challenge is to select the phrase / that introduces us all to each other"[11] and that "inheritance does not exist / without a body-language to transform it."[12] A colleague of EAP's believes that his choice of the signal *cimarronage* has further metalinguistic implications: the maroon is allied with the poet who rebels against the domination of an exclusively Eurocentric literary tradition, and he calls up the figure of the *griot,* venturing to recount the silenced history of the African Diaspora.[13]

The progression of segments in *Signo cimarrón* contains, though without overt chronicling, a skeletal epic, evoking lands of origin, forced passage, labor, mythologies, invention, and art. A clever weaving of the maritime motif, Iberian forebears, and vital Afro-Caribbean sites occurs in "Ciudades" (Cities), which revolves around double iterations of the before-and-after moniker "santiago de cuba de compostela," which wed the port city of eastern Cuba—famous for its heavily Afro-Cuban *carnaval* and for its reception of French/Haitians fleeing the uprising in the early 1800s—with the Galician city made mecca by pilgrimages to the burial ground of St. James, and focal point of the emergence of *cantigas* (sung lyric) in Iberia in medieval times. Musical motifs are fundamental in *Signo cimarrón*; witness such titles as "Concierto," "Cantata," and "Paso doble," which contains the line "me disperso en el continente" (I scatter in the continent), expressing a wide-ranging fraternity. Nowhere is the musical voice of Africans in the Americas stronger than in the three-section poem "Orfeo," which honors the famous Cuban singer Beny Moré and his compatriot Bola de Nieve alongside blues legend John Lee Hooker. Cruz ("Afro-brasilidade" 125–26) believes this set "synthesizes [. . .] connections with both the Diaspora of the 'Black Atlantic' (Paul Gilroy) and classical Oriental culture," unavoidably echoing the prominent Brazilian utilizations of the powerful mythological figure of Orpheus: in the drama *Orfeu da Conceição,* by Vinícius de Moraes, and in its film adaptations (*Black Orpheus, Orfeu*).[14] From a historical point of view, perhaps the poem of greatest impact is "Desaparición de Rosendo Mendizábal y Otros." Its three parts—"Enigma,"

---

11. "el desafio es escoger la frase / que nos presenta unos a los otros" (23).

12. "la herencia no existe / sin un cuerpo-lenguaje que la / transforme" (23).

13. Adélcio de Sousa Cruz, "*Signo Cimarrón*: Diálogos Afro-Poético-Musicais." A *griot* is a West African (itinerant) bard, a treasured repository of oral tradition.

14. Luis (16) concurs. On these all, cf. Perrone "Don't Look Back" and "Myth, Melopeia, and Mimesis."

"Inscripciones," "Desciframiento"—present the establishment and deciphering of the supposed mystery of the disappearance of blacks in Buenos Aires. The title personage, an early mixed-blood tango composer, does not figure in the poem proper; the "protagonists" are the many thousands of Afro-Latin Americans (one-third of the city's population by one estimate) who went missing in the course of the nineteenth century in the main *urbs* of the River Plate. Barbosa (67–76) elucidates how this tripartite poem, which also has epical traces, proves to be a historical intervention in which a musical referent reaffirms metonymically an invisible presence whose formative cultural roles merit acknowledgment. The poem can surely be thought of as an Afro-transamerican act.[15]

As seen in the semiosis of the title itself, the literary horizon of EAP's *Signo cimarrón* is inseparable from its challenging of history. The overall epigraph—"¿Quién canta en las orillas del papel?" [Who sings on the shores of the paper?]—is effective. It is taken from Octavio Paz's *Libertad bajo palabra* (Liberty under Parole), a suggestive title where captivity and language (from oral epic poetry to modern verse) are in play. It also constitutes the first musical motif, while the word *orillas* brings to bear two connected semantemes: maritime travel and margins. Poems within allude to Paz's critical collection *Signos en rotación* and to his experimental text *Blanco* (Luis 18). Indeed, EAP's closing poem is precisely "Blanco," two meanings of which obtain: *white* is an ironic contrast with the theme of black folk, and *target* connotes a goal. The Brazilian poet writing in Spanish admits a fabular discursive function—"alguna narración se narra" [some narration is narrated]—and ends with the image of "otra cadena, más allá de las letras" [another chain, beyond letters], which is a final reminder of the legacy of bondage alongside hopeful links to something other beyond literature. Senses of remembrance and transcendence will follow.

As in most volumes by EAP, the table of contents of *Variaciones de un libro de sirenas* (three parts with respective subdivisions and subheadings) is somewhat intricate, almost implying a sort of cartographical figuration. The poet's preoccupations with memory and history continue, and an inter-Latin American ethic is palpable. In the first part, the epical strain is clear in the sectional rubric "Fábula," the first subheading of which, "Isla" (Island), directly embodies the trope of insularity and, with but one explicit reference (Columbus), speaks with sharp images to invention ("discovery" and fabrications) and colonial experience (including native presence, avarice,

---

15. On EAP's sources, poetics, and blackness, see his interview in Marques (58–79) in Portuguese, and (193–211) in Spanish; the book's bilingual publication is a clear transamerican gesture.

religion, bondage, testimony). The second part "Nave" (Vessel) advances the literal and symbolic utility of navigational figures, narrating an individual African arrival with collective significance on a continental scale in the poem "Anti-Adán": "I reside in the dispersed / continent / I offer sacrifice to no one / but rather doubt / about the life that I invent."[16] The semanteme of dispersion (read diaspora) is, naturally, decisive, even giving title to the whole second section.

This second sequence in Spanish by EAP revisits the lyrical intentionality he initiated in *Caderno de retorno*. Notions of mission also recur: "my task is to educate scarabs, telling them what there is beyond the shadows."[17] *Escarabajos* is a splendid vocabular choice, as it connotes the realm of nature (beetles), human problems (ill-shaped individuals, flaws in a cast), and defective communication (scrawl, poor handwriting). Carrizo (8) underlines the centrality of geographic metaphors of connection, apt indeed in this volume *Beyond Tordesillas*:

> Bridges—not mediations—in the direction of a language that rushes forth into a space without borders, toward a place of relationships, trying to argue with the Western expectation about seduction, seeking to approach the Other as necessarily human: "la estrechez / de los países exige / que me desplace" [the narrowness / of the countries demands / that I move about].

The narrator of this section of *Variaciones* concludes his appearance with a question made affirmation: "where am I? / this is not a doubt / but rather a bridge / to the place without borders."[18] And in the next section, a distinct poetic voice, feminine and mythlike, expresses a similar sentiment of interrelational duty:

> it is my task to become a bridge
> for those who
> do not cross their own fear
>
> •
>
> to enter into slumber is to exit
> the world
> not to live faraway

---

16. "resido en el disperso / continente / no ofrezco sacrificio a nadie / sino la duda / de la vida que invento . . ." (29).

17. "mi tarea es educar escarabajos, diciéndoles lo que hay más allá de la sombra" (57).

18. "¿dónde estoy? / ésta no es una duda / sino un puente / hasta el lugar sin fronteras" (58).

from things
but rather to blend with them.[19]

With his adoption of the language of Octavio Paz and Nicolás Guillén as a means to compose his sequence of poems, and his concern with hemispherically shared historical experience, EAP has lived and written via inter-American imperatives. What the web project *Banda Hispânica* envisioned ten years ago continues to be a work in progress, unfolding with unforeseen energies.[20] Among so many other modes of operation, the transamerican is an aspect of Brazilian lyric increasingly attuned to Hispanic counterparts. Criticism of contemporary poetry and song should continue to leave ample room to explore their interrelations and transnational wishes, following concerns with gender, sexuality, indigenous legacies, human rights, im/migration, travel, technologies, and more, any numbers of paths that lead beyond the symbol of the line of Tordesillas/Tordesilhas, toward increased understanding, cooperation, and artistic enjoyment.

WORKS CITED

Augusto, Ronaldo. "Espiral zeosória." *Afro-Hispanic Review* 29.2 (2010): 296–99.

Barbosa, Maria José Somerlate. *Recitação de passagem: a obra poética de Edimilson de Almeida Pereira*. Belo Horizonte: Mazza Edições, 2009.

Bauer, Ralph. "Hemispheric American Studies." *PMLA* 124.1 (2009): 234–50.

Carrizo, Silvina. "navegación de la palabra." Foreword to Pereira, *Variaciones de un libro de sirenas* 5–15.

Cruz, Adélcio de Sousa. "Afro-brasilidade urbana: poética da diáspora em performance." *Representações performáticas brasileiras: teorias, práticas e suas interfaces*. Ed. Marcos Antônio Alexandre. Belo Horizonte: Mazza Edições, 2007. 120–38.

19.
>   es mi tarea hacerme de puente
>   para quien
>   no cruza su propio miedo
>
>   •
>
>   entrar en el sueño es salir
>   del mundo
>   no para vivir lejano
>   de las cosas
>   sino para confundirse con ellas. (77)

20. The original location has become a set of four interconnected websites, with more nations and critical content included.

———. "Canto-poema e samba-blues: estratégias poéticas afro-descendentes na poesia de Edimilson de Almeida Pereira." Paper presented at XI Congresso Internacional da ABRALIC *Tessituras, Interações, Convergências*, 13–17 Jul. 2008, USP, São Paulo, Brazil.

———. "*Signo Cimarrón*: Diálogos Afro-Poético-Musicais." *LITERAFRO*. 1 Sep. 2011. <http://www.letras.ufmg.br/literafro>.

Luis, William. "Introducción a *Signo cimarrón*." Forward to Pereira, *Signo cimarrón*. 7–19.

Marques, Fabrício. *Dez conversas: diálogos com poetas contemporâneos*. São Paulo / Belo Horizonte: Gutenberg, 2004.

Moisés, Carlos Felipe. *Noite Nula*. São Paulo: Nankin, 2009.

Pereira, Edimilson de Almeida. *As coisas arcas: Obra Poética 4*. Belo Horizonte: Mazza Edições, 2003.

———. *Signo cimarrón*. Belo Horizonte: Mazza Edições, 2005.

———. *Variaciones de un libro de sirenas*. Belo Horizonte: Mazza Edições, 2010.

———. *Zeosório Blues: Obra Poética 1*. Belo Horizonte: Mazza, 2002.

———, ed. *Um tigre nas florestas: estudos sobre poesia e demandas sociais no Brasil*. Belo Horizonte: Mazza Edições, 2010.

Perrone, Charles A. *Brazil, Lyric, and the Americas*. Gainesville: UP of Florida, 2010.

———. "Don't Look Back: Myths, Conceptions, and Receptions of *Black Orpheus*." *Studies in Latin American Popular Culture* 17 (1998): 155–77.

———. "Myth, Melopeia, and Mimesis: *Black Orpheus, Orfeu*, and Internationalization in Brazilian Popular Music." *Brazilian Popular Music and Globalization*. Eds. Charles A. Perrone and Christopher Dunn. Gainesville: UP of Florida, 2001. 46–71.

Read, Justin. *Modern Poetics and Hemispheric American Cultural Studies*. New York: Palgrave Macmillan, 2009.

Spitta, Silvia, and Lois Parkinson Zamora. "Introduction: The Americas, Otherwise." *Comparative Literature* 61.3 (2009): 189–208.

CHAPTER 12

Cantigas de amigo

Galicia and Brazil in the Lusophone Musical Space

FREDERICK MOEHN

> Songs in the tide, sounds of our speech
> Songs in the tide, they are songs and that is all
> Songs of Guinea [Bissau], songs of Cape Verde
> Colors of Brazil, sea from the docks of Portugal
> Moon of Luanda, sound of Mozambique
> The Atlantic immersing the sounds of our speech
> Wind of Fisterra, lands of sand
> The Atlantic immersing the sounds of our speech
> Sails billowing, in the sea of Marola
> Sounds of São Tomé, from the streets of Lisbon
> Ay lele lele, ay lele lele, Songs in the tide
> —"Cantos na Maré," Uxía[1]

> Galicia has a surplus of the past and Brazil has a surplus of the future; the two together form an eternity of past and future.
> —Concha Rousia, President of the Brazil Galicia Cultural Institute[2]

IN MARCH 2010 the Brazil Galicia Cultural Institute (ICBG)—established five months earlier in Santiago de Compostela, Spain—opened a branch in Santa Catarina, in the south of Brazil. The inaugural celebration for it began with a performance of Brazil's national anthem and came to a close with "Os pinos" (The Pines), Galicia's official anthem, followed by a recitation of Gali-

---

I am grateful to Uxía, Luanda Cozetti, Aline Frazão, Lenine, Fred Martins, Xurxo Nóvoa Martins, Serginho Sales, Sérgio Tannus, and Xulio Villaverde, for sharing their musical worlds with me. The Fundação para a Ciência e a Tecnologia of Portugal provided research support through the Institute for Ethnomusicology (INET-MD) at the Universidade Nova de Lisboa. Richard Gordon, Robert Newcomb, and Ana Maria Alarcón provided helpful feedback.

1. The translation of these lyrics and all other translations from Galician and Portuguese sources in this essay are my own.

2. From the opening ceremony for the Brazilian branch of the Brazil Galicia Cultural Institute, as quoted in Silva.

cian poetry with guitar accompaniment and music from the Brazilian group Portal do Choro (*choro* is a Brazilian instrumental genre). The president of the new branch proclaimed that for Brazilians, getting to know Galicia and studying its culture "meant an awakening of their consciousness to the importance of language in our lives and in the culture of our people" (Silva). He was referring to the fact that modern Galician and Portuguese are easily mutually intelligible; they both emerged from medieval Galician-Portuguese, once the favored language of lyric poetry on the Iberian Peninsula. The female-voiced poems about male lovers referred to as *cantigas de amigo* (or *cantigas d'amigo*), such as those composed by the *joglar* (minstrel) Martín Códax and by King Denis of Portugal in the thirteenth century, are evidence of this heritage.

The ICBG's mission includes promoting mutual understanding and cultural, educational, scientific, and business collaboration between Galicia and Brazil in a variety of forums and events. It also seeks to encourage links of "Lusophone solidarity" between Portuguese-speaking countries through publications and digital media.[3] In a sense, the ICBG bypasses Lisbon-centric discourses of Portuguese heritage and claims a direct mother-tongue link between Galicia and the massive, economically dynamic South American country, a connection not freighted with the legacies of colonialism or Lusotropicalism.[4] It could be said that Galicia, with its "excess of history," as ICBG president Concha Rousia put it, is reaching out over the centuries and over the sea to partake of some of Brazil's "excess of future," as if to expunge another Galician history: its incorporation into the kingdoms of Castile and León, and subsequently the Spanish nation-state. Might Galicia offer a fruitful intellectual space for thinking beyond the clefts that we are glossing in this book with the metaphor of Tordesillas? If language is considered the primary basis for Galicia's cultural links with Brazil and Portugal (as with other countries where Portuguese is spoken), what role might music play in this space? The *cantigas de amigo* were, after all, also songs. Likewise, the writer Rosalia de Castro inaugurated the modern Galician language renaissance, or *Rexurdimento,* with a collection of poems labeled as songs: *Cantares Gallegos,* published in 1863.[5]

---

3. The ICBG's mission is wide-reaching; see the statement at <http://icbg.edublogs.org> (last accessed 5 Feb. 2012).

4. Lusotropicalism proposes that the Portuguese were uniquely tolerant and adaptable colonizers open to miscegenation with other "races" in "tropical" countries such as Brazil or the African colonies. The term was coined by Brazilian sociologist Gilberto Freyre in the 1930s and has been associated with the contested claim that Brazil is a "racial democracy." Freyre's ideas were eventually embraced by the Salazar dictatorship in Portugal in the 1950s, partly because they could be deployed to help justify Portugal's continued presence in Africa.

5. The *Rexurdimento* renaissance of the Galician language began in the mid-nineteenth century after the so-called Dark Centuries of Castilianization. At the time, Castilian Spanish

Galicia is officially recognized as an historic nationality within Spain. Since 1981 it has also enjoyed status as an autonomous community. Nevertheless, Galicia's centuries-old subordination to Castile and Madrid, aggravated under Francisco Franco (who was, in fact, Galician), has facilitated the increasing Castilianization of its language. Moreover, many Galicians speak Castilian at least part of the time in their day-to-day routines, especially in urban areas (Suárez). Yet Castilian influence over the community has also fueled the desire to help the Galician language thrive. There is, for example, an active debate over the orthography of Galician, with those of the *lusista* (Thompson) persuasion in favor of excising Castilian influences on spelling and instead adhering to the 1990 Portuguese Orthographic Accord, aimed at standardizing the written language.

Beyond the orthography debates, however, many Galician cultural actors often feel an affinity for Portuguese culture (particularly for that of the Minho region in the northwest of the country, the location of the original Portuguese state founded in the twelfth century by Afonso I). The celebrated Portuguese singer-songwriter José "Zeca" Afonso, for example, was beloved in Galicia. More recently, Brazil too has become increasingly important to those asserting affinities with other "Lusophone" contexts, as suggested by the ICBG platform. Legendary Brazilian singer-songwriter Caetano Veloso drew vociferous cheers of "Bravo Caetano!" when, during a 2008 performance at Quintana dos Mortos, in Santiago, he shrewdly announced on stage that he always speaks Portuguese rather than Spanish in Galicia, "because our language is Galician-Portuguese."[6]

In this chapter I explore how *lusofonia*—the notion that there are durable cultural links between lands where Portuguese is spoken—is put into practice through music making, with a brief examination of some recent musical projects and recordings from Galicia. The musicians I have come to know in this part of Iberia tend to be sympathetic to the "reintegrationist" movement, which advocates affiliating with the Community of Portuguese-Speaking Countries (CPLP). Galicia might be considered a space of friction in Iberian studies, perhaps even one that accentuates the linguistic and cultural differences between Portugal and Spain. At the same time, however, Galicia can serve to draw our attention away from Lisbon and Madrid, and trace alternative relationships between Iberia and the Americas. As Burghard Baltrusch

---

dominated in Galician cities and officialdom, while Galician had become a declining rural, nonliterary language.

6. See <http://www.youtube.com/watch?v=dEUg-IhIrm8> (last accessed 26 Feb. 2012).

has suggested, Galicia can "offer itself as a cultural hinge with its own identity, between the Lusophone and Hispanic worlds" (14).[7]

Indeed, for some of the musicians I researched in Galicia, Madrid and Lisbon might be described as symbolic loci of "embarrassment," to reference anthropologist Michael Herzfeld's framework of cultural intimacy in relation to the nation-state. For Herzfeld, this kind of intimacy occurs in settings where there exist shared aspects of identity about which a social group may feel "embarrassed" but which also foster common ground for engagement with the nation-state—in expressions of nationalism as well as of critique or resistance (3). Galician *lusista* cultural production runs contrary to Madrid's authority to claim it as belonging to a "regional" identity—to an "autonomous community" within the Spanish state. In fact, it prefers to ignore the bureaucratic concentration of power in Madrid and in Lisbon, the former administrative center of the Portuguese Empire. Whereas Galician reintegrationists feel affinity for Lusophone expressive culture—especially music and literature—cultural actors in the former colonial territories may feel ambivalent toward Lisbon as a political capital. "On the level of people's identities," the Angolan singer-songwriter Aline Frazão—who lives in Santiago de Compostela—told me during an interview, "conversation between the South and Portugal is difficult, because their way of doing things is very official in general, especially in Lisbon." Brazilians and Angolans, Aline felt, tended to be more informal, making communication with Portugal difficult. Galicia represents, she said, something of a "neutral territory" in this regard, or, as the Galician singer-songwriter Uxía (Uxía Senlle) put it during this group interview, "virgin territory."[8]

Thus, those forms of embarrassment that seem to have roots in the legacy of colonial domination may be offset by a sense of "cultural relief," as Sérgio put it, when Brazilians learn that there is a linguistic connection with a setting that stands outside of the former Empire, and that actually appears to claim "older" links than Lisbon can. These affinities speak to the "forms of rueful self-recognition" that characterize cultural intimacy in Herzfeld's view (3). In truth, Brazilians seem to have little use for the term *lusofonia*. They tend to perceive "Luso" as attributing primacy to the Portuguese aspect, whereas Brazilian national identity discourse has typically privileged the country's history of miscegenation between Portuguese, Africans, and Amerindians. Brazilian

---

7. Similarly, Hooper and Moruxa see Galicia as situated between "the Atlantic north and the Mediterranean south" and between Europe and America, with ties to both *hispanidad* and *lusofonia* (1).

8. From a group interview I conducted with Aline Frazão, Uxía, Sérgio Tannus, and Xurxo Nóvoa Martins, 8 Mar. 2011, in Santiago de Compostela.

author Luiz Ruffato proposed substituting the term "galeguia" (from *galego*) for *lusofonia*. Galician is the true mother tongue, he suggested; the term *galeguia* "diminishes the weight of the colonial past, and reincorporates, with due credit, Galicia into this shared universe" (214). Meanwhile, cultural actors sympathetic to the reintegrationist movement strive to reverse the effects of a history of state-supported efforts to render the Galician minority language a source of embarrassment.

Consider, for example, the program for a festival of Galician- and Portuguese-language cultural expression called éMundial, held in Vigo in June 2012. The reintegrationist Galician Language Association (AGAL) organized three weeks of events featuring "people and realities that speak our language with different musicalities, colors, and forms" (a phrase which, admittedly, does not translate elegantly into English).[9] The aim was to show that the Galician language represents "a strength and an opportunity, not a problem," and that Galicians "can navigate in a linguistic and cultural world that spans four continents [and] unites 250 million people." The organizers of éMundial sought to demonstrate that Galicians have access to the artistic and business output of this wider world, and that language is Galicia's "competitive advantage in the Spanish and European setting." Uxía prepared a brief video message to help promote the event. The best path for "joining our voices," she said in the clip while accompanying herself on acoustic guitar, "is [through] our music." The tools for advancing this brotherhood, she went on, are "mutual knowledge, melodies, the common language, our rhythms, which guide us on how to reach this dream, which is no longer a utopia." So long as Galicia travels the path of *lusofonia,* of *galeguia,* Uxía concluded, it is worldwide (*mundial*). She ended by singing to a chant-like melody, "Galician is worldwide."[10]

Conceptualizing *lusofonia* as rooted in the tongue of the former "discoverers" and colonizers not only seems to exclude the Galician language; it also cedes no fundamental role for the variety of other languages spoken (not necessarily written) in spaces politically mapped as Lusophone, including indigenous languages in Brazil or Angola, for example, or Cape Verdean Kriolo. The notion of *galeguia* does not actually mitigate this particular problem and perhaps even runs the risk of further essentializing cultural solidarity. Moreover, there exists a conceptual tension between thinking about Galician as a kind of "mother tongue" to Portuguese—or as in some ways closer to medieval Galician-Portuguese—on the one hand, and thinking of it as a dialect

---

9. Website for éMundial 2012 <http://emundial.org/2012/que-e-3> (last accessed 13 Apr. 2013).

10. See <http://www.youtube.com/watch?feature=player_embedded&v=W-bKlkEoi4M> (last accessed 14 Apr. 2013).

that should be "re-integrated" into contemporary Portuguese, on the other. Baltrusch thus cautions that instrumentalizing a particular language "as the ontological vehicle of the identity of a people will always be revealed as a consecration lacking foundation" (11). Orthographic accords cannot reverse the grammatical distinctions that have already occurred between, for example, European and Brazilian Portuguese, he points out. On the contrary, they may continue to diverge, Baltrusch suggests, without this being an impediment to the emergence of new and revitalizing cultural exchanges (9). Language is "merely the shell that surrounds [. . .] the translational dynamic to which myths, ideologies, and other cultural values are subject" (11).

Music, in this context, offers the possibility to move discussions of *lusofonia* (and *hispanidad*) beyond linguistic foundationalism. Indeed, while linguistic affinities are important to musicians sympathetic to reintegration, and while the lyrical component is a salient aspect of the music of Uxía and other singer-songwriters working in Galicia, there are additional dimensions to music making that heighten affective sympathies with—for example—Brazilian musical cultures. These include, as Uxía suggested in the video message just described, melodies and rhythms, as well as specific musical instruments or shared knowledge of repertory. These musicians have studied the musical "language" of *bossa nova* and are familiar with the rhythmic syncopations of Brazilian *samba* percussion, the timbres of Portuguese *fado*, the bluesy melodies of Cape Verdean *morna*, and other key genres that circulate among listeners and practitioners of Lusophone music.

Fernando Arenas has suggested that affective ties represent an important and largely unexamined aspect of *lusofonia*, one that is "fraught with contradiction and ambiguity" because of the legacies of colonialism and the dynamics of globalization (137). He writes of "the draw of affect pulling Brazil simultaneously toward Portugal and Africa" (31) but, as already suggested, Galicia appeals to some as a cultural setting that remains outside of this postcolonial space. Affect speaks to the complex of sentiments, practices, and material objects (such as the nylon-stringed classical guitar, or the tambourine) that allow these creative agents to feel "at home" in a given expressive context, or that promote feelings of solidarity, perhaps a sense that social "conversations"—oral, written, musical, visual—can proceed under the presumption of a certain level of shared cultural heritage. Crucially, however, affective engagement between Galician and Brazilian musicians does not presume complete identification of cultural forms or practices; there is similarity *and* difference. The Galician *pandeireta*, for example, is not played the same way as the Brazilian *pandeiro*, and it sounds different too. Musicians find the juxtaposition of these two similar but distinct instruments to be interesting.

At the same time, economic considerations may also motivate cultural producers who seek to present their work as Lusophone. These would seem to be particularly vital to a minority language community. Thus, for example, the reintegrationist monthly magazine *Novas da Galiza* recently chose to apply the norms of the Orthographic Accord to its articles. Eduardo Maragoto of the magazine explained: "In terms of strengthening the language, applying the OA brings Portuguese and Galician much closer together because people begin to see more economically and politically valuable futures for Galician."[11] Musicians are sometimes the first to admit that they seek to expand their listenership (and perhaps thereby to increase their sources of income). This dynamic is not simply about "massifying" one's product to reach ever-wider publics within a given market. Many musicians in Galicia are not making music for so-called mainstream listening publics. Precisely because their work appeals to niche audiences, they need to find how far those niches extend. Cognizant of Brazil's growing influence in world culture and business, Galician musicians see the South American country as a potential market for their work. Yet they find that most Brazilians know little about Galicia, and so there is a kind of informational campaign built into those projects that seek broader publics in Brazil and other parts of the Portuguese-speaking world.

In sum, for cultural actors in Galicia, genuine and deep-rooted affective sentiments can be accompanied by hopes of reaching new audiences. We are presented with a form of cultural intimacy that spills beyond the stifling confines of nation-states through international musical collaborations, taste communities, and markets. A brief look at the recent work of Uxía, the most prominent musician advocating for Galicia's relevance to the Lusophone cultural space, can help illustrate these points.

PERFORMING *LUSOFONIA*: UXÍA AND THE *CANTOS NA MARÉ* MUSICAL EVENT

As an artist who began her career in the 1980s, when Galician nationalism was emerging from the shadows of the Franco years, Uxía has been at the center of the autonomous community's vibrant folk music scene for over twenty-five years. Since 2003 she has organized an annual Lusophone music festival in Pontevedra (a city and province in the southeast of Galicia, bordering Portugal), called Cantos na Maré (Songs of the Tide), with musicians from various Portuguese-speaking countries, including Brazil (Chico César, Socorro Lira,

---

11. "Jornal galego *Novas da Galiza* aplica novo acordo ortográfico," no author attributed.

Paulinho Moska, for example). The opening epigraph to this chapter presents the lyrics to her theme song for this event. They name various places in Galicia and other countries where Portuguese is spoken—Luanda, Lisbon, Guinea-Bissau, Mozambique, for example—and describe the Atlantic as "immersing the sounds of our speech." Songs of these various places wash up on Galicia's shores "in the tide." The "Ay lele lele" vocables faintly echo the traditional refrain of the *alalá* genre of Galicia.

Uxía recorded her album *Meu Canto* (2011) in São Paulo and Rio de Janeiro with a mix of Brazilian and Galician repertory, and with guest performances from Brazilian musicians such as Jaime Alem, Lui Coimbra, Socorro Lira, Marcos Lobo, Marcelo Martins, Júlio Santin, and Ricardo Vignini. Her musical director, the guitarist and arranger Sérgio Tannus (introduced above), is from Niterói, near the city of Rio de Janeiro. Now living in Santiago de Compostela, Sérgio has taken to calling himself a "Brasilego" (contraction of Brazilian-Galician). In our interview Sérgio related the story of how he ended up in Santiago de Compostela. At home in Brazil in April 2006 he attended a cultural festival titled Niterói Meets Spain, part of a series of annual encounters featuring different guest nations. Sérgio met Uxía and other Galician musicians at the festival, including drummer Luís Alberto and guitarist Marcos Teira. He discovered an immediate affinity for the Galician language and for the music. He had no idea, he recalled, that Galicia had a culture so distinct from the rest of Spain. With an invitation from Pepe Sendón (who, like Marcos Teira, had been a bandmate of the Galician rock singer-songwriter Narf), Sérgio traveled to the capital of Galicia in September 2006 to perform in a duo with Brazilian singer-guitarist Lilian França at the Municipal Theater. He "walked on the stones of Santiago," he remembered, and saw the great cathedral. With the concert "the door opened," as people established in the local arts scene approached him to talk and network after the show. The duo spent six months touring Spain, beginning and ending in Galicia. By the time Sérgio returned to Brazil, he had resolved to move to Santiago de Compostela. "I arrived and they adopted me," he recalls. "I don't stay in any place just for the work," he added. "I stay for the good energy of the people, for the good music. So I thought to myself, 'There's work here. There are good people, there's culture, I'm hearing things that we don't hear in Brazil. I need to spend some time here.'" Aside from working with Uxía, Sérgio also hosted a regular Brazilian music jam session at the Borriquita de Belém bar in Santiago (among other musical collaborations); in 2012 he released a solo album titled *Son Brasilego* (Brasilego Sound), featuring musicians from Brazil, Angola, Portugal, and Galicia performing his own repertoire.

To return to Uxía's *Meu Canto* album, which she co-produced with Sérgio, a promotional text proposes that it "follows the path of a culture that travels and transforms the meaning and nature of borders."[12] It opens with a traditional song, "Verde gaio" (Green Parakeet), heard in Galicia, Portugal, and Brazil. Brazilian singer-songwriter Lenine sings a duet with Uxía for the song "Os teus ollos" (Your Eyes), the text to which is a poem by a late nineteenth-century *Rexurdimento* writer, Manuel Curros Enríquez. Likewise, for "Daquelas que cantan" Uxía wrote a song for a poem by *Rexurdimento* author Rosalia de Castro. It utilizes a kind of *maxixe*/tango rhythm, with accordion accompaniment from Brazilian João Carlos Coutinho (*maxixe* is a Brazilian genre with a rhythm somewhat similar to that of the tango; it was popular in the late nineteenth and early twentieth centuries). For "Alalás encadeado" Uxía and Sérgio wrote a composition in the traditional *alalá* style with lyrics from an unpublished poem by the Galician writer Uxio Novoneyra. This chant-like song form—which, as mentioned, features a refrain with the vocables "a-la-la"—is strongly associated with Galician nationalism, and may be performed with *gaita* (bagpipe) interludes. On Uxía's song, however, guest musician Júlio Santin provides accompaniment on a *viola caipira*, a distinctly Brazilian guitar used in the *cantoria* ballad tradition. For "Menino do bairro negro" (Boy from the Black Neighborhood, by the Portuguese José "Zeca" Afonso, mentioned above), Sérgio plays *cavaquinho*, a small four-stringed guitar-like instrument popular in Brazil and Cape Verde, and believed to have originated in Braga, in the north of Portugal (close to Galicia).

Many Brazilian listeners will recognize Paulo César Pinheiro and João Nogueira's declamatory samba, "Minha missão" (My Mission). Uxía sings the first verse in a commanding voice as she accompanies herself on the Galician *pandeireta*: "When I sing / it is to relieve my tears / and the tears of one who has already suffered so." For the second verse, however, the song switches to samba as Sérgio performs the Brazilian *pandeiro* (as well as guitar accompaniment through overdubbing in the recording studio), making a creative link between the *pandeireta* and *pandeiro* tambourine styles (which are, in fact, quite different, although both instruments likely descend from Moorish / North African frame drums). The comparison—not perfect identification—is what makes the song both intelligible and interesting to the "brasilego." Uxía closes the album with "Alalá das Mariñas," a traditional Galician alalá, with sparse acoustic guitar accompaniment from Sérgio and flute from Marcelo Martins. In the opening moments, Carlos Blanco reads a verse by Xurxo Nóvoa Martins, a writer from Vigo: "In the tide of bod-

---

12. Publicity text from the recording label Fol Música: <http://www.folmusica.com/web.php/seo/?_pagi_pg=26> (last accessed 26 Feb. 2012).

ies / that move through the ins and outs of the city without rest / humanity cries but I remain silent / and the wind, friend in the dawn, brings your song closer to me."

In December 2010, when I attended Uxía's *Cantos na Maré* music festival, Lenine was the featured Brazilian musician; he joined Guadi Galego (from Galicia), Aline Frazão (introduced above: Angolan, based in Santiago de Compostela), and António Zambujo (a Portuguese singer-songwriter) as the other headlining artists (along with Uxía). A scene from the after-party following the concert impressed upon me how familiarity with song repertory can enable performances of *lusofonia*. Concert participants and friends met for a late tapas-style dinner in the old center of Pontevedra. They chose an informal tavern-like establishment in which, soon after eating marinated octopus and cured meats with Albariño white wine from the Rias Baixas, the musicians began to sing and play. Uxía, with Sérgio Tannus on guitar, introduced a medley that the two had arranged for a previous Lusophone musical event in Santiago. She began it by singing a well-known traditional Galician folk melody, "Ven bailar Carmiña" (Come Dance, Carmiña). She followed this with the 1957 Brazilian *baião* "Mulher Rendeira" (Woman Lace Maker, with lyrics purportedly penned in 1922 by the great bandit of the Brazilian Northeast, Lampião), and then Brazilian Luiz Gonzaga's classic anthem of the hard life of the Northeast, "Asa Branca" (White Wing, the name of a local bird).

As Uxía sang Gonzaga's verses, Lenine, who is from Pernambuco, in the northeast of Brazil, and thus has a special connection with Gonzaga's music, extemporized in a call-and-response manner. Aline Frazão then kept the medley going by slowing the tempo to sing the beloved Cape Verdean *morna* "Sodade" (written by Armando Zeferino Soares, but best known in Cesária Évora's voice). Aline improvised her own melody on the verses; she was joined by the entire room on the refrain, "Sodade, sodade, sodade, dess nha terra, São Nicolau" (meaning, roughly, "nostalgia and longing for my land, São Nicolau"). Among the other musicians present were Brazilian singer and former Cantos na Maré artist Luanda Cozetti (a resident of Lisbon); the featured Portuguese musician António Zambujo, whose music draws on the *fado* style; Xulio Villaverde, who teaches Galician percussion in Lisbon; and Brazilian ethnomusicology student Claudia Goes (pursuing graduate studies at the Universidade Nova de Lisboa). Goes joined in on the *pandeiro*. It was an intensely affective, intimate (and unofficial, nonbureaucratic) affirmation of Galicia's place in the "community of Portuguese-speaking countries."

LUSOFONIA AS AN ONTOLOGY OF TRANSLATION

Performative moments like these, of which I have witnessed several in Galicia and Lisbon, have obliged me to take the idea of *lusofonia* seriously, despite the valid critiques that scholars have offered of it.[13] The point is not to disavow these critiques, or to show *lusofonia* as "real" or harmonious. A concept that scholars can reveal to be internally inconsistent, unevenly embraced, or ideologically problematic may nevertheless shape the performance and experience of meaningful, enjoyable sociality. The critical work is to parse the ways in which sameness and difference, understanding and misunderstanding, play out in expressive practices and communities. Contemporary Galician and Brazilian music probably have comparatively little in common in terms of basic structural elements. "There aren't many similarities in rhythm," Sérgio Tannus observed. Instead, affect seems to drive processes of musical translation: "But this power [*força*], this desire, and these roots are very much alike in Brazil and in Galicia," Sérgio asserted, "because we are brothers and sometimes we mix up the rhythms. [So] sometimes we play the Brazilian *pandeiro* [together with] the Galician *pandeireta*." "For Galicians I am different," Sérgio conceded, "and Galicia is different for me." Yet, he claims that he feels more "like himself" in Santiago than in Niterói. Is this paradoxical, or is Sérgio so comfortable there because he found difference *in* sameness (or vice versa)?

Baltrusch argues for an ontology of translation in understanding Galicia's potential place in *lusofonia*. Much of what people like to label as "Lusophone" in their culture, he observes, "is in reality not intelligible to them, whether because of linguistic divergences or because of cultural differences" (10). While there "exists a Lusophone culture and media industry that allows a small group of companies and creative individuals to survive from its production," he observes, "these fundamentally economic (and often subsidized) relations obscure major political, social, and cultural divergences" (10). Uxía is in fact dismayed with how little Brazilians know about Galicia. The Brazilian musical soundscape is today so large and varied that it has no pressing "need" of Galicia, or even of Portugal, for that matter. From a market perspective, Galicia (and Portugal) are insignificant; Lenine, for example, probably sells more and fills bigger performance spaces in France, where he has established ties in the music business, than he does in Iberia.

But Brazilian-Galician cultural exchanges do not presume perfect understanding. On the contrary, there is enough difference to make things inter-

---

13. Some important critical essays on *lusofonia* and the related notion of Lusophone postcolonialism are Almeida, Madureira, Margarido, Sanches, and Santos.

esting, to stimulate feelings of *discovery*, and enough sameness to facilitate communication, to make it seem like heritage, to allow individuals to feel that they are finding or enabling *a part of themselves*. Baltrusch draws on Ludwig Wittgenstein's concept of "family resemblance" (a term in use in the nineteenth century to describe language families). The anti-essentialist concept points to a kind of fabric of similarities in instances where it may seem that there exists one fundamental feature in common (such as language). In fact, many cultural expressions of the "agglomerate called *lusofonia*," he points out, "require translation, explanation, contextualization," or what he calls "paratranslation" (10).[14] Galicia, Baltrusch holds, is well situated for such work. I would add that as cultural agents, musicians can experience the excitement of being among those who are forging such links and discoveries in their creative practice; they and their audiences can immerse themselves, to quote from Uxía's song lyrics for "Cantos na maré," in the "songs of the tide" (as I did at the festival after-party described above, for example).

CONCLUSIONS

Baltrusch may be right that the Lusophone cultural marketplace can obscure "a lack of critical work on the memory of the colonial past and, above all, a significant lack of interest in real translations and adaptations of cultures and values, and of their corresponding criticism" (10). However, musicians work with sound, lyrics, timbres, emotions, performance, and they do so in a cultural marketplace. Brazil seems to offer the potential to expand audiences, and Galician musicians may be interested in doing so both out of genuine affective affinity and because it seems like a good way to promote their work. Meanwhile, some Brazilian musicians, such as Sérgio Tannus, have made Santiago de Compostela their home, feeling comfortable in its *lusista* cultural settings.

At the time of this writing, the crisis of the Euro currency has highlighted national, regional, and other particularities of the European Union. International Monetary Fund / European Central Bank loans to Spain, Portugal, Italy, Greece, and Cyprus demand austerity measures and economic reforms, which

---

14. "Paratranslation" (or para/tradución, as Baltrusch sometimes writes it) is a concept associated with professor Yuste Frías at the University of Vigo, in Galicia, where Baltrusch also works. The basic idea is that there are elements that are parallel to a "text itself" that also require translation (essentially, the cultural context). Nord argues that the neologism is unnecessary because it merely identifies what translators have always done. My point here is simply that *lusofonia* does not presume complete intelligibility from one context to another where Portuguese (or Galician) is spoken.

some perceive as threats to sovereignty, while the political discourse can veer toward stereotypes about lack of fiscal discipline and transparency in the southern European nations. In 2013 youth unemployment in Portugal reportedly reached 40 percent (Minder), and the scenario was not much better in Spain at the time (meanwhile, as the economies of the southern nations contract, governments collect fewer revenues and are unable to meet the terms of the loans). Massive emigration, of course, is not new to Iberia. Galicians, for example, have long overrepresented Spain's ex-patriate community (while they are 6 percent of the population of Spain, one statistic counts them as 27 percent of Spaniards abroad; Hooper and Moruxa 2). At the same time, anti-immigration policies seem to be gaining strength in Europe, which may result in Latin American or Lusophone African nationals finding fewer opportunities in Portugal or Spain.

How *lusofonia* and *hispanidad* will emerge from the Euro crisis is unclear. Baltrusch argues that together these two identifications "form part of a vague and malleable superstructure," or even a "mythical meta-system" called *latinidad,* in "competition with an efficiently predatory anglofonia" (5). This may be true as far as it goes. Today, however, we see Brazil as an economic power competing with China for investments in development projects in Angola and Mozambique, for example. So can emergent Brazil-Galicia musical collaborations help advance the project to move "beyond Tordesillas"? To the extent that they divert our attention from the old capitals of Madrid and Lisbon, highlighting internal frictions and postcolonial resonances in the two Iberian states, I think so. Insofar as they join sincere affective affinities with the potential of do-it-yourself music production and an awareness of contemporary market realities, perhaps they open doors to new discussions about Iberian and Latin American cultural heritage.

However, while the terms *lusofonia* and "the Lusophone world" continue to be called upon to describe a variety of cultural productions and affinities, these ways of framing cultural practices struggle to escape their roots in conservative and somewhat essentialist notions of heritage. Culture flows from various centers and in diverse directions, perhaps especially in popular music. As we continue to research these questions, we would do well to study in greater depth the pronounced Caribbean influence in Angolan music, or in popular music from the north and northeast of Brazil, or the fascination that the hipster singers in the Rio de Janeiro-based big band Orquestra Imperial have for old Spanish-language boleros and cha cha chas, to give a few examples. Also of interest is a recently inaugurated team research project focused on Expressive Culture at the Luso-Hispanic Border, based at the Institute for

Ethnomusicology (INET-MD) at the Universidade Nova de Lisboa, which will generate several publications in the coming years. On Galician identity specifically, the online journal *Galicia21: Journal of Contemporary Galician Studies* is a good resource. The barriers to communication and understanding that we are glossing with the metaphor of Tordesillas have proved surprisingly durable, not least in academia, but there are conversations happening.

WORKS CITED

Almeida, Miguel Vale de. "Pitfalls and Perspectives in Anthropology, Postcolonialism, and the Portuguese-Speaking World." *An Earth-Colored Sea: 'Race,' Culture and the Politics of Identity in the Post-Colonial Portuguese-Speaking World*. New York: Berghan Books, 2004. 101–14.

Arenas, Fernando. *Lusophone Africa: Beyond Independence*. Minneapolis and London: U of Minnesota P, 2011.

Baltrusch, Burghard. "Galiza e a Lusofonía—unha tradución entre a miraxe e a utopía." *Galicia21* A (2009): 4–19.

Herzfeld, Michael. *Cultural Intimacy: Social Poetics in the Nation State*. 2nd ed. New York: Routledge, 2005.

Hooper, Kirsty, and Manuel Puga Moruxa. "Introduction: Galician Geographies." *Contemporary Galician Cultural Studies: Between the Local and the Global*. Eds. Kirsty Hooper and Manuel Puga Moruxa. New York: Modern Language Association, 2011. 1–16.

"Jornal galego *Novas da Galiza* aplica novo acordo ortográfico." *Público*. Web. 10 Feb. 2011.

Madureira, Luís. "Is the Difference in Portuguese Colonialism the Difference in Lusophone Postcolonialism?" Rev. of *Toward a Portuguese Postcolonialism*. Ed. Anthony Soares. *Lusophone Studies 4* (October 2006). *Ellipsis* 6 (2008): 135–41.

Margarido, Alfredo. *A lusofonia e os lusófonos: novos mitos portugueses*. Lisboa: Edições Universitárias Lusófonas, 2000.

Minder, Raphael. "Europe's Reservations on Immigration Grow." *New York Times*. New York Times. Web. 28 May 2013.

Nord, Christiane. "Paratranslation: A New Paradigm or a Re-Invented Wheel?" *Perspectives: Studies in Translatology* 20.4 (2012): 399–409.

Ruffato, Luiz. "Galeguia." *Agália: Revista da Associaçom Galega da Língua* 89/90 (2007): 213–14.

Sanches, Manuela Ribeiro. "'Where' Is the Post-Colonial? In-Betweenness, Identity, and 'Lusophonia' in Trans/National Contexts." *New Hybridities: Societies and Cultures in Transition*. Eds. Frank Heidemann and Alfonso de Toro. Hildesheim and New York: Georg Olms, 2006. 115–45.

Santos, Boaventura de Sousa. "Between Prospero and Caliban: Colonialism, Postcolonialism, and Inter-Identity." *Luso-Brazilian Review* 39.2 (2002): 9–43.

Silva, José Carlos da. "Brasil e Galiza formam uma eternidade de passado e futuro." Portal Galego da Língua, 3 Apr. 2010. Web. 25 Feb. 2012. <http://pglingua.org/especiais/espaco-brasil/2220-brasil-e-galiza-formam-uma-eternidade-de-passado-e-futuro>.

Suárez, Anxo M. Lorenzo. "A situación actual da lingua galega: unha ollada desde a sociolingüística e a política lingüística." *Galícia21* A (2009): 20–39.

Tannus, Sérgio et al. *Son brasilego*. Fol Música, 2012. Compact Disc.

Thompson, John Patrick. "Portuguese or Spanish Orthography for the Galizan Language? An Analysis of the *Conflito Normativo*." *Contemporary Galician Cultural Studies*. Eds. Kirsty Hooper and Manuel Puga Moruxa. New York: Modern Language Association, 2011. 143–65.

Uxía et al. *Meu canto*. Fol Música, 2011. Compact Disc.

PART IV

LUSO-HISPANIC CINEMA, PERFORMANCE, AND VISUAL CULTURE

CHAPTER 13

Cartography of Dissidence

In/visibility and Urban Display in Luso-Hispanic Street Projects

TINA ESCAJA

IN HIS theory of performance, Richard Schechner emphasized the urban, collective, and transcultural nature of street performance, extendable to urban interventions and traveling exhibitions that are common in the new millennium.[1] This element, which Schechner defined as "intercultural, inter-generic and inter-disciplinary," proves applicable to the Luso-Hispanic correlations and their cultural and countercultural paradigms. In this essay I investigate two examples of performance that are related to gender violence, highlighting their Luso-Hispanic correlations in terms of parallel contexts of protest and resistance through art and collective interaction.

The first, "Na Prisão" (In Prison), from the Brazilian Grupo do Trecho, founded in 2007 in São Paulo, presents a cartography of dissidence that, like the international "counter-maps" projects of Unnayan in Calcutta, seeks to make "*visible* through mapping those who are traditionally made *invisible* by mapping" (Sen 13; emphasis in original). In the case of "Na Prisão," within its "Performance 1" entitled "Ausências" (Absences), carried out in July 2010 on

---

For a full version see Escaja. Translation from the original Spanish by Leonora Dodge and Tina Escaja.

    1. For a discussion of the term "performance" in the Hispanic context, here applicable to Brazil, as well as an overview of relevant research, see Diana Taylor and Juan Villegas, *Negotiating Performance: Gender, Sexuality, and Theatricality in Latin/o America* (Durham and London: Duke UP, 1994). Other relevant sources include Hernán Vidal's edition of essays, *Cultural and Historical Grounding for Hispanic and Luso-Brazilian Feminist Literary Criticism* (Minneapolis: Institute for the Study of Literature and Ideology, 1989), and Bonnie Marranca and Gautam Dasgupta (eds.), *Interculturalism and Performance* (New York: PAJ, 1991).

Paulista Avenue in São Paulo as a result of the group's artistic residence in the women's prison of Butantã, the map outlined on the ground in front of a police stand shows the floor plan of the jail, with a space for breastfeeding "*desativado*" (deactivated). A dividing line between DENTRO and FORA (inside and outside) of the jail invites viewers to choose where to stand while considering this request: "Allow the rainy season to erase these strokes, because this is definitely not dirt."[2] The temporary and collective value of the project chalked on asphalt emphasizes the transitory and invisible nature of our collective memory with regard to the oppressive spaces of inequality denounced by this project. This ephemeral discourse of dissidence and reaction contrasts, however, with other urban protests that are of a more permanent nature and which have reached a certain "prestige," such as graffiti, or *pichações* (tags).

The second, "Las bellas durmientes" (Sleeping Beauties), by the "Antimuseo de Arte Contemporáneo" (Anti-museum of Contemporary Art), based in Madrid, promulgates dissidence toward a cultural institution that monopolizes and controls the art industry, reclaiming public spaces through collective art projects. In "Las bellas durmientes," led by Peruvian artist María María Acha, the group presents a collective and itinerant exhibition that pays tribute to female victims of domestic violence. The call to participants on the group's web page, which is presented as "open and permanent," involves stickers printed with numbers and information about the victims, or "sleeping beauties," with the date and cause of their death. With the stickers, which show a bed evoking the well-known fairy tale, the group invites participants to pay homage to the victim and to create a registry that eventually will be transported by the Anti-museum's project coordinators. The goal is identical to that of Grupo do Trecho: to reclaim the public space, to question the ruling mechanisms of the culture industry, to enter into dialogue with the community, to make visible and denounce the dispossession and abuse of repressed social sectors, to question and interact with notions of art and society, with implications that are ultimately poetic.

A comparative investigation will enable an interrelated understanding of the cultural, artistic, and historical contexts of both urban projects. The reflections on gender violence, specifically, arise out of the respective political struggles of the 1970s in both countries. If in Brazil they emerge partially as a result of the debates surrounding violence and torture during the dictatorship, in Spain it is the end of the Franco regime, as a product of debates likewise influenced by feminist currents, that allowed the development of institutional structures to aid victims of violence against women. Finally, the Internet has

---

2. "[...] permitam que o tempo de chuva apague esses traços, que isto, sim, não é sujeira." All translations from Portuguese by Debora Teixeira.

become a collective vehicle to unite, distribute, and document the values of denunciation and art that both projects explore.

GENDER VIOLENCE AS A RESIDUUM OF DICTATORIAL POLITICS

In her detailed report on violence against women in Brazil, Dorothy Q. Thomas describes the first attempts to reform laws concerning domestic violence, which occurred during the 1970s, in connection with the debate on violence under the dictatorship: "Reports on sexual abuse, torture and murder of political prisoners during the dictatorship led to a national debate about violence and, in the mid-1970s, to the creation of a number of non-governmental human rights organizations in which women were very active" (7). As Thomas explains, violence against women and state-sponsored violence were connected (and remain connected) in such a way as to subject women to legal and social discrimination. Despite advances in consciousness-raising regarding violence against women, as well as the proliferation of women's groups beginning in the 1980s and the adoption of laws designed to protect women, violence against women remains widespread, and receives limited or very little attention from the legal system. Thus Thomas explains in her report: "Analysts with whom Americas Watch spoke stressed the continuing failure of Brazil's criminal justice system to treat violence against women as a crime, deserving of investigation and protection with the same vigor as homicide and physical abuse occurring in the general population" (15). A symptomatic example is the persistent perception that the killing of women for reasons of adultery amounts to a "crime of passion" [*violenta emoção*] or "of honor," which justifies the action of the killer and places the blame for the crime on the victim. The rewriting of related laws, which has occurred in recent years, has not eliminated this form of prejudice, which continues to impact the application of justice. "Violent emotion" continues to be perceived as a mitigating factor or "legitimate defense" [*legítima defesa*] in so-called crimes of honor committed by men [*homicídio culposo*], while identical crimes committed by women under the same rubric are considered intentional [*homicídio doloso*], which leads to considerably more severe sentences (Thomas 16–17) and is one of the causes of women's confinement in Brazil's large and insalubrious penitentiaries.

Likewise, Spain revised its laws concerning women during the 1970s, with the country's democratization and the rise of the feminist movement. The Franco dictatorship had mounted a frontal assault on the rights of women, as a patriarchal state that emphasized the subordination of women to men. In fact, *franquismo* marked a significant curtailing of the freedoms that had been won by women during the Spanish Republic (Soto Marco). With Spain's democratization, the laws that had protected men in cases of homicide for reasons of adultery—that is, "crimes of passion"—which had been reinstated during the Franco regime, were revoked, and adultery was decriminalized. The number of women's groups multiplied during the 1980s in direct proportion to women's achievement of social and legal rights. The culmination of this process of consciousness-raising and women's empowerment occurred when the law directly addressed violence against women, the instances of which have nonetheless increased at a disturbing rate over the past decades. In January 2005, the Ley Orgánica de Medidas de Protección Integral contra la Violencia de Género (Organic Law Concerning Means of Protection for Violence Against Women) came into effect. Despite the valuable and innovative aspects of this law, three years after its inauguration the Spanish branch of Amnesty International noted irregularities in the law's application in a report that bore the suggestive title "Obstinada realidad, derechos pendientes" (A Stubborn Reality, Rights Withheld).

The State is ineffective in preventing, and is even complicit in permitting, violence against women—a situation common to many countries. As intellectuals and artists like Sally Gutiérrez have argued, in debates sponsored by the Anti-museum, this complicity and ineffectiveness are quite closely tied to a cultural policy that imposes certain parameters and encourages an acritical and conformist attitude on the part of the citizen *qua* consumer. Resistance to this situation manifests itself in the Luso-Hispanic context in expressions that are necessarily countercultural, and specifically, in urban interventions and alternate cartographies of empowerment and dissidence.

URBAN ART AS SUBVERSIVE IN/ACTION: "ABSENCES" BY GRUPO DO TRECHO

In July 2010, on the doorstep of a theater along the elegant Paulista Avenue in São Paulo, possibly the Teatro do Sesi-SP, a private entity associated with the FIESP (Federation of Industries of the State of São Paulo), which sponsors shows after a video advertising the institution, the passersby/citizens became unsuspecting participants in an urban intervention, "In Prison," by Grupo do Trecho, part of their project entitled "Absences." The double intervention (private/public by the passerby-citizen, and urban/performance by Grupo do Trecho), was especially disquieting and complex since it consisted of a diagram of a women's prison, drawn in chalk upon the elitist Paulista Avenue, right in front of a police stand. The group's objective, as they explain on their website, was "to generate cracks and break through the limits between art and reality as a means of questioning what is normal, in order to catch a glimpse of other possibilities; our desire [is to] incite dialogue between co-existing parallel worlds that interact with each other in the city" (http://www.grupodotrecho.ato.br/).[3]

This urban art-action presented itself as a means of reaction and reflection upon a reality marked by divisive concepts and walls, which, according to the thesis discussed by Teresa Caldeira in her book *City of Walls: Crime, Segregation and Citizenship in São Paulo*, characterize the city. These walls appear breached and eliminated in the intervention by Grupo do Trecho in order to expose "ausências" (absences), realities that, in a perfectly compartmentalized urban setting largely articulated by what Caldeira and James Holston call "disjunctive democracy" (692), are invisible to the citizen. "Disjunctive democracy" refers to the disparity between the successes of Brazil's democratization process—a process in which the social movements of the peripheries had an important impact—and its failures. As Caldeira states in *City of Walls*, "on the one hand, the country has seen regular and free elections [. . .] along with freedom of expression and the end of media censorship. On the other hand, violence—civilian, state-sanctioned, and state-related—has increased considerably since the end of military rule" (52). Ultimately this violence, concludes Caldeira, "helps destroy public space, segregates social groups, and destabilizes the rule of law" (52). In spite of the Grupo do Trecho's desire to denounce and break these dividing walls, the dialogue between those two primordial spaces does not seem possible: center(s) and periphery or peripheries; justice and violence; security and vulnerability; exclusivity and exclusion; cultural production versus lack of access to events such as those at the Sesi-SP theater, even if they are free of charge. And at the same time, the fundamental disconnect discussed by Caldeira and Holston seems even more extreme in this case, since the art-action is about a prison, and a women's prison at that, while it literalizes the appointed spaces of conflict and segregation.

The project "Absences" is inspired by the maps of the American artist Ashley Hunt, and in particular by his project "Prison Maps." In his diagram-artifact entitled "What Is the Prison Industrial Complex?" the artist explicitly denounces the economic and political interests that, according to Hunt, deliberately or coincidentally design and expand the penitentiary system, in which

---

3. "[. . .] gerar fissuras e romper limites entre a arte e o real, de com isso questionar o normal para vislumbrar outros possíveis, nossa vontade de fazer dialogar mundos paralelos que coexistem, mas não convivem na cidade."

"profit is more important than people; [. . .] people are split along the lines of race, gender & culture so that their labor, resources & power can be exploited and monopolized, and prisons make invisible the damage done along the way." In another interactive map, the artist contextualizes social welfare as an "Old Strategy Society (the War on Poverty)," becoming a Police State or "New Society" that promotes "Individualism & the Wars on 'Others'":

> Today, the War on Poverty has been transformed into other wars: the War on Crime, the War on Drugs, the War on Immigrants and the War on Terrorism, all of which are made to appear "just," but ultimately are wars on poor people and people of color. These new wars are paid for with the same money from yesterday's War on Poverty, but they confront the dangers of inequality with systems of control, and target our daily struggles for justice with criminalization, militarization & prisons. ("What Is the Context?")

This prevailing situation of division, militarization, surveillance, and inequality coincides with the structuring of cities such as São Paulo, as Teresa Caldeira has investigated. The Grupo do Trecho emphasizes this oppressive quality by questioning the limits between DENTRO (inside) and FORA (outside) with regard to the space of the prison, metaphorically normalizing divisions while underlining the fact of inequality. The passerby can choose to locate him- or herself either inside or outside of a space that is made equal by its mutual exclusion, and which ultimately limits individual freedom regardless of the choice:

> Prison appears absent from the outside world, and the outside appears absent from the world within the prison. And at the same time, their existences allude to one another—just as the inside depends on the outside. On the inside, mechanisms of oppression and regulation of life are implemented in their highest expression, in the same manner as the somewhat more banal social interactions that occur on the outside.[4] (http://grupodotrecho .blogspot.com/2010/)

Nevertheless, as the makers of this urban intervention state, "the fact is that in prison, there is no space for freedom" (http://grupodotrecho.blogspot

---

4. "A penitenciária aparece como ausente do mundo exterior e o exterior como ausente do mundo da penitenciária. E, ao mesmo tempo, suas existências se remetem—como o dentro depende do fora. Do lado de dentro operam, em sua máxima expressão, mecanismos de opressão e regulamentação da vida que são os mesmos das relações sociais mais quotidianas no lado de fora."

.com/2010/). In other words, inequality ultimately prevails, the separation of spaces is rigorously maintained, the dividing walls persist, and the urban intervention on Paulista Avenue will disappear by explicit design of the group: "allow the rainy season to erase these strokes, because this is definitely not dirt." This deliberately ephemeral character contrasts with the resistance, permanence, and alternative prestige that characterize other urban interventions such as graffiti and *pichações*. As Caldeira explores in her segment about this subject ("Un espacio" 120–36), tagging and graffiti impose their allegory and the mark of discrimination upon the urban space that they reinterpret and reclaim. Women barely intervene in these urban spaces unless as sexualized commodities in the large advertisements that legally invade the public space. It is not in vain that in the tension between visibility/invisibility that reproduces urban, racial, and class tensions, there lies the principal assumed "absence": discrimination based on gender. The great paradox of "disjunctive democracy" is that women constituted one of the principal action groups that contributed to the advent of democracy, through their participation in the social movements of the outskirts (Caldeira, "Sabotage" 104), though they were later dismissed by a social and judicial system that perpetuates violence upon them and makes them invisible. The dynamic of the debate between rights/privileges for delinquents, which grows out of the discourse of democracy, does not appear to reach women in prisons, who nevertheless, as Tim Cahill notes in his investigation for Amnesty International, suffer doubly "because they suffer the human rights violations experienced by male prisoners (torture, appalling conditions, corruption, and violence among prisoners) as well as violations due to the lack of specific protection for women: sexual abuse by guards and prisoners, being held in jails with men, lack of access to maternal health care, etc." (qtd. in Fabiana Frayssinet).[5] In referring to the conversation between Natascha Sadr Haghighian and Ashley Hunt, the editors of *An Atlas of Radical Cartography* conclude the following: "Invisibility is not merely an absence, but an active process of erasure, an agent of repression" (10).[6] The city will end up engulfing the Grupo do Trecho's action-map, returning the reality of women's prisons and their social and judicial implications of gender violence to a place of invisibility and "absence," with precarious residue on the Internet.[7]

---

5. See Cahill's report for Amnesty International Brazil, *Picking up the Pieces: Women's Experience of Urban Violence in Brazil*.

6. Bhagat and Mogel are referring to Natascha Sadr Haghighian's interview with Ashley Hunt.

7. In spite of the complexity of the urban action taken by Grupo do Trecho, the response to their project "Ausências" has certainly been limited. After more than two years of being posted on YouTube, the performance had barely reached 170 views.

ITINERANT PROJECTS OF THE "ANTIMUSEO" (ANTI-MUSEUM): ART, POLITICS, AND COLLECTIVE ACTION

The alternative curatorial group based in Madrid, the "Anti-museum of Contemporary Art," created the project "Bellas durmientes" (Sleeping Beauties) to address similar issues of invisibility and disremembering. Like the "Absences" project, this intervention incorporates performance and the reappropriation of public space, now through a small traveling cart/gallery that moves about Madrid exhibiting photographic "homages" to women who were killed by their partners or ex-partners. The invitation to participate in this project is open and inclusive and aims to involve the community in a process of consciousness-raising and denunciation. As María María Acha, the creator and coordinator of the project, instructs on their website to all who wish to participate, they will receive a sticker that symbolizes the metaphor of the "Sleeping Beauty" fairy tale and represents the memory of a woman killed. The sticker has a handwritten note with an assigned number for the victim, along with the year and cause of death. The number of printed stickers corresponds to that of domestic violence–related killings as reported since 2001 (http://artecontraviolenciadegenero.org/?p=242/%3E).

The photographic registry of the homage, which incorporates the sticker into a variety of forms and media (poetry, performance, maps, graffiti, interventions, etc.), will then go on to be part of the traveling "Anti-museum" and also of its virtual exhibition on the project's website (http://artecontraviolenciadegenero.org/?p=242/%3E). The intent is artistic and explicitly activist: "Sleeping Beauties is a community art project, utilized as a political tool to contribute toward the struggle against gender violence"[8] (http://www.antimuseo.org/archivo/etapa3/femvisual.html). The Grupo do Trecho also called for social reflection and intervention, as well as for a questioning of the conventions regarding the function of art: "to generate cracks and break through the limits between art and reality." Both projects share similar dual purposes that invite reflection regarding the interference between art and society within the Luso-Hispanic context. On one hand, both exhibit the reality of gender violence and the power structure's ineffectiveness/complicity with regard to this violence. On the other hand, they also expose the failing and problematic nature of cultural production and its relationship with urban spaces. "Sleeping Beauties" addresses the latter issue by reflecting upon the control of art exercised by museums, as well as their spatial structure. If police/State violence had been identified by Teresa Caldeira as the principal holdover from Brazil's dictatorship, a violence that permeates the urban inter-

---

8. "Bellas Durmientes es un proyecto de arte comunitario, utilizado como una herramienta política para contribuir a la lucha contra la violencia de género."

vention by Grupo do Trecho in "Absences," now it is the control of culture by the government that Tomás Ruiz-Rivas, co-creator of the Anti-museum, identifies as a residue of Franco's dictatorship: "Politicians' interventionism in culture is one of the many legacies of *franquismo*."9 According to Ruiz-Rivas, Spanish politicians, "in contrast to young creative people, [. . .] firmly believe in the subversive potential of art, and for this very reason [. . .] wield direct and rigorous control over its means of distribution."10

The Anti-museum of Contemporary Art's "Sleeping Beauties" stands against cultural control but also against disremembering, another of the vestiges of the Franco regime that Ruiz-Rivas denounces. In this sense, the project implicitly exposes the State's resistance to admitting forced disappearances during the Franco regime, as well as the delay in opening the mass graves of those assassinated during the civil war and the ensuing dictatorship. In the case of "Sleeping Beauties," the mass (and ongoing) grave is exposed as that of the victims of gender violence, in a process involving historic, social, cultural, and media structures that are complicit in this violence. The traveling cart/gallery, Centro Portátil de Arte Contemporáneo (Portable Center of Contemporary Art; CPAC), with its homages, likewise constitutes one of the contextual enclaves of the Anti-museum. The Anti-museum's website explains that the purpose of this "low-cost moving gallery" is "to detonate creative processes in public space. The CPAC creates a connection between strategies of reappropriation of marginalized collective spaces—racial minorities, street vendors, prostitutes [. . .]—and artistic practices that impact the city directly."11

Once again, the city appears occupied and interrogated by ideological and artistic practices that intend to reconfigure the compartmentalized city, be it São Paulo or Madrid, making it fluid and public, no longer harshly divided by walls (political, social, racial, cultural, or private). The traveling exhibition reclaims this "flow" by moving "between spaces representing cultural hegemony—art biennials, monuments, cultural events receiving broad media coverage—and the rundown urban slums where new social and cultural practices emerge among their working class inhabitants"12 (antimuseo.org). The first traveling cart project took place in Mexico City, involving artists and col-

---

9. "El intervencionismo de los políticos en cultura es una de las muchas herencias del franquismo."

10. "Al contrario que los jóvenes creadores, creen firmemente en la capacidad subversiva del arte, y por esta razón ejercen un control directo y riguroso sobre sus canales de distribución."

11. "[. . .] detonar procesos creativos en el espacio público. El CPAC crea una conexión entre las estrategias de re-apropiación de espacios de colectivos marginados—minorías raciales, vendedores ambulantes, prostitutas [. . .]—y prácticas artísticas que inciden directamente en la ciudad."

12. "[. . .] entre los espacios de representación cultural hegemónica—bienales de arte, áreas monumentales, eventos culturales con gran proyección mediática—y los espacios degradados

lectives who in a variety of ways reappropriated the city with their art, interventions, and activism.

In the specific case of the "Sleeping Beauties" project, the space through which the portable Anti-museum traveled was initially a privileged and institutional urban area: the Complutense University of Madrid. However, its more specific destination was the Tenth International and Interdisciplinary Congress of Women, which took place at the Complutense in July 2008. This massive event included viewpoints and participants from a myriad of countries. The fluctuation of notions of art and resistance between physical and intellectual spaces of a broad spectrum reinforces the concept of "cartographic" mobility. This mobility coincides with the theoretical and practical goal of the Anti-museum as it is outlined in its website under the broader rubric of "Tras los signos en rotación" (After Signs in Rotation), which paraphrases Octavio Paz's famous essay, "Los signos en rotación" (Signs in Rotation): "'After Signs in Rotation' is a collective investigation, structured around a series of meetings in which art experts from all of Ibero-America will map out radical artistic practices and analyze their place within current political, social, and economic transformations."[13] The Anti-museum thus positions itself as a forum for ideas, as an enduring document and project that is in a state of continuous "rotation," fluctuation, and mobility. The "Sleeping Beauties" therefore journey into the electronic space, which registers their presence in debates and conferences such as "Arte frente a Feminicidio" (Art Confronting Feminicide), which took place in Guatemala in April 2010. The limits of the city and its fluctuations thus extend into the global sphere of the Internet, where strategies for raising awareness and resistance are articulated through projects and social networks such as Facebook, YouTube, and Vimeo, all resources used with efficacy and activism by the Anti-museum of Contemporary Art.

The ultimate goal of eradicating women's agency and bodies in that "active process of erasure, [which is] an agent of repression," mentioned earlier in connection with Ashley Hunt's project, is reflected in the violence perpetrated by a complicit State that perpetuates conformist stereotypes upon women, while judicially discriminating against and exposing women to violence based on these very same stereotypes, as Dorothy Thomas states in her investigation

---

de las periferias urbanas donde emergen nuevas prácticas sociales y culturales de las clases trabajadoras."

13. "Tras los Signos en Rotación es un proyecto de investigación colectiva, articulado sobre una serie de encuentros en los que expertos en arte de toda Iberoamérica van a cartografiar las prácticas artísticas radicales y a analizar su lugar dentro de las actuales transformaciones políticas, sociales y económicas."

regarding Brazil's judicial system. The end of the "Sleeping Beauties" performance that took place in Cádiz, Spain (La bella durmiente / Sleeping Beauty), is certainly inspiring: "Una mujer solita se puede despertar" [A woman all alone can awaken herself]. Nevertheless, the creative collectives that intervene, reappropriate, and question social, global, and urban space, such as Grupo do Trecho and the various projects of the Anti-museum, help encourage this awakening in an implicit alliance that reexamines common cultural and countercultural Luso-Hispanic relations.

If two decades ago Richard Schechner articulated his theory of performance in terms of action, fluctuation, and change, and claimed that "these systems of transformations vary from culture to culture and epoch to epoch," nowadays we see a continuation of this active role, now affirmed through a countercultural fluidity and connection that unites projects and cartographies. This is the case with art interventions that address, question, and reappropriate segregated spaces in Madrid, São Paulo, or Mexico City. The historical parallels that led to the reexamination of violence against women and its correlation with the Brazilian and Spanish dictatorships extend themselves to the fluidity of borders made possible by strong social movements that reclaim and intervene by means of virtual networks.[14] The ultimate goal for the "transformation of society into a creative community, a living poem"[15] proposed by Octavio Paz in his well-known essay "Los signos en rotación" (310), which the Anti-museum of Contemporary Art appropriates, therefore reaches a new spectrum through new (virtual) cartographies of dissidence. Exposing, making visible, and underscoring the reality of women in relation to gender violence, from the reclaimed Paulista Avenue to the various streets traveled by the Anti-museum in Madrid, constitutes an artistic goal of questioning and engaging in political resistance, in a continuous process of rotation and fluidity.[16]

---

14. A clear example of a large-scale collective action/performance organized through social networks is the Occupy movement initiated in Madrid on May 15, 2011 (15-M), which extended to cities worldwide, São Paulo among them. See "El M-15 de España se irradia al mundo."

15. "Transformación de la sociedad en comunidad creadora, en poema vivo."

16. Grupo do Trecho continued showing its project "Absences" in performances and collaborations such as that of May 2011, with the activist theater group "Grupo 59" (Presentação). The "Sleeping Beauties" project continues, and the "Anti-museum of Contemporary Art" expanded its activities to Medellín in September and October 2011. María María Acha is presently opening a call for a registry of women's visual expressions in protests coordinated through Facebook (Indignadas/Outraged).

WORKS CITED

Antimuseo. <http://antimuseo.org> Web. 12 Dec. 2012.

———. <http://artecontraviolenciadegenero.org/?p=242/>.

———. "Arte frente a Feminicidio." <vimeo.com/channels/114465>.

———. "La bella durmiente / Sleeping Beauty." <http://youtube.com/watch?v=S_R10MNLiQI>.

———. "Indignadas/Outraged." <http://www.facebook.com/pages/Indignadas/142463485892397>.

———. "Tras los signos en rotación." <http://vimeo.com/user4008222>.

Bhagat, Alexis, and Lize Mogel. Introduction. *An Atlas of Radical Cartography*. Los Angeles: Journal of Aesthetics & Protest Press, 2007. 6–11.

Cahill, Tim. *Picking Up the Pieces: Women's Experience of Urban Violence in Brazil*. London: Amnesty International, 2008.

Caldeira, Teresa. *City of Walls: Crime, Segregation and Citizenship in São Paulo*. Berkeley: U of California P, 2000.

———. "'I Came to Sabotage Your Reasoning!' Violence and Resignifications of Justice in Brazil." *Law and Disorder in the Postcolony*. Eds. Jean Comaroff and John Comaroff. Chicago and London: U of Chicago P. 102–49.

———. "Un espacio público cuestionado. Muros, graffiti y *pichações* en São Paulo." *Espacio, segregación y arte urbano en el Brasil*. Madrid/Barcelona: Katz Ed. / CCCB, 2006. 115–37.

Caldeira, Teresa, and James Holston. "Democracy and Violence in Brazil." *Comparative Studies in Society and History* 41.4 (1999): 691–729.

Escaja, Tina. "Cartografías de disidencia: In/visibilidad e intervención urbana en dos proyectos hispano-lusos." *Ámbitos Feministas* 2.2 (2012): 47–58.

Grupo do Trecho. <http://grupodotrecho.blogspot.com/>. December 12, 2012.

———. "Ausências" <http://youtube.com/watch?v=FCWWRpFimTQ&feature=player_embedded>. 11 Dec. 2012.

———. "A presentação de performances, cenas e intervenções do projeto ausências no tusp." <http://grupodotrecho.blogspot.com/>. 12 Dec. 2012.

Frayssinet, Fabiana. "Gang-Raped Girl in Men's Jail Just the Tip of the Iceberg." *Inter Press Service News Agency*. Web. 28 Nov. 2007.

Gutiérrez, Sally. "¿Cuáles son las claves para una política cultural progresista?" Web. 13 Jun. 2012.

Hunt, Ashley. *Prison Maps*. Web. 12 Dec. 2012.

———. "Representations of the Erased." Interview by Natascha Sadr Haghighian. <http://16beavergroup.org/mondays/2007/03/05/monday-03-05-07-ashley-hunt-representations-of-the-erased/> 12 Dec. 2012.

———. "What Is the Context for Today's Prison Industrial Complex?" <http://correctionsproject.com/prisonmaps/chart1c.html> 12 Dec. 2012.

———. "What Is the Prison Industrial Complex?" <http://correctionsproject.com/prisonmaps/whatis.htm> 12 Dec. 2012.

"El M-15 de España se irradia al mundo." Los Tiempos.com. Web. 22 May 2011.

Paz, Octavio. "Los signos en rotación." *Los signos en rotación y otros ensayos*. Madrid: Alianza Ed., 1983. 309–42.

Ruiz-Rivas, Tomás. "De cómo Madrid llegó a ser una capital sin museos de arte contemporáneo." Web. 12 Dec. 2012.

Sen, Jay. "Other Worlds, Other Maps: Mapping the Unintended City." *An Atlas of Radical Cartography*. Eds. Lize Mogel and Alexis Bhagat. Los Angeles: Journal of Aesthetics & Protest Press, 2007. 13–26.

Schechner, Richard. *Performance Studies Textbook*. 2nd draft. Jul. 1995. Web. 12 Dec. 2012.

Soto Marco, Adela. *La mujer bajo el franquismo*. Universitat Jaume I de Castelló, 2002. PDF.

Thomas, Dorothy Q. *Criminal Injustice: Violence Against Women in Brazil. An Americas Watch Report*. New York; Washington, DC; Los Angeles; London: Human Rights Watch, 1991.

CHAPTER 14

Memory, Youth, and Regimes of Violence in Recent Hispanic and Lusophone Cinemas

LESLIE L. MARSH

> *It is, contrary to what one would expect, the future which drives us back into the past.*
> —Hannah Arendt, *Between Past and Future* (1954)

DESPITE THEIR linguistic, cultural, and geographic differences, Hispanic and Lusophone nations of Latin America and Europe share similar historical experiences of having lived through violent, authoritarian regimes during the twentieth century. In the critical gesture to move between and among these nations, what is at stake is the development of an effective approach to compare and contrast common experiences with violence, authoritarianism, trauma, and social fragmentation while not losing sight of key differences. This discursive gesture draws out pivotal divergences, which might otherwise go less noticed or less regarded, and allows us to see individual and collective pasts anew and more profoundly.

An initial step toward addressing the experiences with violence among these nations may be to look at official archives. Extensive work has been undertaken to provide official records of the atrocities of state-sponsored violence against citizens. Truth and reconciliation commissions in Central and South America have demanded an accounting for the names of victims and the atrocities committed against them. Calculations have been made: 69,000 Peruvians were murdered at the hands of insurgent and state security forces between 1980 and 2000; 30,000 disappeared during Argentina's "Dirty War" (1976–83), approximately 30,000 Chileans went into exile, and tens of thousands more were tortured and detained during the Pinochet regime (1973–90). The atrocities in Central America defy humanity. Over a fifteen-year period (from 1981 to 1996), the Guatemalan state killed nearly 200,000 people and disappeared nearly 40,000.[1] Although these reports and an accounting of violence have been vital for sociopolitical recovery, numbers *imply* that violent, authoritarian regimes can be quantitatively measured.

An official, numerical approach may very well thwart comparative discussions as it impedes an effective Luso-Hispanic comparison. In fact, historians Edson Teles and Vladimir Safatle note Brazil's "exceptional" status, with the country being frequently left out of discussions on dictatorships in Latin America (both at home and abroad), since there were relatively few disappeared or tortured during Brazil's military regime, but also due to the apparent legality of military rule (9–13). Rather, Teles and Safatle assert that past dictatorships should be measured by the marks they leave on the present. In other words, how have political institutions, the rule of law, and faith in government been reconfigured alongside the evolution of social relationships?

Each nation has defined the terms of its own eventual transition to democratic civil society. While some scholars vigorously assert that the (re)establishment of democracy functions as a key transitional moment, others hesitate or disagree. Key transitional moments are defined not by official ends of violent regimes but rather by informal social and cultural shifts. In his book *The Last Colonial Massacre: Latin America in the Cold War*, historian Greg Grandin refers to the nearly three decades of counterrevolution that took place across Latin America as a "Cold War" that targeted common people and their ability to organize politically, and that resulted in the eradication of "homegrown" concepts of social democracy. Similarly, William Robinson raises concerns about the "low intensity" of democracy in post-dictatorial Chile and Nicaragua (146–255). Considering Peru, Jo-Marie Burt asserts that constructing democracy requires more than free and fair elections. It demands mechanisms of accountability to protect citizens from arbitrary actions by state actors (8–18). Meanwhile, Janice Perlman observes low levels of confidence in the political process in Brazil since the ratification of a new constitution in 1988.[2] Further reflections on Brazil prompt some to argue that the dictatorship did not completely end. Jorge Zaverucha asserts that the political stages of *distensão* (political relaxation, 1974–79) and *Abertura* (political opening, 1979–84), followed by redemocratization (1985–88)—during which

---

1. The Guatemalan civil war lasted for nearly four decades. The numbers cited here are provided by historian Greg Grandin. See his *The Blood of Guatemala: A History of Race and Nation* (Durham: Duke UP, 2000) as well as *The Last Colonial Massacre*.

2. Based on data collected between 1999 and 2005, Perlman explains that one finds that younger generations are "increasingly cynical about the fairness of the political system and reluctant to participate in the political process" ("Redemocratization" 258). See also Perlman, *Favela* 200–219.

time selected politicians heeded the calls of the military—allowed for the penetration of authoritarian structures into the post-1988 Brazilian government (43–48, 66–69).

As part of the process of strengthening contemporary democratic practices, one finds a common effort to come to terms with the past. As Elizabeth Jelin has observed in her work on memory, several countries in Latin America (including Argentina, Uruguay, Chile, Brazil, Paraguay, and Peru) began working through violent periods of the past at the turn of the millennium. These efforts, Jelin observes, occurred after years of institutional silence and (unsuccessful) efforts to establish democratic futures without critical contemplation of the past (xiv). Silences were strategically imposed through amnesty and indemnity laws as well as various "pacts to forget,"[3] which were promoted by elite groups, former military insiders, and conservative politicians in favor of national reconciliation and reestablishing democracy (Labanyi 93; Crenzel 3–6; Ribeiro da Cunha 17–18, 31–40; Zaverucha 41–48).

Concomitant to these efforts, Latin American film industries were revitalized in the early 1990s after the development of new funding and distribution programs, which in turn helped (re)position cinema as a transnational outlet for reflecting on the past and questioning the quality of democracy established by transitional governments. Indeed, in recent years there has been a marked growth in the number of films reflecting on past dictatorships and regimes of violence. At the center of their narratives one finds many young characters. It is certainly not a new tendency to find youth central to films that treat darker political or historical moments.[4] A focus on youth is particularly interesting

---

3. Amnesty laws such as those ratified in Spain (1977), Chile (1978), and Brazil (1979) contributed greatly to the denial of the past. Additional laws upheld "forgetting" such as the *Ley de Caducidad* (1986)—which was the cornerstone of the "policies of oblivion" (1985–2001) in Uruguay—and the *Ley del Punto Final* (1986) and *Ley de Obediencia Debida* (1987) in Argentina (note that both Argentine laws were repealed in 2003). In other instances, negotiations took place and agreements were made such that democratic governments would not prosecute perpetrators of past human rights abuses. Consider, for example, the *Pacto del Club Naval* (1984) in Uruguay and political maneuvers by General Augusto Pinochet in Chile, who granted the military a supervisory role in government. Similarly, Jorge Zaverucha notes that the Brazilian Constitution of 1988 did not establish civilian control over the military, which remains outside civilian legal jurisdiction.

4. For instance, in Spain one finds a number of films featuring youth protagonists that reflect on the Franco period, including *El espíritu de la colmena* (1973), *Cría cuervos* (1979), *La lengua de las mariposas* (1999), *Los girasoles ciegos* (2008), and more recently the Catalan film *Pá negre* (2010). Mexican director Guillermo del Toro has directed two films that feature youth protagonists in a reflection on the Spanish Civil War and Franco period, *El espinazo del diablo* (2001) and *El laberinto del fauno* (2006). From Argentina, we find several films that detail the experiences of children whose lives were unknowingly affected by the atrocities of the military regime, including *Los rubios* (2003), *Botín de guerra* (2000), *Los pasos perdidos* (2001), and

in that the youth subject is not yet fully included in the adult world. Owing to this, Karen Lury discusses the child in film as embodying a fundamental "otherness" (2). Similarly, Vicky Lebeau asserts in the text *Childhood and Cinema* that, beyond there being a historic compulsion to represent children in film, these depictions, in turn, are a valuable resource for reflecting on cultural histories. While Lebeau asks what cinema wants of the child and Lury's response might be to provide an outsider's perspective, we must inquire further about the appearance of so many child and adolescent protagonists in recent films from Latin America that reflect on past regimes of violence. This essay aims to do so without falling into the "false symmetries" mentioned by Héctor Hoyos and with an awareness of the importance of paying attention to regional forms and negotiations of identity as underscored by Michael Lazzara—both in this volume.

We have entered a period distant from the indexical moments of dictatorial violence. New generations are coming of age and there is a need to investigate the role of the past in the construction of identities in a context where moving images are increasingly constitutive of modern subjectivities. Vikki Bell asserts that we must rethink the direction of "memory-works" (such as films) and see their stories of the past as a "politics of the present" intended to shape a shared future (209). In doing so, emphasis is placed on strengthening social relationships and imagining political communities. In contrast, Russell Kilbourn suggests several caveats regarding this very possibility. More specifically, Kilbourn raises questions regarding the transnational, transcultural consumability of the past in cinema (9–13, 26–28). With regard to those Hispanic and Lusophone films that reflect on the past, it seems wise to recognize the realities of the current era of transnational co-productions, which should not lead to a dismissal but rather a questioning of the degree to which aesthetic choices and efforts to achieve audience appeal (genre selection, narrative development, talent, etc.) allow for not just culturally specific portrayals but successful negotiation between the local and the global.

After a brief overview of the timing of cinematic responses to dictatorships, this essay will focus on the films *Kamchatka* (Marcelo Piñeyro, 2002, Argentina), *Machuca* (Andrés Wood, 2004, Chile), and *O ano em que meus pais saíram de férias* (Cao Hamburger, 2006, Brazil) to consider three questions: the presumed universal subject position of youth, the role of history as a nodal point for subjectivity in the present, and what these films suggest about the consumability of the past. The second part of this essay considers the transmission of past traumas to the present and focuses on the films *La*

Cautiva (2004). Critiques of government policies and inequality are notably treated in Buñuel's *Los olvidados* (1950, Mexico) and Hector Babenco's *Pixote* (1980, Brazil).

teta asustada (Claudia Llosa, 2009, Peru) and *Quase dois irmãos* (Lúcia Murat, 2004, Brazil) to ask questions about multifaceted processes of memory and how "memory-works" are linked to current democratic developments.

Using broad strokes, one finds important differences and similarities between the Latin American countries in question as to the staging of responses to and reflection on violent authoritarian regimes. The end of dictatorial rule did not translate uniformly into an opening for cinematic reflections on the recent past. For example, in Argentina, a break from military rule was followed by a profusion of cultural production from 1984 to 1987 that addressed the dictatorial period. Reflections on the past in the arts then paused after the passage of indemnity laws by President Menem (1989–99) and a period of hyperinflation (Copertari 20–21). Annulment of the impunity laws during the administration of President Néstor Kirchner (2003–07), which has resulted in a reopening of cases against the Argentine military for human rights violations, has broadly coincided with the reinvigoration of the Argentine film industry during the mid-1990s, the economic crisis of 2001 (itself linked to neoliberal measures begun during the dictatorship), and the emergence of a new generation of filmmakers who have addressed the legacy of Argentina's "Dirty War."

The military dictatorship in Brazil (1964–85) has received far less treatment in film and literature, at least until recently. Ricardo Lísias observes that authoritarian institutions were critiqued in Argentine literature, but that in Brazil these institutions remained untouchable for some time (321). Despite the declaration of Amnesty (1979) and the subsequent beginning of *Abertura*, Brazilian films that critiqued military doctrine or the dictatorship such as *Prá frente Brasil!* (Roberto Farias, 1982) and *Em nome da segurança* (Renato Tapajós, 1984) were banned by the military government (Simões 240–41). By contrast, in Argentina at this time, critical films such as the allegorical *Tiempo de revancha* (Adolfo Aristarain, 1981) were released and well received. From the mid-1970s to redemocratization in Brazil, representing history—especially contemporary history—was a contentious enterprise.[5] In 1970s and 1980s Brazil, cinematographic representation of recent history was generally difficult, as the regime had established a mode of censorship whereby it supported the production of historical films that suited its interests and subsequently diverted funds away from potentially critical pictures (Johnson 117; Bernardet 325–27).

Imposed silences have not lasted. Events in recent years have fueled debates about the dictatorial past. The arrest of former Chilean dictator

---

5. For more on the politics of memory and cinematic representation of history in Brazil during the 1980s, see Marsh, *Brazilian Women's Filmmaking* 87–119.

Augusto Pinochet in 1998 in London and the 2004 Valech Report on torture victims prompted a resurgence of discussion about Chile's authoritarian past. In Argentina, as stated above, the annulment of Menem-era indemnity laws by President Kirchner in 2003 reignited claims against the military. Brazil, as well, has begun to address its authoritarian past.[6] As president of Brazil, Fernando Henrique Cardoso (1995–2002) created a law of "sigilo eterno" (eternal nondisclosure) for those documents from the dictatorship period deemed "top secret." His successor, Luiz Inácio Lula da Silva (2003–10), changed the law but maintained the possibility that access would never be granted to some papers despite a 2005 United Nations request that Brazil open its dictatorship-era archives. Similar to other Latin American nations, the limits of Brazil's 1979 Amnesty Law have also been tested. In 2006, the Almeida Teles family began a civil suit against Carlos Alberto Brilhante Ustra for acts of torture committed while director of the DOI-CODI (Destacamento de Operações de Informações—Centro de Operações de Defesa Interna; Department of Intelligence Operations—Center of Internal Defense Operations) in São Paulo from 1970 to 1974 (Almeida Teles 294–95). Whereas trials of military figures took place in Argentina during the administration of President Raúl Alfonsín (1983–89), this was the first time a member of the Brazilian military had been accused and was forced to be held accountable for his actions. This came after decades of seeking justice. Indeed, in the 1970s in Brazil, family members of the dead and disappeared sought redress through a variety of means, but bureaucratic delays and other embargos denied their right to justice and truth (Almeida Teles 253–94). Despite Cardoso- and Lula-era blockades and perhaps owing to various pressures (from civil society, international agencies, President Dilma Rousseff's own survival of torture during the military regime), President Rousseff (2010–16) officially inaugurated the Truth Commission in May of 2012 on the same day that a freedom of information law went into effect. The installation of the Truth Commission in Brazil to investigate violations of human rights committed between 1946 and 1988 is not only one of the last truth commissions in Latin America—notably Argentina, Uruguay, Chile, Guatemala, and Peru have all had truth commissions long before Brazil—but it only officially operated for two years, leading some to question the degree to which the Commission could reveal the truth of Brazil's recent history.[7]

After political "pauses" and the reemergence of filmmaking in the 1990s, one finds an increasing corpus of feature-length fiction films from Latin

---

6. Note that the focus on Chile, Argentina, and Brazil is because these are the countries addressed by the first three films treated in this essay.

7. It merits noting that the truth commissions in Chile, Argentina, Uruguay, and Peru were all also relatively short-lived, being active from 9 months to 2 years.

America that have reflected on past regimes of violence through the point of view of a (generally male) child or adolescent. Two notable films address the illegal conscription of boys into armed struggle. Addressing the political environment of El Salvador in the 1980s, *Las voces inocentes* (Luis Mandoki, 2004) is narrated through the eyes of ten-year-old Chava, who lives with the impending threat of being abducted by the army and, alongside his family and community, faces the constant fear of being caught in the crosshairs of gunfire and explosions. Similarly, *Paloma de papel* (Fabrizio Aguilar, 2003, Peru) is structured as an extended flashback by a young man (Juan) who recalls his experience of being kidnapped by Communist insurgents as a boy in Peru and being coerced into participating in armed guerrilla warfare. The narrative is framed by his return to his hometown upon his release from jail, where he had been held for years by Peruvian authorities for (alleged) terrorist activities.[8] Although both films circulated on the film festival circuit, they have not managed to secure international distribution, even in light of their important gesture toward engaging in broader dialogues regarding the regimes of violence that ravaged Peru and Central America during the 1980s and 1990s.

Greater attention has been paid to the films *Machuca* (Andrés Wood, 2004, Chile) and *Kamchatka* (Marcelo Piñeyro, 2002, Argentina), which reflect on past dictatorships through the eyes of young boys. Despite several similarities to both of these works, Cao Hamburger's *O ano em que meus pais saíram de férias* (2006, Brazil)—hereafter referred to as *O ano em que*—has been generally left out of discussions. All three had successful runs in their home markets, were nominated for numerous awards, and were picked up by international distributors. While in *Kamchatka,* a young "Harry" (the protagonist's alias) is left with his grandparents as his parents attempt to escape the looming threat of detention during the Argentine *Proceso*, a young Mauro in *O ano em que* is left with his grandfather in the Italian/Jewish neighborhood of Bom Retiro in São Paulo in 1970, while his parents make an unsuccessful run from state authorities. Unaware of political events taking place around him, Mauro focuses on the upcoming World Cup soccer matches and befriends the local kids while his grandfather's neighbor, Shlomo, a Jewish immigrant from Poland who escaped the Holocaust, takes Mauro in after his grandfather unexpectedly passes away. By contrast, *Machuca* focuses on two boys (Gonzalo Infante and Pedro Machuca) from different racial and class backgrounds who form a brief friendship on the eve of the 1973 military coup d'etat in Chile. In cinematic terms, the three films rely heavily on market-oriented aesthetics

---

8. Although it does not involve the conscription of a young male protagonist into armed struggle, another work to consider alongside these two films is the Guatemalan production *El silencio de Neto* (Luis Argueta, 1994).

(i.e., synchronic sound, well-lit scenes, conventional editing, straightforward narratives, etc.), and employ (stereotypically) muted colors to evoke historical authenticity. The boys' voice-over narration—establishing a flashback from an undisclosed present and suggestive of personal testimony—makes additional claims of authenticity and frames the political moment in *Kamchatka* and *O ano em que*. In *Machuca*, intertitles stating "Santiago de Chile, 1973" and initial close-up shots of Gonzalo launch the viewer directly into precoup Chile.

Notwithstanding their differences, these films engage in an uneasy conversation about the role of the past as a nodal point for national identification. Scholars have considered the politics of memory and the aesthetics in *Kamchatka* and *Machuca*. David William Foster asserts that *Kamchatka* evinces an ongoing need in Argentina to process its violent past, but that the film's effectiveness is undermined by a reliance on bourgeois norms and a universalization of human experience (105). In contrast, Amaya and Blair praise *Machuca* for offering perspectives other than that of the white, middle-class, Christian hero common in narratives of human development (52). And Tzvi Tal asserts that both *Kamchatka* and *Machuca* offer a nostalgic reconstruction of the past that draws on conventional cinema aesthetics that neither complicate the reception of the film nor stimulate a critical reading (143). Although *O ano em que* participates in a recent boom of films taking up the dictatorial period in Brazil, it (like *Kamchatka*) tends to depoliticize the past while emphasizing a jubilant "melting pot" nationalism and society-unifying zeal for soccer.

All three films can be rightly critiqued for falling short in their representations of the past, especially if factual, nuanced accounts are demanded. But in these "failings" we see culturally specific differences and similarities in reflections on dictatorial regimes: the impression that the middle class was the most affected by the dictatorship (*Kamchatka*), that race and class differences are insurmountable social destabilizers (*Machuca*), or that racial democracy and cross-class and ethnic harmony can be achieved regardless of political circumstances (*O ano em que*).

In spite of Colin MacCabe's argument that conventional realism (such as that found in *Kamchatka* and *Machuca*) problematically lends filmic images an ontological character of historical "truth" (qtd. in Tal 141), these films are less about seeking historical facts and more about the effects of authoritarianism, of having passed through—with varying degrees of awareness—regimes of violence. These films emphasize questions of affect over full understanding of the past. Indeed, it is through youth protagonists that the films effectively exploit the unknown as a way to address the affective sequelae of authoritarianism. Gonzalo (*Machuca*) and Mauro (*O ano em que*) witness acts of violence (i.e., armed forces beating and detaining street protestors) but neither offers—nor is he able to—an explanation of his observations. Similarly, both Mauro and "Harry" (*Kamchatka*) are oblivious to the stress suffered by their parents, who smoke nervously as they deal with the impending threat of being found by agents of the state. Heavy symbolism and use of euphemisms (e.g., "being on vacation") not only reflect a child's way of understanding but also address a general difficulty of capturing the past clearly.

In these films, the inability to fully comprehend what is going on rehearses the thesis put forth by Argentine director Albertina Carri in *Los rubios* (2003), that memory is a slippery historical surface where facts may not stick and that producing a consensual vision of past events is nearly impossible. If the past is not comprehensible in these films, then what is the role of the past in shaping contemporary individual and collective identities? Not fully included in society, youth are outsiders to the strangeness of the adult world. Again, Lury speaks of the fundamental "otherness" of the child's point of view in film (2). In these films, an incomplete understanding of the past is emphasized, and youth characters bring an affective charge to the representation of past dictatorial regimes that forestalls forgetting yet also underscores distance from this past violence. In one sense, the presence of these youth in dictatorship films suggests that we have entered a new sociopolitical period. In another, the past in the confused eyes of children questions knowledge and understanding of history as a nodal point in forming individual and collective identities.

The youth point of view offers a presumed innocent, universal, ideologically neutral position easily open to intra- and transcultural identification. Thus, we must consider further the transmission and appropriation of these memories. A first point regards the shaping of modern subjectivities. Memory has been theorized as social, external, and relying increasingly on "memory industries" (i.e., films, statues, shrines, etc.) (Kilbourn 1–6, 26–28). Alison Landsberg offers the concept of "prosthetic memory," with film acting as memory prosthesis (148–49). Modern subjectivity is very much shaped by memory agents such as film, and, where natural memory is incomplete, "prosthetic memory" fills the gaps. What is more, Landsberg suggests we think about the ethico-political potential of transcultural transmission and consumption of these prosthetic memories. She notes that memory has become commodified and plays a role in globalization but that it is through memory—among other dramatic instances—that media are able to create empathy, and it is through empathy that one finds the potential for uniting diverse individuals and creating the potential for ethical relationships (147–49). In the particular instance of youth reflecting on dictatorial regimes, one may find the significant potential for mutual, cross-cultural strengthening of democratic accountability and justice based on emotion. We do not come to know the past in these films;

we come to feel it in the perceptions put forth by young protagonists. It isn't common events or knowledge of history that can potentially bond individuals from diverse locations, but affective bonds that arise from a common lack of understanding of violent pasts.

This leads to a seemingly contradictory second point regarding youth and the representation of the past with regard to transcultural transmission. The assumed universality and innocence of the young protagonist's point of view in films such as *Kamchatka, Machuca,* and *O ano em que* may create a point of affective identification for international audiences, but it also affords an opening for important comparative investigations of problems that still haunt a given society. As comparisons are made, the universalization of human experience should be questioned. In other words, it is imperative to consider the culturally specific issues being worked through within the framework of youth common to these films. As Carolina Rocha has noted with regard to two of these films (*Machuca* and *O ano em que*), the youth protagonists "have slightly different roles that mirror the way in which their societies still grapple with their past dictatorships" (85).

In addition to transcultural transmission, we must consider the translation of memory between generations. The concept of "postmemory" has proved to be a fruitful way to approach those works by individuals born during or after the periods of violence in Latin America (Nouzeilles, Kaiser). Marianne Hirsch has advanced the concept of postmemory, defined as "a *structure* of inter- and trans-generational transmission of traumatic knowledge and experience" (106). Whereas the above films "re-witness" past violence, both *La teta asustada* (Claudia Llosa, 2009, Peru) and *Quase dois irmãos* (Lúcia Murat, 2006, Brazil) investigate the transmission of trauma across generations and ask questions regarding democratic potential in current contexts.

While the young male protagonists of both *Kamchatka* and *O ano em que* are phenotypically white and of diverse ethnicities, the young protagonists of *Machuca* allow for an exploration of race, ethnicity, and class divides in 1970s Chile. *O ano em que* does portray an ethnically and racially diverse society but does so more in celebratory than critical fashion. In all three cases, the experience with violence is made distant in time, is not fully comprehended, and is mostly witnessed. In contrast, Claudia Llosa's *La teta asustada* addresses the lingering effects of violence committed at the hands of the state and insurgent groups in Peru during the 1980s and 1990s and is notable for being one of few films to develop its narrative around a female protagonist of indigenous descent and her relationship to the past.[9] The female protagonist

---

9. For some scholars, bringing the work of Claudia Llosa into this discussion gives pause. She certainly owns a subject position as an upper-class, educated, phenotypically white and

of indigenous descent, Fausta (Magaly Solier), embodies the breakdown of social trust brought about by years of violence waged on Peruvians by Túpac Amaru, Shining Path, and state forces. Jo-Marie Burt observes that unlike other nations of South America where the military state exercised "a perverse monopoly of violence," political violence in Peru had "multiple fronts" (5). Peruvians were caught in the crossfire. Both state and insurgent forces routinely raped and committed other acts of sexual violence, predominantly against women (Burt 2).

The opening scene of *La teta asustada* refers to this violent past. An aged woman recounts in song a story of how she was raped years ago while pregnant with her daughter, Fausta. According to the beliefs of indigenous groups, the daughter subsequently began life with an illness of fear ("la teta asustada") passed through a mother's milk to her child. In the opening sequences, the mother dies. Overcome with grief, Fausta faints, and her uncle, with whom she is living, takes her to a hospital, where it is discovered that she has placed a potato in her vagina to protect herself from the threat of rape, which her deceased mother endured. Despite an intense phobia of walking alone, Fausta secures a job as a maid for a wealthy white woman (Aída) in the city to earn the necessary funds to bury her mother in her village. The film thus explores the intersection of class, racial, and ethnic differences in contemporary Peruvian society. Working at Aída's house, Fausta befriends the gardener Noé, who is also of indigenous descent, makes strides to overcome her fears, and discovers that there are contemporary and unexpected ways that people may violate her integrity.

The film poetically addresses the profound experience of suppression that resulted from past years of violence, when legitimate social protest was easily mistaken for insurgent activity and met with state repression. Shallow-focus cinematography and internal framing devices underscore Fausta's being silenced and marginalized from the rest of society. Shots capture her looking off into space or sitting with her back to the camera. Indeed, few images visualize her entire body with all fields (front-to-back) in clear focus. Internal frames (windows, doors) block full view of her. She hides behind people at parties and walks close to fences so as to interact with and be exposed to the world around her as little as possible. Fausta lives out the fears and traumas her mother experienced. The potato, a food staple of indigenous Andean peoples and a symbol of Peruvian culture, is taking root inside her and making her ill. As Jo-Marie Burt has noted, the years of violence "reordered politi-

---

privileged individual, and her film, like any work of art, can be critiqued for its merits and shortcomings. However, she is certainly not responsible for the political viewpoints of her relatives (such as those of her Nobel Prize–winning uncle Mario Vargas Llosa).

cal and social meanings in Peru" (5). Thus, the potato planted inside Fausta speaks to this perverse social reordering and gestures towards the need for civil society to reclaim the nation.

What is more, the film addresses social fragmentation that was exacerbated by the deployment of fear by the state and insurgent forces. Indeed, this fragmentation was "both the condition for and the result of the expansion of these authoritarian projects" (Burt 4). Class-based cleavages are delineated as Fausta is seen traversing serpentine stairs between her poor, hilltop neighborhood and the wealthy city below. Ethnic differences also become apparent. While the Western-influenced doctor attending to Fausta in the hospital is oblivious to her psycho-physical pains, she finds compassion and respect with the fellow Quechua-speaking gardener (Noé). As a maid, Fausta witnesses the ongoing abuses of Peru's elite ruling class. An uninspired pianist, Aída traumatizes Fausta by inveigling her with pearls from a broken necklace to share the songs she sings, plays them publicly as her own compositions, and then reneges on the verbal contract between them. Fausta realizes that the potential for violation of her integrity may appear in the form of current cultural and economic exploitation.

Llosa's film ends optimistically. Fausta returns to Aída's house, gathers the pearls owed her, and then collapses, emotionally exhausted, outside the house. Found by Noé, Fausta pleads to have the potato removed from inside her, indicating her desire to heal and overcome her fears. The final scene shows a potato plant left at Fausta's door by Noé, who had earlier scorned the potato for being cheap and flourishing little. This gesture suggests hope that Peru will continue to recover from its traumatic past and overcome contemporary injustices.

In the case of *Quase dois irmãos*, the transmission of past violence is portrayed as occurring on a broader social scale. In fact, recent cinematic reflections on Brazil's dictatorship are closely linked to questions regarding the current quality of democracy, redefinitions of citizenship, and challenges to the lingering effects of past regimes of violence. By veteran director Lúcia Murat, the film focuses on the story of two men, one white (Miguel) and one black (Jorginho), who are first shown as childhood friends in 1957 and then as inmates in the 1970s—Miguel is imprisoned for political activities and Jorginho for bank robbery. In 2004 they reunite in prison, where Miguel (a lawyer) approaches Jorginho (a jailed drug lord) for permission to start an outreach project in Jorginho's community.

Similar to *La teta asustada*, the past pushes against the present in *Quase dois irmãos*. But, whereas *O ano em que* offers a celebratory look at Brazil's social diversity, Murat's *Quase dois irmãos* offers a view of systemic racial and class divides in Brazil. The film's narrative develops a circular structure, beginning in 2004 and then cutting to sepia-colored images of 1957. Additional cuts on matching graphics and action between the present, the 1950s, and the 1970s weave the three moments together, making causal claims that current sociopolitical problems are linked to past periods of authoritarianism and ongoing discrimination.

This exploration of the past's claims on the present questions the notion of Brazilian racial democracy and other utopic myths. Murat, who has investigated the encounter with difference in several of her films—*Brava gente brasiliera* (2000) and *Maré—nossa história de amor* (2007) among them—juxtaposes the intersecting lives of two men (one white, one black) who live parallel yet markedly divergent lives. Cross-class, racial harmony is not fully achieved in Murat's film. Miguel's childhood neighbors complain about black/white, poor/middle-class social gatherings (i.e., *feijoadas* on Sundays) in the late 1950s. What was an initial bond between Miguel and Jorginho in prison in the 1970s devolves into self-imposed segregation, revealing the limitations of leftist progressive thought. In scenes portraying contemporary Brazil, Juliana (Miguel's daughter) enters the "no-go" zone of Rio's *favelas*. Replaying middle- and upper-class racialized fears, Juliana suffers a brutal beating in the *favela* when she is found in the wrong place at the wrong time. The flashback structure comes full circle as Miguel rushes to the hospital to attend to his daughter. As he drives frantically, his words in voice-over mix past, present, and future, stating: "We all have two lives: the one we dream of, and the one we live." This is one unfulfilled possibility. Similarly, there are two lives—that of Miguel and that of Jorginho—that run parallel to one another. But, the "almost" indicated in the film title suggests an incomplete brotherhood and subsequently an unfulfilled and incomplete imagined community.

While the possibility for creating affective, discursive communities certainly exists, the transmission of memory in cinema remains an ongoing, ever-changing process. It is in these differences in memory processes that we find the most compelling paths to appreciate cultural diversity and the simultaneously overlapping and diverging struggles encountered by humanity. What should remain vitally clear is that these films, which reflect on past regimes of violence in Latin America, take part in a larger process to promote new political cultures in the present and near future.

In conclusion, one of the final images of Fausta in *La teta asustada,* in which she clutches the pearls she was promised, then denied, suggests where discussion of youth and their representation in film and media should be directed. Fausta's act of perseverance and resistance represents not only the overcoming of past traumas but also a break in cycles of oppression, fears of violence, and social immobility. As the world's population is increasingly young and urban, and while young males in some regions are far more likely to die of homicide than of natural causes, it seems vital to complement the discussion of mainstream feature-length fiction films with the resurgence of alternative digital media produced by youth in *favelas, barrios, colonias,* and other marginalized urban spaces in the Hispanic and Lusophone world. In the opening to their edited volume, Lessa and Druliolle refer to memory work as offering counternarratives to official versions of the past. Similarly, alternative media productions by youth working alongside new urban social movements, and dedicated to making audiovisual interventions, demand an examination of youth reflections on violence as counternarratives of the present directed towards achieving more inclusive societies.

WORKS CITED

Aguilar Fernández, Paloma. *Memoria y olvido de la guerra civil española*. Madrid: Alianza, 1996.

Amaya, Hector, and Laura Senio Blair. "Bridges Between the Divide: The Female Body in *Y tu mama también* and *Machuca*." *Studies in Hispanic Cinemas* 4.1 (2007): 47–62.

Bell, Vikki. "The Politics of 'Memory' in the Long Present of the Southern Cone." Lessa and Druliolle 209–21.

Bernardet, Jean-Claude. "Qual é a história?" *Anos 70: Ainda sob a tempestade*. Ed. Adauto Novaes. Rio de Janeiro: SENAC Rio, Aeroplano, 2005. 325–33.

Burt, Jo-Marie. *Political Violence and the Authoritarian State in Peru: Silencing Civil Society*. New York: Palgrave Macmillan, 2007.

Copertari, Gabriela. *Desintegración y justicia en el cine argentino contemporáneo*. Woodbridge, UK: Tamesis, 2009.

Crenzel, Emilio. "Present Pasts: Memory(ies) of State Terrorism in the Southern Cone of Latin America." Lessa and Druliolle 1–13.

Foster, David William. "Family Romance and Pathetic Rhetoric in Marcelo Piñeyro's *Kamchatka*." *Contemporary Latin American Cinema: Breaking into the Global Market*. Ed. Debra Shaw. New York: Rowman and Littlefield, 2007. 105–16.

Grandin, Greg. *The Last Colonial Massacre: Latin America in the Cold War*. Chicago: U of Chicago P, 2004.

Hirsch, Marianne. "The Generation of Postmemory." *Poetics Today* 29.1 (2008): 103–28.

Jelin, Elizabeth. *State Repression and the Labors of Memory*. Trans. Judy Rein and Marcial Godoy-Anativia. Minneapolis: U of Minnesota P, 2003.

Johnson, Randal. *The Film Industry in Brazil: Culture and the State*. Pittsburgh: U of Pittsburgh P, 1987.

Kaiser, Susan. *Postmemories of Terror: A New Generation Copes with the Legacy of the "Dirty War."* New York: Palgrave Macmillan, 2005.

Kilbourn, Russell J. A. *Cinema, Memory, Modernity: The Representation of Memory from the Art Film to Transnational Cinema.* New York: Routledge, 2010.

Labanyi, Jo. "Memory and Modernity in Democratic Spain: The Difficulty of Coming to Terms with the Spanish Civil War." *Poetics Today* 28.1 (2007): 89–116.

Landsberg, Alison. "Prosthetic Memory: The Ethics and Politics of Memory in an Age of Mass Culture." *Memory and Popular Film.* Ed. Paul Grainge. New York: Manchester UP, 2003. 144–61.

Lebeau, Vicky. *Childhood and Cinema.* London: Reaktion, 2008.

Lessa, Francesca, and Vincent Druliolle. *The Memory of State Terrorisim in the Southern Cone: Argentina, Chile, and Uruguay.* New York: Palgrave Macmillan, 2011.

Lísias, Ricardo. "Dez Fragmentos sobre a Literatura Contemporânea no Brasil e no Argentina ou de Como os Patetas Sempre Adoram o Discurso do Poder." Teles and Safatle. 319–28.

Lury, Karen. *The Child in Film: Tears, Fears and Fairytales.* London and New York: Tauris, 2010.

MacCabe, Colin. "Realism and the Cinema: Notes on Some Brechtian Theses." *Theoretical Essays: Film, Linguistics, Literature.* Manchester: Manchester UP, 1985. 33–57.

Marsh, Leslie L. *Brazilian Women's Filmmaking: From Dictatorship to Democracy.* Urbana: U of Illinois P, 2012.

Nouzeilles, Gabriela. "Postmemory Cinema and the Future of the Past in Albertina Carri's *Los rubios.*" *Journal of Latin American Cultural Studies* 14.3 (2005): 263–78.

Perlman, Janice. *Favela: Four Decades of Living on the Edge in Rio de Janeiro.* New York: Oxford UP, 2010.

———. "Redemocratization Viewed from Below: Urban Poverty and Politics in Rio de Janeiro, 1968–2005." *Democratic Brazil Revisited.* Eds. Peter R. Kingstone and Timothy Power. Pittsburgh: U of Pittsburgh P, 2008. 257–80.

Ribeiro da Cunha, Paulo. "Militares e anistia no Brasil: um dueto desarmônico." Teles and Safatle 15–40.

Robinson, William I. *Promoting Polyarchy: Globalization, U.S. Intervention and Hegemony.* Cambridge: Cambridge UP, 1996.

Rocha, Carolina. "Children's Views of State-Sponsored Violence in Latin America." *Representing History, Class, and Gender in Spain and Latin America.* Eds. Carolina Rocha and Georgia Seminet. New York: Palgrave Macmillan, 2012. 83–100.

Simões, Inimá. *Roteiro da Intolerância: A censura cinematográfica no Brasil.* São Paulo: Editora SENAC, 1999.

Tal, Tzvi. "Alegorías de memoria y olvido en películas de iniciación: *Machuca* y *Kamchatka.*" *Aisthesis* 38 (2005): 136–51.

Teles, Edson, and Vladimir Safatle. *O Que Resta da Ditadura: A Exceção Brasileira.* São Paulo: Boitempo, 2010.

Teles, Janaína de Almeida. "Os familiares de mortos e desaparecidos politicos e a luta por 'verdade e justiça' no Brasil." Teles and Safalte 253–98.

Zaverucha, Jorge. "Relações civil-militares: o legado autoritário da Constituição brasileira de 1988." Teles and Safatle 41–76.

FILMS CITED

O ano em que meus pais saíram de férias. Dir. Cao Hamburger. Brazil, 2006.
Botín de guerra. Dir. David Blaustein. Argentina, 2000.
Brava gente brasileira. Dir. Lúcia Murat. Brazil, 2000.
Cautiva. Dir. Gastón Biraben. Argentina, 2003.
Cría cuervos. Dir. Carlos Saura. Spain, 1976.
El espinazo del diablo. Dir. Guillermo del Toro. Mexico, 2001.
El espíritu de la colmena. Dir. Víctor Érice. Spain, 1973
Los girasoles ciegos. Dir. José Luis Cuerda. Spain, 2008.
Kamchatka. Dir. Marcelo Piñeyro. Argentina, 2002.
El laberinto del fauno. Dir. Guillermo del Toro. Mexico, 2006.
La lengua de las mariposas. Dir. José Luis Cuerda. Spain, 1999.
Machuca. Dir. Andrés Wood. Chile, 2004.
Maré—nossa história de amor. Dir. Lúcia Murat. Brazil, 2007.
Em nome da segurança. Dir. Renato Tapajós. Brazil, 1984.
Pá negre. Dir. Agustí Villaronga. Spain, 2010.
Paloma de papel. Dir. Fabrizio Aguilar. Peru, 2003.
Los pasos perdidos. Dir. Manane Rodríguez. Argentina, 2001.
Prá frente Brasil! Dir. Roberto Farias. Brazil, 1982.
Quase dois irmãos. Dir. Lúcia Murat. Brazil, 2004.
Los rubios. Dir. Albertina Carri. Argentina, 2003.
El silencio de Neto. Dir. Luis Arguenta. Guatemala, 1994.
La teta asustada. Dir. Claudia Llosa. Peru, 2009.
Tiempo de revancha. Dir. Adolfo Aristarain. Argentina, 1981.
Las voces inocentes. Dir. Luis Mandoki. El Salvador, 2004.

CHAPTER 15

Cinema in Totalitarian Iberia

Propaganda and Persuasion under Salazar and Franco

PATRÍCIA VIEIRA

FOLLOWING THE establishment of the Portuguese *Estado Novo* (New State) under António de Oliveira Salazar in 1933 and the victory of the Nationalists headed by Francisco Franco in the Spanish Civil War in 1939, the two Iberian dictatorships implemented ambitious propaganda programs that aimed at consolidating their grip on the hearts and minds of the populations of both countries. Salazar's government depended on a precarious balance of power between different factions of Portuguese society, including former Republicans, Monarchists, Integralists, and the Catholic Church. Franco, whose political position was relatively more secure after the end of the war, was still faced with the task of governing a nation profoundly divided by the scars of a three-year conflict. The two leaders quickly realized that propaganda would be a valuable tool of government: Salazar founded the National Propaganda Institute (Secretariado de Propaganda Nacional, SPN) in 1933, and Franco created the Press and Propaganda Delegation (Delegación de Prensa y Propaganda), part of the Falange's Ministry of Government (Ministerio de la Gobernación), in 1937, while the Civil War was still going on.[1]

Cinema soon became a privileged medium in the propaganda machine of totalitarian Iberia. True, Salazar was reportedly not a movie lover and con-

---

1. For an in-depth analysis of the propaganda apparatus in the early years of Franco's government, see Sevillano Calero. For a study of propaganda in Portugal's New State, see Paulo.

sidered films to be "horribly expensive," as he confessed to António Lopes Ribeiro, one of the filmmakers who worked more closely with the New State.[2] However, António Ferro, head of the Portuguese Propaganda Institute for almost two decades, was a cinephile, and fully aware of the propagandistic potential of cinema, "which exerts such a strong influence in the renovation of the soul of a people and in the projection of their character" (Ferro 61).[3] Ferro devised a so-called politics of spirit that aimed to harness the vitality of artistic endeavors so as to generate enthusiasm for Salazarism among the Portuguese, and cinema was regarded as a key element for accomplishing this task (Vieira 157–58).

On the Spanish side, the Nationalists started off their cinematic propaganda during the Civil War at a disadvantage, as the main film industry centers in Madrid, Barcelona, and Valencia remained in the hands of the Republicans until 1939. Nevertheless, the Francoists made use of the film studios in Cádiz and Córdoba, in Italy and Germany, as well as those of Tobis in Lisbon to produce a number of propagandistic films, most notably documentaries that presented the various events of the war as part of a heroic and triumphant march toward a better Spain.[4] To aid the Spanish Nationalists and to contain the sympathy of some sectors of Portuguese society for the Republican cause, the New State financed the feature documentary *On the Way to Madrid* (*A Caminho de Madrid*, 1936), directed by Portuguese filmmaker Aníbal Contreiras, which was shown in several countries outside the Iberian Peninsula and helped rally support for the rebels. Still during the Civil War, in 1938, Franco created the National Department of Cinematography (Departamento Nacional de Cinematografía). In 1939, the Regulatory Sub-Commission of Cinematography (Subcomisión Reguladora de Cinematografía) was born and, two years later, the Francoist government founded the National Delegation of Cinematography and Theater (Delegación Nacional de Cinematografía y Teatro) as part of the Falangist Vice-Secretariat of Popular Education (Vicesecretaría de Educación Popular de FET y JONS). The multiplication of institutions designed to coordinate and foster the film industry during and shortly after the Civil War

---

2. For a collection of texts on the filmography of António Lopes Ribeiro, see José de Matos-Cruz's edited volume *António Lopes Ribeiro*.

3. The author is responsible for this and all other translations from Spanish and Portuguese into English.

4. The imbalance between the cinematic production of the two factions at war becomes clear if we look at the numbers involved. The Republicans produced around 220 documentaries during the war, while the Nationalist output was little more than 30 documentaries (Pereira 123).

attests to the centrality of cinema in Franco's struggle to gain adherents to his political agenda both in Spain and abroad.[5]

Having consolidated their grip on power, the Salazar and the Franco regimes employed similar strategies to foster and, at the same time, control national cinemas. The New State saw the need to "protect, coordinate, and stimulate national film production [. . .] given [film's] social and educational functions, as well as its cultural and artistic aspects" (Law 2 027, 02.18.1948), while the Franco government realized that "the film industry is perhaps one of the industries most in need of protectionist support by the state" (ministerial order, qtd. in Monterde 196). Both states put in place a number of protectionist measures designed to limit the impact of foreign movies on the Iberian market, especially those originating from the powerful Hollywood-based film industry, and to encourage national production. In Portugal, for instance, a 1933 piece of legislation decreed that distributors should buy sound films produced nationally and show them in movie theaters for a number of weeks determined by the government. However, this measure was never very effective, and was later dropped for lack of control on the part of the authorities (see Vieira 13–15). In Spain, movie theaters initially had to project one week of Spanish cinema for every six weeks of foreign films and, after 1944, the six weeks were reduced to five. Further, the lucrative right to distribute foreign films depended, beginning in 1941, upon the production of Spanish films, many of which were, therefore, made only for the purpose of obtaining these licenses. Later, the authorities developed a classification system for movies that depended on their quality and their moral and educational value. According to this system, films ranged from "films of national interest," to first-, second-, and third-category movies. Depending on their classification, these Spanish films would earn their producers a certain number of licenses to distribute foreign films. Films of "national interest" also enjoyed better distribution and had to be exhibited for as long as the audience reached a daily average of 50 percent of the capacity of a movie theater in a given week.

These protectionist measures were combined with a number of financial incentives to stimulate film production. In 1941 Spain created the Fund for the Development of National Cinematography (Fondo para el Fomento de la Cinematografía Nacional), which was managed by the National Trade Union for

---

5. In *Historia del cine español*, a book published during Franco's regime, in 1965, Fernando Mendez-Leite states that Spanish cinema was reborn after the victory of the Nationalists. Mendez-Leite praises the efforts of the Franco government to support national cinema, which, from his point of view, entered a Golden Age in 1939: "The end of the Spanish Civil War led, as was expected, to a true liberation of our cinema, which had been strangled for a long time by all sorts of ignominies and arbitrary measures. Better said: Spanish cinema was reborn [. . .]. In 1939 its Third Period began, which we named 'National Cinema' due to its importance" (1:387).

the Performing Arts (Sindicato Nacional del Espectáculo) and could finance up to 40 percent of the production costs of a movie. Producers had to present the script, the budget, and a list of actors and other staff working on a given film when they applied for funding, and the movie would receive more financial support if deemed to conform to the priorities set by the regime, both thematically and stylistically.[6] Similarly, in 1948 Portugal passed a Law for the Protection of National Cinema (Lei de Protecção do Cinema Nacional), which created a Film Fund (Fundo de Cinema) administered by the Propaganda Institute. All films that adopted the values espoused by the New State were eligible to receive funding, though preference was given to historical movies and documentaries, since these were considered to better embody the image of Portugal that the government wished to disseminate.[7] Together with this funding, both Iberian governments established a system of annual prizes that were awarded to the best film, best actor and actress, best photography, best documentary, and so on. Needless to say, the films funded by the two regimes would collect the majority of these prizes, which usually rewarded productions that faithfully reflected the conservative ideologies of the Francoist and Salazarist regimes.

Protectionism and financial support for the film industry were complemented by a tight control of the movies made on Iberian soil, as well as of those imported. The exhibition of any film in Spain and Portugal depended upon the approval of the work in question by the Censorship Boards of the two countries and, in Spain, the scripts of national films had to be sanctioned before the movie was shot. There were no objective criteria for censorship, but criticism of governmental policies or of public figures, negative portrayals of Spanish and Portuguese history, the endorsement of left-wing ideas, as well as the open display of sexuality, would lead to cuts imposed by the censors. Given the considerable capital investment required to produce a movie, censorship worked, to a large extent, as self-censorship, as producers and

---

6. Emilio Sanz de Soto says the following about movie-making in the 1940s: "In order to receive such generous help [from the government] one had to make the kind of cinema one was asked to make [. . .]. As if in an exam, one had to move up the ladder of power and show, in order to qualify, first the script and then the movie. It was not easy to guess what was meant by 'praising racial values or teaching our moral and political principles'" (103).

7. António Ferro, head of the Portuguese Propaganda Institute, does not hide the bias underlying the distribution of financial support for film projects: "It is natural that this criterion will lead us to protect in principle and *according to principle* certain producers and directors who adapt themselves more fully to our criterion" (70). The decisive criterion that Ferro mentions here is the theme of the movie, which should conform to the principles of the New State. Historical films were given preference both in Portugal and in Spain since, as Virginia Higginbotham points out when discussing this genre, "imperial attitudes of sacrifice, patriotism, and military glory coincide neatly with the values of Franco's fascism" (22).

filmmakers avoided topics that could have drawn the attention of the board of censors.[8] In the case of Spain, dubbing, which became mandatory for all foreign films after 1941, was also used as a censorship tool, as parts of dialogues deemed to be politically or morally detrimental to national audiences were often changed or simply cut in the Spanish version. Dubbing, a practice motivated by linguistic nationalism, proved to be a harsh blow to the already feeble Spanish film industry, which lost its linguistic advantage vis-à-vis foreign productions.

In sum, both Iberian dictatorships employed what might be described as a "carrot and stick" approach to cinema: the two countries created incentives for film production and legislation that would protect national films, in particular movies that conformed to the tenets of the Salazar and Franco governments. Yet, at the same time, state authorities controlled the national film industry through an intricate censorship apparatus that made open expression of dissent virtually impossible. Given the efforts of both countries to stimulate and control Iberian cinema, one might be led to believe that the vast majority of Spanish and Portuguese movies from this time were purely propagandistic works, a mere reflection of the ideology of the two totalitarian regimes. However, in spite of governmental attempts to manipulate the film industry, most movies made in the Iberian Peninsula during this period were not *stricto sensu* propagandistic.[9] The propaganda apparatuses of Portugal and Spain were never as powerful as their counterparts in Nazi Germany or even in Mussolini's Italy, where the state produced a large number of films. In Iberia, cinema was produced for the most part by private companies, even though some of them collaborated with the state, as was the case with the Portuguese company Tobis, or with the Spanish Cifesa. As a result, movies aimed, first and foremost, to be lucrative and, therefore, to appeal to a broad audience, which implied avoiding overtly propagandistic messages that were, in general, not well received at the box office. José Luis Castro de Paz points out that "[Spanish] cinematographic companies refused to be actively integrated into the new political ideals and, apart from certain *compromise* movies, [. . .] they mostly continued to cater to the tastes of the audience" (*Cinema herido*, 55). In the

---

8. Spanish films were often produced in two versions: one version for the internal market, which would avoid explicit sexual scenes; and another for export, where sexuality was more openly displayed (Matos-Cruz, "Roteiro Histórico" 43).

9. For the purposes of this chapter, I adopted a concept of propaganda based on the definition put forth by Garth Jowett and Victoria O'Donnell: "Propaganda is the deliberate, systematic attempt to shape perceptions, manipulate cognitions, and direct behavior to achieve a response that furthers the desired intent of the propagandist" (7). Even though Jowett and O'Donnell's definition encompasses activities such as publicity or public relations, propaganda is here understood solely as an activity sponsored by institutions linked to the government.

same vein, film critic Jorge Leitão Ramos states that cinema produced under Salazar was even less propagandistic than Francoist filmography ("Cinema Salazarista" 387).[10]

The absence of a substantial, overtly propagandistic film output notwithstanding, the Salazar and Franco regimes still made the most of cinema as a means to persuade the population in both nations of the advantages of their respective governments. If one cannot speak of massive propaganda film production, the truth is that most movies evinced what Portuguese historian Luís Reis Torgal defined as an "indirect or contextual ideology" as far as their themes, atmosphere, and social morality were concerned ("Propaganda, Ideologia e Cinema" 71).[11] On one hand, the film industry as a whole was constrained by the need to receive state subsidies and to avoid censorship for its survival. On the other hand, authorities quickly realized that, in addition to the number of openly propagandistic movies, indirect propaganda, enmeshed in the fabric of seemingly non-propagandistic topics, would be an extremely effective form of persuasion. If overt propaganda was sometimes employed in Portugal during the 1930s and in Spain in the aftermath of the Civil War as a way to "convert the unbelievers" (Torgal, "Propaganda, Ideologia e Cinema") and turn them into proselytes of Salazarist and Francoist dogma, a "soft" form of persuasion progressively took over. Many films portrayed idealized versions of Portuguese and Spanish societies modeled on the sociopolitical order the authorities wished to promote. They attempted in this way to naturalize the status quo, which would appear to be the only viable option for the citizens of both countries.

The efforts of the two Iberian totalitarian regimes at cinematic propaganda and persuasion not only employed comparable mechanisms for stimulating and controlling the film industry, but also shared many stylistic and thematic features. In Portugal, most films produced directly by the Propaganda Institute were documentary pieces that touched upon a variety of topics, ranging from public works to official visits of heads of state, military parades, sporting

---

10. José Luis Castro de Paz points out that even the propagandistic works of the 1940s incorporated cinematic traditions from the Republican period and suggests that there was a continuity in the cinematic production from before and after the Spanish Civil War, especially as far as the use of popular culture in movies was concerned (*Cinema herido* 55–58). The author restates this argument for 1950s cinema in the book *Del sainete al esperpento. Relecturas del cine español de los años 50*, written together with Josetxo Cerdán.

11. Emilio Sanz de Soto, contrary to José Luis Castro de Paz, believes that there was a radically new cinema produced in Spain after the victory of the Nationalists in the Civil War: "In such circumstances [i.e., under the government of Franco] a new cinema appeared in Spain. A cinema that was even brand new, since it had nothing to do with that other cinema that had appeared during the Second Republic" (103).

events, and other festivities. Some of these documentaries were feature films, such as António Lopes Ribeiro's *Exhibition of the Portuguese World* (*Exposição do Mundo Português*, 1941), but most were short films aired as part of the newsreel *Portuguese Journal* (*Jornal Português*), produced between 1938 and 1951, and replaced in 1953 by *Images of Portugal* (*Imagens de Portugal*).[12] In Franco's Spain, newsreels were also a significant part of film propaganda. In 1942 the government created the *Cinematic News and Documentaries* (*Noticiarios y Documentales Cinematográficos*, NO-DO), part of the Vice-Secretariat of Popular Education. Like its Portuguese version, NO-DO focused primarily on the achievements of the regime—political events, the inauguration of public works, sporting victories, and so forth—and on a variety of news items on topics that were supposedly representative of traditional Spain: bullfighting, handicrafts, folklore, and so on. These newsreels were the only ones that could be produced in Spain and were shown in all movie theaters in the country before feature films. The monopoly of the NO-DO ended in 1975, but it continued to be produced until 1981.[13]

Beyond documentaries, Portuguese and Spanish fiction films from the 1930s to the 1950s also touched upon a number of common topics. Political propaganda movies were few in both countries and consisted mostly of anticommunist narratives that highlighted the dangers of Soviet influence on the two Iberian nations. *The May Revolution* (*A Revolução de Maio*, António Lopes Ribeiro, 1937), the only film produced and funded exclusively by the National Propaganda Institute, is the most emblematic example of this genre in Portugal. The protagonist is a Portuguese communist who, having lived outside the country for a number of years, returns to Lisbon to overthrow the Salazar regime and to organize a leftist revolution. Faced with the progress brought by the New State, he gives up his plan and, instead, becomes a fervent supporter of Salazarism. The Spanish counterpart to the blatant propagandistic message of *The May Revolution* was *Race* (*Raza*, 1941), directed by José Luis Sáenz de Heredia, a relative of José Antonio Primo de Rivera, founder of the Spanish Falange, who worked closely with the Franco regime.[14] The script of the movie, conceived as a political manifesto justifying the need for the Civil

---

12. For a study about the *Portuguese Journal*, see Piçarra.
13. For a detailed analysis of NO-DO, see Tranche and Sánchez-Biosca.
14. A modified version of the film was released in 1950 under the title *Spirit of a Race* (*Espíritu de una raza*). This version eliminated the more overtly fascistic traits of the movie, in an effort to adjust Spanish propaganda to the new international political situation after the victory of the Allies in the Second World War, a time when the Spanish regime was struggling to be accepted by Western democracies. Thus, fascist salutes were eliminated, some scenes were changed, and dialogue was revised to present an image of Francoism that would be more palatable to an international audience.

War, was written by Franco himself under the pseudonym Jaime de Andrade. The plot, a thinly disguised fictionalized biography of the dictator, narrates the epic story of a Spanish family with a long military tradition, divided along political lines by the war.[15] The Republicans, indiscriminately associated with communism, are portrayed as subhuman, while the Nationalists stand out for their honorable behavior and bravery in combat. The film ends with the victory of the Nationalists, which signified a renewal of Spanish society, now freed from the detrimental influence of the Republicans.[16] Both *The May Revolution* and *Race* included documentary footage of parades in support of Salazar and Franco, which were used to confer veracity upon the events narrated. Documentary images, seamlessly interwoven with fictional footage, suggested that the fictionalized story depicted on the screen was not far from reality and therefore buttressed the propagandistic political message of the films.

The Salazar and the Franco regimes also favored historical movies as a means to disseminate the two governments' views on what Portuguese and Spanish society should be like. These films highlighted the glorious past of Iberia and praised national heroes, who were presented as models to be emulated by the citizens of both nations.[17] In Portugal, two very popular films funded by the state were *Camões* (Leitão de Barros, 1946), about the life of sixteenth-century poet Luís Vaz de Camões, whose epic poem *The Lusiads* is considered to epitomize the adventurous Portuguese spirit that fueled the maritime voyages of the fifteenth and sixteenth centuries, and *Frei Luís de Sousa* (*Friar Luís de Sousa*, António Lopes Ribeiro, 1947; adapted from the homonymous play by Almeida Garrett from 1843), about the sociopolitical consequences of the Battle of Alcácer Quibir (1578), where the Portuguese were defeated by the army of the Sultan of Morocco. The film *Madness of Love* (*Locura de Amor*, 1948), which narrated the unrequited love of Queen Juana for her husband King Felipe, was to set the tone for historical films in Spain. Juan de Orduña, the director of the movie, produced a number of other historical films, such as *Agustina de Aragón* (1950), about a Spanish heroine of the Napoleonic wars, and *Dawn of America* (*Alba de América*, 1951), which depicts Christopher Columbus's 1492 voyage to America under the auspices of the Spanish crown.

Significantly, a large number of Spanish and Portuguese historical films of this period portrayed the two countries' colonial past. Some went back to the

---

15. See Tatjana Pavlovic et al. for an in-depth analysis of the film *Race* (66–73).

16. Alejandro Yarza persuasively demonstrates in "The Petrified Tears of General Franco" how kitsch aesthetics was used in *Race* to disseminate the fascist ideology of Franco's regime.

17. António Ferro considered historical films—"bearded cinema," in the words of their detractors—as "one of the safe and solid paths for Portuguese cinema" (64).

Renaissance, as did *Dawn of America* and *Camões,* and emphasized the central role played by the two Iberian countries in opening up new maritime routes for European trade. Others depicted later moments in the imperial history of the two nations in America and in Africa. The narratives of Sáenz de Heredia's *Bambú* (1945) and Antonio Román's *The Last in the Philippines* (*Los Últimos de Filipinas,* 1945), which inaugurated the Spanish colonial film cycle, take place during the 1898 Spanish-American War. This conflict also provides the initial setting for *Race,* where it is presented as a shameful defeat for Spain that the Civil War is somehow expected to redeem. The Portuguese *Chaimite: The Fall of the Vátua Empire* (*Chaimite: A Queda do Império Vátua,* Jorge Brum do Canto, 1953), is similarly set in the late nineteenth century, and depicts a love story that unfolds against the background of the so-called pacification military campaigns in Portugal's African colonies. Many films about the colonial past include battle scenes that underline the patriotism of Spanish and Portuguese soldiers, who suffered and died to expand and protect their countries' overseas territories. In these movies, the Franco and Salazar regimes are implicitly presented as the heirs to this tradition of bravery, and as the upholders and guardians of a proud colonial legacy.

Nationalism and colonialism are also the hallmarks of the so-called crusade cinema (cine de cruzada), a genre that proliferated in Spain in the 1940s and revolved around the heroic deeds of the Spanish military.[18] Movies such as *¡Harka!* (Carlos Arévalo, 1941), and *¡A mí la Legión!* (Juan de Orduña, 1942) highlighted the bravery of the members of the Spanish Legion in their fight against rebels in Spanish-occupied Morocco. The Legion's support for the Nationalist cause in the Civil War was presented as a continuation of its efforts to defend Spain's colonial heritage, as becomes clear at the end of *¡A mí la Legión!* The emphasis on military courage and on the primacy of military cohesion and camaraderie over civilian values is also present in a number of other films about the Civil War, such as *Squadron* (*Escuadrilla,* Antonio Román, 1941) and *Service at Sea* (*Servicio en la Mar,* Luis Suárez de Lezo, 1950) about the Nationalist air force and navy, respectively.[19] Since Portugal had not experienced a recent conflict, war movies were, understandably, much less common. Still, films such as *João Ratão* (Jorge Brum do Canto, 1940), which

---

18. Leoncio Verdera's book *Lo militar en el cine español* attests to the relevance of this topic in Spanish cinema during the Franco regime and even later. Verdera identifies around 105 Spanish feature fiction films about life in the military produced between 1940 and 1985 (24).

19. Asunción Gómez shows that Spanish military films often displayed a strong misogyny, as women, associated with civil life, were seen as a threat to the soldiers' focus on military matters (576). Fátima Gil Gascón and Salvador Gómez García note that women were primarily presented as wives and mothers in Spanish filmography from the early Franco years, in keeping with the regime's conservative social values.

touches upon the Portuguese participation in the First World War, and especially the above-mentioned *Chaimite*, also highlight the courage and patriotism of Portuguese soldiers.

Literary works were a frequent source of plots for films in both countries, many of which were historical movies based on the texts of popular nineteenth-century novelists. The novels of Portuguese Romantic writer Júlio Dinis, for instance, gave rise to movies such as *The Pupils of the Rector* (*As Pupilas do Senhor Reitor*, Leitão de Barros, 1935), and *The Heiress of Canaviais* (*A Morgadinha dos Canaviais*, Amadeu Ferrari and Caetano Bonucci, 1949).[20] In Spain the writings of nineteenth-century novelist Pedro Antonio de Alarcón inspired films like *The Scandal* (*El Escándalo*, José Luís Sáenz de Heredia, 1943) and *The Nail* (*El Clavo*, Rafael Gil, 1944). Authorities believed that literary texts encapsulated the timeless values of traditional Portugal and Spain. Therefore, the adaptation of these narratives for the big screen was regarded as a means to educate the population in these principles.

Films inspired by religious topics were present in both the Francoist and Salazarist filmographies. However, the genre was much more prevalent in Spain, probably because Franco's regime relied more heavily on the support of the Catholic Church than did the Portuguese New State. A number of Spanish films mixed religion and colonialism, such as Juan de Orduña's *White Mission* (*Misión Blanca*, 1946), about a missionary in Spanish Equatorial Guinea. Another example is *Dawn of America*, which ends with the baptism of several native Americans brought to Spain by Columbus, whereupon Queen Isabella, the Catholic, proclaims the unity of the Hispanic family on both sides of the Atlantic throughout time, and under one faith and one language. Other films presented the Nationalist struggle as a religious war, and noted the anticlericalism of the Republicans. In *The Sanctuary Does Not Surrender* (*El Santuario no se Rinde*, Arturo Ruiz Castillo, 1949), the Nationalists heroically defend the Sanctuary of the Virgin de la Cabeza against an attack by Republican forces, and one of the most powerful scenes in *Race* is the assassination of a group of Catholic priests by Republican soldiers. One very popular religious film was José Antonio Nieves Conde's *Balarrasa* (1951), which narrates the events leading a soldier of the Spanish Legion to embrace religion and become a missionary. As Jean-Claude Seguin points out, the move from military life to religion might be indicative of an evolution in Franco's regime itself, which progressively abandoned its military allies and turned to the Church for political support (37). Spanish filmmaker Rafael Gil also directed a number of religious films, including *Faith* (*La Fe*, 1947), about a priest tempted by the love of a

---

20. For an analysis of the kinds of literary works adapted to the big screen under Portugal's New State, see Luís Reis Torgal's *Estados Novos, Estado Novo* 2:202–8.

young woman, and *The Lady of Fátima* (*La Señora de Fátima*, 1951), depicting the apparition of Mary to three shepherd children in the small Portuguese town of Fátima. This was also the topic of the best-known Portuguese religious film from this period, *Fátima, Land of Faith* (*Fátima, Terra de Fé,* Jorge Brum do Canto, 1943), which narrates the conversion of an atheist doctor and university professor to the Catholic faith after his son is miraculously awakened from a coma by Our Lady of Fátima. Many of these films portrayed the Franco and Salazar governments both as the culmination of a teleological theo-political historical development and as the embodiment of the miraculous spiritual salvation of Spain and Portugal in an age of atheism and materialism.

Folkloric movies set in rural areas were very prevalent during this period. These films foreground the customs and traditions of the different regions of the two countries and often include songs and dances from the countryside. See, for instance, the Portuguese *Village of the Clean Clothes* (*Aldeia da Roupa Branca,* Chianca de Garcia, 1939), which revolves around a clever country girl who fights to bring her childhood sweetheart back from Lisbon to his rural hometown, and the Spanish *Dolores* (*La Dolores,* Florián Rey, 1940), which narrates the love life of the merry country girl who gives the movie its title, and alternates between songs and picturesque images of country life. Among the popular cinematic genres of the time, folkloric movies and comedies were the ones in which propaganda messages were less pronounced. Still, in these movies rural areas were often presented as idyllic landscapes where the population lived in a happy symbiosis with the natural environment. Occasional difficulties could be overcome through hard work and with the help of the whole community, bound by close-knit ties of solidarity. The countryside usually represented the last bastion of true Portuguese and Spanish values, untainted by the corrupting effect of the foreign influences that abounded in the cities.

As for comedies, in Portugal they were mostly composed of escapist narratives that kept the dream of upward social mobility alive for the urban lower middle classes. This genre boomed in the mid-1940s, but quickly declined in the latter part of the decade and came to an abrupt end in the 1950s with *The Great Elias* (*O Grande Elias,* Arthur Duarte, 1950).[21] In Spain, however, comedies were to take a more socially critical attitude from the 1950s onwards, marked by the dark humor of a new generation of filmmakers, including Luis García Berlanga, Juan Antonio Bardem, and the Italian Marco Ferreri. This development paved the way for a new Spanish cinema that would progres-

---

21. Paulo Jorge Granja points out that, even though they avoided political issues, Portuguese comedies reproduced the conservative values of the New State.

sively distance itself from the propaganda and persuasion movies of the early Franco years.

Given the similarities that united the Salazar and Franco regimes, their shared sociopolitical values—traditional Catholicism, authoritarianism, hierarchical and conservative social relations, and a fierce anticommunism—the analogous themes of much of their film production and the geographic proximity of Portugal and Spain, one would expect the development of a close cinematic collaboration between the two countries. In fact, the Spanish cinema magazine *Primer Plano,* with close ties to the government, called in February 1941 for the development of an "Iberian cinema" that would target not only the Spanish and Portuguese markets but also the lucrative Latin American markets. This project was praised by film director and producer António Lopes Ribeiro, who often worked for the cinema division of the Portuguese Propaganda Institute, in the magazine *Animatógrafo,* where he emphasized the benefits of joining forces for the two nations' film industries (Ribeiro 66–67).

Portuguese filmmaker José Leitão de Barros was one of the pioneers of this Portuguese-Spanish collaboration. He directed a Spanish version of his film *Bocage* (1936), about the sentimental misfortunes of the renowned eighteenth-century homonymous Portuguese poet, co-produced with Eugenio González under the title *The Three Graces* (*Las Tres Gracias*). The Spanish movie was filmed simultaneously with the Portuguese one, with the replacement of some of the Portuguese actors by Spanish ones. Barros later directed another co-production, *Inês de Castro* (1944), which depicted the illicit love affair between the Galician noblewoman Inês and the Portuguese prince Pedro. The cast and crew were from the two countries, and there were Portuguese and Spanish versions of the movie. Another popular co-production was *Holy Queen* (*Rainha Santa / Reina Santa,* 1947), about Aragonese princess Isabel, who became Queen of Portugal and was later canonized as a saint. Rafael Gil directed the Spanish version of the movie, and Aníbal Contreiras was in charge of the Portuguese version. These co-productions, focusing on historical figures that crossed borders and became well known in both nations, were supported by the Portuguese and the Spanish governments. Both nations were eager to promote political and cultural ties between the two neutral countries in the uncertain years of the Second World War and its aftermath. Iberian cinematic cooperation thus peaked in the 1940s, with as many as ten films shot in partnership between 1944 and 1949 alone (Pina 110), a collaboration that would dwindle in the 1950s.

The Salazar and the Franco governments used cinema as a means to persuade the citizens of Portugal and Spain of the advantages of the two regimes. The authorities of both countries supported the national film industries through protectionist measures, production subsidies, and film prizes designed to reward the movies that most faithfully mirrored the conservative ideology of the rulers, and they controlled cinematic output by resorting to censorship. Even though few overtly propagandistic movies were made on the Iberian Peninsula, historical films, especially those about the colonial past, films about religion, literary adaptations, folkloric films, and comedies often reflected the traditionalist values of Salazarism and Francoism. In spite of some efforts in the 1940s to foster cinematic collaboration between the two nations, the ambitious plan of creating an "Iberian cinema" was never fully implemented, as the film industries of the two countries drifted apart. Portuguese cinema entered a profound crisis in the 1950s that only began to be overcome with the New Portuguese Cinema movement of the early 1960s. In Spain, a younger generation of filmmakers, influenced by Italian neorealism and armed with a corrosive sense of humor, began to question the cinematic models of the 1940s and paved the way for the emergence of the New Spanish Cinema.

WORKS CITED

Castro de Paz, José Luis. *Un cinema herido. Los turbios años cuarenta en el cine español (1939–1950)*. Barcelona; Buenos Aires; and Mexico City: Paidós, 2002.

Castro de Paz, José Luis, and Josetxo Cerdán. *Del sainete al esperpento. Relecturas del cine español de los años 50*. Madrid: Cátedra, 2011.

Ferro, António. *Teatro e Cinema (1936–1949)*. Lisbon: Edições SNI, 1950.

Gascón, Fátima Gil, and Salvador Gómez García. "Women, Engagement and Censorship in Spanish Cinema 1939–1959." *Revista Latina de Comunicación Social* 65 (2010): 460–71.

Gómez, Asunción. "La Representación de la mujer en el cine español de los años 40 y 50: Del cine bélico al neorrealismo." *Bulletin of Spanish Studies* 79 (2002): 575–89.

Granja, Paulo Jorge. "A Comédia à Portuguesa, ou a Máquina de Sonhos a Preto e Branco do Estado Novo." *O Cinema sob o Olhar de Salazar*. Ed. Luís Reis Torgal. Lisbon: Temas e Debates, 2001. 194–233.

Higginbotham, Virginia. *Spanish Film under Franco*. Austin: U of Texas P, 1988.

Jowett, Garth S., and Victoria O'Donnell. *Propaganda and Persuasion*. Thousand Oaks, CA; London; and New Delhi: Sage, 2006.

Matos-Cruz, José de, ed. *António Lopes Ribeiro*. Lisbon: Cinemateca Portuguesa, 1983.

———. "Roteiro Histórico do Cinema Espanhol." *Panorama do Cinema Espanhol 1896–1986*. Eds. Luís de Pina and José de Matos-Cruz. Lisbon: Cinemateca Portuguesa, 1986. 24–63.

Mendez-Leite, Fernando. *Historia del cine español*. Vols. 1 and 2, Madrid: Ediciones Rialp, 1965.

Monterde, José Enrique. "El cine de la autarquía (1939–1950)." *Historia del cine español*. Madrid: Cátedra, 1995. 181–238.

Paulo, Heloísa. *Estado Novo e Propaganda em Portugal e no Brasil. O SNP/SNI e o DIP.* Coimbra: Livraria Minerva, 1994.

Pavlovic, Tatjana et al. *100 Years of Spanish Cinema.* Malden, MA; and Oxford, UK: Wiley-Blackwell, 2009.

Pereira, Wagner Pinheiro. "Cinema e Propaganda Política no Fascismo, Nazimo, Salazarismo e Franquismo." *História: Questões & Debates* 38 (2003): 101–31.

Piçarra, Maria do Carmo. *Salazar vai ao Cinema. O Jornal Português de Actualidades Filmadas.* Coimbra: MinervaCoimbra, 2006.

Pina, Luís de. *História do Cinema Português.* Lisbon: Publicações Europa-América, 1986.

Ramos, Jorge Leitão. "O Cinema Salazarista." *História de Portugal.* Ed. João Medina. Vol. 12: *O Estado Novo.* Lisbon: Ediclube, 1993. 387–406.

Ribeiro, António Lopes. "Possibilidades dum Cinema Ibérico." *Panorama do Cinema Espanhol 1896–1986.* Eds. Luís de Pina and José de Matos-Cruz. Lisbon: Cinemateca Portuguesa, 1986. 66–67.

Sanz de Soto, Emilio. "1940–1950." *Cine español 1896–1983.* Ed. Augusto M. Torres. Madrid: Ministerio de Cultura, Dirección General de Cinematografía, 1984. 99–141.

Seguin, Jean-Claude. *Historia del cine español.* Madrid: Acento Editorial, 1995.

Sevillano Calero, Francisco. *Propaganda y medios de comunicación en el franquismo (1936–1951).* Alicante: Publicaciones de la Universidad de Alicante, 1998.

Torgal, Luís Reis. *Estados Novos, Estado Novo.* Vols. 1 and 2. Coimbra: Imprensa da Universidade de Coimbra, 2009.

———. "Propaganda, Ideologia e Cinema no Estado Novo. A 'Conversão dos Descrentes.'" *O Cinema sob o Olhar de Salazar.* Ed. Luís Reis Torgal. Lisbon: Círculo de Leitores, 2000. 64–91.

Tranche, Rafael R., and Vicente Sánchez-Biosca. *No-Do: El tiempo y la memoria.* Madrid: Cátedra and Filmoteca Española, 2006.

Verdera, Leoncio. *Lo militar en el cine español.* Madrid: Ministerio de Defensa, Secretaría General Técnica, 1995.

Vieira, Patrícia. *Cinema no Estado Novo: A Encenação do Regime.* Lisbon: Colibri, 2011.

Yarza, Alejandro. "The Petrified Tears of General Franco: Kitsch and Fascism in José Luis Sáenz de Heredia's *Raza.*" *Journal of Spanish Cultural Studies* 5.1 (2004): 41–55.

CHAPTER 16

Globalization and Documentary Film
Luso-Hispanic Reflections

MICHAEL J. LAZZARA

GLOBALIZATION—and its attendant flows of bodies, identities, technologies, goods, and ideas—has, in myriad ways, called up tensions between hegemony and resistance that have fueled sustained reflection and debate among academic disciplines and particularly in the field of Latin American cultural studies. While it is possible to think of the global and the local as a neat opposition wherein the former subordinates the latter in a hierarchical and colonizing relationship, the work of key contemporary Latin American cultural theorists (Mignolo, García Canclini, Martín-Barbero, Richard, Yúdice, and others) has tended, to the contrary, to conceive of the local/global dynamic as a complex set of power relations that is not at all unidirectional (Juhász-Mininberg 214). Néstor García Canclini, for example, points out that "although *hegemony* and *resistance* continue to be useful analytical categories, the complexity and nuances of these interactions also compel us to study identities as processes of *negotiation*, inasmuch as they are *hybrid, flexible,* and *multicultural*" (96; emphasis in original). Regional forms of identity may indeed disappear as a result of globalizing forces, but not necessarily so; more likely local identities will persist, as will localized forms of resistance, though perhaps markedly changed by the uneven ways in which the production and consumption of culture happens in the globalized era.

Studying globalization serves as an invitation to comparative scholarship, mainly because the critiques of globalization that appear in different kinds of cultural production seem to transcend national and even regional boundaries. Heeding this call to comparatism, this chapter situates the reflection on the global and the local in the specific realm of documentary film studies. Historically, documentary film has been obsessed with grasping, recording, explaining, or questioning aspects of "real" life and with making visible the testimony and experience of the "other." In recent decades, however, it has become fertile terrain from which to explore the uneven negotiations that take place between the center and the periphery, the global and the local, the filmmaker and his or her subject, and other such binary constructions. Leonor Arfuch, speaking about documentary and other genres that heavily incorporate first-person discourse—part of what she calls the "biographical space" in contemporary culture—observes that the structure of feeling of our capitalist, media-driven, globalized era is marked not so much by a narcissistic or voyeuristic obsession with micronarratives that can disrupt modernity's master narratives, as by a desire to compensate for and combat the "uniformity, anonymity, and isolation" of contemporary life (26). Many Latin American documentary filmmakers today appear to want to rekindle social bonds and a sense of community that have seemingly been torn asunder by global capitalism's fragmentation of human existence. Many films are narrated in the first person, but almost always with a desire to say something about the broader community. In the face of alienation, exploitation, and the homogenization of experience, filmmakers vindicate difference, situating themselves in a complex relationship with the subjects they film, portraying them not as foreign or exotic "others," but as human beings whose experience is part of a wider, "shared historicity" that includes the filmmaker, even when he or she originates from another place (Arfuch 27). Many of these "new" Latin American documentaries (I am referring to films more or less from the last two or three decades) value alternative experiences and forms of knowledge that combat individualistic, market-driven mentalities.

Thinking about the complex relations that globalization implies, it seems worth noting that *reflexivity* is a key characteristic of new documentary films from Spain, Latin America, and around the world. Moving away from the aesthetic tenets of "direct cinema" or the overtly ideological "third cinema" (as it was known in 1960s Latin America), filmmakers of the 1990s and 2000s have opted for a more personalized, reflexive style that includes increasing meta-cinematic experimentation. In opposition to the "fly on the wall" style of direct cinema (Firbas and Monteiro 86–87), which under the guise of objectivity sought to capture the "real" in ways that appeared unmediated by the camera, the construction of truth has become problematic for today's documentarians who more and more reveal on screen the negotiations that take place between "producer, process, and product" (Ruby 34). Documentarians have intentionally and overtly become part of the mix. If it is true, as Jay Ruby points out, that "the documentary film was founded on the Western middle-class need to explore, document, explain, understand, and hence symbolically control the world"—a need reflected through classic documentary techniques like the so-called voice-of-God narration—reflexive documentarians, perhaps out of an ethical obligation to their subjects, make the camera and their own authorial presence a visible part of the equation (41). More than documents to be naively consumed and accepted at face value, then, the resulting films can best be understood as performative constructions of reality, visibly and logically marked by fiction, power, myth, and silence. One need only look at the work of filmmakers like João Moreira Salles, Andrés Di Tella, Sandra Kogut, Eduardo Coutinho, Juan Carlos Rulfo, Albertina Carri, Mercedes Álvarez, and José Luis Guerín to see this reflexivity at work in recent documentary production from the Luso-Hispanic world.

For the purposes of this chapter, I wish to group together three filmmakers who, working both regionally (across Luso-Hispanic borders) and transatlantically (in Spain), challenge the homogenizing impetus of globalization and ponder, somewhat melancholically, its effects. The films—Eduardo Coutinho's *O fim e o princípio* (The End and the Beginning, Brazil, 2005), Mercedes Álvarez's *El cielo gira* (The Sky Turns, Spain, 2004), and Juan Carlos Rulfo's *Del olvido al no me acuerdo* (I Forgot, I Don't Remember, Mexico, 1999)—dialogue perfectly with one another insofar as they are all obsessed with the difficulties of preserving lifestyles and histories that time and globalization are quickly erasing from the earth, from history, and from collective memory. The three films merit joint analysis because, even though they come from different national contexts, their style and content are strikingly similar—a circumstance that I think urges us to focus more on how the political and aesthetic impulses of these "new" documentaries converge rather than on what differentiates them. All of these films record the testimonies of elderly subjects; all of them are filmed in a reflexive, self-critical style; all of them explore (implicitly or explicitly) the tricky space of encounter between the metropolitan filmmaker and the "other"; and all of them foreground the importance of memory—corporeal, spatial, oral—as weapons against the alienating impulses of the global. In short, the documentaries reflect collectively on the ways in which, to echo García Canclini, the *negotiation* between disappearing local communities and the hegemony of global capitalism is being worked out on film and across geographical and cultural borders.

In the following pages, I will draw out the complexities of these negotiations by focusing on three issues: (1) the encounter between the filmmaker and his or her subject; (2) the work that these documentaries do with ruins, time, and memory; and (3) the accent that these films place on constructing community as a way to combat the individualizing impulses of global capitalism.

THE ENCOUNTER

Having done no prior research and planning, Brazilian documentarian Eduardo Coutinho headed with his crew to São João do Rio do Peixe, in the arid backlands of the state of Paraíba, to make a film, *O fim e o princípio,* about a community of poor farmers seemingly fated to disappear. Plagued by incessant drought, the lives of the backlands inhabitants are difficult but happy. A sense of community exists, but that community seems to be disintegrating as a new generation leaves the region in search of a better life and greater opportunity elsewhere, most likely in the modern, globalized city. Aware of this dynamic, Coutinho captures on film his encounter with the community, negotiating and inventing the film through the loose structures and largely spontaneous interactions that have become hallmarks of his filmmaking.[1] For Coutinho, truth is not something located on the outside to be captured and recorded. Instead, reflexively, he makes his presence felt, occasionally appearing on screen, making his voice audible, revealing his crew's and the camera's presence, in short, documenting the process of creating a reality through film.

Coutinho arrives in the backlands conscious of his position as a privileged metropolitan filmmaker. Consequently, he uses his film to raise the key ethical question of how to represent alterity. The director's approach to the community he wishes to film is admirable. He takes care to keep editing to a minimum, insisting that interviews appear on screen in the order in which they were conducted (an obsession in all of his films). Moreover, instead of scripting the experience according to his own desires, he chooses a fluid approach that subordinates his will and preconceived notions to the knowledge of a go-between from the community. In this sense, Rosilene Batista (or Rosa) plays a key role in facilitating the encounter; she is described in the closing credits as

---

1. In an excellent article on Coutinho, one of the few analyses I have come across in English, Cecilia Sayad calls attention to the centrality of the author in Coutinho's cinema: "What best distinguishes Coutinho's films from the sociological model is the fact that while the latter narrates, he offers a portrait of the nation—privileging tones, color, and the momentary over message, psychology, a sense of progression, and closure. Coutinho produces a cinema of instants and bodies, in which the author *figures* as a central actor, and where the nation, rather than be discussed, is simply rendered present. The director gives flesh to a 'function' that has long been discussed as an abstract concept, and his celebration of presence restores indexicality to the unstable categories of author and nation" (147).

a "mediator." Rosa, who lives in a nearby town, comes from a family that has inhabited the region for over a century. She knows all of Coutinho's potential informants personally and facilitates the "outsider's" contact with them (indeed, that's how she refers to him), urging her neighbors to see Coutinho as trustworthy. Early in the film, Rosa hand-draws a map of the town for Coutinho, cluing him in to her particular *saber,* a local form of knowledge that without her assistance the filmmaker would otherwise be unable to penetrate.[2]

Throughout *O fim e o princípio,* as in other Coutinho films, the director repeatedly upholds and affirms local forms of knowledge, respecting the secrets that local communities keep. His films are riddled with implicit questions: Who can possess knowledge? What forms of knowledge and experience are deemed valuable? To what extent can knowledge and localized experience be revealed or understood by another? For example, Leocaído, an impressive character who lives reclusively in a stable, is an avid reader of the Bible, history books, poetry, and almanacs. His wit and insight speak to the knowledge that even the backlands' most downtrodden residents possess. At times, this knowledge can become overtly political or politicized. In another moment of the film, a resident of the *sertão* named Chico Moisés offers an implicit critique of globalization and a defense of his community's secrets, a reflection that permits us to understand retrospectively the interventions of Leocaído and others who appear on screen:

> CHICO MOISÉS: Today the world is full of lies, ain't it? Can you tell me some news about the world out there?
> COUTINHO: You know as much as we do.
> CHICO MOISÉS: And who is the world?
> COUTINHO: I don't know.
> CHICO MOISÉS: Ain't it us? It appears so.[3]

Likewise, Nato, another interviewee, critiques capitalist accumulation and the "sins" to which it leads: "Nobody ever thinks they're going to die. They just

---

2. One is reminded of Doris Sommer's well-known discussion of how Rigoberta Menchú deployed the secret as a strategy, or even a political weapon, for maintaining the integrity of both the individual and her community in the face of imperial or colonial forms of domination (Sommer). More than speaking *for* the other, then, Coutinho's cinema opens a space in which the other can speak, artfully minimizing his questions so that the interviewee and his or her experience take center stage.

3. All translations from the Portuguese or the Spanish are taken from the English subtitles of the DVD versions of the films studied.

keep having and doing, increasing their pile [. . .]. To have is never enough. And to be greedy is a big source of worry because then you forget to pray."

Although influenced to some extent by globalization—we notice that many interviewees have television sets or wear clothing stitched with globalized messaging—São João do Rio do Peixe appears as a place in which subtle, though powerful challenges to capitalist hegemony are possible. For example, viewers notice when Zeca Amador, another resident, tells Coutinho that he acquired the plot of land on which he lives with a handshake, that is, without a deed. But perhaps the most dramatic defense of local forms of knowledge comes from Zé de Souza, a deaf, widowed man who sits alone all day, forgotten by his own family and the other *sertão* residents. A marginal among the marginalized, he embodies the radical isolation of life in the town. Coutinho forges a special bond with him, taking the time to write down questions for the deaf man. Zé receives the questions with a smile, happy that the metropolitan filmmaker acknowledges him as a subject. After a series of basic inquiries about the deaf man's life, typical of Coutinho's interviewing style, the filmmaker concludes by asking Zé if he would like to say anything else. Zé's reply is memorable: "A man who says everything he knows makes a fool of himself." The secret is preserved. The other's experience resists narration.

Coutinho did not make *O fim e o princípio* to capture an authentic, peripheral Brazil hidden from the view of the metropolitan center. Indeed, there is nothing totalizing about his cinema in general, no compulsion to portray the nation exhaustively. He avoids the temptation to speak for or exoticize the other as the media often do, a detail that seems particularly relevant given that Coutinho began his career as a television director. Instead, Coutinho is content to film snippets of reality, or better said, multiple realities: for example, life in São João; the experience of living in a lower-middle-class apartment building in Rio, as in *Edifício Master* (Master, A Copacabana Building, 2002); or life in the *favela*, as in *Santo forte* (Mighty Saint, 1999). Each testimony he films is unique; each experience forms part of the patchwork of the nation as a complex construct that evades totalizing or reductionist representations. At the same time, each unique human experience dialogues overtly or elliptically with that of every other. This last point is clear when one considers that in *O fim e o princípio*, Coutinho is not just making a film about the other, but about himself; or, perhaps he is simply acknowledging on film that one cannot speak of the other without somehow speaking of oneself. Coutinho, who was tragically murdered in February 2014, was getting older at the time of filming *O fim e o princípio*; it therefore seems reasonable to assume that his aging (or aged) subjects' resistance to capitalist globalization resonated with his own personal politics and worldview. Coutinho is clearly attracted to the discourse of a subject like Leocaído whose rhetoric, in Coutinho's own words, encompasses a kind of "popular metaphysics that almost always manifests in surprising ways" ("O Fim e o Princípio na Terra," n. pag.).

Local forms of knowledge that create tensions with globalization are also celebrated in Mercedes Álvarez's *El cielo gira*. Filming in 2003, the director visits Aldealseñor, her childhood home until age three, located on the plains of Soria, Spain. She was the last baby born in the town, whose residents, like in Coutinho's film, are now all old. They live a sleepy existence in a place that is unlikely to see generational renewal and that is slowly opening up to globalization. In her encounters with her subjects, Álvarez's technique differs from Coutinho's, though her motivation for filming is similar: to capture something raw and authentic about the other's experience. Álvarez does not "interview" her subjects, but rather stages scenes in which the town's inhabitants converse freely. Early in the film, two old men, Antonio and Silvano, chatting on their way home from tending the cemetery—a frequent backdrop in the film that alludes to the impending fate of the town and its inhabitants—offer a subtle critique of capitalist accumulation: "And the dreams we have, how to get more of this and that, what are they for? In the end, you leave it all behind."

In *El cielo gira*, signs of globalization are plentiful. Cranes and bulldozers appear on the scene to impose modernity, a detail that symbolically creates tension around the idea of "progress" and its consequences for local populations. Modern windmills are erected on the plains to provide sustainable energy, replacing the ruinous mills of Don Quixote fame; an abandoned palace transforms into a forty-two-room, five-star hotel. A group of townsfolk talks about plans for the new hotel and worries that it will bring unwanted outsiders to Aldealseñor seeking employment. "Maybe we won't even be allowed in," one woman remarks, understanding the hotel to be a symbol of how capitalist development may eradicate her community's way of life. Here, as in other parts of the film, the question of who has the right to inhabit a given place echoes in the air.

Discussion topics among the *viejos* vary widely, ranging from world political and economic dynamics to imperialism and oil. At one point, the radio, a symbol of modernity, interrupts a conversation, announcing the imminence of the U.S. bombing of Iraq, the presence of weapons of mass destruction, and the tensions between George W. Bush and Saddam Hussein. One townsman comments that "Bush is the most resolute of all," to which another astutely retorts, "but how can Bush know what the other one [Saddam] has or does not have?" They go on to discuss how likely it is that Spain will become involved in the conflict, and reminisce about other moments in their lives that were touched even more directly by war, violence, and trauma. For example, they allude to one "18th of July" when "they" (the Nationalists) killed a woodsman from Magaña, an intimate reference to the Spanish Civil War. Soon thereafter, a woman stares at a television set while bombs fall on Baghdad. The layered message, collectively communicated by Álvarez and her subjects, is that war, abuses of power, and greed constitute a continuum in human experience; this continuum is not at all bounded by geography. Meanwhile, politicians and influences come and go, like the campaign vehicles and posters that disrupt the town's tranquil existence, proselytizing for the masses while two old women pray quietly in church. Disillusioned by empty political promises, one old man jokes that a young socialist politician came to Aldealseñor promising "candy, balloons, and condoms." He quips: "I told him he could keep them."

RUINS, TIME, MEMORY

Mercedes Álvarez once remarked that *El cielo gira* is "a film about ruin and the decadence that precedes disappearance." In a sense, so is *O fim e o princípio*. But perhaps it is in Juan Carlos Rulfo's *Del olvido al no me acuerdo* (1999) that we feel the effects of time's passage most acutely. The director, son of the legendary Mexican novelist Juan Rulfo, who penned *Pedro Páramo*, goes in search of his father's origins and, by extension, his own, which prove to be elusive. One of the greatest lessons the film teaches is that beginnings are almost impossible to pin down and that what constitutes a "life" is overwhelmingly difficult to narrate. Consequently, throughout the film Juan Rulfo's name functions as a signifier that has become dissociated from its signified. The famous author's son interviews a series of old people, none of whom knew Juan Rulfo very well or remember much about him. Instead of telling concrete stories about the legendary writer, they talk about their own relationships, exploits, joys, and hardships, always with much grace and the particular wisdom that comes with age. Their faces leathery, ravaged by time, extreme poverty, and the elements—corporeal testimonies to the hardships of life at the margins— the *viejos* embody memories (individual and collective) that evade direct narrative and frequently take the form of myth, popular sayings, humor, or song: local, *alternative* forms of memory that stand in contrast to mere information, globalized narratives, and media sound bites. Dotted by long aerial takes of Jalisco's burning plains, the documentary recreates the ghostlike feel of Rulfo's famed *Pedro Páramo*. It is a film in which living cadavers sing and dance together and in which the love and solidarity among the plainspeople stand as unique forms of resistance to the (paradoxically) alienating, individualizing impulses of the global.

Juxtaposed with the interviews conducted on Jalisco's plains, Juan Rulfo's widow, Clara Aparicio de Rulfo, wanders through the modern city, forty years later, remembering her courtship with Juan. She notes, quite simply, that "everything has changed," an existential comment that captures both an intimate truth about her relationship with Juan Rulfo and a more collective truth about how globalization is transforming ways of life both in urban spaces and in the remote corners of places like Jalisco. Her thought echoes several of the plainspeople's own observations on the fleeting nature of life and the assuredness of death. Harking back to some of the subtle critiques of capitalism heard in Coutinho's and Álvarez's films, the final testimony in *Del olvido al no me acuerdo* transmits the idea that whether one is rich or poor, death is the great equalizer. Aware of the commonalities of human existence, another old man remarks to his friend that the mesquite tree next to which they sit was once young: "Now it's old like you and me." This image strikingly interfaces with that of the elm tree in *El cielo gira*, which functions as a mute witness to the radical change that Aldealseñor has undergone over time. A montage of black and white photos shows the tree and the skulls of townspeople buried beneath it. Now cut off at the top, the tree is disappearing, like everything else.

Taken collectively, the films of Coutinho, Álvarez, and Rulfo generate tensions between localized memories (microhistories) and the impulses of global capital that detonate their ruination. Álvarez, perhaps, explores the ruins trope most deeply and productively in the third section of her film, "The Submerged Cities." Her focus is on Numantia, a Celtiberian city destroyed by the Roman Empire in 133 BC, which stood on the same site as modern-day Aldealseñor. Today Numantia's ruins are a tourist attraction. In one compelling sequence, a guide walks visitors around the rubble of the ancient city, at once raising questions about the commodification of history while implying Aldealseñor's impending ruination. Will Aldealseñor be done away with by the hegemony of global capitalism in the same way that Numantia vanished at the hands of its imperialist colonizers? The guide explains that when faced with Scipio's invasion, many of Numantia's inhabitants committed suicide and burned their homes in protest. They refused to give their culture over to their captors: an ancient expression that dialogues directly with the modern-day, localized forms of resistance to capitalism that all three of these films have encrypted within them.

El cielo gira, like the other films, ends on a note of ephemerality. It emphasizes life's brevity, the broad sweep of history, and the relative insignificance of human beings in relation to the cosmos. Central to this reflection is Pello

Azketa, a painter from Pamplona who serves as Álvarez's guide through the ruins of Aldealseñor. Azketa is going blind. Consequently, his landscapes, which figure prominently in the film, harmonize with Álvarez's long, vertiginous takes of the misty and desolate Sorian plains; they also fuse imagination and memory in ways that metaphorically evoke Aldealseñor's fated disappearance. However, the film's final image is not of real-life Sorian landscapes, but rather of the *representation* of that reality on canvas, which may suggest that memory traces are all that remain when historical periods or personal experiences pass into ruin.

Might all of these images of ruination (skulls, destroyed cities, works of art, the dinosaur tracks that are fossilized into the earth beneath what today is Aldealseñor) be telling us something more grandiose about the "moment" of global capitalism in which we are living? Might these filmmakers be imagining, however timidly, another time beyond the present? By making films situated on the verge of an abyss, Álvarez, like her Brazilian and Mexican colleagues, seems to imply that change is inevitable and that the present moment is unlikely the end of history. Time will go on, and with luck, new social, political, and economic configurations will emerge that allow us to see beyond the ruins.

COMMUNITY

From where, though, will these new configurations emerge? I want to conclude by rescuing from these films the idea of connectedness, of *community*, which is certainly central to the poetics of all three and which may also encapsulate, implicitly, a politics of resistance to the forces of globalization. Of course, the notion of community closely relates to the preservation of collective memory—and such preservation seems to be a goal that motivates all three filmmakers. However, when I speak of the collective memory that these films preserve, I am not referring to a set of mere historical facts or even to a broad narrative through which a given community imagines itself. Rather, I am referring to the kinds of intimate memories that bind groups together affectively, through song, folklore, myth, or anecdote—the very personal memories that Borges had in mind when he mused about the unique perspective that every human witness has: "What will die with me the day I die? What pathetic or frail image will be lost to the world?" (311).

One of the most frequently heard critiques of global capitalism is that while, on one hand, it brings people closer together through technology, access, and the creation of shared spaces of identification, on the other hand it pushes us farther apart, making us more individualistic, competitive, obsessed with personal gain, and situated at a remove from one another. In other words, while the forces of globalization and consumer culture do generate certain kinds of communities and also produce positive effects, at the same time critics have asked if these are really the kinds of communities in which we want to be living, being often devoid of solidarity and rampant with inequality. Academics like Andreas Huyssen have looked specifically at the ways in which globalization interfaces with memory and have admonished that oversaturation with memory, data collection, and archiving might paradoxically foster an alienating amnesia in contemporary cultures (21). Indeed, memory has to be actualized and made meaningful, not just stored for posterity, if it is to bring people together. Sharing these concerns about the paradoxically alienating forces of the global, Jesús Martín-Barbero suggests that in Latin America today traditional cultures, or localized interests, play a strategic role insofar as they represent "a fundamental challenge to modernization's dehistoricized universality and its homogenizing pressures" (191). It is no wonder, then, that documentary filmmakers are focusing their lenses on such communities.

If we take the films of Coutinho, Álvarez, and Rulfo together, it is clear, as I have shown, that tradition, local practices, forms of resistance, and global capitalism exist in a tense relationship, a complex dialectic riddled with doses of negotiation, resignation, and rebellion. It is undeniable that the three towns depicted in these films belong to and participate in the capitalist order. Yet, at the same time, the behaviors and attitudes of the towns' inhabitants subtly hint at a precapitalist social arrangement, or minimally at a less individualistic form of capitalism that the directors find compelling, likely because of the closer-knit community formations that such arrangements portend. In that sense, community becomes a key notion around which these documentaries register their impassioned resistance to the global order.

In my estimation, the films project two visions (or versions) of community. The first is inwardly focused and has to do with how the members of communities bound for extinction (or minimally, for radical metamorphosis) relate to one another in ways that challenge extreme individualism. The second is outwardly focused and has to do with how the members of those communities relate to the world, that is, to the larger "global" community. Let me say a word about each of these visions.

First, interpersonal relationships in the films of Coutinho, Álvarez, and Rulfo are marked by an admirable solidarity that reminds viewers of people's interconnectedness and of the importance of caring for one another. Children respect their elders. People sit around swapping stories, chatting about the mundane or the political, unhurried by the concerns of modern life. They take time to bury their dead. They know their neighbors. They sing and dance together, imparting wisdom through sayings and songs. They reach out and lend a hand to passersby, rejecting outsiders only when they lack understanding or somehow threaten local life. (Juan Carlos Rulfo's film opens with an old man staring directly at the camera, questioning viewers as to what their role will be: "Hey! Who are you? And your friend? Are you the devil? Oh, then I already know you, so I'll see you later.") Those who don't pose a threat are welcomed with open arms.

A moving example of the solidarity people show one another comes in a sequence of *El cielo gira* in which a Moroccan shepherd living in Aldealseñor randomly encounters a Moroccan competitive runner who is temporarily living in Soria. Both men are Arabs and speak to each other in Arabic. They identify a common, human bond and treat each other with kindness. The fact that they are both Moroccan, symbolic descendants of Moorish Spain, reminds viewers of the Reconquest and particularly of the violence that undergirds current geopolitical configurations and immigration patterns. The ruined Moorish castle that appears on screen at certain points in the film interfaces with this chance encounter. From there, an analogy emerges: what was once the Reconquest that expelled the Moors is today neoliberal globalization, a new form of violence that once again threatens a local, established community. The shepherd shares with his new friend an Arab proverb that speaks to what Mercedes Álvarez has described as *convivencia* (a form of community), the interconnectedness of human beings on both a local and a global scale (Ehrlich n. pag.): "Mountains never move, but men do. Men may move about, but even though twenty years may pass, they can reunite." Time, politics, war, violence, and money may transform places, but people should not lose sight of *convivencia*, the ties that bind human beings together in ethical configurations of community. This seems to be a major takeaway from *El cielo gira*, as well as from the other films.

A second way in which these documentaries create bonds of community is by reaching beyond the villagers' circumscribed realities. Perhaps the most forceful example of this can be found in *O fim e o princípio* and harks back to my earlier discussion of the encounter between the filmmaker and his subjects. Coutinho is able to bring disparate individual realities together and make them play together quite convincingly on screen. He strives to document real dreams, real pain, real problems, and to show what binds people together in a world that in so many ways pushes them apart. His questions to those he encounters are simple. "Where are you from?" "What are your dreams?" In that sense, he serves not so much as an interviewer, but as a prompter and guide who seeks to open space for the other to share his or her experience, all the while preserving the right to alterity to which the other is entitled. In one revealing sequence, Leocaído asks Coutinho three times if he believes in God. Coutinho avoids answering directly, though he acknowledges that it would sometimes be helpful to believe in a higher power. Coutinho's ambiguous response brilliantly reflects his desire not to usurp the space he has opened for his subject; at the same time, he does not breach the implicit ethical pact he makes with his interlocutor to uphold his end of the "conversation."

Coutinho once stated in an interview that "all human beings are born, live, and die [. . .] and aside from that it's simple: sex, marriage, kids, money" (Frochtengarten 128). This common narrative among *all* people harbors for Coutinho something like an ethics of filmmaking, a point of connection that brings even the most disparate of experiences into a relationship with another. One might posit that by saying "you," Coutinho says "I." He plays the role of empathic listener to the other, bringing anonymous people out of anonymity by making them visible on screen and dignifying them as subjects. He doesn't just use his subjects; he humanizes them and relates to them in solidarity. The same can be said of Álvarez and Rulfo. In that vein, toward the end of *O fim e o princípio*, Coutinho promises to return to the backlands one year later to follow up with his characters and let them celebrate their on-screen debut. Significantly, the encounter, a mutual awareness, continues even after the camera stops rolling, and this mutual awareness functions as a powerful weapon, a point of departure for combating the homogenization of experience and the disappearance of the local.

If the films of Coutinho, Álvarez, and Rulfo achieve anything at all, it is not just that they rescue anonymous stories and experiences from oblivion. These films do not simply fetishize otherness or register a lament about global capitalism's dark side. More importantly, and in subtle ways, they challenge us to understand the interconnectedness of the self and the other and to posit community formation as a counterforce to the hegemony of global capital. In so doing, globalization is configured on screen not as a given, but as a question.

Last, the question of globalization begs more comparative research on documentary filmmaking not only within the Luso-Hispanic world, but beyond it as well. What tactics for contesting globalization on screen exist beyond those discussed here? Should we read the reflexive presence of directors in their own films as derivative of capitalist individualism or as a counterforce to it? How are we to understand the rampant interest in localized memories and histories that these documentaries capture? What historical and social experiences traverse the Luso-Hispanic world, necessitating a comparative study of the cinemas of Brazil and Spanish-America? What dialectics exist between the work of Luso-Hispanic documentary filmmakers and artists working in other genres like literature or the visual arts? This study, I hope, might serve as an invitation to carry out additional scholarly work around these questions and on contexts whose synergies have yet to be sufficiently uncovered.

WORKS CITED

Arfuch, Leonor. "Íntimo, privado, biográfico: espacios del yo en la cultura contemporánea." *Estéticas de la intimidad*. Ed. Lorena Amaro. Santiago: Pontificia Universidad Católica de Chile, Facultad de Filosofía, Instituto de Estética, 2009. 17–27.

Borges, Jorge Luis. *Collected Fictions*. Trans. Andrew Hurley. New York: Penguin, 1999.

Ehrlich, Linda C. "Three Contemporary Spanish Films: Landscape, Recollection, Voice." *Senses of Cinema* 46 (2008): n. pag. Web. 10 Jan. 2012.

"O Fim e o Princípio na Terra do Fim do Mundo." *Raiz: Cultura do Brasil* 1. Web. 10 Jan. 2012.

Firbas, Paul, and Pedro Meira Monteiro. *Andrés Di Tella: cine documental y archivo personal*. Buenos Aires: Siglo XXI, 2006.

Frochtengarten, Fernando. "A Entrevista Como Método: Uma Conversa Com Eduardo Coutinho." *Psicologia USP* 20.1 (2009): 125–38. Web. 10 Jan. 2012.

García Canclini, Néstor. *Consumers and Citizens: Globalization and Multicultural Conflicts*. Trans. George Yúdice. Minneapolis: U of Minnesota P, 2001.

Huyssen, Andreas. *Present Pasts: Urban Palimpsests and the Politics of Memory*. Stanford: Stanford UP, 2003.

Juhász-Mininberg, Emeshe. "Local-Global." *Dictionary of Latin American Cultural Studies*. Eds. Robert McKee Irwin and Mónica Szurmuk. Gainesville: UP of Florida, 2012. 211–16.

Lins, Consuelo. *O Documentário de Eduardo Coutinho: televisão, cinema e video*. Rio de Janeiro: Jorge Zahar Editor Ltda., 2004.

Martín-Barbero, Jesús. *Al sur de la modernidad: comunicación, globalización y multiculturalidad*. Pittsburgh: IILI, 2001.

Ruby, Jay. "The Image Mirrored: Reflexivity and the Documentary Film." *New Challenges for Documentary*. 2nd ed. Eds. Alan Rosenthal and John Corner. Manchester: Manchester UP, 2005. 34–47.

Sayad, Cecilia. "Flesh for the Author: Filmic Presence in the Documentaries of Eduardo Coutinho." *Framework* 51.1 (2010): 134–50.

Sommer, Doris. "Rigoberta's Secrets." *Latin American Perspectives* 18.1 (1991): 32–50.

CONTRIBUTORS

ALFREDO BOSI is Professor Emeritus of Brazilian Literature at the University of São Paulo. Considered one of Brazil's greatest literary and cultural critics, Bosi is the author of numerous studies on Brazilian literature, culture, and intellectual history, including *Dialética da colonização* (1992), *Literatura e resistência* (2002), and *Ideologia e contraideologia* (2010). Bosi is a member of the Brazilian Academy of Letters.

TINA ESCAJA is Professor of Spanish and Director of Gender, Sexuality and Women's Studies at the University of Vermont. She publishes on gender, technology, and representation in Latin America and Spain. She is the author of *Salomé decapitada: Delmira Agustini y la estética finisecular de la fragmentación* (2000) and editor of *Compromiso e hibridez: Aproximaciones a la poesía hispánica contemporánea escrita por mujeres* (2007).

EARL E. FITZ is Professor of Portuguese, Spanish, and Comparative Literature at Vanderbilt University. His areas of specialization include Brazilian literature, comparative literature, Spanish American literature, comparative Luso-Hispanic studies, and inter-American studies. His publications include *Translation and the Rise of Inter-American Literature* (with Elizabeth Lowe, 2007) and *Machado de Assis and Female Characterization: The Novels* (2015).

DAVID WILLIAM FOSTER is Regents' Professor of Spanish and Women and Gender Studies at the Arizona State University. His research focuses on urban culture in Latin America, with emphasis on issues of gender construction and sexual identity. He is the author of numerous monographs and edited volumes, and has held Fulbright teaching appointments in Argentina, Brazil, and Chile, as well as visiting appointments at several U.S. universities.

RICHARD A. GORDON is Professor of Portuguese and Spanish-American Literature and Director of the Latin American and Caribbean Studies Institute at the University of Georgia. His research focuses largely on historical film and social identity. His publications include *Cannibalizing the Colony: Cinematic Adaptations of Colonial Literature in Mexico and Brazil* (2009) and *Cinema, Slavery, and Brazilian Nationalism* (2015).

TRACY DEVINE GUZMÁN is Associate Professor of Latin American Studies at the University of Miami. Her research interests include global and transnational indigeneity, South-South relations, and environmental studies. Her book *Native and National in Brazil: Indigeneity after Independence* (2013) won Honorable Mention in the competition for the Latin American Studies Association (LASA) Brazil Section Book Prize.

HÉCTOR HOYOS is Associate Professor of Iberian and Latin American Cultures at Stanford University, where he teaches contemporary fiction and literary theory. He is the author of *Beyond Bolaño: The Global Latin American Novel* (2015). He edited the special journal issues "Theories of the Contemporary in South America" for *Revista de Estudios Hispánicos* (with Marília Librandi Rocha, 2014) and "La cultura material en las literaturas y cultura iberoamericanas de hoy" for *Cuadernos de literatura* (2016).

MICHAEL J. LAZZARA is Associate Professor of Spanish at the University of California, Davis. His research focuses on contemporary literature and cinema of the Southern Cone, particularly Chile and Argentina, and on issues of memory, trauma, revolution, and dictatorship. His publications include the books *Telling Ruins in Latin America* (2008) and *Luz Arce and Pinochet's Chile: Testimony and the Aftermath of State Violence* (2011).

LEILA LEHNEN is Associate Professor of Spanish and Portuguese at the University of New Mexico. Her primary research interests are in twentieth- and twenty-first-century Brazilian and Spanish American literature and culture, and issues of citizenship, human rights, and social justice. She is the author of the book *Citizenship and Crisis in Contemporary Brazilian Literature* (2013).

LESLIE L. MARSH is Associate Professor of Spanish & Portuguese and Director of the Center for Latin American and Latino/a Studies at the Georgia State University. She specializes in Hispanic and Lusophone film and media studies and Hispanic and Lusophone women's cultural production. She is the author of *Brazilian Women's Filmmaking: From Dictatorship to Democracy* (2012).

PEDRO MEIRA MONTEIRO is the Arthur W. Marks '19 Professor of Spanish and Portuguese at Princeton University. His research focuses on Brazilian and Spanish American literature and intellectual history. A specialist in the work of Sérgio Buarque de Holanda, Monteiro is the author of *Signo e desterro: Sérgio Buarque de Holanda e a imaginação do Brasil* (2015) and editor of *Mário de Andrade e Sérgio Buarque de Holanda: Correspondência* (2012).

CONTRIBUTORS • 251

FREDERICK MOEHN is Senior Lecturer in Music at King's College London. His research interests include music cultures of Latin America (especially Brazil) and Africa (especially Angola), jazz, and interconnections between music, race, class, and national identity. He is the author of *Contemporary Carioca: Technologies of Mixing in a Brazilian Musical Scene* (2012). He has taught at several universities in the United States and Portugal.

SARAH MOODY is Associate Professor of Spanish at the University of Alabama. Her research examines Spanish-American *modernismo* and women's writing in Latin American literature of the nineteenth and early twentieth centuries, especially focusing on the relationship between aesthetic systems, and gender and nationalism. Her current book project is entitled *Las raras: Gendered Aesthetics, Women's Writing, and Intellectual Networks in Spanish-American Modernismo.*

ROBERT MOSER is Associate Professor of Portuguese, Brazilian, and Lusophone African Literature and Culture at the University of Georgia. His research focuses on the figure of the dead and expressions of haunting and mourning. He is the author of *The Carnivalesque Defunto: Death and the Dead in Modern Brazilian Literature* (2008) and co-editor of *Luso-American Literature: Writings by Portuguese Speaking Authors in North America* (2011).

ROBERT PATRICK NEWCOMB is Associate Professor of Spanish and Portuguese at the University of California, Davis. His research focuses on comparative Luso-Hispanic studies, Iberian studies, and Portuguese- and Spanish-speaking essayists and public intellectuals. His publications include the book *Nossa and Nuestra América: Inter-American Dialogues* (2011) and a translation of Alfredo Bosi's *Brazil and the Dialectic of Colonization* (2015).

PEDRO SCHACHT PEREIRA is Associate Professor of Portuguese and Iberian Studies at The Ohio State University. His research focuses on imperial and postimperial discourses, Luso-Brazilian fiction (19th–21st c.), and comparative Luso-Hispanic studies. His publications include *Filósofos de trazer por casa: cenários da apropriação da filosofia em Almeida Garrett, Eça de Queirós e Machado de Assis* (2013).

CHARLES A. PERRONE is Professor Emeritus of Portuguese and Luso-Brazilian Culture & Literature and Coordinator of Brazilian Studies at the University of Florida. He is the author of *Masters of Contemporary Brazilian Song: MPB 1965–1985* (1989), *Seven Faces: Brazilian Poetry since Modernism* (1996), and *Brazil, Lyric, and the Americas* (2010).

PATRÍCIA VIEIRA is Associate Professor in the Department of Spanish & Portuguese, the Comparative Literature Program, and the Film and Media Studies Program at Georgetown University and Associate Research Professor at the Center for Social Studies of the University of Coimbra. Her research focuses on Latin American and Iberian literature and cinema, comparative literature, postcolonial studies and ecocriticism. She is the author of several books, including *States of Grace: Utopia in Brazilian Culture* (2017).

INDEX

A Jangada de Pedra (The Stone Raft) (Saramago), 1, 13
Allende, Isabel, 99, 102
Ambiguity and Gender in the New Novel of Brazil and Spanish America (Fitz and Payne), 95
Andrade, Carlos Drummond de, 105, 147
Andrade, Mário de, 138–39, 141, 142, 147, 164
Andrade, Oswald de, 98, 112, 139, 142
Argentina, 38, 42, 43, 44; and Argentine working class, 120n4, 122; and civil rights, 120; democratic transition in, 121; and dictatorship, 208; and disappeared persons, 204; and human rights, 208; and Juan Domingo Perón, 126; and Juan Manuel de Rosas, 128; and Lebanese and Palestinians, 48; and male homosexuals, 56; and military coup, 130; and Néstor Kirchner, 208, 209; and Oliverio Girondo, 139–40; and political rights, 120; social rights in, 120; writers of, 131
Arguedas, José María, 41, 69–70, 74, 75–79, 75n24, 102, 146
art: and aesthetics, 144–45; and Afro-diasporic work, 168; and avant-gardes, 141–42, 144; and cubism, 144; and *Day of the Dead—City Fiesta* (Rivera), 101; and "Death and the Maiden" motif, 96; and Diego Rivera, 164; and expressionism, 144; and Jean Charlot, 101; and Jose Guadalupe Posada's engravings, 101; and "Las bellas durmientes" (Sleeping Beauties), 197–201; in Latin America, 138; and Mexican muralists, 144, 146; and museums, 37, 132; and painting and sculpture, 113; and politics, 16–17; and protest, 191; and queerness, 62; and theory, 49; and urban art, 194–97; and Week of Modern Art, 105

Assis, Machado de, 15, 59n10, 95; and Brás Cubas, 97, 109, 114; and Brazilian literature, 112, 113, 114, 157n17; and the carnivalesque *defunto* (deceased), 96; and *Memórias Postumas de Brás Cubas*, 104, 109, 111, 112, 113, 114; and the New Narrative, 113, 114; and reader's role, 114; and Realism, 113; and verisimilitude, 115

Barthes, Roland, 113–14, 115, 116
Bolívar, Simón, 13, 105
Bolivia, 96, 131
Borges, Jorge Luis: and aesthetics, 138–39; and the "boom," 112; and *Ficciones*, 108–10, 114, 115; and the ghost, 99; and hypercanonicity, 43n6; and language, 114; and magic, 115; and the New Narrative, 108, 113; and queer issues, 57, 57n6, 61, 62; and reader's role, 114; and Realism, 113; short stories of, 15, 42, 99; and Spanish American works, 113; and structuralism, 109–10, 115
Bosi, Alfredo: and Latin American avant-gardes, 11, 15–16; and "The *Parabola* of the Latin American Avant-Gardes," 15–16. See also *Dialéctica da Colonização* (Brazil and the Dialectic of Colonization) (Bosi)
Brazil: and abolition of slavery, 151; and African slavery, 102, 103; and African studies, 27n9; and Afrocentricity, 59n9; and the Americas, 14, 87; area of, 48; and Artur da Costa e Silva, 69; and Asian

people, 48; authoritarian past of, 209; authors of, 98, 105, 131; and Brazil Galicia Cultural Institute, 173–74; and Brazilian literature, 10, 15–16, 27n9, 95, 96–98, 104–5, 106, 108, 110, 112–13, 121, 122, 150, 157–60; and Brazilian Modernism, 87, 105, 138, 154; and carnival, 96–98, 102, 103, 105, 107; and the carnivalesque *defunto* (deceased), 98, 102, 103–4, 105, 106; cinema in, 17, 121; and citizenship, 68, 120; and civil rights, 120; and Constitution of 1988, 68; and death, 100, 101, 102; democratic transition in, 121; and dependency, 89; and dictatorship, 69, 74, 192, 198–99, 201; and disappeared or tortured persons, 205; economy of, 185; and frontier with Uruguay, 1, 11; and Galicia, 174; gay culture in, 59n9; and gay rights, 57; and Getúlio Vargas, 70; and Gilberto Freyre, 146; and Iberian colonization, 2; and importance of Spanish, 9; and indigenous people, 102, 145; and João da Cruz e Sousa, 151, 155–57, 159, 160; and João Goulart, 68; and Jorge de Lima, 144; and Latin America, 2n11, 7, 12, 13, 42; as Latin America's economic leader, 13; and *lusofonia*, 176–77; and Luso-Hispanic studies, 162–63; and Lusophone Africa, 40; and memory, 16–17; military coup in, 106; military government of, 68–69; and modernity, 151; and national identity, 12, 102; and the National Indian Foundation (FUNAI), 72; and nationalism, 70; and native people, 66, 68–74, 85; and novelist Machado de Assis, 5; and *O espelho de Prospero* (Prospero's Mirror), 82, 88; and political rights, 120; politics of, 13, 69, 74, 151; and Portugal, 25; queer culture in, 59n9; and religion, 103; and *Roots of Brazil*, 90; and Sérgio Buarque de Holanda, 10–11; and the Serviço de Proteção aos Índios (SPI), 66, 70–72, 71n15, 71n16, 72n17; social rights in, 120; society of, 95, 97, 98, 103; and South America, 84–85; and Spanish America, 41, 43, 48, 95; and Street Projects, 16; and transformations since the 1960s, 27; and transition to democracy, 205–6; and transnationalism, 44, 49; and Treaty of Tordesillas, 6n6; and urban working classes, 120n4, 122; and women, 109, 110, 111, 112; and Zumbi dos Palmares, 59n9. *See also* Assis, Machado de; *Inferno provisório* (Temporary Hell) (Ruffato); Ribeiro, Darcy; *Roots of Brazil* (Buarque de Holanda); violence

Buarque de Holanda, Sérgio, 10–11; and American race, 85; and colonization, 103n4; and critique of authoritarian thought, 86–87; and *Ibero-Americans*, 87; and intellectual emancipation, 86; and Monroism, 87; and *Roots of Brazil*, 82, 85, 86–87, 89–90; and *secularization*, 89

Budapeste (Buarque), 50

Camões (Garrett), 12n14

Camões, Luís de: and Iberian studies, 32–33; and *Os Lusíadas*, 10n12; as a poet, 3

Candido, Antonio, 97, 98

"*Cantigas de amigo*: Galicia and Brazil in the Lusophone Musical Space" (Moehn), 16

capitalism: and capitalist culture, 77; force of, 76–77; and global capital, 76, 243–44; and *Maíra* (Ribeiro), 73; and modernity, 71; and precapitalist American societies, 78. *See also El zorro de arriba el zorro de abajo* (Arguedas)

Carpentier, Alejo, 139, 140, 144, 146

Cervantes, 86

Césaire, Aimé, 84, 144, 165–66

Chile, 42, 44, 69, 73n19, 131, 204, 205, 209

Cien años de solidad (*One Hundred Years of Solitude*) (Garcia Marquez), 43, 46, 99

cinema: and Argentina, 208; in Brazil, 17, 121, 208, 237–40, 246; and Budapest, 50; and Carvalho's *Budapeste*, 50; and Comparative Luso-Hispanic studies, 3, 11, 246–47; and democracy, 206–7; and documentary film, 11, 17, 50, 234–47; and films cited, 219; in Iberia, 17, 220–32; and *Japón* (Reygadas), 50; and *Kamchatka* (Pineyro), 50, 207, 211, 213; and *La teta asustada*, 208; and Latin America, 16–17, 50, 209–10, 216; and *Machuca* , 207, 210–12, 213; and *Maira* (Ribeiro), 71n14; and memory, 16–17, 212–13, 216, 241–44; and "Memory, Youth and Regimes of Violence in Recent Hispanic and Lusophone Cinemas" (Marsh), 16–17, 206–19; in Mexico, 17; and *O ano em que meus pais saíram de férias*, 207, 210–12, 213; and propaganda, 220–21, 223, 226; and *Quase dois irmãos*, 208; in Spain, 17; and Spanish America, 16–17; in totalitarian Iberia, 220–32; and trauma, 207–8, 213, 217, 241; and truth construction, 17; and *Um passaporte húngaro* (Kogut), 50;

under dictatorship, 11, 16–17, 220–25; and youth subjects, 206–7, 210–13, 217
Cities and Citizenship (Appadurai and Holston), 119–20
Cixous, Hélène, 116
class: and Argentine working class, 120n4, 122; in Brazil, 215–16; in Chile, 213; and Mexican upper class, 101; and middle-class readers, 131; and transnationalism, 43; and working class, 120n4, 121, 122, 123, 124, 126–27, 129, 130
colonization: and Africa, 1, 2, 4, 22, 25; and the Americas, 1, 4, 22, 66, 68, 87, 102; and anticolonial struggles, 68; and Asia, 1, 4; and Brazil, 16, 66, 103; and colonialism, 138; and coloniality of power, 66–67, 69; and colonial themes, 169–70; and death, 100; and former Spanish and Portuguese empires, 5–6; and Iberian colonization, 1–2; and Iberian overseas colonization, 6–7; and imperialism, 1; and Peru, 66, 74; and Portugal, 102; and Spain, 102–3. *See also* Treaty of Tordesillas
Comparative Luso-Hispanic studies, 2–17, 105n6, 162–64
Cortázar, Julio, 41, 43n6, 102, 108, 112
Counterfeit Politics: Secret Plots and Conspiracy Narratives in the Americas (Kelman), 44
Cuba: and Afro-Cuban *carnaval*, 168; and avant-gardes, 140, 146; and critique of modernity, 89; and Cuban Casa de las Américas, 43; and Cuban-Chinese, 48; and the Cuban Revolution, 105; and Havana, 47; and Latin American literature, 43; and Nicolás Guillén, 144; as part of Spanish Empire, 47; and slavery, 167
Cubas, Brás, 97, 104, 105, 109

Darío, Rubén, 44, 62; and Hispanic American *modernistas*, 150, 158; innovations of, 105; and Latin America, 83; and modernism, 151, 152–54; and New York, 82; and race, 159; and the sacred, 89
Death and the Idea of Mexico (Lomnitz), 100
De la Campa, Roman, 45–46
Deleuze, Gilles, 39, 41
Derrida, Jacques, 113–14, 116
Dialéctica da Colonizacão (Brazil and the Dialectic of Colonization) (Bosi), 16

Díaz Quiñones, Arcadio, 84
Don Quijote de la Mancha (Cervantes), 46
d'Ors, Eugeni, 10

El pibe (The Kid) (Saccomanno): and citizenship, 15, 120–22, 127, 128, 130; and the city, 120, 121, 126; and education, 120, 122, 128, 129–30; and homeownership, 120, 122, 127, 128–29; and Juan Domingo Perón, 127; and poverty, 121, 129; and rights, 121, 127; and urban proletarian life, 120, 121, 126–27, 129; and working class neighborhoods, 121, 126, 127–28
El zorro de arriba el zorro de abajo (Arguedas): and capitalist culture, 77; and Incas, 77; and indigeneity, 78–79; and indigenous people, 69, 77–78; and modernity, 77–78; and Peru, 74, 76–79; and politics, 77; and sociocultural transformation, 70, 74
Europe: and authoritarianism, 204; and Brazil, 50; and Bulgarian Dionysian Kouker figure, 96; Central Europe, 50; and colonization, 87; and corruption, 86; divided territory of, 83; and economic crisis, 13; and European traditions, 59; and European Union, 9, 13, 26, 184; and *hispanidad*, 185; and Ibero-Americans, 85; and integration process, 2; politics of, 185; post-Roman Europe, 55n2; power centers of, 5; and Transatlantic studies, 47

Faber, Sebastiaan, 47
Fanon, Franz, 84
Faulkner, William, 99
feminism, 58, 60, 193
Ferreira, Ana Paula, 26
Ficciones (Borges), 108–10, 113, 115, 116
Figueiredo, Fidelino de, 27, 29
Foucault, Michel, 88, 115
Franco, Francisco, 2, 17
Fuentes, Carlos, 99, 102, 108, 112

Galicia: and Brazil Galicia Cultural Institute, 173–74; and *cantigas de amigo*, 174; and Galician identity, 186; history of, 174; and language, 174; and Lusophone and Hispanic worlds, 175–79; politics of, 175, 176
Galvão, Patrícia, 60
Galvez, Imperador do Acre (Souza), 97, 98

García Márquez, Gabriel: and the "boom," 112; and *Cien años de solidad (One Hundred Years of Solitude)*, 43, 46; and the ghost, 99; and the New Narrative, 108

Garro, Elena, 112

gender: and ambiguity, 15, 95; and *Ficciones*, 109; and gayspeak, 56–57; and gender deconstruction, 95; and gender violence, 16, 191, 197; and identification, 56; and identity, 57; and language, 58; and *Perto do Coração Selvagem* (Near to the Wild Heart), 110, 111–12; and transgendered spirituality, 58–59; and transnationalism, 43, 171

globalization: and academia, 14, 21–22, 38–39; and community, 243–46; and documentary film, 17, 234–47; and Latin America, 38–39, 234; and literature, 49n9, 51, 69; and Luso-Hispanic dialogue, 9, 11, 234–35, 236; and transnationalism, 49, 51

Goyen, William, 102

Gramática de la lengua castellana (Nebrija), 54n1

Grande Sertão: Veredas (Rosa), 57

Guattari, Felix, 39, 41

Hawthorne, Nathaniel, 99

Hispanic studies: and comparative approaches, 2–3, 5–9, 10, 11, 12, 17; and disciplinary separation or disjunction, 2, 4–5, 8–10, 12; and Galician artists, 10–11; and Hispanism, 14, 22, 23–24, 26–27, 45–46; and Ibero-American model, 47; and journal *Suroeste*, 33; and Luso-Brazilian studies, 22, 26–27, 35; and Luso-Hispanic interconnectedness, 2, 3, 5, 6, 10; and queer issues, 55n3; reconfigurations in, 21–23; and Transatlantic model, 46

"Hispanism and Its Discontents" (Resina), 23–31

História da Civilização Ibérica (Oliveira Martins), 32

Hoyos, Héctor, 23, 49

Iberia: and the Americas, 11, 47–48; cinema in, 17; and colonization, 5–6; and Comparative Luso-Hispanic studies, 3, 7, 8–9, 12; and competition between monarchies, 22; and composition in Iberian languages, 3; and educational crisis, 9; and emigration, 185; and Iberian Peninsula, 1, 2, 7, 13, 24, 28, 30, 31–32, 33, 34, 46, 47, 48, 55n2, 162, 174; and Iberian Union, 33, 33n19; and Ibero-America, 82; and Ibero-Americans, 47–48, 85; many nations of, 28n11; and medieval and early modern periods, 3–4, 47; and multilingualism, 8; and national identity, 12, 25; and Peninsular identity, 25; and "personal" documentary style, 17; and Portugal, 28n11; and Spain, 28n11; and transnational traditions, 2; and years of dynastic union, 4

Iberian studies: and the 17th century, 33; and Catalan perspective, 24, 25; and comparative approaches, 3–4, 11, 30–31, 33; and Comparative Luso-Hispanic studies, 8, 9, 12; epistemological challenges to, 31; and Hispanic studies, 34, 35; and Hispanism, 23–34; and Iberianism, 27–28, 29, 32, 35; and Iberian writers, 5; and *Iberismo*, 27–28; and Ibero-American model, 47–48; and Joan Ramon Resina, 23–25, 27–35, 47; and Luso-Brazilian studies, 29–30, 34, 35; and medieval and early modern periods, 33, 47; and multilingualism, 8, 23; and nationalism, 31–32; and parallelism and a-synchronicity, 27, 30; and Pedro Cardim, 33; politics of, 29; and Portugal, 28–29; and Portuguese, 14, 23, 26n8, 27, 28, 29–30; and Portuguese literature and culture, 24, 32, 34; and the state, 28, 29, 30

Inferno provisório (Temporary Hell) (Ruffato): and "A expiação," 124, 126; books of, 120n5, 123; and citizenship, 15, 120–25, 131; and the city, 120, 121, 123, 124, 125; and education, 120, 122, 126; and homeownership, 120, 122, 123, 125, 128; and *Mamma son tanto felice*, 123, 124, 126; *O livre das impossibilidades*, 124; and *O mundo inimigo*, 123; and poverty, 121; and rights, 121; setting of, 123; and urban proletarian life, 120, 121, 122; and violence, 124, 125–26

Jameson, Frederic, 50–51, 79

Joyce, James, 112

Kristal, Efraín, 44–45

Kristeva, Julia, 113–14, 116

languages: and Academia de Ciências de Lisboa, 54–55; and Afro-American cultures, 59; and the Americas, 38, 66; Arabic, 46; Aymara, 48; *castellano*, 54n1; Castilian

Spanish, 3, 10, 40, 43, 47; Catalan, 10, 23, 48, 54; English, 55, 151; Euskera, 23; and feminism, 58; French, 4, 38, 115, 151; Galician, 23, 54, 174, 175, 177; and gay-speak, 56–57; and gender, 58; Hebrew, 46; and heteronormativity, 55–57; and *hispanidad,* 4; Iberian languages, 3, 8, 23, 46, 54n1; Latin, 46, 55n2; and literary criticism, 55; and *lusofonia,* 4, 175–86; and Luso-Hispanic studies, 14, 21–22, 23; Magyar language, 50; and "Mairum language," 74; Náhuatl, 48; and Native American cultures, 59; and Peru, 78–79; and poetry, 155, 157, 158, 165; Portuguese, 1, 2, 3, 4–5, 7–8, 11, 14, 20, 21–22, 23, 26n8, 27, 29, 34, 38, 40, 43, 44, 50, 54, 55, 59n10, 131, 144, 174; and Portuñol, 42; and power structures, 45, 54, 55n2; Quechua, 48, 75, 76, 77, 146; and queer consciousness, 55–56; regularization of, 54–55; Romance Languages, 7–8, 38, 40, 46, 54n1, 55n2; and sociolects, 54, 54n1; and Spanglish, 42; Spanish, 1, 2, 3, 4–5, 7–8, 9, 10, 11, 22, 23, 38, 40, 44, 46, 54, 54n1, 55, 59n10, 75, 77; and Spanish or Iberian multilingualism, 8, 23, 46; and translation, 183–84; and transnationalism, 40, 46

La región más transparente (Where the Air is Clear) (Fuentes), 46

LASER (Latino and Latin American Space for Enrichment and Research), 44

Latin America: and the Americas, 14, 44–45, 47–48, 146; and amnesty laws, 206; and Argentina, 38, 42, 43, 44, 48, 56; and Ariel, 87–88; and Asia, 48; and authoritarianism, 204; and avant-gardes, 137–47; and Brazil, 2n1, 7, 12, 13, 42, 43, 44, 48, 49, 57, 82, 87–88, 89; and Caliban, 87–88; and the Caribbean, 38, 47; and Central America, 39; and Chile, 42; and cities, 119–20; and citizenship, 131; and civilization, 82; and colonialism, 16; and Comparative Luso-Hispanic studies, 3, 8–9, 12; and Costa Rica, 38; and critique of modernity, 88–89; and descendants of African slaves, 38; and enigma, 90; and French imperialism, 84; and French symbolists, 149; and globalization, 38–39; and historical processes, 2; and Iberian colonization, 2; and Ibero-American model, 47–48; and immigration to Spain, 48; and imperialism, 138; and indigenous peoples, 38; and Latin Americanism, 42, 43, 44, 47–50; and Mexico, 42; and the Middle East, 48; and orientalist model, 48; and "personal" documentary style, 17; population of, 48; and postcolonialism, 87; and publishers, 131–32; and representations of dictatorship, 16–17; republics of, 1, 2; and Richard Morse, 10–11; and Rodó, 83; and sexuality, 59; social sciences in, 88–89; and subalternism, 45; as a sum of nations, 42–43; and transition to democracy, 205–6; and transnationalism, 38–39, 51; and trauma, 106; and the United States, 84; and Uruguay, 42; and Utopian-dystopian duality, 106; writers of, 102. *See also* cinema; Cuba; LASER (Latino and Latin American Space for Enrichment and Research); Latin American studies; literature; Morse, Richard

Latin American studies, 24n6, 47

Lispector, Clarice: "A imitação da rosa" ("Imitation of the Rose"), 60–61; and *A paixão segundo G. H.,* 61; and Brazilian literature, 113; and *différance,* 116, 117; and individualism, 105; and language, 116–17; and the New Narrative, 114; and *Perto do Coração Selvagem* (Near to the Wild Heart), 15, 108–9, 110, 112, 113, 114–17; and poststructuralism, 114–15; and reader's role, 114; and Realism, 113; and sexuality, 116–17; and structuralism, 116; and the *unheimlich,* 62; and women as creative equals, 112

literature: and aesthetics, 140–47, 150, 158–59; and ambiguity, 95; American literature, 99–100, 102; and "ancestral impulse," 99–100, 103, 105; and the anti-hero, 97; and auto-ethnography, 70–74; and avant-gardes, 137–47; and the "boom," 102, 105–6, 110, 112; Brazilian literature, 3, 5, 6, 10, 11, 14, 15–16, 37, 57, 59n10, 60–61, 69–74, 87–90, 95, 96–98, 103n5, 104–5, 108, 109, 110–17, 121, 154; and Brazilian symbolism, 149–60; and Calibanic genealogy, 84; and *cantigas de amigo,* 175; and the carnivalesque, 95–98, 103–7; and Catalan-language writers, 10; and citizenship, 121–22, 132; and Comparative Luso-Hispanic studies, 3, 7–9, 11; and comparative model, 43–44; and Cuban-American writers, 43; and Cuban Casa de las Americas, 43; and cumulative model, 42–43; and dreams, 147; European literature, 10, 97, 143; and fiction, 37, 95, 98, 99, 104–5,

107, 109, 117, 120–21, 122; and the figure of death, 96–98; French literature, 5, 16, 44, 84, 115, 116, 143, 151, 154, 157–58; and futurism, 141–43; and *Generación del 98*, 25; and German-French dialogues, 44; and the ghost, 99–100, 102, 103–5, 106; and the Golden Age, 22; and hemispheric model, 44–45; and Hispanic American authors, 85; and Hispanic American *modernistas*, 16, 149–60, 151, 154, 159; and Hispanism, 51; and Hispanist model, 45–46, 47; and historical novels, 106; and hypercanonicity, 43; and Ibero-American model, 47–48; and indigenous novels, 69–80; and Indonesia, 43n6; inter-American literature, 11, 12, 108, 117, 163–65, 171; and Jose Enrique Rodó, 10–11, 86, 88; and language, 113–14, 116–17; and Latin Americanism, 51, 164; Latin American literature, 10–11, 14, 15–16, 22, 37–39, 41–51, 95–107, 108–17, 120–32; and *l'écriture féminine*, 116; and literary criticism, 49, 147; and literary revenant, 11, 15, 95, 103–7; and Luso-Spanish American model, 41; and magical realism, 139; and *malandragem* (roguery), 95–98, 105; and medieval and early modern periods, 47; and metafiction, 95; and modernism, 105, 138, 150, 154, 159–60, 164; and *modernismo*, 16, 44, 105, 151; and modernity, 89, 123, 137, 141, 142, 147; and multiethnic literature, 106; and myth, 88, 89, 140, 143; and narrative, 11, 15, 60, 61, 95, 97–98, 100, 103–5, 108–17, 120, 122–32, 169; national literature, 43–44, 109, 139; and nation-state, 42, 45, 47; and non-Castilian cultures, 29; North American literature, 14–15, 64–69; and *novela indigenista*, 43; and orientalist model, 48; Peruvian literature, 74–79; and politics, 44, 50, 64, 70, 73, 74, 75, 79, 105, 122, 146; Portuguese literature, 4, 5, 10, 10n12, 22, 24, 32, 33, 40; and postcolonialism, 84; and postmodern writers, 62; and poststructuralism, 116–17; precolonial literature, 43; and prose, 15, 60, 61, 104, 145; and queer issues, 61; and Realism, 5, 60, 113, 115, 140, 147; and reality, 117, 147, 151; and short stories, 104, 113, 147; and social transformation, 122; sociologies of, 39; Spanish American literature, 3, 11, 13, 14, 15, 16, 37, 45–46, 95, 98, 99–100, 103–5, 108, 109, 110–11, 117, 139; and Spanish American *vanguardismos*, 16; Spanish literature, 5, 10, 22, 40, 45–46; and Spanish nation-state, 10n12; and structuralism, 114–15, 117; and subalternism, 45, 79; and supplemental model, 43; and surrealism, 145, 147; and Symbolists, 16; of the Tawantinsuyu, 42; and "The Dead Narrator in Modern Latin American Prose Fiction" (Cypress), 104; and trans-Atlantic model, 46–47; and transnationalism, 50–51; and the *unheimlich*, 62; at universities, 21, 46, 47; U.S. literature, 10, 11, 40; and verisimilitude, 113, 115; and women as characters, 110–11; and women writers, 112; and world literature, 39, 40, 43, 49–50, 51. *See also* poetry; Queer studies; transnationalism

López-Calvo, Ignacio, 48

Los Recuerdos del porvenir (Recollections of Things to Come) (Garro), 100

Luso-Brazilian studies: and comparative approaches, 2–3, 5–9, 10, 11, 12, 17; and disciplinary separation or disjunction, 2, 4–5, 8–10, 12, 30; epistemological challenges to, 26–27, 30; and Hispanic studies, 35; and Hispanism, 14, 29–30, 34; and journal *Suroeste*, 33; and Luso-Afro-Brazilian studies, 26; and Luso-Hispanic interconnectedness, 6, 10; and Manuel de Oliveira Lima, 25, 25–26n7; in North American universities, 28; and novelist Eça de Queirós, 5; and Portuguese, 29–30, 34; and queer issues, 55n3; reconfigurations in, 21–23, 25–30

Macunaíma (Andrade), 97

Magellan, Ferdinand, 6

Maíra (Ribeiro): and Alma, 72–74; and Brazilian indigenist apparatus, 71, 72; and indigenous people, 69, 70, 72–74; and Isaías, 72, 73; and neocolonialism, 74

Mannoni, Dominique, 84

Marcuse, Herbert, 88

Martí, José, 2, 13; and modernism, 150; and *Nuestroamericanismo*, 43; and texts in *La Nación*, 85

McNickle, D'Arcy, 64–69, 70, 74–75, 78, 79

Melo, Francisco Manuel de, 3

Memórias de um Sargento de Milícias (Memoirs of a Militia Sergeant) (Almeida), 97

memory: and cinema, 207, 208, 236–37; and *El pibe*, 129; and feelings, 145; and the ghost, 99, 102; and *Inferno provisório*, 124; and Latin American artist, 143; and

"Na Prisão" (In Prison), 192; and poetry, 169; and working class, 130
"Memory, Youth and Regimes of Violence in Recent Hispanic and Lusophone Cinemas" (Marsh), 16–17, 204–19
Mexico: and Agustín Yáñez, 143; area of, 48; and artistic expression, 101; and Brazil, 103; cinema in, 17; Cristero rebellion in, 100; and cultural *mestizaje,* 101; and death, 100–102; and Día de los Muertos (Day of the Dead), 96, 100–101, 102, 103; exiles in, 47; and indigenous people, 102; and José Vasconcelos, 146; and Latin American literature, 42, 43; and the Mexican-American War, 105; and Mexican muralists, 144, 146; and Mexican revolution, 100; and modernist movement, 100, 101; and national history, 100; and patriarchy, 101; and Porfirio Diaz, 101; and publishers, 132; revolution in, 105; society of, 100, 101, 103; violent origins of, 101
Mongólia (Carvalho), 50
Morrison, Toni, 99, 106
Morse, Richard, 10–11, 15; and critique of modernity, 88, 89; and *Ibero-Americans,* 87; and *O espelho de Próspero* (Prospero's Mirror), 82, 88, 90; and secularization, 89
music: Angolan music, 185; and "*Cantigas de amigo*: Galicia and Brazil in the Lusophone Musical Space" (Moehn), 16, 173–86; and the Cantos na Maré (Songs of the Tide), 177–82; and Cuba, 146; and Galician and Brazilian music, 10–11, 16; and Galician musicians, 184; jazz, 96, 163, 164; and poetry, 165; popular music, 185; rock, 163; and Spanish America, 165

Nabuco, Joaquim, 85
Native Americans: and the Americas, 66; and citizenship, 68; and colonialism, 66–67; and decolonization, 67, 68; harmful legislation to, 64–65, 65n1; and nationalism, 66; and sexuality, 59; and the United States, 70; and *Wind from an Enemy Sky* (McNickle), 64–69
Native American studies: and Luso-Hispanic studies, 11; and Native Agency, 14–15; and *Wind from an Enemy Sky* (McNickle), 64–69
Neruda, Pablo, 46, 106n7, 147, 162n1
North America: and American Southwest, 46; and Caliban, 83, 84; and civilization, 83; and colonialism, 67; and *hispanismo,* 84, 87; and Latin American poets, 83; and Luso-Hispanic studies, 162–63; and media, 163; and Monroism, 87; and Native North America, 67; and the New Narrative, 108; and North American literature, 14–15, 64–69; power centers of, 5; universities in, 28, 46; and U.S. cities of Boston and Miami, 11; writers of, 99

O'Connor, Flannery, 99
O enigma de Qaf (Mussa), 50
O espelho de Próspero (Prospero's Mirror) (Morse), 82, 88, 90
Oliveira Lima, Manuel de, 25, 25–26n7
Oliveira Martins, Joaquim Pedro de, 32, 35
Ópera do Malandro (Buarque), 97
Ortega, Julio, 46

Paz, Octavio, 100, 147, 171
Pedro Páramo (Rulfo), 100, 101–2, 104
Pereira, Edimilson de Almeida, 165–71
performance: and the anti-hero, 97; and gender violence, 16, 191; and "Las bellas durmientes" (Sleeping Beauties), 192; and Luso-Hispanic studies, 191; and "Na Prisão" (In Prison), 191–92; and politics, 198–201; and street performance, 191; and theory of Richard Schechner, 191, 201. *See also* art
Perto do Coração Selvagem (Near to the Wild Heart) (Lispector): and experimental Brazilian fiction, 15, 109; and freedom, 110, 112; and Joana, 111–12, 114–17; and language, 113, 114, 116–17; and Otávio, 110, 112; and structuralism, 110; and women, 110, 112
Peru, 131; and Asian people, 48; and Bolivia, 77; and Centro Cultural Peruano Japonés, 48; and Ciro Alegría, 143; and demographic transformation, 75; and Francisco García Calderón, 86; and Incas, 67, 77, 146; and indigeneity, 78; and Juan Velasco Alvarado, 68, 69; and modernity, 77; and nationalism, 70; and native people, 66, 68, 69–70; peasants of, 75, 76, 77; and Peruvian Reality, 143; and politics, 74, 78; and Quechua, 76, 146; society of, 75–76; and state murders, 204; and state rapes, 214; and transition to democracy, 205; violence in, 214–15. *See also* Arguedas, José María
Piglia, Ricardo, 44

Plato, 62
Poe, Edgar Allan, 82, 83
poetry: and Afro-descendant musicality, 165; and Afro-diasporic work, 163, 165–70; and the Americas, 164; and Brazilian symbolism, 149–51; and *cantigas de amigo*, 174; and cinema, 163; and D. H. Lawrence, 85n1; and free verse, 151–53; Galician poetry, 173–74; and gender, 58n8; of José Watanabe, 48; and Keats, 51; and language, 62, 162, 166, 171; Latin American poetry, 11, 16, 82–83, 147, 162–71; lyric poetry, 16, 162–63, 164, 165–67, 171, 174; and medieval poetic culture, 3; and mulatto poetry, 146; and Oliverio Girondo, 139–40; and queer issues, 62; and reality, 147; and Ronald de Carvalho, 6; and Ruy Belo, 33n20; and slavery, 165, 166–68; and sonnets of Luis de Góngora, 58n8; Spanish American-Brazilian links in, 16, 162–71; and Spanish and Portuguese, 62; and subjectivity, 149–50; and Tordesilhas-Festival Iberoamericano de Poesia Contemporânea, 162. *See also* music; Pereira, Edimilson de Almeida; "Shared Passages: Spanish American-Brazilian Links in Contemporary Poetry" (Perrone)
Portugal: and Africa, 25, 27; and the Americas, 83; autonomous regions of, 33; and Brazil, 40, 48, 103; and church hierarchy, 103; and cinema, 223; and colonialism, 4–6, 22, 25, 26, 102, 103; and cultures of Portuguese-speaking world, 29, 175; and dictatorship, 2, 11, 17; and Eça de Queirós, 113; and economic reforms, 184–85; empire of, 33; and European Union, 26; and Felipe II, 33n19; and Galicia, 174; and the Golden Age, 32n17; and historic transformations since the 1960s, 27; and Iberian Peninsula, 48; and Iberian studies, 28–29, 32–35, 47; and imperialism, 4, 55n2; and Instituto Camões, 40; and King João IV, 22; and Lisbon, 11, 26, 28n11, 33n20; and loss of Brazil, 25; and *lusofonia*, 4; and medieval and early modern periods, 1, 3, 22; national epic of, 32–33; and national identity, 12, 25–26, 30n15; and *Os Lusíadas* (Camões), 10n12; and role in European Union, 13; and Spain, 29, 32–33, 34, 175–76; and Spanish Hapsburgs, 1–2, 22, 33n19; and Spanish nation-state, 10; and state of Salazar, 220–25; and Treaty of Tordesillas, 6–7; and years of dynastic union, 4. *See also* colonization
Pramoedya Ananta Toer, 43
Pynchon, Thomas, 44

Queer studies: and Brazilian women writers, 60–61; and *candomblé*, 59; and feminism, 58, 60; and Gabriela Mistral, 62; and gayspeak, 56–57; and heteronormativity, 58–60, 61, 62; and lesbians, 58, 59n11, 60; and Luso-Hispanic studies, 14; and Maria Elena Walsh, 57; and Mário de Andrade, 57, 60, 62; and novelist João Guimarães Rosa, 57; and "Queer Aztlán" (Moraga), 58; and Queer English, 55, 59n10; and queer theory, 58, 62; and Shakespeare, 62; and Spanish and Portuguese, 11, 54–62; and transgendered spirituality, 58–59; and use of language, 61–62. *See also* Galvão, Patrícia; Lispector, Clarice

race: and American race, 85; in Brazil, 215–16; and "Brazilian race," 71; in Chile, 213; and cultural universalism, 70; and João da Cruz e Sousa, 157; and *La raza cósmica* (The Cosmic Race), 146; and Latin America, 84–85, 146; and poetry, 158–60, 169; and racism in Peru, 75; and the United States, 97
Real Academia Española, 45, 46
religion: and Afro-Caribbean and Afro-Brazilian practices, 58–59; and Brazil, 103; and Buddhist belief, 100; and Catholicism, 72, 90, 96, 100, 101, 220; and church, 103; and colonial experience, 169–70; and Counter-Reformation, 54, 90; and death, 100; and Judeo-Christian heteronormativity, 59; and Lent, 103; and liberation theology, 76; and *Maíra* (Ribeiro), 72; and Mexican religious conservatism, 101; and missionaries, 72; and Mormon and Pentecostalist practices, 58–59; and native people, 66; and poetry, 147; and rituals, 96, 100; and Yoruba Orisha religion, 59n9
Renan, Ernest, 84
Retamar, Roberto Fernández, 84
Revista Occidental, 32
Reyes, Alfonso, 6, 8, 13
Ribeiro, Darcy, 69–74, 74n22, 75, 76, 78, 79

rights: and citizenship, 68, 119–22, 119n3; civil rights, 119n3, 120, 121, 125, 127; and gay rights, 57; *habeas corpus* rights, 69; human rights, 171, 193, 208, 209; and native people, 68; political rights, 119n3, 120, 121, 127; and religion, 119n3; and self-articulation, 122; social rights, 119n3, 120, 121, 125, 127; and the state, 119n1, 120; and urban spaces, 119; and voting rights, 68, 119n3; welfare rights, 120n7; of women, 194, 197

Rodó, José Enrique, 10–11, 13; and Ariel, 86, 88; and Iberian America, 83; and Ibero-Americans, 84–85; *Mirador de Prospero,* 84–85

Rodríguez, Ileana, 45

Roots of Brazil (Buarque de Holanda), 82, 85; and authoritarian thought, 86–87; and Brazilian political thought, 90; and "Iberian" civilization, 89; and myth, 89; and *O espelho de Próspero* (Prospero's Mirror), 90; and secularization, 89–90

Russia, 100, 141

Salazar, António de Oliveira, 2, 17, 220–25

Saramago, José, 10, 12, 13

Scarlet Letter (Hawthorne), 97

Schwartz, Jorge: and "Abaixo Tordesilhas!" (Down With Tordesillas), 6–7; and Brazilian literature, 10; and Luso-Hispanic disengagement, 8

sexuality: and Afro-American cultures, 59; and Alma in *Maíra,* 73; and Latin American society, 59; and literary criticism, 61; and male homosexuals, 56; and Michel Foucault, 58; and Native Americans, 59; and native people in *Maíra,* 73–74; and *Perto do Coração Selvagem* (Near to the Wild Heart), 112, 116–17; and poetry, 171; and sodomy, 59. *See also* Queer studies

Shakespeare, William, 62; and Caliban, 83, 84; and Calibanic genealogy, 84; and *Tempests After Shakespeare,* 84

"Shared Passages: Spanish American–Brazilian Links in Contemporary Poetry" (Perrone), 16, 162–71

Silko, Leslie Marmon, 102

Silva, José Asunción, 151–52, 158

South America: and MERCOSUR, 9; and the New Narrative, 108

Spain: and American Southwest, 46; and the Americas, 83, 103; autonomous regions of, 29, 33; and the Basque Country, 12, 40, 47–48; and Catalonia, 10, 12, 25, 32, 40, 47; cinema in, 17; and colonialism, 4–6, 25, 46, 48, 102–3; and dictatorship, 2, 11, 17, 192, 193–94, 201; and economic reforms, 184–85; empire of, 33, 47, 48; Entroido festivals in, 96; and Franco's dictatorship, 220–25; and Galicia, 10, 11, 12, 16, 40, 48, 175; and *hispanidad,* 4; and Iberian Peninsula, 10n12, 32–33; and imperialism, 4, 22, 40, 54n1, 55n2, 100; and indigenous civilizations, 106; and Instituto Cervantes, 40; and Juan Valera, 32; King of, 46; languages of, 23, 40, 46, 48; and "Las bellas durmientes" (Sleeping Beauties), 197–201; and Latin America, 48; and Madrid, 11, 33n20, 48; and medieval and early modern periods, 1, 3, 22, 47; and Mexico, 48; modernization in, 25; and national identity, 12, 25; and nationalism, 25, 29; and Occitan, 48; and pan-Hispanism, 40; politics of, 25; and Portugal, 27, 29, 32–33, 34; and role in European Union, 13; and Spanish Civil War, 47, 220, 221–22, 241; and Spanish Hapsburgs, 1–2, 22, 33n19; and Spanish literature, 10; and Spanish nation-state, 10, 12; and Spanish university system, 24–25; and Street Projects, 16; and Treaty of Tordesillas, 6–7; and world politics, 240–41; and years of dynastic union, 4. *See also* colonization; Galicia

Spanish-American War, 25, 84, 87, 105

Spivak, Gayatri, 45

subalternism, 45, 70

Third World Literary Fortunes (Armstrong), 105–6

Torga, Miguel, 10, 12

Transatlantic Studies Association, 47

transnationalism: and academia, 39, 46, 51; and Brazil, 50; and Catalonia, 32; and Comparative Luso-Hispanic studies, 11; and diasporic transnationalisms, 48; and ethnicity, gender, and class, 43; and geography, 41, 49–50; and globalization, 49, 51; and Instituto Camões, 40; and Instituto Cervantes, 40; and Latin America, 51; and Latin American literature, 14, 16, 37–39, 40–51; and literary canons, 6; and the market, 41; and media, 39; and migration, 45; and plurality, 49, 50; and Portugal, 32; and post-dictatorship cultures, 44; and pub-

lishers, 39, 46; and Spanish American works, 50; and subalternism, 45; and transhistoricizing, 50–51; and transnational traditions, 2, 14
Treaty of Guadalupe Hidalgo, 42
Treaty of Tordesillas: and "Abaixo Tordesilhas!" (Down With Tordesillas), 6–7; and artistic expression, 171, 185; and Comparative Luso-Hispanic studies, 17; and Galicia, 174; and Iberian overseas colonization, 6–7, 22; and Latin American literature, 42; and Native American studies, 14–15; and Pedro Meira Monteiro, 15
Trotsky, Leon, 141
Tupac Amaru kamaq taytanchisman (To Our Father and Creator, Tupac Amaru) (Arguedas), 75–76

Unamuno, Miguel de, 4, 32n17
United Kingdom, 47
United States: and Boston, 11, 83; and Brazil, 68; and the Caribbean, 84; and citizenship, 68; and civilization, 82, 87; critique of, 84, 86, 87; and critique of modernity, 88; divided territory of, 83; expressive culture in, 164; and futurism, 141; and gay Puerto Ricans in New York, 55n3; and imperialism, 65, 70, 87; and Indian policy, 70; and Latino culture, 42; and legislation regarding Native lands, 64–65, 65n1; and the Mexican-American War, 105; and Miami, 11; and mining interests, 76; and Monroe Doctrine, 87; and Mormon and Pentecostalist practices, 58–59; and multiethnic literature, 106; and music, 165; and New Orleans, 96; and New York, 82, 83, 85; popular culture in, 163, 165; puritanical foundation of, 97; and religion, 97; as a republic, 86; and revolution, 77; and Transatlantic studies, 47; universities in, 3, 7, 22n3, 40, 47, 49; and *Wind from an Enemy Sky* (McNickle), 64–65, 66; and world politics, 240. *See also* Native Americans; Spanish-American War
Uruguay: and Darcy Ribeiro, 69; and frontier with Brazil, 1; and frontier with Rio Grande do Sul, 11; and Jose Enrique Rodó, 10–11; and José María Arguedas, 69; and Latin America, 42

Vargas Llosa, Mario, 75, 102, 108, 112
Velasco Alvarado, Juan, 68, 69
Verdaguer, Jacinto, 10
Veríssimo, Érico, 96, 104
Vicente, Gil, 3
violence: and Central America, 204–5; and "crimes of passion," 193–94; and domestic violence, 192; and *El pibe*, 130; and Franco, 199; and gender violence, 16, 192–94, 197, 198; and Latin American literature, 121; and "Memory, Youth and Regimes of Violence in Recent Hispanic and Lusophone Cinemas" (Marsh), 16–17, 204–17; and modernity, 80; in *Pedro Páramo* (Rulfo), 101; and rape, 214; and transition to democracy, 205; and truth commissions, 209; and use of torture, 209; and war, 241. *See also* cinema; *Inferno provisório* (Temporary Hell) (Ruffato)

Watanabe, José, 48
Wind from an Enemy Sky (McNickle): and Adam Pell, 64, 65, 67–68; author of, 64, 66, 67, 68, 69; and indigenous people, 68, 69; and legislation regarding Native lands, 64–65; and Little Elk people, 64–65, 66, 67–68; and medicine bundle, 65–66, 65n3, 67; and neocolonialism, 74; and Peruvian Inca figurine, 67

Zabus, Chantal, 84
Zamora, Lois Parkinson, 99, 102, 103–4

TRANSOCEANIC STUDIES
ILEANA RODRÍGUEZ, SERIES EDITOR

The Transoceanic Studies series rests on the assumption of a one-world system. This system—simultaneously modern and colonial and now postmodern and postcolonial (global)—profoundly restructured the world, displaced the Mediterranean *mare nostrum* as a center of power and knowledge, and constructed dis-centered, transoceanic, waterways that reached across the world. The vast imaginary undergirding this system was Eurocentric in nature and intent. Europe was viewed as the sole culture-producing center. But Eurocentrism, theorized as the "coloniality of power" and "of knowledge," was contested from its inception, generating a rich, enormous, alternate corpus. In disputing Eurocentrism, books in this series will acknowledge above all the contributions coming from other areas of the world, colonial and postcolonial, without which neither the aspirations to universalism put forth by the Enlightenment nor those of globalization promoted by postmodernism will be fulfilled.

Beyond Tordesillas: New Approaches to Comparative Luso-Hispanic Studies
   EDITED BY ROBERT PATRICK NEWCOMB AND RICHARD A. GORDON

In Search of an Alternative Biopolitics: Anti-Bullfighting, Animality, and the Environment in Contemporary Spain
   KATARZYNA OLGA BEILIN

Prophetic Visions of the Past: Pan-Caribbean Representations of the Haitian Revolution
   VÍCTOR FIGUEROA

Transatlantic Correspondence: Modernity, Epistolarity, and Literature in Spain and Spanish America, 1898–1992
   JOSÉ LUIS VENEGAS

Conflict Bodies: The Politics of Rape Representation in the Francophone Imaginary
   RÉGINE MICHELLE JEAN-CHARLES

National Consciousness and Literary Cosmopolitics: Postcolonial Literature in a Global Moment
   WEIHSIN GUI

Writing AIDS: (Re)Conceptualizing the Individual and Social Body in Spanish American Literature
   JODIE PARYS

Learning to Unlearn: Decolonial Reflections from Eurasia and the Americas
   MADINA V. TLOSTANOVA AND WALTER D. MIGNOLO

Oriental Shadows: The Presence of the East in Early American Literature
   JIM EGAN

www.ingramcontent.com/pod-product-compliance
Lightning Source LLC
Chambersburg PA
CBHW021847300426
44115CB00005B/54